LETTERS TO THE PRESS

THE UNKNOWN CONAN DOYLE

---◆---

LETTERS TO
THE PRESS

---◆---

COMPILED WITH AN INTRODUCTION BY
JOHN MICHAEL GIBSON AND
RICHARD LANCELYN GREEN

SECKER & WARBURG
LONDON

This edition first published in England 1986 by
Martin Secker & Warburg Limited
54 Poland Street, London W1V 3DF

Introduction and notes © 1986 by John Michael Gibson
and Richard Lancelyn Green

This edition © 1986 by Martin Secker & Warburg Limited

British Library Cataloguing in Publication Data

Doyle, *Sir* Arthur Conan
Letters to the press.
1. Doyle, *Sir* Arthur Conan—Biography
2. Authors, English—19th century—Biography
I. Title   II. Gibson, John Michael
III. Green, Richard Lancelyn
823′.912   PR4623

ISBN 0–436–13303–2

Typeset by Inforum Ltd, Portsmouth
Printed in Great Britain by
St Edmundsbury Press Ltd, Bury St Edmunds

CONTENTS

INTRODUCTION

───── ◆ ─────

When Sherlock Holmes said that the Press was a most valuable institution if one knew how to use it, he was echoing the sentiments of his creator. Probably no other popular writer has ever before revealed quite such a wide range of interests or believed so fervently that he had the ear of society, and therefore the right to address it on a diversity of topics, as did Arthur Conan Doyle. From his early days as a doctor when he wrote to the medical journals about a self-experiment with drugs or the suspension of the Contagious Diseases Acts (which prevented the compulsory examination of potential carriers), through the period of his greatest literary success when he dealt with what he considered to be malpractices such as self-advertisement, multiple reviewing, and the power of boycott exercised by the circulating libraries, and on to the early years of the new century when he voiced the public's concern about matters of state and of political and national integrity, such as the rights and wrongs of the Boer War, the efficiency of the British Army, the situation in Ireland, or the Belgian misrule in the Congo, he showed himself again and again as a man of sound common sense and independent mind, one whose views or schemes for the improvement of his fellow countrymen deserved a hearing.

Conan Doyle was born in May 1859. His uncle was the illustrator, Richard Doyle, who designed the famous *Punch* cover, while his father, Charles Altamont Doyle, also did a number of book illustrations, and his grandfather was the cartoonist 'HB'. But his contacts with the literary world were almost entirely of his own making. In September 1879 he had his first story published in *Chambers's Journal* and it was also during that month that his earliest known letter appeared in the Press. This concerned the drug Gelseminum and was published in the *British Medical Journal*. Before that, his writing had been for private consumption. At

1

Stonyhurst College he had won a prize for a poem on 'The Crossing of the Red Sea', and at university in his native town of Edinburgh, he had composed a student song, 'Portobello Beach', which remained popular long after he had left.

Many of the major influences on his work dated back to his youth. There was the poverty of his childhood and the problem of his father's growing alcoholism. There was the period spent at Liberton Bank in the care of John Hill Burton's sister, Mary, and his friendship with William Burton, which led to the series of photographic essays which were among his earliest works. There were also walking tours through Scotland, visits to Arran and the Isle of May, and trips to southern Ireland to visit his mother's relations. His schooldays at Stonyhurst and at Feldkirch in Austria were also important, as were his years at Edinburgh University where he studied under Joseph Bell and Professor Rutherford and where he made many of his closest friends. He also had practical experience with doctors in Shropshire, Sheffield, and Birmingham, and went on two sea voyages, one in 1880 on a Greenland whaler and another a year later down the west coast of Africa.

Early in 1882 he went into partnership with a student friend, George Budd, who practised medicine in an unconventional way and who provided Doyle with some of his more unusual ideas. It was an uneven partnership, and it soon collapsed. By July 1882 Doyle had moved to Southsea where he was to remain in practice until 1890. His stories had been appearing in a variety of magazines, including *London Society*, *All the Year Round*, *Temple Bar*, and the *Cornhill Magazine*. There were also the articles in the *British Journal of Photography*, another, 'Life and Death in the Blood', which had appeared in *Good Words*, and his first novel, 'Girdlestone & Co.' which he started in 1884.

At Southsea, Doyle was a stalwart of the local sporting clubs, playing cricket, football, and bowls, and he was politically active as a Liberal-Unionist. He was also a regular attender at meetings of the Portsmouth Literary and Scientific Society, at which he read papers on his Arctic voyage, on Carlyle, and on George Meredith, and of which he was later made Honorary Secretary. It was in Southsea that he created Sherlock Holmes and that he wrote his first historical novel, *Micah Clarke*, and by 1890 he had gained considerable experience as an author. He had also made many contacts with the literary world, one of the most important being his friendship with James Payn of the *Cornhill* who had accepted a story in 1883 and had then invited him to a contributors' dinner at Greenwich. Payn was to be one of the first to read *A Study in Scarlet* and was also indirectly responsible for the second Sherlock

2

Holmes story, as he recommended Doyle to the representative of *Lippincott's Magazine* in 1889. Another useful friend was Hugh S. Maclauchlin, variously editor of the *Hampshire Post* and of the Portsmouth *Evening News*. He devoted a leading article to Doyle's first book at the time of its publication in *Beeton's Christmas Annual* and remained an admirer of his work. Doyle also made himself known to a number of other editors by offering them the second serial rights of *The Sign of Four*. By his own efforts he succeeded in having the story reprinted in the *Bristol Observer*, the *Glasgow Citizen*, the *Hampshire Telegraph*, and the *Birmingham Weekly Mercury*.

Weekly papers were then a major forum for popular fiction and served a wide readership. They had the ingredients of a magazine with novels, short stories, household and gardening hints, fashion gossip, theatrical and sporting notes, and other such features, but their domination was being threatened by a new type of penny paper. The first was George Newnes' *Tit-Bits* which was soon followed by Alfred Harmsworth's *Answers*, *Pearson's Weekly*, and a host of lesser rivals. They were so successful that the proprietors went on to scale greater and greater heights. George Newnes founded the *Strand Magazine* and other periodicals, while Harmsworth went on to found the *Daily Mail* and, as Lord Northcliffe, became one of the country's greatest press barons. Pearson also achieved success with illustrated magazines and with his newspaper, the *Daily Express*.

At the end of 1890 Doyle went to Berlin as a representative for W.T. Stead's *Review of Reviews* to witness Dr Koch's consumption cure and to write a character sketch of him. He was not able to meet Dr Koch, nor to attend any of the important lectures, but he did acquire sufficient information to be able to write to the *Daily Telegraph* to warn the public that the success of the treatment was not assured. He was among the first to do so and his doubts proved well-justified. He also met journalists such as Lowe of *The Times* and Saunders of the *Morning Post*, and his discussion with Malcolm Morris, a Harley Street dermatologist, was to have far-reaching results. Morris advised him to give up his practice and move to London as an eye specialist, that being a subject which had long fascinated him. And this was what Doyle did. At the beginning of 1891 he went to Vienna and Paris to bring himself up to date, and on his return he established himself in Upper Wimpole Street. While he waited for patients, he wrote the first of the short stories about Sherlock Holmes and these were taken by the new *Strand Magazine*. They were so successful that he was able to give up his medical career and devote himself wholly to literature.

He had moved to South Norwood and was soon well known in literary circles. Jerome K. Jerome and Robert Barr, who were joint editors of the *Idler*, became close friends, and his cricketing ability brought him into contact with J.M. Barrie, A.E.W. Mason, and his future brother-in-law, E.W. Hornung. He was elected to various literary societies, including the Vagabonds and the Authors' Club, and became a member of the Reform Club. He there joined the circle of literary men headed by Sir John Robinson, editor of the *Daily News*, and Wemyss Reid whose magazine, the *Speaker*, published a number of his articles and poems.

In the Autumn of 1894 he went on a lecture tour of America where the name of Sherlock Holmes had made his own familiar. He was made to feel very much at home in the literary circles which centred on the major cities such as New York, Chicago, and Boston. He met many of the rising men-of letters, including Howells, Eugene Field, Riley, Hamlin Garland, and John Kendrick Bangs, and he paid tribute to the earlier generation which had had such a profound influence upon him, among them Oliver Wendell Holmes, Mark Twain, Bret Harte, and Edgar Allan Poe. He also met various editors and publishers, one being S.S. McClure whose newspaper syndicate had published many of his early stories and who was then publishing a magazine in which Doyle agreed to invest some of the proceeds of his tour.

During the 1890s Doyle enjoyed greater and greater affluence, marred only by the illness of his wife, though even that was turned to his advantage. One year he took her to Switzerland where he spent his time experimenting with Norwegian cross-country skis, then at the end of 1895 they went to Egypt where, early the following year when war against the dervishes seemed imminent, he offered to go as a special correspondent for the *Westminster Gazette*. He joined the other members of the Press, E.E. Knight of *The Times*, Scudamore of the *Daily News*, Beaman of the *Standard*, Julian Corbett of the *Pall Mall Gazette* and H.C. Seppings-Wright of the *Illustrated London News*, and went up the Nile to Wady Halfa. There was little to report, but he thoroughly enjoyed the experience and in 1898, when war with France was threatened, he again offered his services, this time to the Central News Agency. Had war been declared, he would have proceeded without delay to a special dispatch boat in the Mediterranean. But it never materialised. Back in England he built himself a large house at Hindhead where his neighbours included Grant Allen, Bernard Shaw, and Grant Richards.

The next turning point in his life came in 1899 with the outbreak of the South African War. In December he tried to get a commission in the army and when that failed offered his services as a doctor to Archibald Langman who was fitting out a private field hospital. This provided him with the means of getting to

4

South Africa and he arrived at Bloemfontein just in time to deal with a major outbreak of enteric fever. He also wrote a history of the war which was published in September 1900 and revised during the years that followed, and a highly successful pamphlet, *The War in South Africa: Its Cause and Conduct*, for which he first sought support through *The Times* and which was then translated into many different languages. He was to call it 'an incursion into diplomacy' and it proved so successful in combating the adverse propaganda that he was offered a knighthood in the Coronation Honours of Edward VII (who, it was said, had contributed anonymously to the fund set up to finance the project).

Also during the Boer War, he became interested in the idea of local rifle clubs and home defence. In 1900 he stood for Parliament with an Edinburgh constituency and he put his name forward again in 1903 for the Border Burghs, fighting the first on a patriotic platform and the other as a reluctant protectionist (though winning neither). He became a keen motorist, went up in a balloon, and in 1904 was made a life member of the Crimes Club. It had been founded by Arthur Lambton, while the members included George Sims and Churton Collins. The first was responsible for the campaign in the *Daily Mail* which cleared Adolph Beck, while the other helped Doyle to attempt to do the same for George Edalji. There were two long articles about the case in the *Daily Telegraph* in January 1907, followed by a series of letters and three further articles, making it Doyle's most sustained investigation and the one which made the greatest impact upon the public. For the *Daily Mail*, he described the 1908 Olympic Marathon at which the Italian, Dorando, who had led most of the way, was helped across the finishing line and disqualified. And for the same paper he was to describe the funeral of Edward VII (as he had done with Queen Victoria's funeral for the *New York World*).

In 1909 he was made President of the Divorce Law Reform Union; in the same year he publicised the Belgian misrule in the Congo and by writing a booklet, *The Crime of the Congo*, and by lecturing on the subject with E.D. Morel; then in 1912 he wrote a pamphlet on the Oscar Slater Case, which he felt had involved a serious miscarriage of justice and which was to remain unsolved until the last years of his life. He was also made a member of the British Olympic Committee, to which he was elected at the suggestion of Lord Northcliffe; its aim was to raise money for the doomed 1916 Berlin Olympic Games. All these subjects and others, such as Kent Coal, Irish Home Rule(to which he was converted in 1911), and the sinking of the *Titanic* (which led to a famous exchange of letters with Bernard Shaw), were raised and discussed in the newspapers.

5

Like many others, he realised that war was imminent, but his article in the *Fortnightly Review*, 'Great Britain and the Next War', was one of the first to warn of the danger of a submarine blockade and to press for a Channel tunnel. With the outbreak of war, he immediately set about the establishment of a civilian volunteer reserve and did everything in his power as a propagandist. There was a recruiting pamphlet, *To Arms!*, a series of articles in the *Daily Chronicle* which were issued as *The German War*, and in June 1916 he visited the Italian Front, along with the British and French Fronts, being accompanied on the last part of his journey by Robert Donald, the editor of the *Daily Chronicle*. Throughout the war he wrote letters and articles, including towards the end a series for the *Evening Standard*, and, as with the Boer War, he produced a history of the campaigns.

In 1916, after thirty years of study, he was converted to Spiritualism and soon became one of its leading exponents. He gave lectures throughout Great Britain and visited Australia, America, South Africa, and Scandinavia in his attempt to convert others. In 1925 he opened a Psychic Bookshop which also incorporated a Psychic Museum and acted as a publisher, and in 1928 he write a weekly column of 'Psychic Notes' for the *Sunday Express*. He took many editors and other men of affairs into his confidence and, though he did not always succeed in making them share his belief, he did invariably win their respect. For the public at large, however, some of the subjects with which he dealt appeared preposterous, none more so than the ridiculous fairy photographs to which he gave undue prominence by publishing them in the *Strand Magazine*. To those who do not share a belief in spiritualism, it is doubtful whether anything that he said about it will have any validity, but he did at least argue his case well and many of the subjects do have a curiosity value. He was often confronted by fraud and trickery and chose to accept many things which defied logic and science, but in other respects his judgement was as sound and as balanced as ever. On the day that he died, the *Daily Telegraph* published his last letter to the press. It concerned Winston Churchill's account of the British failure to take Constantinpole, and suggested that this had, in retrospect, proved beneficial.

Doyle's letters to the Press stand well on their own as he put his case carefully and always tried to give both sides of the argument, using facts and figures where necessary to support his claims. The letters are arranged in chronological order and are printed in full as originally published. A uniform style has been adopted for the opening, which in the original varies between, 'Sir', 'Dear Sir', 'Gentlemen', or whatever, and for the address which either appeared at the head or foot of the original. Most of the headings are those used by the newspapers, though some have been shortened, with the subheadings omitted.

In making this selection, a large number dealing with spiritualism have been excluded, as well as others which either repeat the argument of an earlier letter or concern small points of detail. It is to be hoped that this book will illustrate the energy and integrity of Conan Doyle, and also help to explain why he was occasionally annoyed by those who thought of him solely as the creator of Sherlock Holmes. It provides a reflection of the times in which he lived, much of which is still pertinent today, and the writer comes across as a warm-hearted and tolerant person, and as a man who had seen life from many angles and who had lived it to the full.

RICHARD LANCELYN GREEN
JOHN MICHAEL GIBSON

LETTERS TO THE PRESS

1879–1890

THE BRITISH MEDICAL
JOURNAL   20 September 1879

Gelseminum as a Poison

SIR, – Some years ago, a persistent neuralgia led me to use the tincture of gelseminum to a considerable extent. I several times overstepped the maximum doses of the text-books without suffering any ill effects. Having recently had an opportunity of experimenting with a quantity of fresh tincture, I determined to ascertain how far one might go in taking the drug, and what the primary symptoms of an overdose might be. I took each dose about the same hour on successive days, and avoided tobacco or any other agent which might influence the physiological action of the drug. Here are the results as jotted down at the time of the experiment. On Monday and Tuesday, forty and sixty minims produced no effect whatever. On Wednesday, ninety minims were taken at 10.30. At 10.50, on rising from my chair, I became seized with an extreme giddiness and weakness of the limbs, which, however, quickly passed off. There was no nausea or other effect. The pulse was weak but normal. On Thursday, I took 120 minims. The giddiness of yesterday came on in a much milder form. On going out about one o'clock, however, I noticed for the first time that I had a difficulty in accommodating the eye for distant objects. It needed a distinct voluntary effort, and indeed a facial contortion, to do it.

On Friday, 150 minims were taken. As I increased the dose, I found that the more marked physiological symptoms disappeared. To-day, the giddiness was almost gone, but I suffered from a severe frontal headache, with diarrhoea and general lassitude.

On Saturday and Sunday, I took three drachms and 200 minims. The diarrhoea was so persistent and prostrating, that I must stop at 200 minims. I felt great depression and a severe frontal headache. The pulse was still normal, but weak.

From these experiments I would draw the following conclusions.

1. In spite of a case described some time ago in which 75 minims proved fatal, a healthy adult may take as much as 90 minims with perfect immunity.

2. In doses of from 90 to 120 minims, the drug acts apparently as a motor paralyser to a certain extent, causing languor, giddiness, and a partial paralysis of the ciliary muscle.

3. After that point, it causes headache, with diarrhoea and extreme lassitude.

4. The system may learn to tolerate gelseminum, as it may opium, if it be gradually inured to it. I feel convinced that I could

have taken as much as half an ounce of the tincture, had it not been for the extreme diarrhoea it brought on.

Believe me,
Yours sincerely,
A.C.D.

Clifton House, Aston Road, Birmingham.

THE LANCET   25 March 1882

Notes on a Case of Leucocythaemia

SIR, – As the causation of this rare and curious disease has been as obscure hitherto as its treatment has been futile, your readers may be interested by a case which seems to throw some light upon both points.

The patient, a well-built man, twenty-nine years of age, came to my friend Mr. Hoare complaining of a large tumour, which extended across his abdomen from the right costal border to the left anterior superior spine of the ilium. This proved upon examination to be an enormously hypertrophied spleen, the hilum being represented by a deep notch a little above the level of the umbilicus. The account of the patient was that some years before he had had a sharp attack of ague at Aspinwall, on the American coast, and that he had never entirely shaken off its effects. The swelling, however, had appeared recently, and attained its large proportions in the course of a few weeks. On examining the blood under the microscope we found that the leucocytes were enormously increased in number, almost filling up the interspaces of the rouleaux, while the coloured corpuscles were ill-formed, and diminished not only relatively, but also in the aggregate. The proportion of white to red was calculated at one to seven. None of the other blood glands were affected, and the only symptoms complained of were referable to pressure of the tumour, principally dyspepsia and vomiting from its interference with the stomach, and pain in the legs from compression of the lumbar plexus. The liver was slightly enlarged and tender, but the secretion of bile appeared to be unaffected. The heart was weak and had a well-marked functional murmur. Excessive marasmus was another leading feature of the case, the patient having fallen from fourteen to eleven stone in a few weeks. Having given both iron and quinine a fair trial, and found them equally inefficacious, we have now had recourse to arsenic in large doses, in combination with the iodide and chlorate of potash. This mode of treatment, combined with a liberal diet, and strict attention to the state of the bowels, has been remarkably efficacious. The tumour

14

has already diminished in size, and some of the more distressing secondary symptoms have been alleviated. The principal interest of the case lies, I think, in the connexion to be traced between the malarious poison and the subsequent leucocythaemia, a connexion which seems to show that this obscure disease is intimately allied to ordinary "ague-cake," if not a mere modification of that pathological condition, determined by some idiosyncracy of constitution or temperament.

I am, Sir, your obedient servant,
A. CONAN DOYLE

Aston, March, 1882

THE MEDICAL TIMES   16 June 1883

The Contagious Diseases Acts

SIR, – As an ounce of fact is proverbially superior to an indefinite quantity of theory, I think that I am justified in citing one or two instances of the effects of the present suspension of the Acts. Being in practice as a medical man in the town most affected by the measure, I am able to speak with some authority on the subject. Last week a large transport entered Portsmouth Harbour with time-expired men from India. Upon the same day several diseased women left the hospital presumably with the intention of meeting that transport, and there was no law to prevent it. I say that if an unfortunate soldier, coming home to his native land after an absence of years, and exposed to such temptations, should yield to them, and entail disease upon himself and his offspring, the chief fault should not lie at his door. It surely emanates logically from those hysterical legislators who set loose these bearers of contagion, and their like, upon society. For fear delicacy should be offended where no touch of delicacy exists, dreadful evils are to result, men to suffer, children to die, and pure women to inherit unspeakable evils. Loose statements and vague doctrines of morality may impose upon hasty thinkers, but surely, when the thing is reduced to its simplest terms, it becomes a matter of public calamity that these Acts should be suspended for a single day, far more for an indefinite period. The apostles of free trade in infection have worked to such good purpose that within a few weeks the streets of our naval stations have become pandemonia, and immorality is rampant where it lately feared to show its face. Property has depreciated near all the public-houses since the suspension of the Acts, on account of the concourse of vile women whose uproar and bad language make night hideous. I venture to say that, were the old laws enforced again to-morrow, there would

still in a hundred years' time be many living who could trace
inherited mental or physical deformity to the fatal interregnum
which the champions of the modesty of harlots had brought about.

A. CONAN DOYLE

Southsea, 1883

THE EVENING NEWS,
PORTSMOUTH   27 March 1884

The Portsmouth Young Men's Christian
Association and their Rev. Critic

SIR, – I read with much interest the three letters which appeared in
your issue of yesterday in defence of the action of the Rev. Lindsay
Young re. the Young Men's Christian Association, and was
tempted to exclaim with Shakespeare, as I perused each, "Why,
this is a more beautiful song than the other!" The trio, taken
together, would be of interest to the antiquarian. There is a
mediaeval smack about them which wafts us back to the
enlightened days when so-called Christianity took its stand
against quoit playing, the maypole, and plum-pudding, upon
Christmas day. What! because Mr. Young is Vicar of St. John's,
shall there be no more cakes or ale in the land? Think you that the
mild man-god of Galilee looked stern when those children played
whom he invited to come to him? "Worldly" is a word which the
narrow-minded unimaginative bigot is only too ready to employ.
The Roman Pro-Consul, steeped in the vices of the rising Empire,
the Instful Sadducees, preaching temperance to the masses, and
living in luxury – these were the men to whom Christ applied the
term. Who thinks now that He would mean it to apply to earnest
and God-fearing young men, deriving intellectual and moral
amusement from the lips of a lady who is above slander? As
"Veritas" remarks, Mr. Young probably cannot be shamed; and
yet, unless his moral digestion is very strong, surely he cannot but
feel some qualms when he thinks of the broad liberalism of our
Saviour in the corn field and compares it with his own petty
straw-splitting view of things around him. Is the designation of
"Christian" to be withdrawn from a body of men because they
listen to an account of how a child sacrifices its life in the hope of
shedding a gleam of happiness upon the deathbed of a little mite
younger than itself? This is the theme of "Billy's Rose"; but of
course Mr. Young has not read it, because it is (save the mark!)
worldly and un-Christian. Thank God that there are not many
who accept Mr. Young's definitions of Christianity, for if they held

16

good one would have to choose between Mohametanism and Atheism.

I remain, Sir, yours truly,

A.C.D.

THE EVENING NEWS,
PORTSMOUTH   23 September 1884

American Medical Diplomas

SIR, – In ventilating the question of sham degrees and American diplomas you do the public a great service. In all other trades and professions an incompetent man is a mere inconvenience, of more harm to himself than to others. It is different, however, in medicine. There, a blunder in diagnosis or an error in treatment means death to the unfortunate sufferer. It is obviously impossible for the poor and uneducated to distinguish between a qualified practitioner and a quack who has appropriated some high-sounding title. In order to protect them, therefore, it is necessary that the law and the force of public opinion should be brought into play.

The so-called "University of Philadelphia" might stand as a type of these sham examining boards. The university consisted of a small body of speculative parchment-mongers who did a roaring trade in worthless diplomas until the Government of the United States discountenanced them. They then established agencies in Europe and continued their dishonest traffic. Anyone who could muster the necessary dollars was free to their degree and might then pose as the equal of the *bona fide* practitioners who had expended hundreds of pounds and years of his life in obtaining his qualification. It is true that in practising on the strength of their bogus degree they rendered themselves liable to the Apothecaries Act. This, however, is seldom put in force, for the reason that the prosecutor too often finds his opponent a man of straw, and has to bear the expense of the proceedings. There is a body called the Medical Defence Association, which occasionally comes down upon these gentry and gibbets one to act as a scarecrow to the others. The public Press, however, is the best of all defences, for by ventilating the question it opens the eyes of those who might become dupes. It is no question of the comparative merits of British and American degrees. An M.D. of a good Transatlantic college is always respected in England, and any man might be proud to hail from the school of which Gross, Sayre, and Austin Flint are shining lights. It is against sham degrees that we protest, which enable a man to cover his ignorance by an imposing title,

17

and to decide matters of life and death without being competent to do so.

I remain, Sir, sincerely yours,
A.C.D.

THE LANCET   29 November 1884

The Remote Effects of Gout

SIR, – I read with much interest the description of the relation of certain diseases of the eye to gout, as reported last week in the *Lancet*. Mr. Hutchinson has remarked in his lecture on the obscure non-arthritic effects which gout may produce in the children of gouty parents, without any ordinary gouty symptoms. I have had two cases lately in my practice which illustrate his remarks so well that I cannot forbear from quoting them. A Mr. H — came to me suffering from chronic eczema and psoriasis. He attributed it himself to the great changes of temperature and profuse perspirations incidental to his business. I put him on arsenic and afterwards on iodide of potash, without much benefit. He told me that he had never had any gouty symptoms in his life. Shortly afterwards his married daughter, Mrs. B —, consulted me on certain intense pains in her eyes, accompanied by temporary congestion and partial blindness, which attacked her whenever her digestion was deranged. Recognising this to be a gouty symptom, and bethinking me of the obscure skin disease which afflicted the father, I made somewhat minute inquiries into the previous family history. I then found that the grandfather of Mrs. B — and the father of Mr. H — had been a martyr to gout for many years, and had eventually died of a form of Bright's disease, which I have no doubt from the description was the "contracted granular kidney" so intimately associated with gout.

These cases are, I think, interesting as showing the protean character of the disease, extending over three generations. The grandfather was thoroughly gouty; the father had skin affections without any other gouty symptom; the third generation exhibited eye symptoms and nothing else. I may mention that both cases improved rapidly upon calchicum and alkalies.

Yours sincerely,
A. CONAN DOYLE, M.B., C.M.

Southsea, Nov. 24th, 1884.

Carlyle: His Character and Philosophy

SIR, – I do not know whether your editorial columns are a final tribunal, beyond which there is no appeal, or whether you will have the courtesy to allow me to say a few words in reply to your remarks upon Carlyle. The cold douche of criticism which you have directed against my views is most bracing and invigorating; and, as you justly observed, a little more dissension at the meetings of our Society would add a piquancy to the proceedings which is at present wanting. The remarks upon Carlyle's character, however, which appeared in your article seem to me to show such a misapprehension of the man, and such a false view of his philosophy, that it would be hardly fair to allow them to pass unchallenged.

I know of no incident in literary history which is more petty, and at the same time more pitiable, than the onslaught made upon Carlyle's character and memory after his death. As long as he was alive, who cared to breathe a word against him? The moment that the old lion lay still and silent, however, there was no jackal too small to take a snap or pinch at him. Had it been clearly established that he had broken every commandment in the Decalogue, there could not have been a greater yelping and outcry. No more bitter words could be found to describe the private life of Goethe or a Byron than have been applied to that of Carlyle. Had he combined the licentiousness of Heine, the intemperance of Coleridge, and the vindictiveness of Landor, what harder terms could have been used? And yet, after all, what was the head and front of his offending? When the whole 85 years of his life are examined with the uttermost minuteness of criticism, the flaws in it are so small that it seems almost ludicrous to enumerate them. Let us examine Froude's *Life*, Mrs. Carlyle's *Letters*, the *Journal of Caroline Fox*, and the leading article of the *Hampshire Post*. Having sifted these authorities, let us see what the enormities are of which the man has been guilty, and which invalidate his teaching.

The first and most prominent indictment is a grave one. He abominated the crowing of cocks, and became irritable when his work was interrupted by it. This is sad indeed! The second charge is almost as bad. He disliked the jingling of his neighbour's piano and the playing of street organs. After this, of course, it is impossible to accept him as a moral reformer.

But there are other and more insidious crimes to be considered.

He judged some of his contemporaries hardly, and wrote his convictions in his private journal, which was afterwards published without these passages being erased. In it he describes Charles Lamb as a drunkard; Leigh Hunt as a sloven; and Coleridge as a dreamer. It is true that Lamb was a drunkard, Hunt a sloven, and Coleridge a dreamer; and that Carlyle said so openly and in the light of day, besides writing it in his journal. But this, in the eyes of the critics, is no extenuation but rather an aggravation, of his offence. He has committed the unpardonable crime of speaking the truth; and of all errors, that is the last to be forgiven in this world. You wrong him, however, when you insinuate that he depreciated the majority of his contemporaries. His admiration for Tennyson, Ruskin, Owen, Sterling, Emerson, and others was sincere, and expressed with characteristic energy.

Then there is the terrible question of his temper. If a man ever existed who had at the same time a highly strung nervous system, chronic dyspepsia, and a sweet temper, that man was a psychological monstrosity. To say that the philosopher had not such is simply to admit that he was human. His irritability, however, was a very superficial and transient trait in his character. We have his letters to his wife, written when they were both grey-headed, and breathing as much passion and tenderness as though she was still the Haddington lass of 41 years before. This temper, of which so much has been said, could not have been such a terrible thing if, after enduring it for four decades, his wife and he could still correspond in such a strain. There is no man who has not, somewhere in his composition, what the American humourist described as his "redeeming vices." Assuredly, however there is no one of whom we have any record who possessed them in so infinitesimal a degree as Carlyle. I leave it to any unbiased mind whether it would not be ludicrous, were it not humiliating, that, on such charges as these, this great man's character should be gravely stated to have suffered by the publication of the volumes mentioned in your leading article.

If I take exception to your remarks on Carlyle's character, I do so even more emphatically in the case of your exposition of his philosophy. His was no Gospel of Despair. To point out and bewail evil is not to despair of it. No philosopher, ancient or modern, has even taken so broad and so hopeful a view of the universe. This is wrong, and that is wrong, according to him: but all things are directed to an ultimate good end, which they will surely and infallibly attain. Here is one passage out of a hundred similar ones:—

"One way or another all the light, energy and order, and genuine *thatkraft*, or available virtue, we have does come out of us, and goes very infallibly into God's treasury, living and working through eternities there. We are not lost, not a single atom of us – of one of us."

Is that a cry of "despair?" Might not the Gospel of Optimism be a better name for such a creed?

It is hard within a limited space to answer so sweeping and trenchant an attack as that which appeared in your columns, I have touched upon a few points; but there are many which I have neglected, not because they are impregnable (for all are equally weak), but because I feel that your space must not be trespassed upon too much. You remark that Carlyle's lament was monotonous, and always the same. Consistency, I admit, is not a crime. Again, you say that his influence is on the decrease. Anything further from the fact I can hardly imagine. Not only is it on the increase, but it has become the only modern influence among the younger generations. In 300 years Carlyle will stand out above the writers of the Victorian era as Shakespeare does among those of the Elizabethan.

The mere question of the merits of his teaching is one which time will settle. What concerned me more particularly in writing this letter was the defence of his private character. As flies settle upon the least sound portion of the meat, so critics love to dwell upon the weaker side of a great mind. By reading their strictures, those who have not examined the question for themselves might go away with a false impression. In the hope of lessening that possibility I have troubled you with this long letter.

Faithfully yours,
A. CONAN DOYLE, M.D.

Southsea, 26th Jan., 1886

THE EVENING NEWS,
PORTSMOUTH   7 May 1886

The Proposed Recreation Ground
at North End

SIR, – In considering the question of the proposed recreation ground at North-end, it appears to me that there are two points which have hardly received the attention which they deserve. The first is the principles on which it should be established, and the second, how far it might be made a self-supporting institution. I am inclined to think that it would be no difficult matter for the ground to pay the interest upon the loan without there being any need to fall back upon the already over-weighted resources of the borough. Perhaps if this could be made clear it would remove the scruples of some of the present opponents of the scheme, who are very properly anxious to avoid incurring additional expense. In the first place, as regards the management of the ground, since the scheme has been ostensibly put forward in the interest of the numerous athletic bodies of the town, they should be allowed a word in the matter. There has been talk of a free park open to all, in which all ages and sexes may play or walk without let or hindrance. If such a scheme were adopted, the ground would at once lose its whole *raison d'etre*. What hope would there be of good cricket upon a pitch which was cut up and scarred by indiscriminate playings? What would be the value of a bicycle track where the rider could never be certain of a clear course, but must be continually on the watch for children or perambulators? Those who merely wish for fresh air and open space have already the Common, the Victoria Park, and the Portsdown Hills, over which they may ramble. The desertion of the former by cricketers and football players is typical of what would occur in the new ground were it thrown open to the public without restriction or reserve. It is useless to assert that the scheme is undertaken for the benefit of the athletic clubs, and then to couple it with conditions which would deprive it of all value to any athletic body. On the other hand if the ground were regulated in a manner which would make it really useful, there is every prospect that it would be able to pay its way. Let there be a first-class cricket field with every appliance for keeping it in the best of order, a good cinder track for runners and cyclists, lawn-tennis courts round the edges, and a neat little pavilion, to which the gate keeper's lodge might be attached. Then let every club which takes advantage of these arrangements, including the various cricket, football, cycling, running, tennis, and other Societies, pay either so much per year or so much per match for the use of the ground. There is no desire among the different Clubs to make the public pay for their amusements. All they want is to have the chance of such a ground, towards which they are very willing to contribute, and their payments would assist in defraying the annual interest. Again, if the cricket pitch were kept in perfect condition there should be no difficulty in arranging that some of next season's county matches should be played upon it. A three days' match, reckoning the attendance at a thousand a day and the entrance money at one shilling, should bring £150 into the fund. If a few such matches could be arranged, and if all athletic sports, cup ties at football, bicycle and harrier competitions, &c., were to devote a portion of their gate money to the ground, there should be no difficulty in making it self-supporting. It cannot be too strongly impressed upon the Council, however, that any attempt at making the park a public lounge and at the same time a field for athletics, will simply end in danger to the loungers, discontent among the players, and financial responsibility to the borough. The question will arise why such a field should be provided by the town. Simply because it is too large an enterprise for private individuals, and because it will be a permanent addition to the many attractions of the borough. No ratepayer can reasonably complain that he is excluded from it, since by affiliating himself to any local club he can at once have the full use of it. If this opportunity be lost, I fear in a year or two a ground will be taken which may be less convenient and more expensive.

I remain, Sir, faithfully yours,
A. CONAN DOYLE, M.D.

Bush Villa

THE EVENING NEWS,
PORTSMOUTH   6 July 1886

The Unionist Platform

SIR, – As a man holding Liberal opinions upon many of the leading questions of the day, I should like to explain why I and many more are about to vote for the Unionist candidates. The whole controversy may, it appears to me, be summed up in the following six propositions, which I have never heard controverted:–

1. That since the year 1881 the agitation in Ireland has been characterised by a long succession of crimes against life and property.

2. That these murders and maimings have never been heartily denounced by any member of the Irish Parliamentary party.

3. That politicians who could allow such deeds to be done without raising their voices against them cannot be men of high political morality – and are, therefore, however talented, unfit to be trusted with the destinies of a country.

4. That Michael Davitt, whose influence in Ireland is hardly second to that of Parnell, has publicly stated that this shall *not* be a final settlement.

5. That Ireland ought in justice to have the same privileges as England, Scotland, or Wales, but that there is no reason why she should have more than the three law-abiding sister countries.

6. That a grand scheme of Imperial Federation is nearly ripe, by which every country should manage its own local affairs, leaving Imperial matters to a central Parliament, in which every division of the Empire should be represented. That any exceptional Irish legislation of the nature proposed would hamper this just and symmetrical design, which we owe largely to the genius of that eminent Radical – the late Mr. W.E. Forster.

23

I trust that by publishing this short statement you may give another proof of that good feeling which has characterised this political campaign. If we differ from men whose opinions we share on many other subjects, it is not from any narrow class or party feeling, but from an honest conviction that an Irish Parliament would not conduce to the strength or prosperity of that Empire which all parties are anxious to uphold.

I remain, Sir, sincerely yours,
A. CONAN DOYLE

THE EVENING MAIL, PORTSMOUTH   26 March 1887

Working Men's Loyal Jubilee Memorial

SIR, – It appears to me that General Harward's idea of a small personal memorial to the Queen, in the shape of a bust or statue to Her Majesty, is one which is well worthy of public support. In this utilitarian age it is, I know, difficult to enlist sympathy for any scheme which involves an outlay without any practical return; but surely if ever there was a time when some little sentiment was excusable it is on this the fiftieth year of the Victorian era. A hundred years hence both the Portsmouth Hospital and the Colonial Institute will no doubt be standing; but how many of those who pass these buildings will care to enquire what was the occasion upon which they were erected. A statue, however, with a suitable inscription tells its own tale, and will record, as long as granite will hold together, the loyal affection with which the people of this historical borough regard a sovereign whose conduct of affairs may serve as a model to every future occupant of the British Throne. It is no exaggeration to say that since the days of Edward the Confessor no English monarch has ever led so consistently virtuous a life or has had so beneficent an influence upon the domestic lives and social habits of her subjects. It is only fitting, therefore, that some small tribute of personal affection and admiration should be offered to Her Majesty herself, apart from the two other undertakings which are, after all, rather presents to ourselves as a town and as a nation, than to Queen Victoria, in whose honour they are said to be inaugurated. Loyalty is not the prerogative of any one party – as might be seen in democratic Birmingham the other day – and Liberals should be the first to honour a monarch whose leading characteristic has been her compliance with every constitutional safeguard, and her ready and uniform acquiescence to the will of the people as declared by their representatives. In conclusion, I may suggest that the statue might adorn the new Town Hall. The sum which is required is so small that it could not possibly make any appreciable difference to the other schemes which are already before the public.

Yours faithfully,
A. CONAN DOYLE

Bush Villa

LIGHT   2 July 1887

A Test Message

SIR, – I believe that it has been found a useful practice among revivalists and other excitable religionists of all types, for each member to give the assembled congregation a description of the manner in which they attained the somewhat vague result known as "finding salvation." Now among Spiritualists there is really a good deal to be said for such a practice, for the first steps of the inquirer after truth are along such a lonely and treacherous path that it must always be of interest to him to hear how some other wanderer has stumbled along it, uncertain whether he was following a fixed star or a will-o'-the-wisp, until at last his feet came upon firmer ground and he knew that all was well. To the humble inquirer, distrustful of self and fettered with the prejudices of early education, it is of no avail to speak of psychography, materialisation, or advanced phenomena. He yearns for some proof which shall be more within the range of his own personal experience and which shall be decided enough to convince his reason without being so overwhelming as to stagger and confuse it. This must be my apology, therefore, for dwelling upon the incident which, after many months of inquiry, showed me at last that it was absolutely certain that intelligence could exist apart from the body.

Some months ago I read Judge Edmonds' *Memoirs*, and I have since read Alfred Russel Wallace's book, Major-General Drayson's tract, and other writings on the subject. After weighing the evidence, I could no more doubt the existence of the phenomena than I could doubt the existence of lions in Africa, though I have been to that continent and have never chanced to see one. I felt that if human evidence – regarding both the quantity and the quality of the witnesses – can prove anything, it has proved this. I then set to work to organise a circle of six, which met nine or ten times at my house. We had phenomena such as messages delivered by tilts, and even some writing under control, but there was never anything which could be said to be absolutely conclusive. That complicated machine, the human body, is capable of playing strange tricks, and what was the possibility of unconscious cerebration, of involuntary muscular action, and of the effect of a dozen heavy hands on one light table, I was never entirely satisfied. I was convinced that others had obtained the phenomena, but not that I had done so myself.

Last week I was invited by two friends to join them in a sitting with an old gentleman who was reputed to have considerable mediumistic power. It was the first time that I had ever had the opportunity of sitting with anyone who was not a novice and inquirer like myself. I may remark here that for some days I had been debating in my mind whether I should get a copy of Leigh Hunt's *Comic Dramatists of the Restoration* – the question being whether the mental pollution arising from Messrs. Congreve, Wycherley, and Co. would be compensated for by the picture of the manners and customs of those days to be gathered from their pages, and which I had particular reasons for wishing to be well up in. I had thought the matter over, but had dismissed it from my mind a day or two before the séance. On sitting, our medium came quickly under control, and delivered a trance address, containing much interesting and elevating matter. He then became clairvoyant, describing one or two scenes which we had no opportunity of testing. So far, the meeting had been very interesting, but not above the possibility of deception. We then proposed writing. The medium took up a pencil, and after a few convulsive movements, he wrote a message to each of us. Mine ran: "This gentleman is a healer. Tell him from me not to read Leigh Hunt's book." Now, sir, I can swear that no one knew I had contemplated reading that book, and, moreover, it was no case of thought-reading, for I had never referred to the matter all day. I can only say that if I had had to devise a test message I could not have hit upon one which was so absolutely inexplicable on any hypothesis except that held by Spiritualists. The message of one of my friends, referring to his own private affairs, was as startlingly correct as mine.

Let me conclude by exhorting any other searcher never to despair of receiving personal testimony, but to persevere through any number of failures until at last conviction comes to him, as come it will. Let him deserve success by his patience and earnestness, and he will gain it. Above all, let every inquirer bear in mind that phenomena are only a means to an end, of no value at all of themselves, and simply useful as giving us assurance of an after existence for which we are to prepare by refining away our grosser animal feelings and cultivating our higher, nobler impulses. Unless a man starts with that idea the séance-room sinks to the level of the theatre or the opera – a mere idle resort for the indulgence of a foolish, purposeless curiosity. Let a man realise that the human soul, as it emerges from its bodily cocoon, shapes its destiny in exact accordance with its condition; that that condition depends upon the sum result of his actions and thoughts in this life; that every evil deed stamps itself upon the spirit and entails its own punishment with the same certainty that a man stepping out of a second floor window falls to the ground; that there is no room for deathbed repentances or other nebulous conditions which might screen the evil doer from the consequence of his own deeds, but that the law is self-acting and inexorable. This, I take it, is the lesson which Spiritualism enforces, and all phenomena are only witnesses to the truth of this central all-important fact.

Pray excuse my encroachment upon your space.

Yours faithfully,
A. CONAN DOYLE, M.D.

Southsea

THE EVENING MAIL,
PORTSMOUTH   15 July 1887

Compulsory Vaccination

SIR, – From time to time some champion of the party which is opposed to vaccination comes forward to air his views in the public Press, but these periodical sallies seldom lead to any discussion, as the inherent weakness of their position renders a reply super-fluous. When, however, a gentleman of Colonel Wintle's position makes an attack upon what is commonly considered by those most competent to judge to be one of the greatest victories ever won by science over disease, it is high time that some voice should be raised upon the other side. Hobbies and fads are harmless things as a rule, but when a hobby takes the form of encouraging ignorant people to neglect sanitary precautions and to live in a fool's paradise until bitter experience teaches them their mistake, it becomes a positive danger to the community at large. The interests at stake are so vital that an enormous responsibility rests with the men whose notion of progress is to revert to the condition of things which existed in the dark ages before the dawn of medical science.

Colonel Wintle bases his objection to vaccination upon two points: its immorality and its inefficiency or positve harmfulness. Let us consider it under each of these heads, giving the moral question the precedence which is its due. Is it immoral for a Government to adopt a method of procedure which experience has proved and science has testified to conduce to the health and increased longevity of the population? Is it immoral to inflict a passing inconvenience upon a child in order to preserve it from a deadly disease? Does the end never justify the means? Would it be

27

immoral to give Colonel Wintle a push in order to save him from being run over by a locomotive? If all these are really immoral, I trust and pray that we may never attain morality. The colonel's reasoning reminds me of nothing so much as that adduced by some divines of the Scottish Church, who protested against the introduction of chloroform. "Pain was sent us by Providence," said the worthy ministers, "and it is therefore sinful to abolish it." Colonel Wintle's line of argument is that smallpox has been also sent by Providence and that it becomes immoral to take any steps to neutralise its mischief. When once it has been concisely stated, it needs no further agitation.

In the second place is the mode of treatment a success? It has been before the public for nearly a hundred years, during which time it has been thrashed out periodically in learned societies, argued over in medical journals, examined by statisticians, sifted and tested in every conceivable method, and the result of it all is that among those who are brought in practical contact with disease, there is a unanimity upon the point which is more complete than upon any other medical subject. Homoeopath and allopath, foreigner and Englishman, find here a common ground for agreement. I fear that the testimony of the Southsea ladies which Col. Wintle quotes, or that of the district visitors which he invokes, will hardly counter-balance this consensus of scientific opinion.

The ravages made by smallpox in the days of our ancestors can hardly be realised by the present sanitary and well-vaccinated generation. Macaulay remarks that in the advertisements of the early Georgian era there is hardly ever a missing relative who is not described as "having pock marks upon his face." It was universal, in town and in country, in the cottage and in the palace. Mary, the wife of William the Third, sickened and died of it. Whole tracts of country were decimated. Now-a-days there is many a general practitioner who lives and dies without having ever seen a case. What is the cause of this amazing difference? There is no doubt what the cause appeared to be in the eyes of the men who having had experience of the old system saw the Jennerian practice of inoculation come into vogue. When in 1802 Jenner was awarded £30,000 by a grateful country the gift came from men who could see by force of contrast the value of his discovery.

I am aware that Anti-Vaccinationists endeavour to account for the wonderful decrease of smallpox by supposing that there has been some change in the type of the disease. This is pure assumption, and the facts seem to point in the other direction. Other zymotic diseases have not, as far as we know, modified their characteristics, and smallpox still asserts itself with its ancient virulence whenever sanitary defects, or the prevalence of thinkers of the Colonel Wintle type, favour its development. I have no

28

doubt that our recent small outbreak in Portsmouth would have assumed formidable proportions had it found a congenial uninoculated population upon which to fasten.

In the London smallpox hospital nurses, doctors and dressers have been in contact with the sick for more than fifty years, and during that time there is no case on record of nurse, doctor, or dresser catching the disease. They are, of course, periodically vaccinated. How long, I wonder, would the committee of the Anti-Vaccination Society remain in the wards before a case broke out among them?

As to the serious results of vaccination, which Colonel Wintle describes as indescribable, they are to a very large extent imaginary. Of course there are some unhealthy children, the offspring of unhealthy parents, who will fester and go wrong if they are pricked with a pin. It is possible that the district visitors appealed to may find out some such case. They are certainly rare, for in a tolerably large experience (five years in a large hospital, three in a busy practice in Birmingham, and nearly six down here) I have only seen one case, and it soon got well. Some parents have an amusing habit of ascribing anything which happens to their children, from the whooping-cough to a broken leg, to the effects of their vaccination. It is from this class that the anti-vaccinationist party is largely recruited.

In conclusion I would say that the subject is of such importance, and our present immunity from small pox so striking, that it would take a very strong case to justify a change. As long as that case is so weak as to need the argument of morality to enforce it I think that the Vaccination Acts are in no great danger of being repealed.

Yours faithfully,
A. CONAN DOYLE, M.D., C.M.

Bush Villa, July 14th, 1887

THE HAMPSHIRE COUNTY TIMES,
PORTSMOUTH   27 July 1887

Compulsory Vaccination

SIR, – Colonel Wintle's second letter appears to me to contain a jumble of statistics and quotations, some of which do not affect the question at all, while others tell dead against the cause which he is championing. If there is such a consensus of testimony that there was a marked diminution of pock-marked faces between the years 1815 and 1835, is it not a fact that these are the very years when the fruits of Jenner's discovery might be expected to show itself upon the rising generation? Colonel Wintle's argument appears to be that it was a mere coincidence that the disease should begin to diminish at the very time when the new treatment was adopted by a considerable section of the public. The medical profession holds that it was cause and effect – an explanation which has been amply borne out by subsequent experience.

The Colonel seems to think that because we still suffer from occasional epidemics of smallpox that proves the system of vaccination to be a failure. On the contrary, the most clinching argument in its favour is furnished by these very epidemics, for when their results come to be tabulated they show with startling clearness the difference in the mortality between those who have and have not been vaccinated. The unvaccinated not only contract the disease more readily, but it attacks them in a far more virulent form. The Sheffield case recorded by "Common Sense" is a remarkable and recent example of this well-known fact.

The protection afforded by vaccination is in exact proportion to the thoroughness of the original inoculation. I suppose the most determined anti-vaccinationist would hardly venture to suggest that the statistics of hospitals are cooked in order to annihilate their particular fad. Here are Marson's tabulated results of the cases treated at the Smallpox Hospital during twenty years, and if Colonel Wintle can ignore them, I am puzzled to know what evidence would be accepted by him as conclusive. A glance at the subjoined table will show that there is a most exact correspondence between the degree of vaccination and the degree of mortality:–

Of those with 4 vaccine marks .... .5 per cent died
     ,,   ,, 3   ,,   ,, ... 1.9
     ,,   ,, 2   ,,   ,, ... 4.7
     ,,   ,, 1   ,,   ,, ... 7.7
With none, but professing
to have been vaccinated 23.3
Non-vaccinated patients   37

Here it will be seen that the death-rate varies from less than one in a hundred among the well-vaccinated to the enormous mortality of 37 per cent. among Colonel Wintle's followers. These figures, remember, are taken from no single outbreak, where phenomenal conditions might prevail, but they represent a steady average drawn from twenty years of London smallpox. I might quote other corroborative tables of statistics, but I feel that if the foregoing fails to convince no other evidence is likely to succeed.

Colonel Wintle remarks that London and Liverpool are more afflicted by smallpox than any other towns and deduces from that an argument against vaccination. The reason for the prevalence of the disease is of course that they have a larger floating population than any other English city and that therefore it is more difficult to enforce the vaccination acts. With all the zeal in the world a public vaccinator cannot eliminate smallpox in a large port with a constant influx of foreigners and seamen.

Anti-vaccinationists harp upon vaccine being a poison. Of course it is a poison. So is opium, digitalis, and arsenic, though they are three of the most valuable drugs in the pharmacopaeia. The whole science of medicine is by the use of a mild poison to counteract a deadly one. The virus of rabies is a poison, but Pasteur has managed to turn it to account in the treatmemt of hydrophobia.

As to fatal cases following vaccination, medical men are keenly alive to the necessity of using the purest lymph, and no candid enquirer can deny that some deplorable cases have resulted in the past from the neglect of this point. Such incidents are as painful as they are rare. Every care is now used to exclude a possibility of a strumous or syphilitic taint being communicated, these being the only constitutional diseases which have been ever known to be conferred. As I said in my previous letter, there are some children who will fester and inflame if they are picked with a pin, and these occasionally have their hereditary weakness brought out by the vaccination. Such stray cases, however, even if we allowed Colonel Wintle's extreme estimate of one a week, bear an infinitesimal proportion to the total amount of good done. At present if a child dies of any cause within a certain time of its vaccination the anti-vaccinators are ready to put it down as cause and effect. Convulsions, whether arising from worms, or teething, or brain irritation, are all ascribed to the pernicious effect of what the literature of the league terms "that filthy rite."

In conclusion, there is no reason why Colonel Wintle should not hold his own private opinion upon the matter. But he undertakes a vast responsibility when, in the face of the overwhelming testimony of those who are brought most closely into contact with disease, he incites others, through the public press, to follow the same course and take their chance of infection in defiance of hospital statistics. Only the possession of an extremely strong case can justify a man in opposing medical men upon a medical point, and this is of all points the one which should be most cautiously approached, as the welfare of the whole community is at stake. Should I put forward some positive and dogmatic views upon the rifling of guns or the trajectory of a shell, Colonel Wintle, as an artillerist, would be justified in demanding that I should produce some good reasons for the faith which was in me. The tendency of the scientific world, if we may judge from the work not only of Pasteur and Koch, but also of Burdon-Sanderson, Toussaint, and others, lies more and more in the direction of preventive methods of inoculation to check zymotic disease. In opposing that tendency

Colonel Wintle, however much he may persuade himself to the contrary, is really opposing progress and lending himself to the propagation of error.

To anyone who wishes to know exactly the evidence upon which the practice of vaccination is based I should recommend "The Facts about Vaccination," published by the National Health Society, 44, Berners-street, London.

Yours faithfully,
A. CONAN DOYLE, M.D., C.M.

Bush Villa, Southsea

THE HAMPSHIRE POST, PORTSMOUTH 27 April 1888

The Liberal Unionists

SIR, – As I had the honour of acting as Secretary to the Liberal Unionist organisation in connection with the recent demonstration, it is perhaps fitting that I should answer the letter of "An Old Liberal." Here, as elsewhere, the Liberal Unionists have found a difficulty in perfecting their organisation, as everything had to be begun *de novo*. They have now, however, a central Committee, and they have a list of some hundreds of electors who are pledged to Liberal Unionist views. The Committee is well aware, however, that this list is a very imperfect one; and they will be most happy to add to it the name of "Old Liberal" and the names of any of his friends who may desire to join us. If there is any further information which "Old Liberal" or any other elector might desire, I should be glad if he would call either upon me, or upon Mr. Sherwin, at 23, High Street.

Yours faithfully,
A. CONAN DOYLE

Bush Villa, Elm Grove, 21 April, 1888

THE EVENING NEWS, PORTSMOUTH 20 November 1889

Mr. Shutte's Critic

SIR, – I have read with much interest the very moderate letter of "Broad Churchman," and the answers which it has called forth. From my own point of view he errs rather in the direction of narrowness than of breadth, but it is well that every phase of religious thought should have its champions. From the friction of many views a spark of truth may be elicited.

"A Southsea Curate's" position appears to me to be a very untenable one. He upholds the absolute and entire inspiration of the Bible. But does he not know that there are in the Bible statements which we *know* to be untrue? Are these untruths to be put down to the Deity? The supposition is absurd. Was it He, the possessor of all knowledge, who fell into errors that a modern school child would smile at? Was it He who was the author of the statement that the world was created in six days, that the creation was some five thousand years ago, or that Joshua commanded the sun, which was never moving, to stand still? If it was, then alas for our conceptions of the Deity. If it was not, then what becomes of the absolute inspiration of Scripture?

Winwood Reade in his *Martyrdom of Man* remarks that at the time of the Reformation men pulled down idols of stone and wax, in order to put up in their place an idol of paper and printer's ink. Let us take the good of the Bible and make the most of it, but let us, in the name of reverence and reason, forbear from ascribing to the All-wise that which would represent Him as a magnified man, full of the petty angers, jealousies, and revenges, which we condemn in our fellow mortals. We need no book and no inspiration to tell us of His wisdom and His power. The starry heavens, where a hundred million worlds are circling above us, are enough to bring it home to us far more closely than the words of any Jewish prophet, and there is a moral sense within us which guides the agnostic as well as the Christian. The broader our views the better, for the broadest that human mind can attain to must yet be infinitely narrow when compared to that final truth which must embrace the universe, and all that dwells upon it. In the meanwhile our best aspiration must be,

"That *nothing* walks with aimless feet,
That not *one* life shall be destroyed,
Or cast as rubbish to the void
When God has made the pile complete."

Yours faithfully,
A Southsea Physician.

P.S. – One gentleman, I observe, wants to know how modern thought is superior to that of the 16th century. One sign of progress is that a discussion of this sort may be courteously carried on without any of the disputants having the power, or, I hope, the desire, to make a bonfire of their opponents.

Income Tax Assessment

SIR, – I should like to ask through the medium of your paper whether some change might be introduced by a strong expression of public feeling, in the preposterous system of assessment. At present the infliction is divided into two stages, that of the yellow paper and that of the blue. On the yellow paper you are requested to state under a number of headings which appear to be purposely and most ingeniously contrived for the purpose of puzzling the taxpayer, what your income is, and whence derived. This you do, and return the document, prepared to pay tax on the amount which you have ascertained to be correct.

Presently the blue paper trouble begins. You receive your tax paper, and find that the Assessor has had the insufferable impertinance to disregard your return completely, and to assess you at a purely arbitrary sum, fixed by himself. It amounts to this that income tax is levied not upon a man's income, but upon what some gentleman or gentlemen in the background considers that a man's income ought to be. Would it not be better for this gentleman to put forward his guess in the first instance, and so avoid the farce of the yellow paper altogether. Such an arrangement would save both time and temper, for it takes time to accurately fill a complicated form, and it is a little trying to the temper to have it tacitly assumed that one's statement is a misrepresentation.

And then you are assured that it is open to you to appeal. But what does appealing mean? It means standing before a quorum of one's fellow citizens, like a prisoner before magistrates, and going through the humiliating ordeal of exposing one's private books, and most intimate personal concerns to their criticism. The assessor, when he takes such a liberty as to alter the return which is sent to him, must know very well that nine out of ten of his victims would rather suffer an injustice than have it redressed by such a means. I recollect that some years ago, on the occasion of the assessor's guess being peculiarly outrageous, I took the trouble to appeal, and, of course, obtained my reduction, but three times the sum would not tempt me to go through the experience again.

If the Assessor has fault to find with the figures returned to him, then the onus of disproving them rests with him. But to ignore the taxpayer's return, and to place him in the dilemma of either suffering an injustice, or of going through a degrading ordeal is an intolerable scandal, and one which can only be removed by some wide and forcible expression of public opinion.

I remain, sir, faithfully yours,

A. CONAN DOYLE.

THE DAILY TELEGRAPH

20 November 1890

The Consumption Cure

SIR, – It may, perhaps, be not entirely out of place for an English physician who has had good opportunities of seeing the recent development of the treatment for tuberculosis in Berlin to say something as to its present position and probable results. Great as is Koch's discovery, there can be no question that our knowledge of it is still very incomplete, and that it leaves large issues open to question. The sooner that this is recognised the less chance will there be of serious disappointment among those who are looking to Berlin for a panacea for their own or their friends' ill-health.

I have seen the cases under Professor Bergmann's treatment, those under Professor Bardeleben at the Charité Hospitul, and those of Dr. Levy at his Clinical Cluss, in the Prentzlauer Strasse. This series of cases, taken together with the observations of the assistant physicians and students who have seen most of the treatment, enables one to form some opinion, however imperfect, as to the weaker and stronger points of the system.

In the first place, as to the obtaining of the all-important lymph. I called upon Dr. A. Libbertz, to whom its distribution had been entrusted, and I learned that the present supply is insufficient to meet the demands of the German hospitals, and that it will be at least six weeks before any other demands could be supplied. A pile of letters upon the floor 4ft across and as high as a man's knee gave some indication of what the future demand would be. These, I was informed, represented a single post.

Now as to what may fairly be expected from the lymph when this initial difficulty has been got over. It must never be lost sight of that Koch has never claimed that his fluid kills the tubercle bacillus. On the contrary, it has no effect upon it, but destroys the low form of tissue in the meshes of which the bacilli lie. Should this tissue slough in the case of lupus, or be expelled in the sputum in the case of phthisis, and should it contain in its meshes all the bacilli, then it would be possible to hope for a complete cure. When one considers, however, the number and the minute size of these deadly organisms, and the evidence that the lymphatics as well as the organs are affected by them, it is evident that it will only be in very exceptional cases that the bacilli are all expelled. By the

35

cessation of the reaction after injection you can tell when the tubercular tissue is all cleared out from the system, but there is no means by which you can tell how far the bacilli have also been got rid of. If any remain they will, of course, cause by their irritation fresh tubercular tissue to form, which in turn may be destroyed by a new series of injections. But, unfortunately, it is evident that the system soon establishes a tolerance to the injected fluid, so that the time must, apparently, come when the continually renewed tubercle tissue will refuse to respond to the remedy, in whatever strength it may be applied. Here lies the vast difference between Koch's treatment of consumption and the action of vaccine in the case of smallpox. The one is (for a time at least) conclusive, while in the other your remedy does not touch the real seat of the evil. To use a homely illustration, it is as if a man whose house was infested with rats were to remove the marks of the creatures every morning and expect in that way to get rid of them. Professor Koch himself admits that the bacillus is untouched, and there has not been time yet to see how far its presence will re-establish the old state of things. There is, however, grave reason to fear that it may at least possibly have the effect which I indicate.

Another objection – though a much slighter one – is that the process stirs into activity all those tubercular processes which have become dormant. In one case which I have seen the injection, given for the cure of a tubercular joint, caused an ulcer of the cornea, which had been healed for twenty years, to suddenly break out again, thus demonstrating that the original ulcer came from a tubercular cause. No doubt the ultimate effect of the injection would be beneficial to the corneal ulcer, as well as to the joint, but it is none the less somewhat trying to the patient to have all his varied ailments brought to a head simultaneously. It may also be remarked that the fever and reaction after the injection is in some cases so very high (41° Centigrade, or over 108° Fahr.) that it is hardly safe to use it in the case of a debilitated patient.

So much as to the more obviously weak points of the system. Others may develop themselves as more experience is gained. On the other hand, its virtues are many, and it represents an entirely new departure in medicine. There can be no question that it forms an admirable aid to diagnosis. Tubercle, and tubercle alone responds to its action, so that in all cases where the exact nature of a complaint is doubtful a single injection is enough to determine whether it is lupus, scrofula, phthisis, or any of the manifold forms of tubercle. This alone is a very important addition to the art of medicine.

Lupus and joint affections (scrofulous) undoubtedly get great benefit, but Koch himself cannot tell how far this is temporary and how far permanent. In the early stages of phthisis, again, it causes a rapid change for the better. When cavities are formed, however, Koch himself says that the aid of the surgeon should be employed, which means an extensive and serious operation.

Whatever may be thought of the system, there can be but one opinion as to the man himself. With the noble modesty which is his characteristic, he has retired from every public demonstration. Leaving other men to expound his views, he immures himself once more in his laboratory, and I can say from experience that it is impossible for the stranger in Berlin to see the man whom, of all others, he would most wish to meet.

I hope that perhaps these remarks may be of some practical value to those of your readers who may have some personal reason for desiring to know exactly what is thought in Berlin of the recent discovery.

I am, Sir, your obedient servant,
A. CONAN DOYLE, M.D.

Central Hotel, Berlin, Nov. 17

1890–1914

"For Nelson's Sake"

SIR, – I had waited in the hope that some one else would have answered "R.N.'s" letter, but I prefer to intrude upon your space a second time rather than to leave it unanswered. If your correspondent's signature means that he is an officer of the Royal Navy, we may be allowed to hope that his seamanship is better than his logic. He states that our desire to save Nelson's flagship for the nation shows that we are ignorant of naval history. Most people would have thought that it proved the contrary. If, as he states, others of Nelson's ships have been sold in days gone by, surely the obvious deduction is that it is the more important that this one, almost a last survival, should be retained. As to Nelson's mental or moral state during the time he commanded her, that is quite beside the question. The point is that we have only two ships that ever carried his flag, and that one of them has been sold for an insignificant sum to a foreign nation.

The talk of the expense of keeping the old ship up will not bear discussion. We must, as long as our Navy lasts, have store and depôt and receiving ships in our harbours. The *Foudroyant* can always earn her keep as one of those. Supposing that it takes £10,000 to give her a fresh lease of life. If we can afford £70,000 for an old master, we can also find money to preserve our national relics.

Yours faithfully,
A. CONAN DOYLE

12, Tennison-road, South Norwood.

Britain and the Chicago Exhibition

SIR, – A graceful act of courtesy may do more than the most elaborate statecraft. A capacity for such actions has never shown itself to be part of our national genius. Such a proceeding, for example, as the presentation of the Statue of Liberty by France to America is, as far as I know, unparalleled in our annals. And yet if there are any two races upon earth between which such courtesies should prevail they are our own and our kin of the United States.

At present their heart is set upon making their exhibition a success, and any help which we might give them in achieving this would be very welcome to them. Much after-dinner oratory has been expended upon both sides of the water upon our common origin and common sympathies. Our Government has an opportunity now of showing some practical sign of good will.

The German Government has just refused to the Americans the use of any of their military bands. It would be a graceful action upon the part of our authorities to offer, say, three of our own crack regimental bands, including one of the Guards, to play in the British section of the exhibition. If, in addition to this, a squadron of our Life Guards was sent over to take part in the opening procession the compliment would be the greater. German and French regimental bands have played in London exhibitions and American regiments have visited Canadian towns, so that the idea has no claims to novelty. It appears to me, however, to be just one of those occasions for cementing international friendship which seldom present themselves and which are too valuable to neglect.

Yours faithfully,
A. CONAN DOYLE

Reform Club, Pall Mall, S.W., Dec. 22

THE CRITIC,
NEW YORK   2 December 1893

A Protest from Dr. Conan Doyle

SIR, – I have seen reviews in American papers of a collection of stories under my name, entitled *My Friend the Murderer*. Would you have the goodness to allow me to state in your columns that the book is published without any sanction of mine, and that the tales in it were written many years ago, and were meant to have the ephemeral life that they deserve? It is a matter of very little interest to anyone else no doubt, but it is slightly annoying to an author when work which he has deliberately suppressed is resuscitated against his wish.

A. CONAN DOYLE

Reform Club, London, 13 Nov., 1893

THE CRITIC,
NEW YORK   27 January 1894

Another Letter from Dr. Doyle

SIR, – I note that Messrs. Lovell & Co. state in your columns that they bought the stories which they have recently published from "an agent of mine, Mr. Hogg, and paid twenty-five pounds for them." I have no doubt that Messrs. Lovell & Co. have as much to complain of as I, but I would suggest to them that an agent should be asked to furnish some credentials. I have never employed any agent of that name, and my first intimation of the appearance of the book was a review in an American journal.

A. CONAN DOYLE

Davos Platz, 7 Jan., 1894

THE DAILY CHRONICLE   1 May 1894

"Esther Waters" and the Libraries

SIR, – Whatever action the Society of Authors may take on the question of the exclusion of *Esther Waters* from the railway bookstalls, it is, I think, the duty of every newspaper which has the interests of literature at heart to comment upon it. It may be argued that Messrs. W. H. Smith and Son are a private firm and may do what they like in the matter. As a matter of fact, however, through the huge monopoly which they hold the firm is practically a public institution, and is far too great a thing to be managed upon lines of individual caprice or intolerance. A huge power rests in their hands. Exclusion from their stalls and their library means that the work is cut off at the meter as far as the country consumer goes. Such a power must be used with forbearance, otherwise it becomes unfair both to the author and to his public.

Esther Waters is, in my opinion, a great and a very serious book. It is great because it draws many aspects of life, and every one of them with an attention to detail and a thoroughness of workmanship which put the book on the very highest plane of fiction. It is serious because it deals with a succession of vital questions, and because the most frivolous reader cannot fail to have his conscience touched by it – to have it brought home to him that humble tragedies surround him on all sides, and that he may not have to go further than his own kitchen to find a field for his benevolence. It is the greatest sermon against gambling that has ever been preached, and though in the course of the story it deals with matter which, if coarsely treated, would become objectionable, I do not think that any literary critic would accuse Mr. Moore of bad taste. To draw vice is one thing, and to make it attractive is another.

On what ground, then, can Messrs. Smith and Son inflict so serious an injury upon this author and his book as to exclude it from a large share of its natural market? The obvious duty of a distributing house is to distribute, and not to act as an illegal and unauthorised censor upon literature. It may seem to their advisers immoral to draw certain sides of life, but to many others it seems equally immoral that a great branch of literature should be devoted entirely to frivolity. If the book is objectionable there are recognised means for suppressing it, but both authors and public have a right to complain of a monopoly being used in such a fashion that it becomes a law within the law. *Esther Waters* is a good book – good both in literature and in ethics – and if it is to be placed outside the pale of legitimate fiction, it is difficult to say how any true and serious work is to be done within it.

Yours faithfully,
A. CONAN DOYLE

Reform Club, April 30

THE DAILY CHRONICLE   3 May 1894

The Boycott of "Esther Waters"

SIR, – The defence of the firm in the matter of the non-circulation of *Esther Waters* is founded upon an obvious fallacy. It proceeds throughout upon the assumption that the firm chooses the reading of the public instead of their choosing their own. If the firm was requested to *push* a book of which it disapproved, then at once every word which Mr. Faux has said would become perfectly logical. But nothing of the kind is asked. It is only claimed that the book should have the same fair play as other books. If Mr. Smith's subscribers don't want it, then, of course, they will not ask for it. If they do, they have a right, and the author has a right, that it should be supplied.

Mr. Faux must not think that silence means approval on the part of his subscribers. To take the readiest example, I have myself been a subscriber to his library for years, and yet I have never lodged a complaint against his "Index Expurgatorius." If this is to be the test, I would beg any subscriber who may chance to read this letter to take the trouble to register his protest. The question is not one of this novel or that. It is whether our literature is to conform to the standard of the Glasgow Baillie, or whether it is to claim the same privileges as every great literature of which we have any record. If a book errs in morality let the law of England be called in. But we object to an unauthorised judge, who condemns without trial, and punishes the author more heavily than any court could do.

Mr. Faux wonders that I do not see the fatal blemishes in *Esther Waters*. I would remind him that all the critics whose verdicts I have seen have been equally blind. It is not frankness of expression, but the palliation of vice which makes a dangerous book. If Mr. Faux has read this book carefully, he cannot but acknowledge that the principal impressions which it leaves are a horror of gambling and a deep sympathy with and pity for the humble sorrows of the poor. These are not the fruits of an immoral book.

Yours faithfully,
A. CONAN DOYLE

12, Tennison-road, South Norwood, May 2

THE DAILY CHRONICLE   1 January 1895

Mr. Conan Doyle and America

SIR, – I observe some impressions of America attributed to me in *The Daily Chronicle* which are quite unauthorised and largely incorrect. I formed no such sweeping opinion as to the institutions of the two countries, and I saw many points in which I thought that we had much to learn. As to the better feeling between England and America I was convinced that it was on the increase, and I believe one of the chief obstacles which it has to encounter is the irritating criticisms made by travellers, who generalise upon a short experience, and who fail to allow for the fact that conditions which are dissimilar to our own must evolve different types and different methods.

Yours faithfully,
A. CONAN DOYLE

Davos Platz, Dec. 27.

THE AUTHOR   July 1895

Lecturing in America

SIR, – I observed a passage in last month's *Author* which speaks of the gains to be made by lecturing in America. It is a subject upon which there has been a great deal of exaggeration, and I think that a few words upon it may not be amiss – the more so as my name was coupled with the remarks.

Anyone who goes to America with the intention of seeing the place and the people, and counts on no more from his lectures than the payment of his expenses, will have a most enjoyable experience. He will come back with enlarged ideas, with a pleasant remembrance of hospitality received and with new

45

friendships, which he will hope to retain until they are old ones.

But if he goes with the primary idea of making money he will be disappointed. Thackeray and Dickens made money, and when we have another Thackeray and Dickens they may do the same; but the British lecturer whose credentials are more modest will find that the margin left over, after his expenses are paid, is probably a less sum than he could have easily earned in his own study.

In the extract to which I refer from your American correspondence, the sum of 500 dollars a lecture is mentioned. This is nonsense. Taking an average a fifth part of it would be nearer the mark, which is no more than could be obtained from the better class provincial societies in Great Britain. For argument's sake, however, let us put the American average at 125 dollars. When the agent's commission of 15 per cent. and the high travelling and hotel expenses have been paid, the lecturer will probably have from 80 to 85 dollars clear. Allow him four lectures a week, and we have from 320 to 350 dollars as his gain. Two months of this will leave him something under 3000 dollars. From this he has to subtract his double passage-money, and about a month extra spent in the journey and preparations. If the balance will exceed what he would earn in the same period by his pen, it is then worth his while to go to America for money.

If any brother author should go, however, I strongly recommend him to put his affairs in the hands of my friend, Major J. B. Pond, in whom they will find a very sympathetic comrade as well as a keen business manager. My own trip to America was one of the most pleasant experiences of my life, but if it had been the wish to earn more than I could have done at home which had attracted me thither, I should certainly have been disappointed. This would be a merely personal and unimportant matter, were it not that the mention of exaggerated sums in your pages might mislead and cause disappointment to some of your readers.

A. CONAN DOYLE

Grand Hotel Belvedere, Davos-Platz, Switzerland

THE CRITIC,
NEW YORK   21 September 1895

A Letter from Dr. Doyle

SIR, – I notice that you allude to my recent lecturing tour in America as though it had been unsuccessful. In justice to my most able manager, Major J. Pond, will you allow me to say that it was successful beyond all possible expectation, that I had crowded houses nearly everywhere, and that I could have easily doubled the list of my engagements. My remarks about American lecturing were impersonal, and I repeat that an English author should go there with the primary idea of seeing the country and the people, and that the making of money should be a secondary one.

A. CONAN DOYLE

Maloja, Switzerland, 2 Sept. 1895

THE CRITIC,
NEW YORK   26 October 1895

"Strange Secrets"

SIR, – Will you allow me through your columns to warn your readers against a book called *Strange Secrets*, which is being sold with my name upon the cover? Out of a large number of stories, only one is mine – a very short one in the middle of the book.

A. CONAN DOYLE

Grand Hotel, Caux, 30 Sept. 1895

THE TIMES   7 January 1896

England and America

SIR, – An Englishman who travels in the United States comes back, according to my experience, with two impressions, which are so strong that they overshadow all others. One is of the excessive kindness which is shown to individual Englishmen. The other is of the bitter feeling which appears to exist both in the Press and among the public against his own country. The present ebullition is only one of those recurrent crises which have marked the whole history of the two nations. The feeling is always smouldering, and the least breath of discussion sets it in a blaze. I believe, and have long believed, that the greatest danger which can threaten our Empire is the existence of this spirit of hostility in a nation which is already great and powerful, but which is destined to be far more so in the future. Our statesmen have stood too long with their faces towards the East. To discern our best hopes as well as our gravest dangers they must turn them the other way.

As to the cause of this feeling, it is not so unreasonable as Englishmen usually contend. It is the fashion among us to apportion the blame between the Irish-American and the politician who is in search of his vote. But no such superficial explanation as this can cover the fact that the Governors of 30 American States should unhesitatingly endorse a Presidential

Message which obviously leads straight to war. A dislike so widely spread and so fierce in its expression cannot be explained by the imported animosity of the Celtic Irishman.

To understand the American's view of Great Britain one must read such an American history as would be used in the schools, and accept the statements with the same absolute faith and patriotic bias which our own schoolboys would show in a British narration of our relations with France. American history, as far as its foreign policy is concerned, resolves itself almost entirely into a series of wrangles with Great Britain, in many of which we must now ourselves confess that we were absolutely in the wrong. Few Englishmen could be found now to contend that we were justified in those views of taxation which brought on the first American war, or in the question of searching neutral vessels, which was the main cause of the second. This war of 1812 would possibly only occupy two pages out of 500 in an English history, but it bulks very large in an American one, and has left many bitter memories behind it. Then there was the surly attitude which England adopted towards the States after they had won their independence, the repeated frictions during the Napoleonic epoch, and the attack upon an American frigate by a British 50-gun ship in time of peace. After the war there was the Florida dispute in the time of Andrew Jackson, the question of the Oregon line, the settlement of the Maine and New Brunswick line, and, finally, the hostile attitude of most of our Press at the time of the Civil War. Since then we have had two burning questions, that of the Alabama claims and that of the Behring Sea fisheries, culminating in this of Venezuela. The history of his country then, as it presents itself to an American, is simply a long succession of quarrels with ourselves, and how can it be wondered at if he has now reached that chronic state of sensitiveness and suspicion which we have not quite outgrown ourselves in the case of the French?

If we are to blame as a community for some at least of these unfortunate historical incidents, we are even more to blame as individuals for the widespread bitterness which is felt against us. We have never had a warm, ungrudging word of heartfelt praise for the great things which our kinsmen have done, for their unwearying industry, their virtues in peace, their doggedness in war, their unparalleled clemency when war was over. We have always fastened upon the small, rude details and overlooked the great facts behind. In our shocked contemplation of an expectoration upon the floor we lost sight of universal suffrage and equal education. Our travellers, from Mrs. Trollope and Dickens onwards, have been surprised that the versatile hard-working men, who often combined ten trades in one to adapt themselves to the varying needs of a raw-growing community, had not the manners of Oxford or the repose of Sussex. They could not understand that this rough vitality and over-bearing energy which carried them through their task implied those complementary defects which must go with unusual virtues. Of all English travellers to the States, there was hardly one who did not make mischief with his reminiscences until, in our own days, Mr. Bryce did something to rectify the balance. And our want of charity and true insight are the more inexcusable since no one has written more charmingly of England than Washington Irving, Emerson, and Holmes.

These personal and political causes of bitterness may each be small in itself, but in the aggregate they have assumed a proportion which makes them of national importance. Our journals and public men are in the habit now, as a rule, of alluding to America and Americans in the most friendly way, and that must in time have its effect, if recent unhappy events do not change it. One must have travelled in America to appreciate how kindly is the temper of the people – "angelic" is the adjective which Monsieur Bourget employs – and it is impossible to think that they can continue for ever to feel vindictively towards a kindred nation which has a friendly feeling for them. But the shadow of the past still lies between us, and it may be long before it is lifted. In the meantime we should, in my opinion, lose no opportunity of doing those little graceful acts of kindness which are the practical sign of a brotherly sentiment. Opinions may differ as to the value of Bartholdi's Statue of Liberty as a work of art, but there can be no gainsaying that as a visible sign of French friendship it carries its message to every American who enters New York Harbour. We have our opportunities occasionally of showing a friendly feeling. We had such a one a couple of years ago, when I ventured to point out in the columns of *The Times* that an offer of the Guards' bands for the opening of the Chicago Exhibition might do something towards a better feeling between the nations. The chance was missed, but others will arise. Above all I should like to see an Anglo-American Society started in London, with branches all over the Empire, for the purpose of promoting good feeling, smoothing over friction, laying literature before the public which will show them how strong are the arguments in favour of an Anglo-American alliance, and supplying the English Press with the American side of the question and *vice versa*. Such an organization would, I am sure, be easily founded, and would do useful work towards that greatest of all ends, the consolidation of the English-speaking races.

Yours faithfully,
A. Conan Doyle

Mena House Hotel, Pyramids, Cairo, Dec. 30

The Case of Mrs. Castle

SIR, – Might I implore your powerful intercession on behalf of the unfortunate American lady, Mrs. Castle, who was condemned yesterday to three months' imprisonment upon a charge of theft? Apart from the evidence of medical experts, it is inconceivable that any woman of her position in her sane senses would steal duplicates and triplicates – four toast-racks, if I remember right. Small articles of silver with the hotel mark upon them, so that they could neither be sold nor used, were among the objects which she had packed away in her trunk. It can surely not be denied that there is at least a doubt as to her moral responsibility, and if there is a doubt, then the benefit of it should be given to one whose sex and whose position as a visitor amongst us give her a double claim upon our consideration. It is to a consulting-room, and not a cell, that she should be sent.

Yours faithfully,
A. CONAN DOYLE

Greyswood Beeches, Haslemere, Nov. 7

THE SATURDAY REVIEW   2 January 1897

"Dr. Conan Doyle's Latest Case"

SIR, – I observe that Mr. Max Beerbohm differs very widely from me in his conception of the dandy of the early part of this century. The lists are open to all, and if he wishes to depict a fop of his own it will, no doubt, meet with the success which it deserves. But in the meanwhile you will perhaps allow me space to point out some of the historical and social errors which appear in his short article.

Mr. Beerbohm is severe because I do not describe the younger Pitt. There was no reason why I should describe him, as he does not – save for a reference in conversation – appear in the book. But, in order to show me how it should have been done, Mr. Beerbohm quotes what he describes as the well-known description by Thackeray. It is a well-known description – but it is evidently not a well-known one to Mr. Beerbohm, for it does not refer to the person of whom he is talking at all. "An awful figure in a chair," says Thackeray. "A livid face . . . powdered wig . . . a Roman nose. There he is! There is the great Commoner." How could any one imagine that this was the younger Pitt, who probably never rode in a chair or wore a wig in his life – and who certainly never had a Roman nose! The description is of Pitt's father, afterwards

Earl of Chatham. It may be a venial offence to confound the one Pitt with the other, but what are we to say of the failure to recognize the internal evidence which is contained in the quotation itself? I trust that Mr. Beerbohm will "scatter no more paper flowers" about that epoch until he has read something more reliable than D'Aurevilly's lively but inaccurate essay.

Mr. Beerbohm is contemptuous because a fop has been described in the text as standing with his thumb in his armpit. He also alludes to Brummell in terms which suggest that he knows something of him. If so, he must know that this was one of the Beau's characteristic attitudes. Contemporary sketches depict him in it. The student can refer to one of them in the frontispiece of the second volume of Gronow's Memoirs. There the Beau stands, thumb in armpit, in this impossible attitude for a fop.

Mr. Beerbohm then alludes to "the old exploded fable" that the "Regent was warned off the Turf." After the foregoing specimens of Mr. Beerbohm's historical accuracy, it will take more than his mere assertion to establish that this is a fable. He cannot even state the case without blundering, for it was in 1791 – twenty years before George became Regent – that the incident occurred. It is true that the Prince of Wales was not warned off by name – this would have been too daring even for the autocrats of the Jockey Club – but his jockey, Sam Chifney, was suspended, which answered the same purpose. Chifney's own account of the matter will be found in the little pamphlet by him called "Genius Genuine."

Mr. Beerbohm denies that the Prince had an upturned nose. He must settle that with Mr. Lawrence the painter, who has depicted him with one. Mr. Beerbohm in commenting upon my picture of the times implies that, though I may have the facts, I have not caught the spirit. I cannot say the converse of him, but, at least, I can assure him that he is very far from having caught the facts. He may be upon safe ground when he refers to my bedside manner and gold-rimmed glasses, but he is very ignorant of the period about which he writes.

Yours faithfully,
A. CONAN DOYLE

Reform Club, Pall Mall, S.W.

THE SATURDAY REVIEW 9 January 1897

"Dr. Conan Doyle's Latest Case"

SIR, – I note the various concessions which have to be made to Mr. Beerbohm in order to save the situation. If his conscience will pass them I will do the same. And I especially applaud his excellent contention that because George was at one time of his life a Regent, it is permissible to describe him at all times as the Regent. I would suggest that the same argument would justify us in describing any historical character as "The Baby" – which would simplify matters very much.

Here's "good hunting" for the New Year to Mr. Max Beerbohm.

Yours faithfully,
A. CONAN DOYLE

Greyswood Beeches, Haslemere, 4 Jan., 1897

THE DAILY CHRONICLE   7 August 1897

Literary Etiquette

SIR, – When Mr. Kipling writes such a poem as his "Recessional," he does not state in public what he thinks of it, and how it came to be written. When Mr. Barrie produces so fine a work as *Margaret Ogilvie*, there are no long interviews and explanations to advertise it before it appears. The excellence of the literature commends the poem or the tale to the discerning reader, and the ordinary advertising agencies present its merits to the general public. As a literary man, I would beg Mr. Hall Caine to adopt the same methods. Whether his work is of the best or not is a matter of private judgment. Personally, I have a high opinion of some of it. But that is beside the question. What he has never seemed to realise is that in every high profession – be it law, medicine, the Army, or literature – there are certain unwritten laws – a gentlemanly etiquette which is binding upon all, but most binding upon those who have a claim to stand among the leaders of the profession. If those who are successful advertise their own wares, and use the machinery of the Press in order to whet curiosity about their own book before it has come into the hands of the critics, the young aspirant naturally comes to imagine that this is the cause of the success, and by his imitating the same tactics the whole tone of the profession becomes lowered. Mr. Hall Caine's book has not yet appeared – when it does appear I wish it every success – but I do think it unworthy of the dignity of our common profession that one should pick up paper after paper and read Mr. Caine's own comments on the gigantic task and the colossal work which he has just brought to a conclusion, with minute descriptions of its various phases and of the different difficulties which have been overcome. Surely in the case of another man Mr. Caine would clearly perceive that it is for others to say these things, and that there is something ludicrous and offensive about them when they are self-stated. Each successive book of Mr. Hall Caine's has been self-heralded in the same fashion. All these wire-pullings and personalities tend to degrade literature, and it is high time that every self-respecting man should protest against them, on no narrow individual grounds, but because it rests with us to preserve the honourable traditions which have been handed down from those great men who have preceded us.

It would be preferable if we could leave such questions of etiquette to the critics, but every body of men is the guardian of its own honour, and if we do not sustain an etiquette of our own there is no reason why the critics should interfere to do so. The discipline of every self-respecting profession must be self-enforced, and cannot proceed from outside pressure. That discipline has of late years been sadly relaxed, and some of us hope that the day may come when the Authors' Society may deal with it, as legal or medical societies enforce a high standard of professional etiquette. At present we can do nothing but protest.

If I do not sign my name it is because I do not desire to import personalities into what is an impersonal matter. I have no desire, however, to make an anonymous attack, and I enclose my card, with full permission that it should be forwarded to Mr. Hall Caine should he so desire.

Yours faithfully,
AN ENGLISH NOVELIST

Authors' Club, Aug. 6

THE TIMES   20 October 1897

Nelson Day

SIR, – Might I suggest to the Navy League through your columns that they might reunite public opinion and remove every possible objection to their annual commemoration if they were to hold it on September 29, the date of Nelson's birth, instead of upon that of his death at Trafalgar? The latter, in spite of every disclaimer, must be offensive to our neighbours. If the French were annually to hold public celebrations in honour of Marshal Saxe and the victory of Fontenoy no explanations would prevent us from feeling that it was a national insult. It is un-English and unchivalrous to exult over a beaten foe. But if we kept Nelson's birthday it would answer every purpose which the Navy League has in view, and it could not be open to these objections.

Yours faithfully,
A. CONAN DOYLE

Morley's Hotel, Trafalgar-square, London, W.C.

Nelson Day

SIR, – I regret to find myself at variance with Admiral Hamilton and the other gentlemen who have replied to my letter, but I am still of opinion that a day to celebrate Nelson – his birthday for choice – is in better taste than an annual celebration of a victory over what are now two friendly neighbours. It is beside the question, as it seems to me, to argue whether the French ought or ought not to resent it. What we have to recognize is the fact – amply proved by their Press comments – that they *do* resent it, as we should most certainly do if the cases were reversed. If we can attain our ends of honouring the memory of the hero and of stimulating public interest in the Navy in an inoffensive manner, why should we resort to a provocative one? It is a sound old British maxim never to hit a man when he is down, and all celebrations of days which are to our foemen days of disaster appear to me to be an infringement of this. With all sympathy for the general aims of the Navy League, I still feel that the great words of Lord Rosebery at Stirling, when he said that Britain had so many victories that she had neither the time nor the memory to celebrate them, strike a higher and a nobler note.

Yours faithfully,
A. CONAN DOYLE

Reform Club, Pall-mall, S.W., Oct. 22

The Ethics of Criticism

SIR, – You have more than once been good enough to put your columns at my disposal when I had occasion to broach some subject which appeared to concern the general interests of literature in this country. May I be allowed once more to draw attention to what seems to me to be a growing scandal, and to invite some expressions of opinion from my brother authors upon the subject? I refer to the publications of reviews upon the same book by the same reviewer in many different periodicals, so that what to the uninitiated might seem to be a general burst of praise or blame may really when analysed prove to be the work of a single individual.

I am aware that the subject has been discussed before now; but it becomes year by year a more crying evil, and things seem to me to have now come to such a pass that some attempt must be made to find a remedy. I have no desire to descend to personalities; but one cannot state a case in a convincing manner without giving a concrete instance, which I shall do with as little offence as possible.

There is an excellent and useful monthly, *The Bookman*, in the columns of which the editor, a well-known critic, is naturally able to express his opinion of any new book. The same editor sends – or has until recently sent – a letter to the New York *Bookman*, and so exercises a double influence on each side of the Atlantic. This seems to me to be quite legitimate and fair.

There is a well-known weekly, the *British Weekly*, which is edited by the same gentleman. It is the chief exponent of Nonconformist literary opinion. In this journal this same gentleman can, and does, review the same volume. The reviews are anonymous and there is no reason why the outside public should connect the one review with the other. To it they appear to be two important independent judgments.

In the same paper there are two different columns of paragraphs devoted to literary comment and chat, which are signed respectively by "Claudius Clear" and by "A Man of Kent". I am credibly informed that both of these noms de guerre cover the individuality of the same critic who has already had his opportunity of literary criticism in three other forms. If all these strings are pulled simultaneously a prodigious consensus of opinion seems to exist. And yet there is only the one pair of hands to pull them.

Turning now from these more serious papers to their somewhat frivolous contemporary the *Sketch*, we come upon a colum of literary criticism signed by yet another symbol, "O.O." Yet, incredible as it may seem, the opinion of "O.O" is still the opinion of "Claudius Clear," of "A Man of Kent," of the critic of the *Bookman*, of the critic of the American *Bookman*, and of the critic of the *British Weekly*. This, I hold, is not legitimate criticism.

And now when I add that this same critic frequently expresses his opinion of any important new book in the anonymous columns of a daily paper, and thus adds a sixth to his possible methods of influencing public opinion, I think that I have said enough to show that a protest is needed. I have not chosen this example as being the only case, though perhaps it is the most notorious; but there are other groups of papers controlled by a single opinion, and any two of these groups by forming an alliance can at any time exert an enormous influence upon the fate of a book. It is not too much to say that the property of authors and of publishers comes in this way to be at the mercy of a very small clique of men. To revert to the instance already given, it is obvious that four or five such critics would cover the whole critical Press of London, and no beginner could gain a hearing without their sanction. I hold that such a state of things is intolerable.

The question now is by what possible means we can check such an abuse. Perhaps the mere ventilation of it with a free expression of opinion may do something in this direction. Perhaps also we may appeal to the good feelings of editors, and ask them whether it is not right that the opinion of their paper should be the opinion of their paper, and not the echo of some other paper. But in the last resort we have one final method of ensuring fair play. It is so powerful a weapon that I should be loth to see it used unless it were necessary for the higher interests of literature. Authors and publishers have between them the regulation of advertising, and literary papers are dependent upon advertising. A combination of authors who are opposed to wire-pulling and pluralism would easily, either acting independently or through the Society of Authors, break down this pernicious system.

Let me repeat, in conclusion, that it is not adverse criticism which I deprecate. We do not get enough of it, though it is sometimes misapplied. But it is the system by which one man writes many notices which are quoted as separate opinions. This is the great danger, as it seems to me, of modern British literature.

Yours truly,
A. Conan Doyle

Reform Club, Pall-mall, S.W.

THE DAILY CHRONICLE   16 May 1899

The Ethics of Criticism

Sir, – An omission, which is no doubt accidental – since the proofs were correct – has been made in my letter, which has weakened and altered my point. The real serious abuse is that such criticism *may* not be honest criticisms, but may, consciously or not, be influenced by commercial considerations. That a critic of many voices and numerous noms-de-plume should also have an interest in the success of certain books is, I hold, a scandal.

Yours faithfully,
A. Conan Doyle

Undershaw, Hindhead, Haslemere

THE DAILY CHRONICLE   18 May 1899

The Ethics of Criticism

Sir, – In the face of Dr. Nicoll's assurances, I unreservedly accept his statement that he has never, directly or indirectly, used his very powerful position upon the critical Press to further any personal or commercial end. I will say, also, that after his denial I am sorry that even in the most guarded way the possibility of such a thing should have been suggested. It will serve, however, to bring home to Dr. Nicoll's mind how vicious a system must be, and what unjust suspicions it may excite, when the same gentleman who has so many openings for influencing opinion holds a paid position in an important publishing house. I can assure Dr. Nicoll that I have done him a service by giving him an opportunity of finally setting all such speculations to rest.

I end where I began by repeating that it is obviously wrong that several opinions upon a book, some signed in one way, some signed in another, and some not signed at all, should all really represent the opinion of one man. I believe that Dr. Nicoll has wielded an influence of this kind, and my general facts have not been disputed. Mr. Bullock says there are other and worse groups of papers. It is very possible. Let him name them, as I have done, and he will do good service to literature.

As to the quality of my own work, however deplorable, it is entirely beside the question. I fully subscribe to the time-worn adage which Dr. Nicoll has quoted.

Yours faithfully,
A. Conan Doyle

Reform Club, Pall-mall, S.W.

THE TIMES   18 December 1899

Volunteers and the War

Sir, – The suggestion comes from many quarters that more colonials should be sent to the seat of war. But how can we in honour permit our colonial fellow-civilians to fill the gap when none of our own civilians have gone to the front? Great Britain is full of men who can ride and shoot. Might I suggest that lists should at least be opened and the names of those taken who are ready to go if required – preference might be given to those men who can find their own horses? There are thousands of men riding after foxes or shooting pheasants who would gladly be useful to their country if it were made possible for them. This war has at least taught the lesson that it only needs a brave man and a modern rifle to make a soldier.

Yours faithfully,
A. Conan Doyle

Undershaw, Hindhead, Haslemere

The War Office and Inventors

SIR, – In the coming reform of the War Office there is one department which will, I trust, undergo a complete reorganization – or rather I should say organization since it does not appear to exist at present. I mean the board which inquires into military inventions. I have heard before now of the curt treatment which inventors receive at the hands of the authorities. As I have myself had a similar experience I feel that it is a public duty to record it.

The problem which I was endeavouring to solve was how to attain accuracy – or approximate accuracy – for a dropping, or high angle, rifle fire. It appears to me to be certain that the actions of the future will be fought by men who are concealed either in trenches or behind cover. In the present war it has been quite unusual for our soldiers ever to see a Boer at all. Direct fire is under these circumstances almost useless. The most of your opponent which shows is only the edge of his face, and his two hands. When he is not firing he is entirely concealed. Under these conditions except at close quarters it appears to be a mere waste of ammunition to fire at all.

There is only one side upon which the man in the trench or behind the rock is vulnerable. That side is from above. Could a rain of bullets be dropped vertically all over the enemy's position your chance shot has the whole surface of his body to strike, while the direct chance shot has only a few square inches. There is no escape from this high angle fire. No trench or shield is of any avail. Human life can be made impossible within a given area.

In this system it is not the individual at whom you shoot, but at the position, the ridge, the kopje, whatever it is that the enemy holds. If you search this thoroughly enough you will find the individuals. For example, suppose that a kopje occupied is 1,000 yards long and 100 yards deep, 100,000 bullets falling within that area gives one bullet for every square yard. But 100,000 bullets are nothing – only the contents of the magazines of 10,000 men. It can be judged then how untenable a position would be, if only fire of this sort could be made at all accurate.

But at present there is no means by which it can be regulated. If you were to say to the best marksman in the British Army "Drop me a bullet on that kopje 500 yards off" he would be compelled to look helplessly at his rifle and confess that there was nothing to enable him to do this. He might hold his gun up at an angle and discharge it, but it would be pure guess work, and the probability is that he would be very far out, nor could he correct his error, since he would have no means of knowing where his bullet fell.

My experiments have been in the direction of affixing a small, simple, and economical apparatus to the rifle by which a man would know at what angle to hold his rifle in order to drop a bullet at any given range. It would weigh nothing, cost about a shilling, take up no space, and interfere in no way with the present sights, so that the rifle could be used either for direct or high-angle fire at the discretion of the officer. Having convinced myself that my idea was sound, I naturally wished to have it examined at once in order that, if it should be approved, the troops might have the use of it. I therefore communicated with the War Office, briefly stating what my idea was, and my letter was in due course forwarded to the Director-General of Ordnance. I have just received his reply:–

"War Office, Feb. 16, 1900.

"Sir, – with reference to your letter . . . concerning an appliance for adapting rifles to high-angle fire, I am directed by the Secretary of State for War to inform you that he will not trouble you in the matter.

"I am, Sir, your obedient servant,
(Signature illegible)
"Director-General of Ordnance."

Now, Sir, my invention might be the greatest nonsense or it might be epoch-making, but I was given no opportunity either to explain or to illustrate it. It may be that the idea has been tried and failed, but, if that were so, why not inform me of it? I have shown it to practiced soldiers – one of them with a Mauser bullet wound still open in his leg – and they have agreed that it is perfectly sound and practicable. And yet I can get no hearing. No wonder that we find the latest inventions in the hands of our enemies rather than of ourselves if those who try to improve our weapons meet with such encouragement as I have done.

Yours faithfully,
A. CONAN DOYLE

The Reform Club, Feb. 19

THE WESTMINSTER
GAZETTE   26 February 1900

Mr. Conan Doyle and High Angle Fire

SIR, – My attention has just been called to an interview in the *Westminster Gazette*, concerning my failure to induce the War Office to listen to my views on the question of high angle fire, or to examine the means by which I propose to regulate it. In this I observe that Captain Kenyon declares that I have received three letters upon the subject, of which I have only published the last. He adds that this will be the official answer if a question on the subject be asked in the House. I trust that this is not so, as Captain Kenyon is entirely mistaken in his statement.

I have received two letters from the Ordnance Department upon the subject, of which the one published is the first. The reason why the second was not published also was that it was almost a verbatim reproduction of the first, save that after the words "will not trouble you in the matter of an apparatus for high angle fire from rifles" there is added "as it was not considered desirable to adopt that means of fire." I have therefore had two letters which were practically the same letter. What, then, becomes of the three letters which were said to have been sent to me?

The *Westminster Gazette* misquotes me when it says that I claim success for my idea. On the contrary, I state that there may be a fallacy. But I do claim that the principle is right, and that the detail is worthy of careful examination. If such a use of rifle fire were in vogue, and if approximate accuracy could be attained, it is quite certain that Cronje's force, surrounded in a confined space by 20,000 Lee-Metfords, could not possibly have held out. Every square yard of his position could be searched by a dropping fire, while each Boer had only to dig a hole in order to be safe from a direct one.

As to Captain Kenyon's statement that a wind would render the fire uncertain, and possibly unsafe, it is perfectly correct. But as the rifle remains with its present sights intact, it would not be used for a dropping fire unless the conditions were favourable. A special cartridge with a heavier bullet and less cordite would of course ensure greater accuracy. The height to which the bullet goes with the ordinary service cartridge is such that 55 seconds elapse before its return to earth.

No doubt Captain Kenyon would claim that the replies from his office are in the usual official routine form; but I object, not merely in my own name, but in that of every man who wishes to try to aid his country, that this form should be so offensively curt.

Yours faithfully,
A. CONAN DOYLE

The Reform Club

THE BRITISH MEDICAL JOURNAL

7 July 1900

The Epidemic of Enteric Fever at Bloemfontein

SIR, – You were good enough to suggest when I left England that I should send you some notes upon any points which might strike me. The pressure of work has prevented me from complying with your request, and even now I feel that you will find these comments of a very scrappy character.

When the nation sums up its debt of gratitude to the men who have spent themselves in this war I fear that they will almost certainly ignore those who have done the hardest and the most essential work. There are three classes, as it seems to me, who have put in more solid and unremitting toil than any others. They are the commissariat, the railway men, and the medical orderlies. Of the three, the first two are the most essential, since the war cannot proceed without food and without railways. But the third is the most laborious, and infinitely the most dangerous.

The outbreak of enteric among the troops in South Africa was a calamity the magnitude of which had not been foreseen, and which even now is imperfectly appreciated. We naturally did not dwell too much upon it while the war was in progress. But it was appalling in its severity, both in quantity and quality. I know of no instance of such an epidemic in modern warfare. I have not had access to any official figures, but I believe that in one month there were from 10,000 to 12,000 men down with this, the most debilitating and lingering of continued fevers. I know that in one month 600 men were laid in the Bloemfontein Cemetery. A single day in this one town saw 40 deaths. These facts would have stiffened the resistance at Pretoria if they had been generally known. It is only now, when the worst is past, that they can be talked of.

How was this unforeseen and unprecedented crisis grappled with? Entirely by the efforts of the medical men and by the devotion of the orderlies. When a department is confronted by a task which demands four times more men than it has, the only way of meeting it is for each man to work four times as hard. This is exactly what occurred, and the crisis was met. In some of the general hospitals orderlies were on duty for thirty-six hours in forty-eight, and what their duties were – how sordid and obscene – let those who have been through such an epidemic tell.

He is not a picturesque figure, the orderly, as we know him. We have not the trim, well-nourished army man, but we have recruited from the St. John Ambulance men, who are drawn, in this particular instance, from the mill hands of a northern town. They were not very strong to start with, and the poor fellows are ghastly now. There is none of the dash and glory of war about the sallow, tired men in the dingy khaki suits – which, for the sake of the public health, we will hope may never see England again. And yet they are patriots, these men; for many of them have accepted a smaller wage in order to take on these arduous duties, and they are facing danger for twelve hours of the twenty-four, just as real and much more repulsive than the scout who rides up to the strange kopje or the gunner who stands to his gun with a pom-pom quacking from the hill.

Let our *personnel* speak for themselves; and we make no claim to be more long-suffering than our neighbours. We have 3 on the staff (Mr. Gibbs, Mr. Scharlieb, and myself). Four started, but one left us early in the proceedings. We have had 6 nurses, 5 dressers, 1 wardmaster, 1 washerman, and 18 orderlies, or 32 in all, who actually came in contact with the sick. Out of the 6 nurses, 1 has died and 3 others have had enteric. Of the 5 dressers, 2 have had severe enteric. The wardmaster has spent a fortnight in bed with veld sores. The washerman has enteric. Of the 18 orderlies, 1 is dead, and 8 others are down with enteric. So that out of a total of 34 we have 17 severe casualties – 50 per cent. – in nine weeks. Two are dead, and the rest incapacitated for the campaign, since a man whose heart has been cooked by a temperature over 103° is not likely to do hard work for another three months. If the war lasts nine more weeks, it will be interesting to see how many are left of the original *personnel*. When the scouts and the Lancers and the other picturesque people ride in procession through London, have a thought for the sallow orderly, who has also given of his best for his country. He is not a fancy man – you do not find them in enteric wards – but for solid work and quiet courage you will not beat him in all that gallant army.

There is one mistake which we have made, and it is one which will not, I think, be repeated in any subsequent campaign. Inoculation for enteric was not made compulsory. If it had been so I believe that we should (and, what is more important, the army would) have escaped from most of its troubles. No doubt the matter will be fully threshed out in statistics, but our strong impression, from our own experience, is that although it is by no means an absolute preventive it certainly modifies the course of the disease very materially. We have had no death yet (*absit omen*) from among the inoculated, and more than once we have diagnosed the inoculation from the temperature chart before being informed of it. Of our own *personnel* only one inoculated man has had it, and his case was certainly modified very favourably by the inoculation.

Of the courage and patience of the soldiers in hospital it is impossible to speak too highly. We have had 500 cases pass through our hands, and can speak now from a fairly large experience. I had always imagined that in every large army there must be a minority of skulkers and shirkers, but they are singularly absent in the South African Field Force. I have not had more than two or three cases in my wards which bore a suspicion of malingering, and my colleagues say the same. They are uniformly patient, docile, and cheerful, with an inextinguishable hope of "getting to Pretoria." There is a gallantry even about their delirium, for their delusion continually is that they have won the Victoria Cross. One patient, whom I found the other day rummaging under his pillow, informed me that he was looking for "his two Victoria Crosses." Very touching also is their care of each other. The bond which unites two soldier pals is one of the most sacred kind. One man shot in three places was being carried into Mr. Gibbs's ward. I lent an arm to his friend, shot through the leg, who limped behind him. "I want to be next Jim, 'cos I'm lookin' after him," said he. That he needed looking after himself seemed never to have occurred to him.

I do not think that any men have ever expended money better than those who fitted out the private hospitals. The officers of the Army Medical Department freely admit that they do not know what they would have done without their aid. They arrived out here at the very moment when the sickness was becoming alarming, and they took their share of the strain when the epidemic was at its height. The large general hospitals found it difficult to get to work on account of the pressure on the line which prevented them from getting up their bulky equipment, but the private hospitals, more compact and mobile, got to work almost at once after their arrival. The pressure was severe. Our own hospital, with equipment and *personnel* for 100 cases, had 150 cases, most of them virulent Paardeburg enterics, shot upon them, and had to cope with them as best they might. But the men had come out to work, and the orderlies, though untrained, never once grumbled at the great exertions which were called for. Without the Yeomanry, the Portland, the Irish, the Scotch, the Welsh, and the other hospitals fitted up by private effort, and manned by volunteers, it is difficult to see how the epidemic could have been met.

There is sure to be some adverse criticism of the Army Medical Department after the war, because they have had to meet so difficult a situation with such inadequate resources that it is impossible that there should not be particular instances where the machinery has broken down. A captious critic could quote cases of an overfilled, undermanned hospital without medical necessities in one place or of hardships endured by the sick and wounded in another. How can it be otherwise, when a Department which is sufficient for the needs of two army corps has to provide for the wants of 200,000 men with typhoid raging among them? Taking it on the whole, the Department has been well organised and well worked, and has met an unforeseen and exceptional state of things with remarkable success.

The statistics of the campaign are likely to be vitiated by the

employment of the vague and unscientific term, "simple continued fever," so largely used in the army returns. A great number
of cases were classified under this head, and such forms as "veld
fever," "camp fever," etc., were freely used. I think that nearly all
medical men have come to the conclusion that all, or at least most,
of these cases were really enteric of varying types and degrees of
severity. Our senior surgeon, Mr. Gibbs, performed *post-mortems*
on several cases which presented abnormal features, but never
without finding the characteristic ulcers.

A. CONAN DOYLE, M.D.

The Langman Hospital, South African Field Force, Bloemfontein,
June 5th, 1900

THE EDINBURGH EVENING
DISPATCH   25 September 1900

To the Electors of
Central Edinburgh

GENTLEMEN, – In asking you for your votes and your help in my
Candidature, I do not come before you as a stranger. I was born in
Edinburgh. I spent my boyhood there. I was educated at the
University, and I graduated there. I owe much to the old City, and
my proudest ambition would be that I should have the honour of
representing its Citizens in Parliament.

The circumstances of this election are exceptional. All other
questions are overshadowed by that prolonged and terrible war
which has called for such national sacrifices, and plunged so many
of us into mourning. Now at last we have won our way through
many struggles to success and we will prove whether the wisdom
of our people can secure that which the valour of our soldiers has
gained, or whether at this last hour a great political mistake is to
impair the results of our victory. That is the issue before the
Electors.

At the outset of this war, I took upon myself the task of writing a
history of it. This compelled me to examine the evidence with care,
and I became deeply convinced of the Justice and Necessity of the
struggle. There came a time of stress when each felt called upon to
do what he could to help. I found myself in South Africa. My
duties led me both to Bloemfontein and to Pretoria. I heard from
their own lips the views of British loyalists, of Africanders, of Boers
of every shade of opinion, of British officers, and of British officials.
I returned with strong convictions as to the situation. The chief of
these is that a final and satisfactory settlement can only be hoped
for by strong national support for the Government, which has

amid many difficulties carried the war to a successful conclusion. Any appearance of vacillation or change of purpose must encourage our enemies, dishearten our own people, and alienate the great Colonies which have stood by us so loyally in the struggle. Canada, Australia, and New Zealand have given their gold and their blood to the Cause. Will you not give your votes and your work? The soldiers have done their part. It is our turn to do ours. It is not possible that in a struggle where Scottish troops have fought so heroically, the Electors of the Central Division of the Scottish Capital will be lukewarm or hostile.

Gentlemen, many have made sacrifices of home, of comfort, of life itself, in this war. I ask you also to make one. It is to sacrifice the other questions which may be dear to you in the face of this great question, which is essential and urgent. For the sake of your special interest in any one domestic subject, be it Temperance or Education or religion, do not give a vote which may weaken your country in the one paramount problem which has to be solved. How can you place the settlement of this question in the hands of a party, half of whom blame the Government for not having made war more vigorously, while the other half attack it for having made war at all?

My views upon Social questions will always be in favour of freedom, tolerance, and progress, following the lines marked out in the past by the great Whig party which was so long associated with Edinburgh. If I am returned upon a question of patriotism, I shall feel pledged to oppose all narrow or reactionary legislation, and to keep the interests of all my Constituents before my mind.

Hoping that you will vote upon broad national grounds, unprejudiced by other issues,

I am, GENTLEMEN,
Your obedient Servant,
A. CONAN DOYLE

Dunard, Grange Loan, Edinburgh, Sept. 24, 1900

THE DAILY
CHRONICLE   28 September 1900

Dr. Doyle and the Reform Club

SIR, – I have just seen a letter in your columns from some gentleman who has omitted to sign his name, to the effect that I have broken the principles of the Reform Club by standing as a Liberal Unionist candidate, and accepting the support of the Conservative portion of the electorate. My impression was that the Reform Club contained as many Liberal Unionists as

Radicals, and I am not aware of any regulation which prevents those members from standing for Parliament and accepting such support as they can get. Should there be, as your anonymous correspondent suggests, any such rule, I should, of course, accept the decision of the Club committee upon the point.

Yours faithfully
A. CONAN DOYLE

Sept. 27

THE SCOTSMAN   3 October 1900

Dr. Conan Doyle and his
South African Services

SIR, – I observe that at Sir Lewis McIvor's meeting last night someone, on his referring to my work in South Africa, calls out that I had gone there "on business principles." It is not a point which I could have raised, but since this statement has been made, you will permit me to say that I have never received a shilling for those services which I very gladly gave to my country. Far from profiting by them, my expedition cost me £200. I am sorry to intrude these personal details, but the point was not of my raising.

I am, &c.
A. CONAN DOYLE

Old Waverley Hotel

THE IRISH TIMES   3 October 1900

South County Dublin

SIR, – Will you permit me, as a man of Irish blood living outside Ireland, to say a word upon Mr. Plunkett's candidature, and the opposition which he is meeting? Viewed from outside, it appears that the one thing which Ireland wants, and has wanted for many years, is a central party, a party free from bitter sectarian or political feeling, who will be ready to extend a hand to the left and a hand to the right, and so in time make every Irishman, North and South, recognise that he has a common country, and that there is no reason why the inhabitants of that country should be for ever divided into two camps. With some relaxation of dogmatic theology and of political bitterness upon each side, it would be possible to unite Ireland upon a basis of national unity and Imperial loyalty. Such a party is one of the greatest necessities, as it seems to me, in our political life. The one man who has stood for it in recent years is Mr. Horace Plunkett, who recognises that some compromise must be made, and that Irishmen of all creeds must learn to drop their minor differences, and look upon each other as brothers, before any permanent peace and prosperity can come to the country. We earnestly desire a body of reasonable and temperate men who will intervene between the bigots and fanatics of either party. I am myself a Unionist candidate for Parliament, but it fills me with sadness that Unionists in Ireland can be so narrow and intolerant as to oppose the candidature of the man who has, of all living Irish politicians, done the most practical good for the country. By such an attitude they alienate from themselves the sympathy of many men, who like myself care nothing for the bolstering up of any sect or of any narrow party, but who are whole-souled in one desire that Ireland should become prosperous, happy, and reconciled to that great empire which has been so largely built up by Irish valour and Irish intellect.

Yours, &c.,
A. CONAN DOYLE

Undershaw, Hindhead, Haslemere

THE SCOTSMAN   16 October 1900

Dr. Conan Doyle and the Catholic Church

SIR, – I have waited for the rush of the elections to pass before addressing a letter to you, and through you to the electors of the Central Division, upon the subject of the recent contest there.

It will be within the memory of those who have followed the events in that Division that upon the morning of the election three hundred posters were exhibited upon the walls, in which I was stated to be a Papist conspirator, a Jesuit emissary, and a Subverter of the Protestant Faith. These posters confronted the workmen as they went to their work in the morning, and there is no doubt that they did me considerable harm at the polls. When I say that there is not one truthful statement in the whole placard, and when I report that it vitally affected the election, it is evident that the incident was a very grave public scandal. At the last instant, when no time was left for contradiction, the electors were influenced in their voting by a statement which was both false and malicious.

My own religious beliefs are things which I should not have obtruded upon the public, but the issue has been so directly raised that I cannot avoid it. Let me state my position once for all. I am not, and never have been since my school days, a Roman Catholic.

For more than twenty years my strongest convictions have been in favour of complete liberty of conscience, and I regard hard-and-fast dogma of every kind as an unjustifiable and essentially irreligious thing putting assertion in the place of reason, and giving rise to more contention, bitterness, and want of charity than any other influence in human affairs. I have hardly ever written a book in which I have not indicated this view, and in one work, *The Stark Munro Letters* it is the main thesis of the book. When I add that the church which I attend in London is that of Mr. Voysey, in Swallow Street, it will be obvious that my religious views are broadly tolerant, founded upon a Reverent Theism, rather than upon the special teaching of any particular sect. The process of religious thought in the future, and the best one for the happiness of the human race, lies, in my opinion, in the various creeds directing their attention to those things which they have in common instead of eternally accentuating the things which hold them apart — matters of dogma and ritual which are not the essentials of Christianity.

So much about a subject to which I shall not recur. My early association with the Catholic Church leaves me with no bitterness toward that venerable institution, which contains many of the most saintly men and women whom I have ever known. My own recent experience is enough to show me the vile slanders to which they are subjected. But a man's soul and reason are his own and he must go whither they beckon. That path has in my case been an open and a straight one since I emerged from boyhood.

This being my religious position, I leave it to the judgment of your readers how unjust were the terms applied in this unscrupulous placard. I am advised by the highest authorities that under the recent Illegal Practices Prevention Act of '95, a legal remedy is within my reach. No punishment, however, which could be inflicted upon the person who is responsible for the bill could undo the harm which has been done. I prefer, therefore, to leave the facts upon record and to trust that the publicity which I give to them may prevent the recurrence of so gross a scandal.

As a last word may I once again thank my friends of the Central Division for the loyalty and energy with which they stood by me in the contest.

I am, &c.
A. CONAN DOYLE

Reform Club, London, October 13, 1900

The South Dublin Election

Sir, – Will you permit me as one of Irish descent, though living outside Ireland, and also as one who has done his best for the Union in the recent elections, to say a word about how the South Dublin election strikes me? The one thing needed above all other things in Ireland, the necessary condition for any improvement, appears to me to be the formation of a central party – a party which shall be as far removed from the narrow and provincial patriotism of the south as it is from the intolerance of the north. The island is, and has long been divided into two clearly marked camps, containing two opposing forces who from racial, religious, or social causes can never amalgamate. While things remain so, and while every fresh statute is used as a weapon by one party against the other, it is difficult to see how legislation can improve matters. The last way of all is certainly by Home Rule, which would concentrate into one chamber the bitter antagonism which animates the two parties. It is bad that they should shake their fists at each other from opposite ends of the island, but it would be infinitely worse if they did so across the table.

The first requisite for any improvement is a party of reasonable, moderate men, with their hearts filled with that true Irish patriotism which would subordinate religious or racial prejudice to the great and holy task of uplifting their country and assuaging those bitter hatreds between Irishman and Irishman which have distracted the island from time immemorial. Such a party would consist of men who were swayed by no selfish interest, who had no sympathy with bigotry or intolerance, whether Catholic or Protestant, who were loyal to their own country and also loyal to that Empire which has been largely built up by Irish valour and Irish brains. Having established such a party, it would soon come to hold the scales between the two extreme sections, and in that way it could exercise a moderating influence upon them. It would attract to it the reasonable and enlightened men from the whole community. If a nucleus were but formed I believe that such a party would rapidly assume considerable dimensions, for it is impossible to conceive that Ireland is the one country in the world which is inhabited entirely by extremists. There must be a large moderate section if a means could be found by which they could express themselves. In their development and growth lie, as it seems to me, the best hopes for the future of the country, and for the healing of that wound which is always a drain upon the strength of the Empire.

The best chance which has appeared in our time for the formation of such a nucleus lay in the candidature of Mr. Plunkett, a man who was a patriot without being a partisan. He had done more for Ireland than any of the noisy mischief-makers. His mind was broad enough and his heart was big enough to prevent him from losing sight of his country amid the strife of factions. He would make those concessions which a moderate party must make, and he would make them because they were reasonable and because the judgment of an impartial man must endorse them. He would let bygones be bygones, for the eternal raking up of the past is the most fruitful cause of Irish trouble. He would accept a Secretary who was a capable Irishman, be his religion and his politics what they might. He would vote for a University which would bring up Irish young men in the prevailing Irish faith, although he might not himself share that faith. He would organize the butter-making industry and care no more for the politics of the farmer than for those of the cow, so long as the national industry prospered. Here was the ideal man for the central party, the man with the impartial judgment, for whom Ireland and the Empire have equally been waiting. And this was the man who has been defeated in Dublin with the acquiescence of some of our most weighty organs of public opinion, who draw the moral that Government impartiality does not pay, and that this election is a proof that we have attended too little to the Unionist party in Ireland. Although I am under existing circumstances a strong Unionist myself, I think the lesson rather is that the Unionists in Ireland have in this matter acted in a way which has shocked some of their most ardent supporters, and that they have shown themselves incapable of taking a broad and statesmanlike view of the Irish question. Imagine, for example, the perverted state of mind of one who, like "An Irish Loyalist" in your issue of to-day, upbraids Mr. Plunkett for having twice voted during the last Parliament for measures proposed by the Nationalists. Must a man, then, always vote with his party? Is his mind to be inaccessible always to reason if it come from an opposing faction? How contemptible is the view of the politician which is disclosed in such a complaint! Mr. Plunkett's attitude is best appreciated by the fact that he has earned the abuse of such fanatics as Davitt on one side and of ultra-Orangemen upon the other. An Irishman could have no more honourable epitaph upon his tombstone.

Yours faithfully,
A. CONAN DOYLE

Undershaw, Hindhead, Haslemere, Oct. 17

Dr. Conan Doyle on Early Closing*

Sir, – In reply to yours of 25th, I shall be pleased to receive such a deputation as that to which you allude almost any afternoon between five and six.

The matter of shorter hours for shop assistants is one in which I take the deepest interest, believing that in a country which has no compulsory military service physique and well being of members of the class to which you allude can only be guaranteed by a universal adoption of short hours and frequent holidays. Personally, I do not feel that this end can be altogether gained by legislation, but I think that the constant ventilation of this subject, and the continued education of the public, will prove in themselves a sufficiently irresistible force to oppose to the few remaining opponents of progress in this direction.

Believe me, dear sir,
Yours faithfully,
A. Conan Doyle

* A reply sent to the Edinburgh secretary of the *Grocers' Assistant* who had requested a meeting with Conan Doyle.

The Lessons of the South African War

Sir, – I have read Colonel Lonsdale Hale's letter in your columns disagreeing with my views upon military reform. I can assure him that I have no desire to "teach" professional soldiers, but my contention is that free discussion should be permitted and encouraged upon military matters. A civilian's argument cannot be disposed of by merely writing "(sic)" after it.

I think that Colonel Lonsdale Hale does less than justice to the manhood of his countrymen when he fears for the result of an invasion unless we had an army of professional soldiers to oppose it. The little country of Switzerland is surrounded by four great military Powers, and yet for centuries it has preserved its independence. For its defence it depends upon a militia force, but an attack upon it would be regarded, even by Germany, as a very serious military operation. In South Africa we have ourselves experienced how difficult has been the task of conquering a militia of 50,000 men. Now an essential part of the scheme which I outlined in the last chapter of my "Great Boer War" was that the number of riflemen in the country should be raised to a million, and that they should be supported by a strong artillery. The numbers of an invading force must be limited, and it must be hampered for want of transport and supplies. It could not make flanking movements against the masses of men who oppose its advance, and it could not, on the other hand, afford the losses which must come from a series of frontal attacks. At the same time it must move or starve. I cannot picture the situation of such an army without repeating, even at the risk of Colonel Lonsdale Hale's displeasure, that I believe that the bugbear of invasion is for ever past.

Critics will reply that it would be impossible to raise a million riflemen. If necessary, we could do so compulsorily by an extension of the Militia Act, and I believe that there would be little popular opposition to such a measure if an appeal were made to the patriotism of the people. But it is probable that the numbers could be obtained without any compulsion. Apart from the Militia and Volunteers, there is a great untapped source of military strength in that large portion of the population who would willingly learn the use of the rifle, but who are unable to join any organized body of Volunteers. In most country villages it is impossible for the peasant to become a Volunteer, but he would willingly spend a couple of hours in shooting upon a Saturday afternoon if facilities were offered to him. But the Government must encourage such a movement. It must appoint inspectors to go round the country and to confer with the local authorities as to the opening of parish butts, and it should not sell but give a rifle to every man who will join a rifle club and learn to shoot. There are few places where a 200 yards range cannot be opened, and with modern low trajectory rifles a man who shoots really well at that range will be of some use at any range. Where proper butts cannot be erected a Morris tube range can always be started, and the men grounded in the use of fire-arms. I am myself at present engaged in organizing such a range upon Hindhead, on the model of one started near Guildford by my friend Mr. St. Loe Strachey. I believe that I shall have no want of members and that we shall soon be able to form a local corps of irregular riflemen from among men who could not serve as Volunteers. Should such a movement spread all over the country there would be no difficulty in getting the million men for home defence. I grant that they would be raw levies, but they would be formidable in numbers and in spirit, and the strongest lesson of the Boer war seems to me to be that a brave man with a good rifle very soon makes a formidable soldier.

As to the other details of this scheme, I shall not enumerate them, but must refer those who are interested to the chapter in which I deal with them. The substance of it all is that the professional soldiers should be fewer in number, more highly paid, more highly trained (especially in shooting), and that they should be used entirely for the defence of the outer Empire, since the island can very well take care of itself. The advantage would be that at the point of contact we should always have an absolutely efficient force, that there would not be the waste which there is at present, when we are always feeding and paying large bodies of men who are seldom wanted, and that we should have a reserve from which at any time we could construct a very much larger army than our present system can give us. I think that all this could be done on the lines which I have indicated, but I realize that I talk as an amateur, and I am anxious for professional criticism, whether it be favourable or adverse.

As to the question of the Imperial Light Horse, which seems to me to be the type of the mounted soldier of the future, Colonel Lonsdale Hale may call him cavalry or mounted infantry. It is immaterial which he is (Major Karri Davis, who raised the corps, calls them mounted infantry), but the essential thing is that they should look upon the rifle as their weapon and be trained to fight on foot. It is new to me that any dismounted cavalry ascended Elandslaagte Hill with the Imperial Light Horse – but that also is immaterial.

Yours faithfully,
A. CONAN DOYLE

Reform Club, Pall-mall, S.W.

THE TIMES   6 November 1900

The Lessons of the South African War

SIR, – I hesitate to trouble you with another letter, but perhaps you will permit me to say a few words in answer both to "Custos" and to the second letter of Colonel Lonsdale Hale.

It is evident that "Custos" has read my letter but not the article to which that letter was supplementary. He is under the impression that I advocate a merely defensive army. He will see, if he refers to the last chapter of my *Great Boer War*, that this is not so. I maintain that our Regular Army should be the most efficient, the most highly trained, and the best equipped in the world. This I propose to effect by roughly halving their numbers, doubling their pay, and keeping them entirely for the foreign service of the Empire. Under such a system every man would be worth feeding, paying, and transporting. We should not when the pinch comes be compelled to leave 92,000 men at home because they were too immature to go upon active service. By saving the pay and keep of these useless men we could raise the rest of the Army to the highest standard. "Custos" will see, therefore, that he has misunderstood me in thinking that I favour only defensive measures.

But if this highly-trained force is to be entirely available for the service of the Empire, then we must take our own measures against invasion at home. It would be a good thing for the country and for individuals that every man should be made to understand that he is not to trust to others, but to himself, for protection. I see several reasons against compulsory military service, but I see none against compulsory rifle practice, if the authorities would take the question of ranges seriously in hand. Without compulsion, however, I believe that a very large force of riflemen could be enrolled, apart from the Volunteers and Militia. With such a force, and a strong artillery, I am still of opinion that the Regular forces could be set free with perfect safety for offensive purposes.

I am sorry that Colonel Lonsdale Hale derived a wrong impression from a sentence of mine. It was certainly expressed too loosely. I did not mean to assert that if unlimited invaders were permitted to land under their own conditions we could beat them off, but I meant that, given the actual conditions, the temporary loss of command of the sea or the absence of most of our Regular Army would not be fatal to us if we had a million men accustomed to the use of the rifle in the island. This I still think.

Colonel Lonsdale Hale thinks that our task of subduing Boer militia is very much more difficult than the task of an invader in subduing English militia because the distance is greater. His argument here appears to me to be unsound. It is true that we had a far greater distance to convey our men and stores, but having got there we found ourselves at a friendly base where we could organize before advancing, with a population from which we were able to raise 15,000 excellent troops. The invader of England, on the other hand, lands under our guns and has no foothold save what he can win for himself. I think the invasion of England far the more difficult operation, and, if carried out against an armed and organized population, an impossible one.

With apologies for my frequent trespasses upon your space,

Yours faithfully,

Reform Club, Pall-mall, S.W.   A. Conan Doyle

THE WESTMINSTER
GAZETTE   12 November 1900

Mr. Conan Doyle and Army Reform

Sir, – In his very generous estimate of my *Great Boer War* your critic has stated that my scheme of Army reorganisation is to have a highly-trained home army of a hundred thousand men, and he pertinently asks where the defence of the Empire would come in. The plan which I put forward is the exact opposite. It is to have an army of a hundred thousand well-trained and well-paid men on the defence of the Empire, and to retain no regular soldiers save artillery and the Guards at home. Let the island be defended by the million of militia, volunteers, and riflemen, who could easily be raised if the public were taught that they were to rely entirely upon themselves for self-protection. We should then be stronger both at home and abroad than we are at present, and in war time we should have an enormous reserve of men who knew something of the use of weapons, and who could rapidly be turned into good soldiers. It is deplorable that our young men should all be playing games or shooting rabbits when they might so easily be doing something to strengthen their country. Apart from the Volunteer force there are great numbers of men who could very well learn the use of the rifle if some effort were made to provide facilities for it. At no great expense we could make ourselves invulnerable at home if we will only shake ourselves free from the ideas of the old-fashioned disciplinarian soldier, who will never admit how far a good spirit will atone for a scanty training.

I entirely agree with your critic as to the impossibility of writing a complete history of the war at present, but I make a rule with each fresh impression of my book to make additions and corrections so as always to incorporate into it the latest information on the subject. In this way I hope to minimise those objections which he urges.

Yours faithfully,
A. CONAN DOYLE

Undershaw, Hindhead, Haslemere.

THE GLASGOW EVENING NEWS   19 December 1900

"Burghers of the Queen"

SIR, – I feel most strongly about this matter, and I only regret that it is not possible for me to be at Glasgow on the date you name.

The idea I am working with at Hindhead is simply riflemen, drawn from the resident civilians. I find them very keen, and quite ready to pay for their own cartridges, which, with the Morris tube system, can be sold at three a penny. I made range for them at 50, 75, and 100 yards, the latter representing 600 without the Morris tubes, and twice a week I have a muster. Then on holidays I will give them a prize to shoot for, and I believe that in a year or two there will not be a carter, cabman, peasant, or shop-boy in the place who will not be a marksman. The whole expense of targets (5), mantlets, rifles (3), and tubes is not more than about £30. The system, I hope, will spread to the surrounding villages until all that district is full of possible fighting men. The Southern counties of England are most open to attack, and it is there that the movement should receive universal support. Considering that it is all done by voluntary effort, I think that the least which the Government should do is to satisfy themselves by a test as to the efficiency of each man who has passed through the rifle club, and then, having thoroughly tried him, to give him a rifle and bandolier of honour, for his patriotic exertions, which he could keep in his own home. It would still remain the cheapest military force in the world. Men from 16 to 60 should be enlisted – the older the man the better soldier he makes. The bayonet I am not so sure about. It puts false ideas into the men's heads as to what they are for. No red tape, no uniform, no swagger – a broad-brimmed, looped hat with a badge, and no other distinction. I am convinced that there are half-a-million of men to be had on those terms, and that it would help, not hinder, the Volunteer movement.

Wishing you all luck,
yours very truly,
A. CONAN DOYLE

THE WESTMINSTER
GAZETTE   27 December 1900

Civilian Riflemen

SIR, – Your Military Correspondent has a most unfortunate habit of criticising other people's views without having taken the preliminary trouble to ascertain what they are. Some weeks ago he attributed a scheme to me which was the exact opposite of that which I had advocated. I pointed out his error at the time in your columns. Instead of learning some modesty by this absurdly absent-minded proceeding, he now writes a very energetic diatribe against the Civilian Rifleman movement without in the least understanding what it is that he is attacking.

The object of the movement, as has been pointed out again and again, is not to supplant the regular soldier but to supplement him. The more regular soldiers we can have the safer we shall be, but as it is evident that in order to get the best and most intelligent material we must pay them more highly, there comes a limit to what the country can afford. The Navy must remain our most important service, and therefore the funds for the Army must be kept within certain limits.

It is not a very wild idea, then, to imagine that since the present war has shown that brave men with rifles which they know how to use are very formidable when acting on the defensive, such a force might be enrolled to help in the defence of this country. The idea may seem very preposterous to the Military Correspondent of the *Westminster Gazette*, but that merely shows that instead of being, as we had hoped, a reformer, he is himself the victim of prejudice and routine. Can he or any other sane man seriously say that the country would not be stronger if it had a half-a-million more men trained to the use of arms within its borders. If he believes that no man can fight save one who has been drilled in a barrack yard, then I say that he has missed the lesson which we have spent so much in blood and money to learn. It is good for the country to have these men, and it is good for the men to learn that they owe a duty to the country. They are there to be had, and, in spite of your correspondent and of all other obstructionists, a very few years will, I believe, show that the movement has come to stay.

In the most absurd passage your correspondent asks why the men should wear a broad-brimmed hat, and why a badge. They must wear a hat of some sort, and why should they not wear one which will enable them to recognise each other, and which is adapted to screen their eyes from the sun. As to the badge, the men, of course, belong to different corps and clubs. How can one be told from another save by a badge? It is a waste of time to answer such questions, and yet they are the difficulties which appeal to a military expert.

It was Lord Salisbury who first appealed for the formation of Civilian Rifle Clubs, and it was Lord Dundonald, with the lessons of the war fresh in his mind, who said last week that Britain would be safe from invasion if she had riflemen to line her hedgerows, which are as formidable as the kopjes of South Africa. The advice of the Premier and the opinion of the practical soldier may be set against the criticisms of the gentleman who is so puzzled about hat-badges, and who cannot understand why, if a man may be a serviceable soldier (as the Boers are) up to sixty, there should be any age limit at all.

I have stood all day to-day marking for our own corps of civilian riflemen. Gentlemen, shopboys, cabmen, carters, and peasants were all shooting side by side. The prize, at a range which was equivalent to six hundred yards, was taken by 83 out of a possible 90, and 82, 81 and 80 were the next. Fifty men spent their bank holiday at my butts, and the scene was like a village competition in Switzerland. Conceive the stupidity which would refuse such military material as that, when all that it will ever ask from the country is a rifle and a bandolier!

Yours faithfully,
A. CONAN DOYLE

Undershaw, Hindhead, Haslemere

Dr. Conan Doyle Supports Our Cause

SIR, – I have a very strong opinion – which I expressed when I was
a candidate for Parliament – that shop assistants, both male and
female, are much too hard worked. In some trades, and the
grocer's particularly, it is in my opinion a crying evil. I should like
to see a bill passed by which a two-thirds majority of any trade
could compel every shop to shut at reasonable hours. It is a
national question, for surely it is of great importance to the nation
that so many young men and young women should have time to
improve their physical health and to cultivate their minds. The
inconvenience to the customer in shopping an hour or two earlier
is nothing when compared to the welfare of so many thousands.
Your organisation has, therefore, my heartiest sympathy.

Yours truly,
A. CONAN DOYLE

Civilian Riflemen

SIR, – I observe that your Correspondent says that his allusions to
the civilian rifleman movement were made in chaff. That is all
very well, but the matter is from our point of view a serious one,
and we would rather have serious criticism than chaff from
military experts.

In his last article, however, he has stated his case against the
movement, and so has your correspondent "Imperial Defence," so
we have something more solid than chaff to discuss. The fallacy
into which both these critics fall is to take it for granted that
civilian riflemen must always under all circumstances remain
civilian riflemen. The object of the movement, as I see it, is to
cover the country with clubs which will teach the average Briton to
shoot, and to shoot well. When he has learned this lesson he
becomes valuable material which is at the disposal of the country.
He has learned the chief lesson of soldiering, and the one most
difficult to acquire. In time of war he will crowd in to strengthen
the Regular, the Militia, and the Volunteer battalions. A residue
would be left, no doubt, in every part of the country who would be
prepared to act as irregulars, but the great majority would join the
recognised forces.

The critics may ask why they should not join these forces now.

The answer is that they don't, and that we must take facts as they are. Some are kept out by their hours of work, some by their distance from a centre, some by their dislike to uniform or drill. But you can get them to shoot, if facilities are provided, and when once they have learned to shoot they will then in time of national danger, when public spirit runs high, take their places in the ranks, not as raw recruits but as expert marksmen. Your Correspondent says that we have already plenty of men to line our hedgerows. So we have in time of peace, but suppose that we were fighting Russia desperately in the North of India; would we then have plenty of men to meet an invasion from France? We should, if we could replenish our ranks from a huge reserve of trained riflemen, but not otherwise. This is the way and the only way, short of conscription, by which we can get such a reserve.

The first thing that we have to do is to get the riflemen. To discuss transport and all the other questions raised by your correspondents is premature. Having got, as we will get, a large number of civilians who can shoot, the military authorities can then decide how best to employ them in time of need. My own idea has always been that they would for the most part go to strengthen the recognised forces, so that they would need no separate organisation of their own.

Your Correspondent suggests a large number of other reforms, most of which are no doubt very excellent ones, but the most important of all, as it seems to me, is to broaden the base upon which our military system rests by taking more of the population into it. That want of interest in military things and subsequent want of public spirit which your Correspondent remarks upon and deplores is due to the fact that we alone among the nations of Europe have continued to set a certain class aside for the purpose of war, instead of all sharing in the common duty. The average citizen has been made to feel that it is no business of his. Such a movement as this of civilian riflemen will spread to the small country villages and will quicken the patriotism and the manhood of the nation, as it does now in Norway and in Switzerland.

As to the help which the War Office can give to such a movement, the less it is fettered by officialism the better. Every parish is capable of organising its own butts, and I find that the men will pay readily for their ammunition. In the present stage it needs no help, but the Chancellor of the Exchequer might very well remove the tax upon private rifles unless they are used for sporting purposes. As the law stands at present, the rifleman who is so keen that he buys his own rifle is at once fined ten shillings by his grateful country. After a time, when the movement has shown that it has vitality, the authorities might then serve out rifles and bandoliers of honour to those who have attained a high standard of efficiency. But that is in the future.

Your Correspondent asks me to divert my attention from this movement and turn it to cyclist corps and to the finding of officers for Volunteer regiments. No doubt there is plenty of room for work in both these directions, and patriotic workers will be found. But the adoption of the wise advice of the Prime Minister seems to me to be infinitely more important than these smaller details. For this reason, because I believe that it is a vital thing for the country to accustom more of its citizens to the use of arms, I prefer to put any surplus energy I have into furthering such a movement as far as my limitations will permit.

Yours faithfully,
A. CONAN DOYLE

Undershaw, Hindhead, Haslemere

THE FARNHAM, HASLEMERE &
HINDHEAD HERALD   5 January 1901

The Undershaw Rifle Club

SIR, – Would you permit me through the medium of your columns to acknowledge the help which I have had in the formation of this rifle club. Through the kindness of Mr. Harman, Mr. Ingham Whitaker, Mr. Charles Maclaren, M.P., Mr. Barrie, Mr. Bernard Hamilton, the Rev. J. M. Jeakes, Mr. Jackson, Mr. Turle, Dr. Lyndon, Mr. Henslowe, Mr. Anderson Wells, Mr. Bulley, and Miss James, the task has been very much lightened, while I must also acknowledge the courtesy of Mrs. Tyndall in permitting me to place the butts upon her ground. The Club has been a very great success, and we hope soon to have a hundred good riflemen. There is, however, room at the firing points for many more, and all are welcome from 2 to 4.30 every Wednesday and Saturday. None need hesitate to come because they have never used a rifle, for those are the very men we want. The age limits are from sixteen to sixty.

I hope to see similar clubs started at Headley, Churt, Tilford, Witley, Chiddingfold, and especially at Haslemere. If any gentleman desires to organise one, and so help in what is a very urgent public duty, I will be happy to furnish him with full information as to the methods by which we have brought our own to success.

Yours faithfully,
A. CONAN DOYLE

South African Cricketers

SIR, – It is announced that a South African cricket team is about to visit this country. The statement would be incredible were it not that the names are published, and the date of sailing fixed. It is to be earnestly hoped that such a team will meet a very cold reception in this country, and that English cricketers will refuse to meet them. When our young men are going from North to South to fight for the cause of South Africa, these South Africans are coming from South to North to play cricket. It is a stain on their manhood that they are not out with rifles in their hands driving the invader from their country. They leave this to others while they play games. There may be some question even in England whether the national game has justified itself during this crisis, and whether cricketers have shown that they understood that the only excuse for a game is that it keeps a man fit for the serious duties of life. There can be no question, however, that this South African visit would be a scandal. I trust that even now it may be averted.

I am, Sir, &c.,
A. CONAN DOYLE

Undershaw, Hindhead, Haslemere

South African Cricketers

SIR, – I admit that I wrote with some heat upon this subject (*Spectator*, April 20th). Perhaps you will kindly permit me to restate the case more temperately, but not less firmly. Do Mr. Boughey, and others who differ from me, seriously contend that it is seemly or opportune that a body of picked young men should leave their country at a time that it is invaded in order to play games at a distance? Will they uphold that position? If they do, then our standard of public duty has indeed fallen. Mr. Boughey contends that the same objection would apply to theatres, races, &c., – by which he apparently means theatres and races in England. But this is a confusion of thought. The point is that this is a South African war waged in South Africa very largely for the benefit of British South Africans. While the war is still going on these same South Africans send a team to play cricket in England leaving the defence of their country mainly in the hands of strangers. Is this right? I have no doubt that some of the African team may have served in the war. They have probably all served in the town guards, since service in them was almost universal. But that does not affect the question. As long as South Africa is full of British and Australian volunteers who are ready to give up their comfort, and sometimes their lives, for the sake of the cause, South Africans are bound in honour, as it seems to me, to see the thing through, and not to come away upon a pleasure trip. Mr. Boughey says that so small a body of men can never be missed. Individually that is true. But collectively, coming in a public capacity, their journey must have a discouraging effect upon our own men who are fighting in South Africa. Take the case of the original Imperial Yeomanry, the noblest body of men, in my opinion, that ever left this country. They are still in the field. What do you suppose they think of this cricketing venture? Is it likely to allay the irritation which they feel at their unexpectedly long detention in the field? Our young men took this war to be a very serious and earnest thing when they sacrificed their own comfort and careers for the sake of it. They are still in South Africa, and these South Africans are coming over to play cricket. I am sorry that my views should have caused amazement to Mr. Boughey and to one or two journalists. I can assure them that the emotion is mutual. I should not have imagined that so elementary and obvious a position needed to be justified.

I am, Sir, &c.,
A. CONAN DOYLE

The Athenæum, Pall Mall, S.W.

THE TIMES   5 September 1901

The Derailing of Trains

SIR, – Would it not be perfectly feasible to put a truck full of Boer irreconcilables behind every engine which passes through a dangerous part of the country? Two of these dastardly affairs in the last few weeks have cost us 40 men killed and wounded, while the sum total of men who have been maimed in this fashion during the war amounts to many hundreds. Such a practice as I suggest would infallibly put an end to it, and is so obvious that it is difficult to imagine why it has not been done. The Germans in 1870 continually carried French hostages in the trains.

Yours faithfully,
A. CONAN DOYLE

Undershaw, Hindhead, Haslemere

Train-wrecking

SIR, – With all courtesy to Mr. Mackarness, I cannot imagine what the doings of Attila and the Huns, or of Wellington in the Peninsula, have to do with the question of the ethics of railway-wrecking and its prevention. Our first duty is to our own soldiers, and if there are any means which have been sanctioned by military usage by which we can shield them from such danger it is for us to use them. Had we continued to do so from the first some hundreds of men would probably have been saved from death or mutilation. Mr. Mackarness asks me why I call the wrecking of a railway train at this stage of the war a dastardly outrage. I do so because it is indiscriminate in its character, and may involve the lives of non-combatants, of women and of children. In this last case a woman was one of the victims. On a previous occasion it was a party of sick soldiers who were on their way to hospital who suffered most severely. I do not deny that the Boers are within their rights as belligerents in doing this, inhuman as it may seem, but why in the name of common sense should we not be permitted to take such steps as are within our power to prevent them?

Mr. Mackarness points out that it is only by such means that a small Power can hope to hold its own against a larger one. Very possibly, and it is only by such means that the larger Power can retort. Let both sides wear the gloves, or let both sides take them off.

Yours faithfully,
A. CONAN DOYLE

The Athenæum, Pall-mall, S.W.

Dr. Conan Doyle on his Defence

SIR, – My attention has been called to a letter by Mr. Marks, in which he traverses some statements of mine as expressed in my pamphlet on the South African war. After reading some severe remarks upon my own inaccuracy, I was prepared to learn something important from Mr. Marks, but in this I have been disappointed, as most of what he says is entirely irrelevant, and in no way affects my conclusions. I can assure him that if he can ever convict me of error I shall be happy to receive his correction and to alter my text.

On the point of the suzerainty I can only quote my own words:

"The discussion is a barren one, since both parties agree that Great Britain retained certain rights over the making of treaties by the Republics, which rights place her in a different position to an independent sovereign State. Whether this difference amounts to a suzerainty or not is a subject for the academic discussion of international jurists. What is of importance is the fact, not the word." Holding these views, it is immaterial to me or to my argument whether the Crown lawyers or Sir Edward Clarke were right in their contention.

Mr. Marks, the stickler for accuracy, then begins his second indictment by the sentence: "Dr. Conan Doyle has a chapter, consisting of little more than two pages, on 'Expansive and Explosive Bullets." As a matter of fact I have nothing of the kind, for it is only a small subsection of Chapter IX. Mr. Marks is, of course, correct in saying that in warfare there is practically no such thing as an explosive bullet. Heavy game ammunition of an explosive type used to be manufactured, and it is possible that some of this is still in the hands of old Boer hunters, but the word "explosive" may convey a wrong impression, and had better be eliminated. There remain, however, expansive bullets of many varying degrees of deadliness, slit bullets, hollow bullets, and soft-nosed bullets. It is notorious, as Mr. Marks states, that the British, whose wars are usually against savages, had prepared large quantities of soft-nosed bullets. If Mr. Marks has, indeed, read all my pamphlet he will know that I am no apologist for the Government, and that I express my dissent from the view taken by the British and American representatives at The Hague Conferences upon the subject of expansive bullets. It is only just to say, however, that they were never intended to be used against white races, and that a War Office order forbade their use in the South African war. How some of them did get into circulation there, and how they were withdrawn eventually, is explained in my pamphlet, and is not contradicted by Mr. Marks. What he means by his statistics about their manufacture, etc., I cannot imagine. It has nothing to do with the question, and does not conflict with anything which I have stated. I will willingly accept Mr. Marks's text – "From the manner in which Dr. Conan Doyle had dealt with these things your readers may estimate the value of his testimony on other matters." I ask no more.

Yours faithfully,
A. Conan Doyle

Athenæum Club, S.W., Jan. 30, 1902

The Lizzie Van Zyl Photograph

Sɪʀ, – I observe that Miss Hobhouse, in a letter to the *Daily Chronicle*, throws doubt upon my statement that the child, Lizzie Van Zyl, was the victim of her own mother, rather than of the British authorities. She will find the fact stated in to-day's Press by Nurse Kennedy, who was present. I had already heard it from two other sources.

Miss Hobhouse deplores in passionate language that such matters should be referred to in such a pamphlet as mine. I leave this to the sense of justice of your readers. The Boer children and their treatment in the camps have been the favourite weapon of the anti-national party. If I had not referred to them in my pamphlet it would naturally have been said that I had no answer to make to these charges.

> Yours faithfully,
> A. Cᴏɴᴀɴ Dᴏʏʟᴇ

Undershaw, Hindhead, Haslemere, Jan. 31

"The Cause and Conduct of the War"

Sɪʀ, – So many of the public have taken an active interest in the project of spreading my booklet upon the war in those countries which have never heard the British side of the question that I should like to tell them through your columns how our common cause progresses. When the work is done, I will, with your permission, give a final account of my venture in the same fashion.

A large amount of money was needed to carry my plan into execution. The public, however, has responded – and I hope will respond – in a very generous manner. The unexpectedly large demand for the book in Great Britain, (250,000 copies were called for in a week) has simplified the financial question. While wishing to make no profit upon it, we had retained a small rebate upon each copy, to cover expenses of postage and of free distribution. This trifle has mounted up to such an extent that we shall have some hundreds of pounds to add to the translation fund. The public have also subscribed several hundreds of pounds, particulars of which will in due course be published. We are certain, therefore, of being able to carry out our plans (I speak for Mr. Reginald Smith, my publisher, as well as for myself), but how thoroughly we can carry them out will depend upon the public continuing to support us.

The sums which I have received range from the fifty pounds of Lord Rosebery to the sixpence of a schoolboy. The letters which enclose these hundreds of donations are eloquent of the depths of feeling aroused by the attacks upon the conduct and honour of the soldiers. Many sums – sums which could, I fear, in many cases be ill spared – have come from the wives and mothers of those who have lost their lives in their country's quarrel. A very remarkable proportion of the subscriptions have come from the clergy. The reason which some of them have given for this is that ever since the war began they have been pestered by anti-national literature, which has been sent them free, and that they send their cheques now as a protest against it.

It is a significant fact that, in spite of the protests of many Germans residing in England against the outrageous attacks upon us which have disgraced the German Press, there has – with one or two honourable exceptions – been no help on the part of these gentlemen towards a practical attempt to undo some of the mischief which has been done. "Money talks," as the Americans say, and a few guineas would have been more eloquent than many letters of regret, and proposals for meetings which do not come off. However, it is better so, no doubt.

So rancorous is the feeling in Germany against us that we have been unable, so far, to find a publisher who dare publish a moderate account of the British case, although all expenses were guaranteed by us. Could anything be more suggestive of the complete absence of elementary fair play which has marked all this monstrous agitation? The one fair-minded German whom we have met is Baron Tauchnitz, who has included the book in his English library. Meanwhile, the German translation is nearly ready, and if we are unable to find a publisher in Germany, we shall print 5,000 copies in London and send them ourselves to those whom we desire to influence.

The French translation is also nearly ready. It was most patriotically undertaken by Professor Sumichrast, and it will be published by Galignani. We propose to order 10,000 copies for distribution in Belgium, Switzerland, and France.

The Scandinavian translation is ready, and the book is on the point of appearing. We have found a friend in Mr. Thomassen, of the paper *Verdensgang*, the chief Norwegian journal, who has interested himself most kindly in the matter. His own political views were against us, and I should be indeed proud if I could think that some relaxation in his attitude, which has been apparent lately, was due to my exposition of British views. Some thousands of copies will be distributed in Norway, Denmark, and Sweden.

In Holland we find the same difficulty as in Germany, but the translation will be printed in London, if we can find no publisher there. This translation is delayed through circumstances which are beyond my control.

The Italian translation has also been delayed, but will soon be ready now. We propose to strike 5,000 of this. The Spanish and the Russian are also in hand. The Hungarian and the Portuguese are delayed, but they will both eventually be done. The book is also being translated into Welsh, where we hope to distribute 5,000 copies.

In America and Canada efficient steps have been taken to send free copies to all leaders of public opinion. A large correspondence with foreigners from all over the world shows me that a change of opinion is going on, and that their common sense at last revolts at the idea that the main body of a nation will go on uncomplainingly making such sacrifices of blood and money for so long a time over any cause which is not really a vital one.

I have said enough, I hope, to convince those who have entrusted us with their money that we are endeavouring to use it to some purpose. At a later date I hope to give them a more detailed account of my stewardship.

Yours faithfully,
A. Conan Doyle

Undershaw, Hindhead, Haslemere

THE DAILY MESSENGER,
PARIS   23 February 1902

The War and Continental Opinion

Sir, – My book, *The Cause and Conduct of the South African War*, is about to appear, published in the French form by the house of Galignani. May I say a few words to your readers upon the subject? It is an attempt to tell the true facts of the case to the French public and to dispel the cloud of lies which has obscured the issue. Our funds will enable us to send copies free to all politicians, journalists, and leaders of public opinion. But to get at the main body of the nation I wish to secure the co-operation of the British residing in France who can help me in this fight for truth.

I suggest that in each town, beginning with Paris, a local Committee be formed who will collect funds to buy the book at wholesale prices. It will be issued at half a franc, I believe, and sent to those quarters where it is most needed. If in each town I can get one Briton to organise such a Committee I have not the slightest doubt that the rest will easily follow. May I appeal to the patriotism of your readers that they will help me in this fashion for the sake of truth and of their country?

Yours faithfully,
A. CONAN DOYLE

Undershaw, Hindhead, Haslemere, February 20, 1902

THE GERMAN TIMES, BERLIN

3 March 1902

Dr. Conan Doyle to our Readers

SIR, – Will you permit me to say a few words through your columns to your readers.

The translation of my *Cause and Conduct of the War* is nearly finished, and in a week or so it will be issued from your publishing house.

It is an attempt to put the true facts of the South African war before German readers and to make them understand how egregiously they have been misled and humbugged by interested parties.

Arrangements have been made to send the book free to all politicians and journalists. I wish now to ensure its local distribution in each town of Germany. This I leave in the hands of the local British. They would in my opinion be doing a service to truth and to their country if in each case they would form a committee, collect funds, buy the book which can be had for a few pfennige, and distribute it in those quarters where it will be most useful. Only in this way can we meet this systematic lying which has gone on unchecked and uncontradicted all these years.

If the British in Berlin would communicate with their British friends in other German towns the thing could be easily organised.

I should especially wish to see copies sent to those Rhenish pastors who signed the absurd petition some months ago.

I have had many bitter letters from British people in Germany complaining of their treatment. Here is the means by which they can make their own case heard.

Yours faithfully,
A. CONAN DOYLE

Undershaw, Hindhead, Haslemere

THE TIMES

11 April 1902

"The Cause and Conduct of the War"

SIR, – Some time ago I promised that I would give an account in your columns of my attempt to present a statement of the British case to our Continental critics. I cannot do this in a final form, as the story is not yet done, but with your permission I should be glad, as I am about to leave England for a time, to give some account of our work to those numerous friends who entrusted me with their money. So hearty was the response to my appeal that a sum of more than £2,000 was sent to me – enough to carry out handsomely the whole of our original programme.

First, I would say a word or two about the results of the criticism to which the book has been subjected. Most of this is mere noisy scolding; but wherever a fact has been attacked, I have been ready to examine, and if necessary, to modify it. I find, however, that, setting aside matters of opinion and methods of expression, the errors have been few and trivial. I have misquoted Mr. Charles Hobhouse, M.P., who did not say that Miss Hobhouse's statements would not bear investigation, but that it was a pity that she had not verified them. The other corrections have to do with such matters as the amount of Dutch which Miss Hobhouse can speak, one apocryphal ancedote about Judge Gregorowski, and a technical confusion between expansive and explosive ammunition. No doubt among so many thousand points some others may be open to criticism, but these are all which I could verify, and they have been corrected.

Of the British edition there is little to be said save that it has amounted to 300,000 copies. I am indebted to the South African Imperial Association for their co-operation in sending 25,000 copies to the clergy of Great Britain, who have been bombarded, since the beginning of the war, with anti-national literature. I have had many pleasing letters from honest men whose opinion I had the good fortune to change. "I am heartily ashamed of myself to think that I should ever have thought so ill of my own fellow-countrymen." So ran the manly confession of one of them.

The editions in the United States and in Canada needed no subsidizing, and have had very large circulations. Sheaves of newspaper comments and articles have reached me, so that the facts of the case have certainly been well disseminated. A Welsh edition of 10,000 has also been distributed.

The Norwegian edition, for use in Norway, Sweden, and Denmark, was the first to appear upon the Continent. The publication was attended by some curious difficulties. At the last moment the special preface which I had written for the Scandinavian peoples could not be sent from the translator to the publisher on account of the heavy snowstorms which had interrupted all communication. It was heliographed therefore from hill to hill for 100 miles, and so was in time to accompany the edition. This preface was reproduced by many of the Scandinavian papers, and considerable publicity was given to the little book, which was sent free to every one who could influence public opinion. A Norwegian gentleman, Mr. Knudsen, in London with the help of several other Scandinavians subscribed a sum of money which will go far to pay for this edition. If we have had occasion to deplore the way in which some Britons have played their country false at the greatest crisis of her history, we must console ourselves with the recollection of the whole-hearted friendship which a certain number of generous foreigners have shown to us and to our cause.

In Holland we have met with considerable difficulties which we will overcome. There is no copyright law in that country – which is a serious blot upon their national honour. There is, however, a close association of publishers, who take turns to steal foreign books. A publisher who puts his name down for such a book is left in undisputed possession by the others. On the appearance of this pamphlet a firm at once put its name down for it, so as to block any one else from translating it. This put an end to all chance of our being able to publish it in that country. We have taken other means, however, and I hope that within a few days our Dutch edition will be in the hands of all politicians, journalists, and Professors in the United Provinces. The remaining copies will be sent to South Africa.

The French translation has been out for some weeks. It was admirably done by Professor Sumichrast of Harvard University, a gentleman of French-Canadian birth. In his patriotic desire to uphold the honour of his country he has refused any sort of remuneration for many weeks of arduous work. Ten thousand copies were distributed free, and 10,000 kept on sale. The pessimistic fears expressed by many Britons that the Continental Press would under no circumstances listen to the British case, have been shown to be ill-founded. Many papers commented in a fair spirit upon the book. Sympathy and justice might be expected from M. Yves Guyot in *Le Siècle* but it was as unexpected as it was pleasing to find the powerful *Indépendance Belge* devoting a whole sheet to an impartial and discriminating discussion of the British case. Many private letters, some sympathetic, some argumentative, but none bitter, show that the book has not missed its mark. The French translation has been distributed over French Switzerland, and it had been intended that the German edition should be sent to the German cantons. A pleasing development caused us to modify our plans. A number of eminent and public-spirited Swiss gentlemen, annoyed by the persistent and malignant anti-British agitation, which is so inexplicable in a country which has been our fellow pioneer in European freedom, made up their minds to have an edition of their own. The translation was made without charge by Mr. Toggenburger, of

Zurich, and the organization was largely due to Dr. Angst, British Consul in that city. The result is an edition of 2,000 copies, beautifully got up, with many additions and a map. It has just come out, and was distributed free in the proper quarters. This charming act of international justice and courtesy has relieved our German edition to that extent.

I now come to that which we looked upon as the most important part of our enterprise, and which has certainly caused us most trouble and vexation – namely, the German issue. The translation was done in an exceedingly leisurely way, and was found at the last moment to be so imperfect that it was necessary to practically re-do a good part of it. In this we have had the most loyal and energetic support from Mr. Musgrave of the *German Times*. Mr. Musgrave is a patriotic German, of British ancestry, and is so ardent a champion of the Pan-Teutonic idea that he travelled at great personal inconvenience from Berlin to Seaford in order to persuade me to soften some passage in which I had faintly reflected the deep indignation which is felt by Britons at the abominable conduct of the German Press and people during this war. By his help all difficulties were at last overcome, and the pamphlet has been issued in Berlin to-day.

There has been some advantage in the delay in this as in some other cases, as it has allowed me to append all the fresh evidence about the way in which Lord Kitchener was forced to form the concentration camps, and also the evidence of Baron Huebner as to the conduct of British soldiers.

Before its appearance the book, in its English form, was commented upon by the German Press in a way which leads me to hope that the British case will finally obtain a fair hearing. The *National Zeitung* contained an analysis and discussion of the book which left nothing to be desired. Committees have been formed in the German towns, and when the 20,000 copies have been absorbed we hope to send out a fresh supply.

The Italian and the Spanish editions should be out within a week or so, and will be widely distributed both in Europe and in South America. A Portuguese edition should also be ready for the press. The Russian also is nearly ready.

In Austria the German edition will be well distributed, and already, through the help of Dr. Ernst, a portion of the book has appeared in the chief democratic paper, the *Wiener Tageblatt*. A special Hungarian edition has also been printed and will appear at Budapest within the next few days. A Rumanian edition has also been prepared by the industry and patriotism of an English gentleman, Mr. A. H. Synge, who has taken the whole burden of it upon his own shoulders.

These are the results which my publishers and I have to show for the money with which we have been entrusted. It is too soon yet to say how far we have succeeded in influencing to any appreciable degree public opinion upon the Continent, but at least we have carried out to the full our original programme of placing in the hands of every Deputy and of every journalist a statement of the British case in his own language. If he still chooses to distort facts he can no longer urge ignorance as an excuse.

Yours faithfully,
A. CONAN DOYLE

Athenæum Club, April 9

THE TIMES   5 June 1902

"The Cause and Conduct of the War"

SIR, – The time has come when I can give a final account of this venture, and inform those who subscribed to the fund what I have done, and what I intend to do, with the money which has been entrusted to my care.

Events move so rapidly now that it is already difficult to realise that at the end of the year 1901 the British view of the war and of the causes which led to it was absolutely unstated upon the Continent. Our case was laid forth in Blue-books and in bulky volumes which were inaccessible to the foreign reader and ignored by the foreign Press. Some effort had been made here and there by leaflets to correct some of the more outrageous errors, but these dealt with single points. What seemed to be needed was a statement which should be short and clear, but at the same time should cover the whole field of the controversy. The need of such a book became more apparent when the malignant anti-British campaign in Germany, which had lasted during the whole war, became suddenly more intense, reaching a height which must modify the relations between the two countries for many years.

It was at that period that, with the co-operation of my friend and publisher, Mr. Reginald Smith, I endeavoured to put the British case into an easily-understood form, and to raise a fund which would enable us to place a translated copy of the book in the hands of every man of any importance in the civilised world. We had no delusions, and expected no wholesale conversions, but we would at least ensure that the plea of ignorance could not be used in mitigation of the just resentment which this shameful campaign of slander had produced.

The public responded to our appeal most generously, and sent in over £2,000. The pamphlet was sold at a very low price in the English edition, but even so, the sale was so great that where we had wished to make no profit we found ourselves with a further balance of £2,000. These sums together gave us ample means for carrying out our design.

Editions have appeared in every language and have been sent free, not only to every deputy and journalist, but also to professors, mayors, schoolmasters, regiments, clubs, hotels, and such other people or places as seemed best.

The only hitch in our plans was with the Russian edition, which was vetoed by the local censor in Odessa, and is only now on the eve of appearance. But for this misfortune we have done all, and more than all, that we proposed. A great number of Press notices showed that our work had not been in vain. Such important papers as the *Verdensgang* in Norway, *National-Zeitung* in Germany, *Tageblatt* in Vienna, *Indépendance Belge* in Brussels, and the whole Hungarian Press gave the book a sympathetic reception. There can be no doubt that during the months which have passed there has been a steady fall in the Anglophobia of the Continent, and that the extreme libels which were once common could not now be issued in any country without ridicule and rebuke from the decent papers. It may be too much for those who have helped us to claim that this is due to our efforts, but at least it is a very pleasing coincidence that it should have so closely followed them.

Finding that we had funds in hand we widened our methods of work. In March, I bought 600 copies of "Recht und Unrecht im Burenkrieg," an excellent Austrian statement of the British case, and I had it distributed where I thought it would be most effective. At the same time I sent free copies of the pamphlet to all the parish priests and municipal councillors in Ireland.

We now find ourselves with the work done and with a considerable sum of money still in hand. This cannot be exactly stated, as the accounts are not yet all to hand, but it will probably be not less than £1,400. Far the greater part of this is money actually earned by the sale of the pamphlet, and we feel that we have a free hand in dealing with it, but that we should like to use it for some public purpose which would meet with the approbation of those who supported the original fund. We propose, therefore, to set apart £1,000, the interest of which shall form a scholarship for enabling some poor South African, Boer or British, to pursue his studies at Edinburgh University. From the sum which remains we hope to send a small souvenir to a few friends of Great Britain abroad who have stood loyally by her at a time when many of her own children played her false. The balance, if any, I should like to retain in my hands and to use at my own discretion for the encouragement of the movement for civilian riflemen.

I thank you, Sir, for your powerful aid in permitting me to use your columns in order to address those who have helped to carry our project to success. Especially I would thank Mr. Reginald Smith for the invaluable help which he has given me. The whole resources of the firm have been used to arrange this complex and difficult business without any question of profit or reward.

Yours faithfully,
A. Conan Doyle

The Athenæum, Pall-mall, S.W.

THE SPECTATOR   4 July 1903

The New Protection

Sir, – Since you have opened your columns to a discussion upon the new tariff proposals, perhaps you will permit me, as an old reader and occasional contributor, to say a few words. I am aware that they possess no weight; but this seems to me to be just one of those large national questions upon which a man owes a duty to his country first to examine the evidence, and then to put his own opinion upon record. I have approached the question with at least one advantage, which is a perfectly unbiassed mind and no prejudices. I have read all I could find on both sides of the question – your own articles included – and the result has been to turn me into a Protectionist and an advocate for Imperial reciprocity, though to me the case for the former seems stronger than for the latter.

I have never yet seen a statement which presents both sides perfectly fairly, so that the reader could weigh the one against the other. A writer who would treat the subject at length in a judicial and impartial spirit would perform an important national service. Certainly such a writer in stating the Free-trade case might well lay great stress upon a point raised by the *Spectator*, – namely, the possibility of corrupting our politics when large money issues depend upon the framing of the law. Some such charge has been freely made against the Protectionist Republics. On the other hand, I have never heard that Sweden or Germany were the worse morally for their commercial policy. A second very serious point is that the British Empire, which is at present regarded with no very friendly feeling by the world at large, would arouse active hostility when it was realised that it meant to establish reciprocal trading tariffs. It would then become the obvious interest of the whole world to prevent the Empire from enlarging. To those who think, as I do, that it is quite large enough already this is not an unmixed evil, but the fact that we would provoke active ill-feeling is not to be overlooked in the argument. Then, again, there is the very strong reason that we have practised Free-trade for sixty years, that our entire commercial system is based upon it, and that we have on the whole done well. So much is incontestable. If in spite of an appreciation of these facts I am still a Protectionist, I should like to state the case for the other side.

The main point in that case seems to me to be the fact that we *must* do something now that Canada has shown her readiness to frame a reciprocal treaty with a foreign nation unless we reciprocate with her. The other Colonies would probably follow her example. Now for many years back the stagnation of decline in our foreign exports has been made up for by the increase in our Colonial exports. If those are to be reduced, then there will be no compensation for our steady loss elsewhere, and we shall be very hard hit. If you exclude coal from our exports (and the export of coal seems to me to be like a man living on his capital), then our sales to the Continent of Europe have fallen from £100,000,000 in 1872 to £79,000,000 in 1902. Such a result of thirty years' trading would have been disastrous indeed if our Colonial exports had not during the same period risen from £60,000,000 to £108,000,000. I say again that we *must* preserve this trade, for our commercial pre-eminence depends upon it. If it can only be preserved on certain conditions, then to those conditions we must submit.

When we are told that if we try to foster the £200,000,000 worth of trade which we have in the Empire we will imperil the £800,000,000 worth of trade that we have with the world the statement sounds alarming, but I do not think that it will bear examination. So far as our export trade with foreign countries goes, everything that could be done to cripple it has already been done. What remains will hold its own so long as we do not tax raw materials, and so increase the cost of production. This we shall not do, because it is not our interest to do it. There remain our imports, amounting to something over £500,000,000. Which of them will be affected? About £160,000,000 represent raw materials, cotton from America, flax from Russia, hemp from the Philippines, &c., which it would be suicidal to tax, and which would therefore be affected. There remain £350,000,000 or so of imports. Now of this, £100,000,000 represent *manufactured* articles sent into the country. The whole essence of the Protectionist argument is that if we could dislocate that portion of our trade, we should be in a stronger position, keep that £100,000,000 at home, and give much more work – which means higher wages – to our own people. I fear that all the wit of the Free-traders will not convince me that when I pay £1,000 to a Paris maker for a motor-car, and that £1,000 duly figures among our imports, I am doing my country as good a turn as if I made out my cheque to a Birmingham manufacturer, in which case our total trade returns would seem to be £1,000 less. It is that transaction, infinitely

95

repeated, which accounts for most of that £100,000,000, and I cannot bring myself to believe that it is anything but a drain on our resources.

There only remain now the £220,000,000 or so which we pay a year for imported food, so that the £800,000,000 which bulked so large has come down to more moderate proportions. Now of the food-stuffs there are many, such as barley and oats, the importation of which from our Colonies is very small, so that these trades would be unaffected. The real contention would centre round wheat, maize, wines, and meat. I confess that I cannot believe that any of these things can be taxed without raising their price *pro tanto*, but what fraction of a penny per loaf a five-shilling duty on corn would represent I have been unable to work out. Surely a remission of taxation upon tea and tobacco, which could be done without injury to any one, would go far to compensate the working man for his minute loss on the loaf. When you put that doubtful loss on one side, and on the other the help to our agricultural industries, the redress to Ireland, which as an agricultural country has suffered severely through our Free-trade policy, and finally the forging of a bond of interest between ourselves and our Colonies, as there is between the States of the Union, then I think that our interests as a nation can lie only in one direction.

I am, Sir, &c,
ARTHUR CONAN DOYLE

Undershaw, Hindhead, Haslemere

THE SPECTATOR   18 July 1903

The New Protection

SIR, – I observe that two of your correspondents in the *Spectator* of July 11th have been good enough to comment upon my illustration of the motor-car, and perhaps you will permit me to show as briefly as I can why these comments fail to convince me. My point was that the introduction of manufactured goods which could be produced in the country was an evil, and I quoted as an illustration the instance of a £1,000 motor-car, and asked whether the country was more benefited by my ordering it in Paris or in Birmingham. The reply of both your correspondents was that I was stimulating the trade of the country more by ordering it abroad, a conclusion which is to me unthinkable. Surely, Sir, presuming that the cars are of approximately the same merit, it is against all common-sense to say that it is better to send this £1,000 to encourage a foreign industry. I am aware that it has been received as an axiom that trade begets trade, but that seems to me to be the very theory which is now upon its trial. Your correspondents both take the view that my £1,000 is not lost to Great Britain, but that it returns in payment of British products. The benefit of a concrete case like this is that one might make an attempt to trace approximately the channels through which the money continues to flow. M. Panhard, for example, pays in my cheque, and transfers my money eventually to his banking account. Some proportion of it is expended in the upkeep of his factory, which becomes a valuable taxable asset for the French Government. The balance of the money is divided between the employers and the workpeople. In the expenditure of the employers certain articles of British manufacture may have a place. In that of the workman, with his blue blouse, his *vin ordinaire*, his sabots, and his whole French outfit, there is very little that could come back to us. He saves some of the money, and it may go to the next Russian loan. Surely it would be a fair statement to say that of that £1,000 not £20 would ever filter back to England. In the other case the whole £1,000 is being devoted to the employment of our own people. Surely it is better to retain that certain £1,000 within the country than to send it forth on the chance of some small proportion of it coming back in trade. It may be fairly argued that this is a special case, and that the balance of trade asserts itself in larger transactions. We buy from America £100,000,000 worth of goods, and return £18,000,000. Where is the balance? But perhaps there is something exceptional here. From Holland, however, we take £32,000,000 and return £9,000,000. Where is the balance? In this case it cannot be accounted for by interest on investments or by shipping charges. Belgium gives £24,000,000 and takes £8,000,000. Again, there is no sign of a balance of trade. And all the time the United States, Germany, and even France are improving their position as compared to ours in defiance of all our accepted axioms of political economy. I can understand the attitude of those stalwarts who refuse to be converted by these considerations, but I confess that I cannot conceive how any one could deny the need for an inquiry.

I am, Sir, &c.,

ARTHUR CONAN DOYLE

Undershaw, Hindhead, Haslemere

THE SPECTATOR   1 August 1903

Sir Conan Doyle and the Motor-car

SIR, – When you had done my motor-car the honour of making it the text of a leading article in the *Spectator* of July 18th, I felt that it would be an anti-climax to pursue the matter further. Since a fresh crop of letters have been elicited, however, by my illustration, I feel that I should like to add a word, if only to acknowledge the extreme good humour and courtesy which your correspondents have shown. Of these letters some seem hardly to meet the point. For example, I would freely admit that an author would waste his time if he made his own clothes, because it is not his trade to make clothes. But we *do* make motor-cars, and make them well. If a £100 tax were levied on every one that entered the country, then either the State would be a £100 richer each time, or the order would go to sustain a British industry. This industry is not an exotic one, such as the cultivation of wine would be, but it is a purely natural one. It has, however, some lost ground to make up, and I cannot even now admit that it would be a national evil if it were aided by the State to keep within the country the large sum which was spent last year on foreign motors. As to Mr. Allhusen's interesting illustration, I presume that a Protective tariff would be drawn up with discrimination, and that such productive machinery as he describes would be exempt from taxation. Even if the advocates of Protection gained the day, there would certainly be so powerful a minority in the country that there would be no danger of high-handed or unreasonable action on the part of the govern- ment. I was much struck by the remark in your leading article that our artisans were limited in number, and that there was no room for any great expansion of productive industry. This hardly tallies, however, with Mr. Charles Booth's statistics, which show over 30 per cent. of the workers receiving less than 23s. a week. There is here a broad margin of labour which could be worked up into higher forms. And finally, one always comes back to the assertion that the imports are the payment for the exports, and the greater the discrepancy, the greater the profit. If it is so, then I must admit that the country flourishes amazingly. But I look at other lands, and I see countries which send out more than they take in, and which should, therefore, be in evil case. And yet they are not so, – they present every sign of prosperity. When a fact will not fit in with a theory, then the theory must go by the board. I am told that no gold passes in return for imports, and yet I read of the American market being restored by the huge cash payments for the American crops. Among all your correspondents not one has spoken authoritatively upon this question of the transfer of bullion, and it does certainly appear to lie deep at the root of the matter.

With apologies for my repeated intrusions upon your space,

I am, Sir, &c.,

Undershaw, Hindhead ARTHUR CONAN DOYLE

98

Completion of Twenty-five Years of the "B.O.P."

SIR, – I wish the *Boy's Own Paper* another 25 years of useful activity. Personally I owe it a debt of gratitude, for it was one of the first papers which grew tired of returning my MSS., and began to print them instead.

With all good wishes,
Yours truly,
ARTHUR CONAN DOYLE

Undershaw, Hindhead, Haslemere, Sept. 5, 1903

THE HAWICK
EXPRESS   18 December 1903

Sir Arthur Conan Doyle on the Tweed Acts

SIR, – I beg to acknowledge your letter asking me for my opinion upon the subject of the Tweed Fishery Acts. I paid some attention to the matter during my recent pleasant visit to the Border Burghs. So long as the law is on the statute book the police have no option but to enforce it; but the law itself, dating back, as it does, for nearly fifty years, seems to me to need either fundamental alteration or absolute repeal. All private legislation seems to me to be open to criticism, and these Acts contain some particularly vexatious provisions. I should like to see no law upon the subject of fishing save the general Salmon Fishery Law of Scotland. This does of course at present apply; but it is complicated by the existence of the private Acts. Even the general law of fishing should be administered in a broad and liberal spirit, and a marked distinction made between the man who transgresses it out of pure love of sport, and the man who does so in order to resell the fish which he takes.

Yours faithfully,
ARTHUR CONAN DOYLE

Dec. 14th, 1903

THE TIMES   29 December 1903

Mr. Balfour and the City of Bradford

SIR, – Mr. Harold Cox has contested upon several occasions Mr. Balfour's statement that Bradford has no exports to the States.

99

Mr. Cox is certainly right, for he can point to the fact that within the last few weeks Bradford has exported one of its largest spinning mills with capital and plant to Rhode Island. How the instance helps Mr. Cox's position or weakens that of Mr. Balfour is another question.

Yours faithfully,
ARTHUR CONAN DOYLE

Undershaw, Hindhead, Haslemere, Dec. 28

THE SOUTHERN REPORTER,
SELKIRK   4 February 1904

The Tweed Trade

SIR, – In reference to your editorial remarks about the decline of the tweed trade, you seem to imply that my figures are unreliable. I repeat what I said in my speech that I have no knowledge of the politics of the gentlemen who sent me those returns, but their names must necessarily remain confidential, as no firm wishes to advertise the fact that its trade is declining. Should any more fortunate firms be kind enough to let me have their more pleasing returns, which you say exist, I shall be happy to give them the same publicity. I observe, however, that the more complete figures collected by the industry of Mr. Ainslie, and quoted in debate the other night, corroborate and extend my own. I understand that the fast loom had been largely adopted before 1890, and that 8 per cent. would be a fair estimate of the amount of the displacement of labour since that date through mechanical improvements.

I am, &c.,
ARTHUR CONAN DOYLE

North British Station Hotel, Edinburgh

THE DAILY
CHRONICLE   4 February 1904

A Plea for Protection

SIR, – My attention has been called to a paragraph in the *Daily Chronicle* in which it is stated that the Hawick Boroughs must be flourishing because more money has been deposited in savings banks. I should think that the real reason of this phenomenon may be that the people see hard times ahead of them. Many of the mills are working half-time, and the population of the three towns has decreased by 5,000 since the last census returns. It is difficult to reconcile these facts with prosperity. How can any branch of the woollen trade be prosperous in Britain when we import £12,000,000 of textiles and yarns every year? Since our export outside the Empire is only about £7,000,000, a clearer case for Protection could not be imagined. If we can keep our home and Colonial markets then we can afford never to sell a yard elsewhere, and still have a far larger output than at present.

I am, &c.,

Athenæum Club, Feb. 3   ARTHUR CONAN DOYLE

THE DAILY
CHRONICLE   6 February, 1904

A Further Plea for Protection

SIR, – The reason why I do not admit the present prosperity of the Hawick Boroughs is that it is not true. I have just returned from them, and I find both employers and employed much dissatisfied with the present state of things. The whole South of Scotland wool industry is in a bad way, as may be shown by the fact that the number of hands engaged fell from 40,034 in 1891 to 24,906 in 1901. In the single town of Galashiels, which is one of the Hawick Boroughs, the decrease was 30 per cent. Trade is bad and tends to become worse. Many of the mills are working half time. And yet, while these our countrymen are forced either to emigrate, as many of them do, or to accept half wages, enough foreign woollen goods come toll-free into our markets to give employment to 200 large factories and fifty yarn spinning mills. The estimate is by Mr. Charles John Wilson, of Hawick, a well-known authority upon the subject. Is it not repugnant to one's reason and one's sense of justice that the nations which bar our own goods should flood our own market unopposed, and drive our people from their work?

Your short article appears to me to be quite a microcosm of Free Trade fallacies and fancies. Because of one single incident, the receipts of the Hawick Banks, a cocksure theory is put forward which has absolutely no relation to the actual facts. Let the gentleman who wrote the article go to the Hawick Boroughs and explain their exceptional prosperity to the half-time workmen – or rather let me earnestly advise him not to do so, for they are practical people with no sympathy with abstract reasoning.

So far as the figures go, we do not seem to start from any common ground. I have no information more recent or more accurate than the Board of Trade return for 1902, as expressed in the Blue-book of August 1903. I append the figures with references to the page so that they can readily be verified. I deal with manufactured woollen goods in the first instance. Our total export (p. 36) was £15,264,000. Of this £6,996,000 (p. 45) went to British

101

possessions, leaving £9,195,000 (p. 41) for foreign countries. Now the inroads into our own markets amounted to £10,326,316 imported from Protectionist countries (pp. 77–89). The balance, therefore, between what we send to these countries and what we receive from them is £1,131,316 against us. I therefore repeat what I said in my previous letter that if we never sold a yard or woollens abroad, and if we kept our own trade (home and colonial), our output would be greater than it is at present.

There follows the old discredited argument that if we increase that output we must decrease our output of something else. The only things that we would decrease are our poor rates and our totals of emigration. The first essential for a nation, as it seems to me, is to hold tight to its own home market. The reason for this is that every gain in your home market in any commodity involves an increased output of some other home commodity in order to pay for it. If, for example, Hawick tweeds are being sold in Sheffield, it needs an increase of Sheffield steel in order to pay for them. But if Hawick tweeds are being sold in Liege, only one set of British workers instead of two sets are reaping the advantage. Let us regain our own home market, and then we may hope to share that rate of advance which Germany and America have enjoyed during the last twenty years. It is a deplorable thing to think that our export of woollens in 1901 was exactly what it was in 1859, forty-two years before. At present under our rotten system there is only one really flourishing trade in this country, and that is coal-mining, which drives our people underground, causes them to spend their lives in unhealthy and low-class labour, squanders our capital, and gives our rivals the material by which they may wrest from us those highly specialised trades in which we used to excel.

I am, &c.,
ARTHUR CONAN DOYLE

Undershaw, Hindhead, Haslemere, Feb. 5

THE TIMES   28 November 1904

The Case of the Caroline

SIR, – Statements have been made in the papers, all of them uncontradicted, and some of them confirmed, that two gentlemen, a Mr. Sinnett and a Mr. Roche, were concerned in running a torpedo-boat out of the Thames and handing it over to the Russians.

I would ask if there is no law to touch these men who have caused us to break the law of nations. If there is not, then there is a grievous want in our Code which should be speedily amended.

We have earned throughout our history the reputation of being an unstable ally. We abandoned Prince Eugene and we abandoned Frederick the Great in the midst of a joint war. I can forgive a Japanese who, seeing us run a torpedo-boat to Russia, supply the Russian fleet with Welsh coals, and allow that fleet to coal at Port Said, believes that we are following our worst traditions.

Yours faithfully,
ARTHUR CONAN DOYLE

Undershaw, Hindhead, Haslemere, Nov. 25

THE BORDER ADVERTISER,
GALASHIELS   11 April 1905

Mr. A. L. Brown and Sir Arthur Conan Doyle

SIR, – A year or so ago Mr. Brown challenged some figures of mine – indeed he was in such haste to do so that he interrupted a meeting for the purpose. Consequently, I went over the figures again, as did several other competent statisticians, and they proved to have been absolutely correct. This incident should have warned him to be more careful, and not to endeavour to controvert remarks which he did not hear, and which he can only know through a very condensed report.

His so called "mistakes" prove in this case, as in the last, to be absolute mares' nests. In talking of the lamentable drop in our exports, I did not confine myself in a hard and fast way to single years, but I prefaced my remarks by saying –, "If you go back for thirty years or so," and finally I took 1871 as a concrete example. I chose this year because I had rather understate my case than overstate it. 1872 is, of course, a more favourable year for my argument. I now give the figures of manufactured woollens and worsteds, including yarns, for two periods of six years, with a thirty years' interval, so that every reader can judge for himself. If Mr. A.L. Brown can derive any consolation out of them he is the Mark Tapley of politics.

Exports of woollen and worsted manufactures, including yarns, taken from Statistical Abstract of the Blue Books, and confirmed by Mr. Hooper's statistics of woollen and worsted trade, kindly sent me by Mr. Brown:–

1870	26,600,000	1899	19,100,000
1871	83,300,000	1900	20,100,000
1872	39,500,000	1901	17,700,000
1873	80,700,000	1902	18,700,000
1874	28,800,000	1903	20,000,000
1875	26,700,000	1904	22,200,000

Mr. A. L. Brown then goes on to point out the difference between the results in price and in bulk. This difference I carefully explained to my audience. Mr. Brown is not, however, an equally frank controversialist, as he fails to point out in his letter that this same difference between price and bulk made the increase in the foreign imports twice as great as would appear from the tables.

In dealing with the loss of population in these Burghs, I appear to have again understated the case – which I should always prefer to do – for I find that Hawick has lost 2,000 souls in addition to nearly 4,000 gone from Galashiels. Mr. Brown appears to say that there is some consolation to be found in the fact that the general population of the country is increasing. If some high class industry was indeed increasing rapidly, then I could follow his statement, but the textile trades, the iron trade, and nearly all productive trades appear to have either fallen or been stagnant. I write at a distance from books of reference, but as far as my memory serves me the only trades in Great Britain which are progressive are coal mining (a trade open to many grave objections), engineering (depending greatly on the motor car development), and ship-building. The reason of this general decline lies in foreign tariffs, and there is no hope for improvement until we are in a position to bargain on equal terms with those who erect them.

Mr. Brown's next argument is that low wages in Belgium are due to its protective tariff. Then how about the high wages of America? Are they due also to a protective tariff? There is a very low rate of wages in many parts of Ireland, and yet Ireland is a free trade country. Germany used to be a free trade country till 1880, and so I think was Belgium, but wages did not fall when they adopted Protection. In Germany they increased at a swifter ratio than in Great Britain. Wages increase in proportion to the demand for labour, and everything which spreads our foreign market or holds our home one helps to send up wages. Tariff Reform would certainly act in that direction.

Mr. A. L. Brown appears to take a cheerful view of the cheap Belgian yarn, produced by sweated labour. I do not think he would find many British yarn spinners to agree with him.

Finally, Mr Brown is exulted at the prospect of a 10 per cent. duty on yarns. As a matter of fact, by the only scheme before the country, the duty on yarns (as on all half manufactured goods) would be only 5 per cent. The Belgian and other yarns would either have to contribute this sum, and so mitigate our taxation, or else keep out, and so give more work for the British workman. If they came in in spite of it, as Mr. Brown says they would, then it would be so much the better for the exchequer, and it would give us a means of bargaining by which we might attain what we all desire, true free trade – that is, a trade in which we are free to sell as well as to buy. I should think, in spite of Mr. Brown's protest, that this is the chief desire of a manufacturing district, and that they will prove it at the next election.

I am &c.,
ARTHUR CONAN DOYLE

Balmoral Hotel, Edinburgh, 8th April, 1905

THE TIMES   14 June 1905

Rifle Shooting as a National Pursuit

SIR, – Will you permit me, as one who has had some small experience of the founding and working of such clubs, to say a few words, now that Lord Roberts's splendid appeal to the nation is likely to give the movement a fresh impetus, and to turn what has been a sporadic development, depending upon local spirit and generosity, into a truly national organisation?

The first point which is worth insisting upon is that a man trained at a miniature range (whether Morris tube or otherwise) does become an efficient shot almost at once when he is allowed to use a full range. What with the low trajectory and the absence of recoil in the modern rifle the handling of the weapon is much the same in each case. I am speaking now of an outdoor miniature range, a hundred yards long, where a man must allow for windage, and where he must raise his sights to fire. Such a range is not a mere toy, but can and does produce riflemen who speedily become excellent service shots. If the country were covered with such ranges we could soon realise Lord Roberts's ideal of a nation of marksmen. Since it is becoming more and more clear that our alternative in the future will lie between some form of actual compulsory service (a hateful but possibly an inevitable measure) and a great development of the rifle club movement, it is a very serious matter to consider what are the easiest and most practical steps to bring the latter into existence.

This leads me to the second point worth insisting upon, which is that the miniature rifle range, besides being efficient, is exceedingly cheap. Given the land, which should be not less than a hundred yards long and twenty yards broad, with a natural or artificial bank at the end of it, the remaining cost of rifles, targets, markers' pits, and the rest of it should not come to more than £50. There are few parishes, one would hope, where some landowner would not spare a strip of his land for a patriotic purpose. Common land or heath land which has no other value, is exactly that which is best adapted for a small range. Therefore, in many cases the young club would only be faced by 'the necessity of finding the small sum already mentioned, with some additional subscriptions for the purpose of providing small prizes or badges for successful riflemen.

At present, in hundreds of places, this money has been found by local effort, and the club has been duly started. In many cases it has gone on running successfully. In many others it has languished after the first novelty was past. The reason for the latter state of things is sometimes, as in the district where I reside, that most of the young men have actually learned to shoot to some extent, and the clubs have therefore done their work. But indifference is also due to the fact that the man has to pay some small fee towards the upkeep of the club, and has also to pay for the cartridges which he uses. A poor working man feels very naturally, that instead of paying he should rather be paid, since he is giving up his time to the services of the State. With free clubs and free cartridges a great stumbling-block would be removed. As the long Morris tube cartridges, which are, in my opinion, the best for the purpose, can be retailed at four a penny, the drain upon the public purse would not be a serious one.

If the ranges are, as I have tried to show, both efficient and cheap, the next point is to determine how they could be best organised as a public institution all over the country. As Lord Roberts says, it was the skill acquired at the parish butts which made England the first military Power in Europe during the fourteenth century. My suggestion is that the parish butts be restored in the shape of a parish miniature range. For the establishment and control of this we have an existing organisation in the shape of the parish council. I think that if the matter were handed over to the parish councils in rural England, and to the town councils (or committees thereof) in the small towns, with definite orders to construct such ranges and with power to levy a small rate towards their formation and upkeep, we would within a twelvemonth have exactly such a network of rifle clubs as is needed to realise that condition which is our alternative to national service. With a controlling head in London and a local inspector in each county to check or encourage the parish councils, a great question could be solved with a *minimum* of friction and expense.

What would be needed then to attain this great end? Simply a law by which each parish council must establish a rifle club, with power to levy the money for that end. Also a trifling addition to our war budget for the inspectors and central authority. It seems a very tiny matter when compared to the revulsion of our habits and dislocation of our lives implied in national service. Having got the butts, would it be necessary to pass a further law making some use of them compulsory for every adult in the parish? We could only answer that question when we saw how far they were voluntarily used when a couple of hundred rounds were given free to every applicant. But suppose that it was eventually necessary to pass such a law, it is surely the very smallest demand that any country in Europe makes upon its citizens.

In conclusion, we should have to consider the question of Sunday shooting. It was the Sunday shooting which gave the nation the benefit of the archery butts in the Middle Ages. What is the use of the most perfect machinery if the individual has no time in which to use it? So long as the workmen have only one half holiday a week it is, I fear, useless to hope that any but a very small proportion of them will voluntarily spend it at the butts. Sunday shooting, out of church hours, is equally permitted in Catholic and Calvinistic countries – indeed, it is more characteristic of the latter – so that its reprobation seems to be not so much a matter of religion as of local custom and prejudice. For my own part it seems to me that our young men would be better employed in learning to serve their country than in standing round doing nothing at the road corners. No doubt this introduces another and very controversial subject; but I am convinced that it is bound up with the first, and is very essential to its solution.

Yours faithfully,
ARTHUR CONAN DOYLE

Undershaw, Hindhead, Haslemere

THE BORDER ADVERTISER,
GALASHIELS   5 September 1905

Sir Arthur Conan Doyle's Platform

SIR, – My attention has been called to a note in your issue of the 29th ult., in which surprise is expressed that a gentleman of Socialistic views, who is a Home Ruler, should address an audience on my behalf. I hope that the incident will emphasise the fact, which I have frequently asserted, that this election will, so far as I can make it so, not be a matter of Tory, Radical, or Socialist, but will be a contest between those who wish to improve the conditions of British trade and those who desire to leave them as they are. All other subjects are secondary to this, and all minor differences may be sunk in pursuit of the one main object. The presence upon my platform of such gentlemen as Professor Robertson Watson, Mr. Samuel Storey, and others will show how an economic question can cut across the lines of ordinary political strife.

Yours faithfully,
ARTHUR CONAN DOYLE

Undershaw, Hindhead, Haslemere, September 2nd, 1905

THE DAILY MAIL   21 September 1905

More Motorphobia

SIR, – I have observed some caustic comments in your recent issues upon the action of the Andover Bench, who appear to be assuming a position not unlike those feudal barons who exacted tribute from all who passed through their territories.

A similar band of reactionary officials have terrorised this Guildford district during the summer. The energy of the police in seizing motorists, and that of the magistrates in taking their money, is exactly equal in both places, for there were seventy-one captures and seventy-one convictions in each. Surely these figures speak for themselves.

Can any sane person imagine that policemen, with their promotion in view and every human motive to make them lean towards an aggravation of the evidence, would be right on every single occasion? Even with a perfectly impartial mind it is no easy task to measure a fast machine exactly over a furlong, where a few seconds one way or the other make all the difference on the estimate of the mile. The least slowness in taking time at one end, or the least fastness at the other, vitiates the whole result.

But in the face of such figures motorists plead guilty, for there is clearly no discretion and no hope of fair play. They simply note the fact, now notorious, that it is dangerous to drive with any speed upon a lonely country road, but that it is safe elsewhere, for it is only on the lonely roads that traps are set. Such is the result of administering a law according to the letter and not the spirit.

To show the length to which the police will go to secure a catch I may quote my own experience recently at Folkestone, a town of which motorists should beware.

I was approaching it for the first time along a wide and deserted road when I was stopped by the usual vidette. On turning back I discovered three other constables lying with their instruments in a graveyard which skirted the road. It was a Sunday, and these skulkers upon consecrated ground seemed utterly blind to the fact that if I had indeed exceeded by a few seconds the legal time they had themselves, if words have any meaning, been guilty of the rather more serious offence of sacrilege. The magistrate in taking my money remarked with heavy jocularity that unless I were mulct I would no doubt kill several people – I, who have never hurt nor frightened a soul in three years' constant driving.

Yours faithfully,
ARTHUR CONAN DOYLE

Undershaw, Hindhead, Haslemere

THE TIMES   31 October 1905

Fiscal Policy

SIR, – Lord Avebury's letter might give the impression that our export of woollen manufactures was increasing. This effect is produced by taking the figures of the last five years, which mark a slight recovery from a period of deep depression.

As a matter of fact, so great has been the fall in our export of woollen manufactures that we send out considerably less than we did in the early seventies. The figures, omitting yarns, were in value £27,000,000 in 1871, £32,000,000 in 1872, and £25,000,000 in 1873, as against the £18,000,000 in round numbers which Lord Avebury quotes for 1904. It must be admitted that the amounts exported do not show so marked a decline as the values would indicate, but this cuts both ways, as it affects the figures of the foreign imports, which have risen from about four millions to nine in the same period.

France, not Germany, is our chief opponent in the woollen industry. As she takes from us on an average £1,500,000 of woollens, and imports to our market more than £5,000,000 worth, it would seem that her protection has not harmed her.

I should not venture to criticize Lord Avebury's letter were it not that as tariff reform candidate for a woollen-manufacturing constituency I have had to look at the facts. There are a small number of manufacturers who maintain the present system, but they are all, so far as I know, men who were previously well known as political partisans. I have not met one non-political who is satisfied with the state of the trade.

Yours faithfully,
ARTHUR CONAN DOYLE

Undershaw, Hindhead, Surrey, Oct. 28

The Free Trade Debate

Sir, – We Tariff Reformers had no occasion to complain of our treatment by our opponents at this meeting. Mr. Chamberlain's views were continually travestied, and a dummy Mr. Chamberlain was badly knocked about, but that is so in political warfare all the world over. We did feel, however, that there was something jarring in Mr. Aitken's final remarks. He took the extraordinary line that a grave moral question was involved in the contest between free imports and tariff reform. He might with as much truth have said that it was a moral question whether one bought jam at the grocer's or made it from one's own fruit. Does Mr. Aitken seriously contend that such men as Charles Booth – who has spent his life among the London poor – or Alfred Moseley – who took the commission to America at his own expense – are of a low moral calibre? Both of these gentlemen are strong supporters of Mr. Chamberlain – or does he mean to imply that we stand upon a higher moral plane than our forefathers in the days of Protection? Let him look, not only at the United States and at Germany, but at such countries as Switzerland, Sweden and Holland. Does he find that the moral standard in these countries is lower than ours? Where then does the moral question come in?

A German friend of mine remarked that the Boers began the war "by commandeering the Almighty." It seems to me to be the habitual practice of a certain section of British politicians. We have already seen it in connection with education rates and with Chinese labour – now it appears even in tariff reform. I do not myself believe that the Higher Powers are always on the side of the opposition.

I would utter a mild word of protest also against the harshness of Mr. Aitken's observations concerning an alleged misstatement which he claimed to have discovered in the remarks of Mr. Hutchinson. Mr. Hutchinson's argument so far as I followed it, was that German wages had increased at a quicker ratio than British. Mr. Aitken waved a Blue Book, and asserted that this was not so. If he had cast his eyes to the bottom of the very page from which he was quoting he would have seen printed in large letters "It will be seen that the table indicates a rise in wages in all four countries. *The rise is greatest in Germany,* and least in the United States." It must be admitted that the difference is very slight, and that there is little political capital for either side to make out of it, but the incident does not appear to justify the severe remarks which Mr. Aitken thought proper to make.

Yours faithfully,
ARTHUR CONAN DOYLE

December 2nd, 1905

THE FARNHAM, HASLEMERE & HINDHEAD HERALD

30 December 1905

The Fiscal Controversy

SIR, – I see that Mr. Methuen still persuades himself that the angels are on the side of the Free Importers. Why not, if it makes him happy? But it is a little unkind to our forefathers and to all the continental nations. In our solitary virtue we are like the recalcitrant juryman who declared that he had never met eleven such obstinate men before.

At present according to our highly moral regulations, diamonds, velvet, silk and motor cars come free into the country, while tea and sugar are heavily taxed. I suppose there is some virtuous principle at stake in this, and that it proves our standard to be higher than that of our neighbours, but on the face of it it seems a little strange.

Mr. Methuen says that the change will make manufacturers richer. If he can show any possible process by which manufacturers can be enriched without a corresponding advantage coming to their workmen, he will have rendered a service to political economy. Manufacturers can only flourish by turning out more stuff, this means more demand for labour, and that in turn regulates the price which the worker gets.

To show that the German worker, after 25 years of commercial life, is not quite up to the British standard, which is the fruit of centuries, is beside the question. The only fair comparison is between the German under a tariff and the German under free trade. He has tried both, and there can be no possible comparison. Both the nation and the individual have prospered best under a tariff.

Our own rates of wages, quoted in the Blue Book, are unfortunately as illusive as those of the man who proudly boasted that he got 7s. 6d. a day, but admitted, on enquiry, that he only got one day's work a week. In the woollen trade, which is that with which I am best acquainted, about a quarter each year may be deducted for half-time, and most trades suffer in a similar manner. The total export, and the number of hands employed, have sunk

111

steadily for 20 years, in this, the oldest of British industries.

The man who makes anything, be he a manufacturer, an artisan, or a farmer, by virtue of the fact that he adds to our stock of wealth, has, in my opinion, more right to consideration than the consumer, who may be a mere parasite and drone. The country cannot do without the former, and very often could dispense with the latter. But I do not think there is any real conflict of interests, for if you look after the trunk, all the branches and leaves will look after themselves.

The very moral results of our present system are that we have, on the authority of the Radical leader, twelve million people on the edge of hunger, and far the largest rate of emigration of any industrial country. What is the state of morality or civilisation among these submerged masses? They are the fruits of sixty years' competition with the sweated labour of Europe, and of the destruction of trade after trade which have been ruined by causes which our stupid pedantry has prevented us from arresting. The skilled worker, be he silk weaver, tin plate worker, glass bottle blower, or whatever trade you like, sinks down, his occupation gone, and joins the sediment down below. In Germany, no trade could ever be ruined, because the tariff wall will always ensure a home market of 60 million people.

One word before I finish as to that plausible supposition that for all the articles brought in and depriving our people of their work, something goes out in return. Nothing of the kind. If it were true, our exports and imports would balance instead of the latter being nearly double. Half our imports represent payment of interest on capital, and for services as carrier on the sea. We can take this in any form. It will come in the easiest. If we make manufactured articles difficult (by taxing them), it will come in food and raw material, which is what we want. At present the poor man's work is sacrificed to the interest of the capitalist, and will be so long as we admit free what we can ourselves make. There was never a more democratic movement than that of Tariff Reform.

Mr. Methuen says that the price of everything will be increased. I do not admit that ten per cent. on manufactures would increase the price by anything. I hope that internal competition would keep the price where it is. But suppose, for argument's sake, that everything did increase ten per cent., that ten per cent. is kept in the national money-box, and goes to alleviate taxation, so you get it all back again. In America there is no income tax and little direct taxation of any kind – as a result of their tariff.

I shall be away until after the election, so it is not out of want of courtesy if I do not answer any further letters on this subject.

Yours faithfully,
ARTHUR CONAN DOYLE

To the Electors of the Border Burghs

GENTLEMEN, – I claim your support mainly upon the Fiscal question, which I put in the forefront because I consider it far more important than any purely political question. We give free imports to all the world, and are flooded with manufactured articles which should be made by our own workers, while all round us the tariff walls of our neighbours grow higher and more impassable. By a small tariff we will certainly do one of two things – either preserve our own home market, or else be able to bargain that foreign nations give us better terms. Whichever we do must bring greater prosperity both to manufacturers and to workmen, for the success of the one means better times for the other. To no industry in Great Britain does this apply more than to the woollen trade, which is the staple manufacture of the Border Burghs.

I am in favour also of acceding to the unanimous suggestion of all the Colonial Premiers as expressed at the London Conference of 1902, to the effect that preference should be given in matters of trade throughout the Empire. I believe that no further argument is needed for this policy than the fact that the present improved outlook in trade, especially in the woollen industry, is the visible first fruit of a preferential policy. The preferences now granted by British Colonies have proved of great value to our trade, but it is certain that they will not continue to grant them if we show no desire to reciprocate. I am in favour, therefore, of taking the tax as far as possible off those food stuffs which we do not ourselves produce and putting it on the foreign imports of those food stuffs which we do produce. By this rational readjustment of taxation both our Colonies and our own farmers will derive some benefit, while the rest of the community will in no way be the worse, but will have the benefit of the increased trade due to the Colonial preference for our manufactures.

I am in favour of a special taxation of objects of luxury. I consider it a scandal that diamonds, motor cars, velvets and silks should come free into the country, while the necessities of the poor man are heavily taxed.

The Irish question is before us once more. My views upon it are the same as in Central Edinburgh in 1900. Since that date the events in Norway and Hungary have given us a fresh object lesson in the danger of two parliaments within one realm. I will never consent to a separate legislature for Ireland. At the same time I am strongly in favour of every meliorative measure short of Home

Rule which can improve the relations between the two countries. I believe that the present Unionist policy of planting the people upon their own acres is a wise one, and that in conjunction with the discouragement of foreign agricultural imports, by which the Irish farmer will for the first time derive some benefit from his connection with Great Britain, it will go far to build up a more friendly and cordial feeling. I am also in favour of meeting the wishes of the majority of the Irish people in the matter of a Catholic University. I believe such a course to be just and expedient – just because Irish money should be used so far as possible as the majority of Irishmen desire, whether we agree with their point of view or not, and expedient because every fresh grievance removed weakens the agitation for that Home Rule which it is against our national interests to grant. Home Rule itself would, I am convinced, be even more hurtful to Ireland than to Great Britain.

As a Liberal I am in favour of complete religious equality. I recognise, however, that great historic institutions, such as the Churches of Scotland and of England should not be disestablished as a side issue, and I should not support any legislation of the sort until the question had been definitely brought before the public in a fresh election.

I am in favour of universal adult suffrage for men and the franchise for those women who contribute directly to Imperial taxation. To deny the latter is taxation without representation.

I am against any fresh taxation of agricultural land, since this is already the most depressed as well as the most important of our industries. It is illogical to talk of adding fresh burdens to it and yet of settling people upon it. In the case of town lands, however, where an increased value has been given by the growth of the town, I think that it is just that the landowner, on the renewal of leases at a higher figure, should contribute a portion of his profit to the municipality in which the land is. This reform applies to England rather than Scotland, but in Scotland I favour the taxation of land held back from building for speculative purposes.

In temperance legislation I believe in local control with a provision for just compensation for the dispossessed publican.

On all other points I shall, as occasion serves, convey my views to the electors, but I would again impress upon them in conclusion that no question of party politics can be so intimate or so pressing as that great trade question which must determine the prosperity of these burghs and the well-being of the inhabitants, as well as the comparative position of our country among the nations of the world.

ARTHUR CONAN DOYLE

Undershaw, Hindhead, Surrey, December 27th, 1905

Mr. Chamberlain and Mr. Burns

Sir, – I observe that Mr. Burns states that Mr. Chamberlain has left no result of the war. He has left a united South Africa under the Union Jack, and he has gained the respect and love of every Briton in that country. What man of our age can show such a monument as that? When I read in history of the little men who in their day threw mud at the great Empire builders, at Chatham and at Pitt, it makes one realise that the world moves in circles and comes ever back to the same point.

Yours faithfully,
ARTHUR CONAN DOYLE

Grand Hotel, Trafalgar-square, W.C., Jan. 26

Sir Arthur Conan Doyle on Tariff Reform*

Sir, – Pray give my kindest greetings to all assembled friends. I have a very lively recollection of the personal kindness which I met with during my two years' work in the Border Burghs. I think that it is the question of Tariff Reform in which they, as well as I, are principally interested. When we remember that every University in the kingdom, the City of London, and the whole of the industrial Midlands have gone straight upon it, we must recognise that, if quality could outweigh quantity, we have won our battle already. If you take in the manhood of the colonies we have at the present moment, treating the Empire as a whole, a large majority in mere quantity. No cause which has progressed so far in so short a time can possibly fail to win ultimate success. I am sorry that the Border Burghs are not among the chosen band who are carrying forward the flag of industrial progress. I believe that the issue there as elsewhere has been obscured by that Chinese slavery, which has already been admitted by the Under Secretary of the Colonies to be a lie or a "terminological inexactitude," to quote his foolish phrase. I said this throughout the election, and now the Government themselves confirm it. I fancy the election of 1906 will live in history as the great Chinese hoax. I suppose that those cartoons of Chinese slaves have hardly had time to be removed from the walls of your burghs before their authors have been forced to admit that they are false. However, they have served their turn. There are some political fanatics who would look upon such proceedings as a mere move in the game of politics, but surely the average voter when he finds that his feelings have been played upon, and his support obtained under such circumstances, will bear it in his memory for the future. Once more wishing all my friends a most pleasant evening and every happiness,

Yours very truly,
ARTHUR CONAN DOYLE

P.S. I hear there was a rumour that I was in hospital after the contest. That was a terminological inexactitude.

Undershaw, Hindhead, Surrey

* Letter read to a Unionist social gathering in Selkirk.

Motor-cars and Coast Defence

SIR, – There is a body called the "Legion of Frontiersmen" which is at present endeavouring to organise some of those civilian forces in the nation which might be of service in time of war. There is one great body to whom they have not appealed which could as a matter of fact be easily organised and which might be of vital importance at a critical moment. I mean the motorists of Great Britain. I will suppose such a contingency as a sudden invasion or raid. The news reaches London that a hostile force has established itself on the south or east coast. Everything depends upon swift action so as to prevent any cavalry that force may possess from pushing on in small parties, seizing junctions, cutting wires, blowing up bridges, and generally disorganizing the defence. It might be some days before a sufficient military force could be on the spot, and in the meantime much mischief would be done and the enemy more strongly established.

My suggestion is that a thousand motorists, a number which I am sure could be trebled or quadrupled, should organise themselves, and should pledge themselves, on the first news of such invasion, to instantly fill up their cars with picked riflemen drawn from their own immediate neighbourhood, and to convey them, with a week's food, their rifles, and their ammunition, to the danger point. Food, rifles, and motor-cars are already to hand, and the only factor missing is the ammunition, 2,000 rounds of which should be given by the Government to the keeping of the motorist who signifies his willingness to serve – such ammunition to be stored in his garage in time of peace. In this way, within a very few hours, such a fringe of irregular, self-supporting riflemen would be formed round the enemy that they could not push swiftly on, or collect supplies, without their patrols being cut off, and an immediate line of resistance would be formed behind which the regular defence could be prepared – all this without putting any tax upon the railways.

I recognise, of course, the risk which such improvised troops would run under the laws of war, but I am convinced that such risk would be cheerfully met in so grave a crisis.

To test the efficacy of such an organisation would be most easy. Let it be formed, and let the War Office telegraph the place of landing upon a given day to every motorist upon the rolls. Let their representatives be upon the spot, and let them count for themselves how many thousand riflemen with arms and provisions would report themselves within five hours.

I should be much obliged if every motorist who reads of this scheme and approves of it would send a card to that effect to the secretary, "Legion of Frontiersmen," 6, Adam-street, Adelphi, W.C.

Yours faithfully,
ARTHUR CONAN DOYLE

Undershaw, Hindhead, Surrey

THE FARNHAM, HASLEMERE
& HINDHEAD
HERObjectType   28 April 1906

Sunday Rifle Shooting

SIR, – I observe in your columns a protest against our action in opening our range on Sundays, so courteously and temperately expressed, that I feel it calls for some word of explanation and justification on our part.

In the first place, I may say that this action has been taken, after mature consideration, by the unanimous vote of the whole committee, some ten in number, representing men of all shades of religious opinion. I need not say that we foresaw opposition, and that we intend to live it down.

At the same time, nothing is further from our wishes than to assume a defiant or offensive attitude towards the religious sentiments of the general community. The range is only open at such an hour in the afternoon as will clash with no religious service. The firing entails work to no-one, but harmless occupation to all. The noise in a Morris tube is so small as to cause no public inconvenience.

In these days when Sunday cycling, motoring, boating, and even golf, are universal, it is difficult to see any logical cause for an

117

objection to the one form of amusement which may serve an important public purpose.

As to the general question of the uses of the Sabbath, I would remind you that our Protestantism came from Germany and our Puritanism from Holland and from Switzerland. In all three countries, and especially in the land of Calvin, it is quite usual to shoot on Sunday, indeed, Sunday is the day specially set apart for that purpose. In the time of James I of England, although this country was Protestant, shooting was, I am informed, *compulsory* on the Sunday. Our present views of Sunday observance, or rather, the views of our fathers – for the last twenty years have materially altered them – have no warrant in the history either of England or of Protestantism, but are the outcome of that somewhat local Puritanism which lingered as a last legacy of the theological disputes of the 17th century.

I am, Sir, yours faithfully,
ARTHUR CONAN DOYLE

Undershaw, Hindhead, Haslemere

THE DAILY EXPRESS   7 August 1906

Are We Becoming Less Religious?
Sir A. Conan Doyle's Views

SIR, – It appears to me that one fallacy runs through a great deal of the correspondence about religion in your columns, and that is the postulate that any form of ritual, including the ritual of going to a large stone building for the purpose of communion with the great Unseen, has any bearing upon true religion.

The lesson which life has taught me is that it has none.

I have known most admirable people who did these practices, and I have known most wicked ones. I have known most admirable people who did not do such things, and I have known most wicked ones. Never yet have I known a person who was good because he went to church, or evil because he did not. And yet in most of your letters such practices are taken as a test whether religion is waning or increasing. There is no relation between them.

The true tests of progress in true religion are (1) Is there a kinder and broader view of such subjects, enabling all men of all creeds to live in amity and charity? (2) Are the criminal statistics better? (3) Are the drink returns better, showing that man is acquiring greater animal self-control (4) Are the illegitimacy returns better, showing the same thing? (5) Is there more reading, more demand for lectures, more interest in science, showing that the mind is gaining upon the body? (6) Are the savings bank returns better, showing thrift and self-denial? (7) Are the trade returns better, showing greater industry and efficiency? (8) Are there more charitable institutions, and does man show more clearly his sense of duty towards the lower animals?

Such practical tests as these, which do actually for the most part show progress, are worth more than the ritual observances which may or may not go with a good life.

There is an aggressive form of religion, calling itself Dogmatic Faith, which has done far more harm to the human race than pestilence or famine. Directly to its door must be laid, not only all the bloodstained history of Mahometanism, but all the murderous doings which have in turn disgraced every sect of Christianity.

In the name of Christ, the Apostle of Peace, this dreadful school of thought, within a few centuries of His death, brought about such quarrels and such murders as had never been heard of in pagan days. Over the Homoiousian question, a theological point depending upon a diphthong, it has been reckoned that a hundred thousand people lost their lives, champions and victims of Faith. The Crusades, the murders of the Albigenses and of the Cevennes, the Thirty Years' War, the Inquisition, the outrages of Catholics on Protestants, the no less detestable outrages of Protestants on Catholics, the persecutions of Nonconformists by the Church, the persecutions of Quakers by the Nonconformists, the manifold domestic tragedies and tyrannies, embittering the lives of countless numbers – surely when all these are considered, the reader must admit that Faith in the positive aggressive sense, has wrought more mischief than famine or pestilence.

All sects have been misled by men of the same acrid frame of mind, and have incurred the same blood-guiltiness. I only know four cults – the original Buddhists, the Quakers, the Unitarians, and the Agnostics – who can, I think, say that they have no blood on their hands. Certainly the Atheists cannot, for their excesses in France – in the Revolution, and also in 1870 – have been as bad as those of the Churches.

And what has been the root cause of it all? Saying you believe what your mind cannot grasp, and what your free reason would frequently reject. A makes his proofless assertion and calls it his faith. B has the right to do the same. Then A and B hate each other with a holy hatred, and there is the epitome of the blackest chapter in the history of the world. We, who are like ship-wrecked

119

mariners upon this little raft of a world, moving upon the face of the infinite ocean, have enough to do to live kindly among ourselves without quarrelling bitterly about that which is beyond the horizon.

Perhaps you say that even in these very words I myself show religious want of charity. But surely it is not so. If the Catholic finds the Pope, or the Anglican the bishop, or the Nonconformist the minister a help upon his path, then in every case it is a good thing – a splendid thing – if it causes that man to be a better, more noble, human creature. Every form of belief is admirable so far as it does that. But when, as in the letters of some of your correspondents, it turns to want of charity, and the reviling of those who have other methods, then it is a petty twentieth-century exhibition of that which ranks in history among the gravest and most bloodthirsty of human crimes.

ARTHUR CONAN DOYLE

Ashdown Forest Hotel, Aug. 3

THE DAILY EXPRESS   11 August 1906

Are We Becoming Less Religious?
A Reply from Sir A. Conan Doyle

SIR, – I had no desire to be led into the morass of a theological discussion; but in answer to Mr. Pollock's categorical question as to my view upon a series of texts, I would answer by reminding him of the words of the Founder of the Christian Faith, that it is the letter which kills, and the virtue lies in the spirit.

This insistence upon the literal meaning of texts is, in the words of Winwood Reade, "to pull down idols of wood only to replace them with idols of paper and printer's ink." They are the weapons by which theologians from the earliest days of Christianity have spread disunion and strife. Every creed can found its position upon a text, and every other creed can find some other to controvert it.

When, for example, the Catholic founds his doctrine of transubstantiation upon the plain text, "This is my body and this is my blood," it seems that nothing could be worded more clearly. And yet the Protestant stoutly denies its validity, and insists upon a metaphorical meaning. To the Unitarian there are many texts which make it appear to him that Christ did not claim the attributes of Deity.

When we consider the origin of the gospels, their translation from language to language, and the fact that every revision has shown the text to be faulty, it is inconceivable that any absolutely hard-and-fast incontrovertible system of theology can be built from them.

But the spirit of the New Testament is clear enough, and there lies the justification of Christianity.

ARTHUR CONAN DOYLE

THE DAILY EXPRESS   31 August 1906

Are We Becoming Less Religious?
Summing Up

SIR, – I had not intended to intervene again in the interesting controversy which has occupied your columns, but so many of the controversialists have alluded to my original letter that it might seem discourteous if I took no notice of their objections.

These objections have come for the most part from clerical correspondents. In all ages any attempt at breadth of thought and at wide charity in the interpretation of the relations between man and his Maker have always met with the same clerical opposition; but history records that, though it has often retarded, it has never checked the gradual emancipation of the human reason from iron-bound ritual and dogma. We are fortunate in the present age in having, on the other hand, many clergy of all denominations who recognise that their creeds must grow more tolerant and more comprehensive lest they be left behind entirely by civilisation.

Those who know how large a proportion of the most earnest-minded and thoughtful men in this country are already outside all dogmatic creeds will admit that the contingency is not a fanciful one.

Throughout this controversy the term "religion" has been continually used where, as it seems to me, "ritual" was a more appropriate expression. Religion is the relation between any human soul and the Creator, and is shown outwardly by the actions of the individual. All canonical observances, rituals, and dogmas are aids to the soul in its developments. So far as they do aid it they are justified. So far as they do not, but become petrified forms which prevent life and growth, they stand condemned. But always "by their fruit shall you know them," and by that standard England has enormously improved, and is, therefore, more truly religious.

What are these pious days to which so many of your correspondents allude? Are they the days drawn by Hogarth and described by Fielding? When was England ever so sober, so intelligent, so well educated, so thrifty, and so industrious as at present. As to this decay of forms and ceremonies, while some depore it others may regard it as the sunrise of saner, better, and more charitable days. I believe that our descendants, looking back at this age, will regard it as one of darkness and superstition, but will admit that it is an advance upon the even darker ages which preceded it.

Insistance upon dogma and ritual, or "religion" in the sense in which your correspondents have misused it, must infallibly result in the human race being eternally divided into rival factions, since it is impossible to conceive that any sect will absorb all the others. It is all very well for one of your correspondents to talk about our little earthly raft having a compass given it. We know by experience that no two people can see alike how the compass is pointing. The Divine Creator has indeed given us one compass, and that is reason, the noblest of all faculties. It is reason which tells us that if each sect would abate something of its rigid doctrine, and insist upon the points which unite it with its neighbours instead of accentuating those which divide it there would be some hope for the gradual extinction of those theological differences, which have, as I hold, nothing to do with true religion, and have been the source of more bloodshed and misery than any other single cause in the world's history.

Several of your clerical correspondents term me an Agnostic. What my individual faith may be is a matter of microscopic interest to others, but since the term has been used I may say that I am not an Agnostic though I extend to that body the respect which I feel for all earnest-minded men. I am a believer in the Christian system in its simplest and least dogmatic form as being on the whole the noblest which the world has evolved, though it has been so overlaid by the bigots and the formalists that it is difficult sometimes to see the original outlines at all. It is not a shaven head, but it is wide charity in the heart which is the essence of that creed. I am a convinced Theist also, and a profound believer in the direct action of a guiding force in the affairs of this world.

Finally, I may say that I do not believe that the Divine Message to the human race was delivered once for all two thousand years ago, but I hold that every piece of prose and verse which has in it anything which is helpful to the individual soul is in some sense a message from Beyond – a message which grows and expands as all vital things must do.

Let me end this letter by a quotation from verse of this character:–

"Our little systems have their day;
    They have their day and cease to be;
    They are but broken lights of Thee;
For Thou, oh Lord, art more than they."

ARTHUR CONAN DOYLE

Crowborough

The Book War
Protest by Sir A. Conan Doyle

SIR, – Would you kindly publish the enclosed. When you consider that this provision in the contract is a traditional courtesy for the convenience of the author in supplying his friends with copies it seems hard to find a word which would express the meanness involved in using it as a weapon – or suggesting it as one – against the publisher himself.

I am, Sir, your obedient servant,
ARTHUR CONAN DOYLE

(Enclosure)
The "Times" Book Club, London, W.

16 November 1906

Sir Arthur Conan Doyle, Hindhead, Surrey

DEAR SIR, – We should be glad to order from your publishers, Messrs. Smith, Elder, and Co., a large number of copies of *Sir Nigel* at the trade price, but they have refused to supply us with their publications. We greatly regret their action, as we know that our subscribers would be glad to read your book if we could circulate it freely among them.

There is, we believe, in the usual form of author's agreement, a clause to the effect that the author may purchase from the publisher copies of his book at trade price; and it occurs to us that you may have this right in respect of *Sir Nigel*. Should that be the case, we should be glad, if you see no objection, to obtain direct from you 1950 copies, as 1800, upon the usual trade terms, provided that we can obtain them at once.

Yours faithfully,
THE "TIMES" BOOK CLUB

Sir Arthur Conan Doyle and Mr. Perris

SIR, – A critic has the traditional licence of making uncontradicted remarks, be they wise or otherwise. When an outside correspondent, however, takes it upon himself to join in the discussion an author may surely say a word in reply. I could not have conceived it necessary to inform any educated man that if a writer draws the customs of any age with such spirit as he may, he does not necessarily mean that he thereby endorses the ideals of that age.

In the preface to *Sir Nigel* I have guarded myself carefully against such an impression. It would be as reasonable to say that I was a Cromwellian Puritan because I drew such types in *Micah Clarke* as to accuse me of mediaeval militarism because I have every sympathy with the knights of old. The first duty of a writer of historical romance is, so far as he can, to forget himself and his own age, and to look at the days of Froissart with Froissart's eyes.

Your correspondent recommends me to turn to the *Piers Plowman* side of the question, but it is clear that he cannot have read my book, since I have actually introduced the author of *Piers Plowman* into it, so that he might state his own case from a sympathetic point of view. Should anyone desire a modern author's ideals upon modern subjects he will naturally find them in those of his books which deal seriously with modern life.

Yours, etc.
ARTHUR CONAN DOYLE

Undershaw, Hindhead, Surrey, Nov. 22

The Case of Mr. George Edalji
Special Investigation by Sir A. Conan Doyle

SIR, – I have been engaged for some time past in investigating the case of Mr. George Edalji, a young solicitor of Parsee origin, who was condemned at the Stafford Quarter Sessions of October, 1903, to seven years' penal servitude for the maiming of cattle. I should be much obliged to you if you would aid the cause of justice by publishing the results of my inquiry in an early number of The *Daily Telegraph*. You would add to the favour if you would permit the statement to be headed "No Copyright," for I hope that in that case other papers – and especially Midland papers – would copy it in extenso. Only an appeal to the public can put an end to a course of injustice and persecution which amount, as I hope that I shall show, to a national scandal.

Yours faithfully,
ARTHUR CONAN DOYLE

Monkstown, Crowborough, Jan. 7

The special article written by Sir A. Conan Doyle – extending to about fourteen columns in length – was published in two parts. The first appeared on the 11th January and the second on the following day.

It was a complete investigation by Sir A. Conan Doyle of this case.

THE DAILY TELEGRAPH   15 January 1907

The Question of Eyesight

SIR, – I regard the optical part of my argument as so important that, with your permission, I will at once answer the remarks of Mr. Aitchison.

I fear that I expressed myself clumsily in the paragraph in which I showed how the normal eye might be reduced to the condition in which Mr. Edalji's eyes always are. Every minus sign in the prescription would, of course, become a plus. My own sight is normal, and I can answer for the feeling of helplessness which such a glass produces. I tried it upon a Press man, and defied him to reach the lawn-tennis ground in front of the house. He failed. Mr. Aitchison underrates the degree of myopia, though it is quoted in full in my paper. On one axis it becomes – 10.50, which surely is a very high degree, and the more serious when combined with astigmatism.

The effects of correction are beside the question, as Mr. Edalji did not wear glasses. I have a police admission to that effect.

To my mind it was as physically impossible for Mr. Edalji to have committed the crime as it would have been if his legs, instead of his eyes, were crippled. I have asked the editors of three of the leading medical papers to put the question of possibility before those of their readers who practise eye work. When the replies have come in we shall see what the opinion of the oculists of Great Britain is upon the subject.

Yours faithfully,
ARTHUR CONAN DOYLE

Undershaw, Hindhead, Surrey, Jan. 14

THE BRITISH MEDICAL
JOURNAL   19 January 1907

The Edalji Case

Sir, – Might I ask you in the cause of justice to permit me to put the following question to those of your readers who are engaged in eye practice?

"Do you consider it physically possible for Mr. George Edalji, whose degree of myopic astigmatism as determined by retinoscopy under homatropine is

Right eye – 8.75 diop. spher.
          – 1.75 diop. cylind. axis 90°.
Left eye – 8.25 diop. spher.

to have set forth without glasses on a pitch dark night with neither moon nor stars; to have crossed country for half a mile, climbing fences, finding gaps in hedges, and passing over a broad railway line; to have found and mutilated a pony which was loose in a large field, to have returned half a mile, and to have accomplished it all under thirty-five minutes, the limit of the possible time at his disposal?"

A consensus of scientific opinion upon this point would greatly aid me in getting justice for this young professional man, condemned for an offence which in my opinion he could not possibly have committed.

I am, etc.,
Arthur Conan Doyle

Hindhead, Surrey, Jan.13th

THE DAILY
TELEGRAPH   19 January 1907

The Edalji Case

Sir, – Would you have the kindness to give publicity to the following incident, which may have a very direct bearing upon the Edalji case?

On Oct. 1, 1903, the police received the following letter, bearing the postmark of Southend-on-Sea:

Seeing in yesterday's issue of *Daily Mail* concerning the cattle-maiming case. You refer to the vicar receiving anonymous letters some years back, and someone sending out goods from various tradesmen for jokes. I think I could inform you who the party was, as I have heard from his own lips that he helped to play the joke upon the vicar. He has been a writer of several annoying letters. Not only has he wrote them himself, but he had got other people. If you think this could help you in any way I will send you address as to where you may find him.

Yours truly,
A Young Housemaid.

P.S.–Please answer through *Daily Mail*

No steps were taken by the police.

There is always the possibility of a hoax, but there is, I think, some internal evidence that this letter is genuine. I have endeavoured to pick up the lost thread by advertisement through the *Daily Mail*, but without success. It occurs to me, however, that this woman, if still alive, must retain her interest in the case, and must therefore be following its development in the *Daily Telegraph*. If this should meet her eye I would beg her to communicate with me at this address, and I give her the assurance that she shall be put to no personal loss or inconvenience if she will aid the cause of justice.

Yours faithfully,
Arthur Conan Doyle

Grand Hotel, London, Jan. 18

THE DAILY
TELEGRAPH   26 January 1907

The Edalji Case
Summing Up

Sir, – I am unable now to find any points which have not been already dealt with in my original articles or in the long correspondence which has ensued. I claim that every point has been fairly met, and that an impartial man must do violence to his reason in having any doubts as to the propriety of a public inquiry into all the circumstances of the case.

Council has been somewhat darkened by the multitude of opinions, conjectures, and false statements which have been made. May I be permitted for the last time to remind your readers of those points of defence, briefly stated, which combine to make up the case:

1. The inherent improbability of a man of Edalji's virtuous, studious, and retiring habits committing these brutal crimes.

2. The proofs that a long conspiracy, extending back for fifteen years, had existed against the Edalji family.

3. The fact that Edalji's evening up to 9.30 is fully accounted

for, save for fifty minutes between 8.35 and 9.25. That in this time it was not possible for him to have walked first a mile along the road and then half a mile each way over difficult country, including the finding of the pony and its mutilation. The evidence of the veterinary surgeon proved the wound to have been inflicted in the early morning.

4. The impossibility of Edalji having done it after 9.30. His father, sleeping in the same room, his mother, and his sister, and the maid, all agree that no one left the house. There is the strong probability that the house was watched outside, and the certainty that twenty watchers were scattered round. There was heavy rain that night, and every garment must have been soaking wet.

5. The fact that the evidence was nearly all police evidence, open, as I have shown, to the gravest suspicion, and contradicted at every point by reputable witnesses.

6. The fact that the writing expert was shown to have blundered in the Beck case.

7. The physical disability produced by the myopia from which Mr. Edalji suffered.

Those are the main headings which I have previously elaborated, and they are all immensely strengthened by the continuance of the letters and the outrages after Mr. Edalji's arrest, and by the connivance at the flight of Green, who had confessed to a similar offence. This is the case which I present in favour of a miscarriage of justice having occurred. I claim that it is a very strong one, and has in no respect been shaken by subsequent inquiry or debate.

Dealing with point 7, I would say that I would by no means wish that this technical professional point should take undue prominence over all the other considerations which I have alleged. Perhaps having myself some special ophthalmic knowledge, and having been over the ground, I was inclined to make too much of it, forgetting that others could not appreciate obstacles which they had not seen. To me the idea of a myope of eight dioptres doing in so short a time, upon a pitch-dark night, what I, a fairly active man, did not do so quickly in daylight, is inexpressibly absurd. I have really suffered somewhat by understating my case, for I might well have taken the broader ground that a normal man could not have done it in the time. My argument really was that, à fortiori, a myope could not have done it. Many correspondents have ignored this, however, and, taking for granted that the normal man could have done it, have contented themselves with drawing comparisons between the powers of the normal and myopic eye, and how far deftness of touch can make up for dimness of vision. I am sending in the opinions to the Home Office to-day. The great majority are to the effect that such a crime, with such eyes, under such circumstances, is either "quite impossible" or "highly improbable." Both Sir Anderson Critchett and Mr. Nettleship have favoured me with opinions.

I have now done what I could, drawing largely upon the stores which Mr. Yelverton had ready for me, to present this case to the British public and also to the Home Office. I do not know that more can be done until we hear from the authorities.

Yours faithfully,
ARTHUR CONAN DOYLE

Grand Hotel, Jan. 25

THE DAILY TELEGRAPH   11 March 1907

The Edalji Case

SIR, – I observe from this week's *Truth*, and also from the *Police Review*, that both Mr. Voules and Mr. Kempster, two of the warmest champions of the Edalji cause, take a pessimistic view of the chances of any good result springing from the present Committee of Inquiry. I may say at the outset that neither Mr. Edalji nor, so far as I know, any one of his friends or advisers knew anything of the formation of this committee, nor of its terms of reference, until they read of it in the newspapers. Taking it as it stands, however, I am more hopeful of good results coming from it than those two gentlemen appear to be.

I think that their conclusions are largely founded upon the idea that the papers to be examined by the Committee consist merely of those official reports which have been the principal material at all previous reconsiderations of the case. This, however, will not be so. Pains have been taken that Mr. Edalji's case should be very fully represented. Among the evidence which will be laid before the three distinguished and independent gentlemen who form the Committee there will be,

1. The full statement of the case as it appeared in the *Daily Telegraph*.

2. The opinion of some twenty experts upon the question of eyesight and its relation to the crime.

3. An alternative theory of the outrages, with evidence in its support.

4. A considerable amount of further evidence throwing a light upon the affair.

It will be seen, therefore, that this inquiry differs very much from all preceding onces, in that it is independent and that it contains much new matter.

There are four courses, as it seems to me, any one of which the

Committee may choose. They may leave things as they are, though that is, I trust, most improbable. They may advise a re-trial; they may advise a Royal Commission; or, finally, they may advise a "free pardon" with compensation. We do not stand to lose in any case. A re-trial or Commission is what we desire. The last supposition (a free pardon) would give us at least a large instalment of that for which we are working. Therefore, on the whole, I am hopeful as to our prospects from the Advisory Committee.

We may still need all the funds subscribed, so I trust that those who have so generously supported the cause of fair play and justice will be content to leave their money in the fund until we see what turn things may take.

Yours faithfully,
ARTHUR CONAN DOYLE

Monkstown, Crowborough, March 4

THE DAILY TELEGRAPH

20 May 1907

Edalji Case

SIR, – While the friends of Mr. George Edalji rejoice that his innocence has at last been admitted (though in the most grudging and ungracious fashion), they feel that their work is only half done so long as compensation is refused him. It is clearly stated in the report of the Committee that: "The police commenced and carried on their investigations, not for the purpose of finding out who was the guilty party, but for the purpose of finding evidence against Edalji, who they were already sure was the guilty man."

The result has proved that he was not the guilty man, and this inversion of all sane methods upon the part of the police has given untold mental agony to himself and to his family, has caused him to undergo the ordeal of the double trial, the three years of incarceration, and an extra year of police supervision. Apart from the misery which has been unjustly inflicted upon him, he has been unable to exercise his profession during that time, and has been put to many heavy expenses, which only the self-sacrifice of his relations has enabled him to meet. And now, though all these results have been brought about by the extraordinary conduct of the police, and the stupidity of a Court of Quarter Sessions, the unfortunate victim is told that no compensation will be made him.

The position is absolutely illogical and untenable. Either the man is guilty or else there is no compensation which is adequate for the great wrong which this country, through its officials, has inflicted upon him. It is hard, indeed, that such compensation should be drawn from the pockets of the taxpayer. It might well be levied in equal parts from the Staffordshire police, the Quarter Sessions Court, and the officials of the Home Office, since it is these three groups of men who are guilty among them of this fiasco. But since there is no means by which those who are responsible can be forced to pay, it lies upon the conscience of this country to do what is just in an endeavour to right this grievous wrong. Could anything be imagined meaner or more un-English than that the mistake should be admitted but reparation refused.

The Committee, while setting right the other faults both of the police and of the court, have, unhappily, stated "that they are not prepared to dissent from the finding of the jury," that the letters of 1903 were in the writing of George Edalji. Their cautious phrase means, I take it, not that they are by any means convinced that it is so, but that they have not sufficient evidence to enable them to contradict it. I do not know how the matter was laid before them, but I will undertake in half an hour, with the documents before him, to convince any reasonable and impartial man, that George Edalji did not write, and could not possibly have written, those letters. Of that I am absolutely certain, and there is no room for doubt whatever. Not only the character of the writing, but the internal evidence of the allusions to people and things, which were beyond his knowledge, show that he was not the author. Since the letters accused him of the crimes it is impossible to imagine how, save on the supposition of insanity (of which there has been no evidence in his life), he could possibly be imagined to have written them. On this subject of the letters I should like, with your permission, to deal further at some length on a future occasion.

As soon as possible after the holidays a meeting will be called of the committee appointed to administer the *Daily Telegraph* Fund. As this money was subscribed for legal expenses, and none have been incurred, the committee has not felt justified in spending it on any other object, and it is still intact. After the meeting the course of action advised by the committee, which consists at present of Sir George Lewis, Mr. Horace Voules, Professor Churton Collins, Mr. Jerome, Mr. J. Hall Richardson, and myself, will be laid before your readers.

I am, Sir, yours truly,
ARTHUR CONAN DOYLE

Edalji Case

Sir, – Upon Monday, the 27th, I received a letter and a postcard, both unstamped, from the unknown correspondent whose writing runs right through the whole Edalji affair from 1892 onwards. They were written in pencil, and addressed to me at the Grand Hotel. The letter was in a coarse yellow envelope, gummed up with stamp paper. A crease in both documents seems to show that though marked London, N.W., they may have been sent up under cover, or possibly in somebody's pocket – a railway guard or other – and then posted. Should this be so one might hope to follow them back to the writer; and I hereby offer a reward of £20 to anyone who will enable me to say for certain whence they came. I should be much indebted to Midland papers if they would give publicity to the facts.

Yours faithfully,
Arthur Conan Doyle

Grand Hotel, Trafalgar-square, May 28

The Edalji Case
Statement in the House

Sir, – I observe that Mr. Gladstone, in the House of Commons yesterday, waived away the question as to whether Mr. Edalji could be re-admitted to the roll of solicitors, by saying that it did not come within his department. This may be an excellent debating point, but it must strike the public as the very essence of red tape. By a decision of the Home Office it has been decreed that Mr. Edalji has been wrongly condemned of maiming cattle, but rightly of having written abominable letters. It is evident that if he is guilty of the latter offence he is no fit member of an honourable profession. It follows, therefore, that as the direct consequence of the act of Mr. Gladstone, Mr. Edlaji is condemned to ruin. What a quibble, then, to say that it is something outside the department!

As matters stand at present, Mr. Edalji has suffered three years' imprisonment in the past, and has to face ruin in the future, when the only thing which is still alleged against him has never been pronounced upon by judge or jury. Could any position be more illogical or unjust?

I have had, within the last few days, the opinion of the gentleman who exposed the forgery in the Dreyfus Bordereau upon the Edalji papers. He says, without reserve, that Mr. Edalji did not write, and could not have written, the 1903 letters.

Yours faithfully,
Arthur Conan Doyle

Undershaw, Hindhead, Surrey, May 30

THE DAILY
TELEGRAPH   11 June 1907

The Edalji Letters

Sir, – In answering a question of Mr. F. Smith's Mr. Gladstone is reported as having said, "The letters themselves formed part of the evidence, and it was after most carefully examining them and forming their own opinion that the jury gave the verdict." This verdict was that Mr. Edalji had killed a horse, a decision which has been since set aside. I emphasise the fact because the casual reader of the Home Secretary's reply might imagine that the verdict to which he alluded was that Mr. Edalji had written the letters, which is the subject now under discussion. This has never been pronounced upon by any jury, and has been declared by the Committee to be entirely distinct from the charge of killing the horse. The late Clerk of the Peace of Stafford, Mr. Matt. F. Blakiston, writing on March 8, 1905, to the Rev. S. Edalji, said: "The indictment proceeded on was that for horse maiming and wounding, and on that the jury returned the verdict of guilty. The other indictment," which involved the letters, "was consequently not proceeded with."

It is certain, therefore, that this young professional man has endured without apology or compensation three years of restraint, and is debarred his profession, and financially ruined in the future, for an offence for which he has never been publicly tried. The conscience of this country cannot be satisfied until there has been some inquiry upon the authorship of these letters, which shall be so held that Mr. Edalji's friends can be assured that his interests are properly represented. At such an inquiry his advisers would be prepared to put up the most weighty expert testimony to show that the letters are not, and could not have been, written by Mr. Edalji.

I have just received a most careful and weighty report upon the Edalji documents from Dr. Lindsay Johnson, the well-known expert who assisted Maitre Labori to unravel the mysteries of the Dreyfus bordereau. In the Dreyfus inquiry, as in this one, Dr. Lindsay Johnson's methods have been to procure photographic positives of the writings in question and to project them immensely enlarged (20–50 diameters) on a screen by means of two lanterns. By having one of the lanterns on a stand provided with all azimuth motions, one can bring any word or line underneath or above the line of comparison. By these elaborate methods even the pulse beat can in many cases be detected, and a minuteness of comparison be effected unknown by any previous method.

Dr. Lindsay Johnson's inquiry has, in this instance, been divided under several heads, but at present I will deal only with that one in which he discusses whether the Greatorex letters of 1903 could possibly have been written by Mr. George Edalji. The report is exceedingly voluminous, painstaking, and minute, but I may present your readers with some general conclusions. "The letters signed Edalji and Greatorex have nothing in common. The former are those of an educated man; they exhibit no errors in spelling or style – the handwriting is that of a man who has written continuously for years, being set, i.e., the same words are always written precisely in the same way, which shows a writer of regular and orderly habits, and every full-stop is inserted. The latter, 'Greatorex's' letter, is in a cramped and apparently disguised hand. It is unquestionably the style of an uneducated man, irregular in his habits. It is practically unpunctuated throughout."

After elaborately comparing a great number of letters, and pointing out the radical difference between them, Dr. Lindsay Johnson continues:

"Further examples are unnecessary, as, look where you will, you will find no points in common between them. As regards the pulse jerks, I counted seventy-eight in thirteen consecutive words when highly magnified, whereas in Edalji's writing they cannot be continuously counted. This shows that the former wrote his letter at about thirteen words a minute, allowing seventy-five to eighty beats for the normal pulse, and had a trembling hand, whereas Edalji had a remarkably firm hand, and wrote very much more rapidly. The inference is that Edalji is a very temperate man, and the other is addicted to drink and dissipation, but I give this with reserve."

Having shown very clearly that Mr. Edalji did not write those letters for which he has been so cruelly and unjustly punished, Dr. Lindsay Johnson, under a separate heading, reports upon the whole series of anonymous letters, which may be classed under the head of the Martin Molton letters, beginning with the boyish effusions of 1892, which had their origin apparently in or near Walsall School, down to a fresh anonymous letter received by me last week. His conclusion is that those documents are all undoubtedly from the same hand. The third point presented for his consideration is how far this handwriting of the Martin Molton letters corresponds with those letters of 1903 for which Mr. Edalji has suffered. On this all-important point the report states: "We notice that out of thirty-four large and small letters of the alphabet, twenty are closely alike, eight have some resemblance, two have very slight agreement, and four are entirely different, but of these four, three occur in two forms, the one form agreeing closely or partly, the other obviously disguised, while the remaining letter 't' is certainly written to deceive. Hence, out of thirty-four letters, large and small, twenty-eight are either closely alike or have some resemblance, while two alone have very slight points in common, the remaining four being well accounted for. We thus become practically certain that the 'Greatorex' letters are disguised epistles written by the same person as all the other letters."

Dr. Lindsay Johnson remarks in a covering letter: "I have purposely avoided reading your articles in the papers lest they should bias my mind." I need not point out to readers of the *Daily Telegraph* that the conclusions to which he has come are exactly the same as my own, though founded upon a far closer scrutiny and upon more elaborate methods. When I say that the report covers nineteen pages of manuscript, it will indicate how exhaustive it is. I must add that Dr. Lindsay Johnson has done this considerable task without fee or reward of any kind.

Yours faithfully,
ARTHUR CONAN DOYLE

Undershaw, Hindhead, Haslemere, June 10, 1907

THE DAILY
TELEGRAPH

25 June 1907

The Edalji Debate

In connection with the expected debate upon the Edalji case the following memorandum has been issued to members of Parliament by the committee:

As the question of George Edalji's compensation will come up on the Estimates, his committee venture to refresh your memory by the following short statement of the position.

George Edalji was condemned for killing a horse.

This conviction has been revoked.

He is, therefore, an innocent man.

He has served three years in gaol and demands compensation for his ruined professional career.

This compensation is refused him on the ground that he wrote certain anonymous letters.

This is strenuously denied by himself, his parents, and his friends.

He has never been tried for the offence.

Therefore he is being severely punished for an offence of which he has never been proved to be guilty, which is against the whole spirit of English law.

All other means of redress having failed, we venture to beg that members of the House, of either party, will bring such pressure as they can to bear upon the Home Office in order to right this wrong. (Signed for the Edalji Committee)

GEO. LEWIS
H. VOULES
CHURTON COLLINS,
ARTHUR CONAN DOYLE,
JEROME K. JEROME,
J. HALL RICHARDSON
(Hon. Treasurer).

Ely-place, Holborn, E.C., June 24

THE DAILY
TELEGRAPH   20 July 1907

Case of George Edalji

SIR, – Mr. Gladstone's reply to Mr. F.E. Smith's admirable exposition of the injustice done to Mr. George Edalji was to declare that the House of Commons should not constitute itself a Court of Appeal. To whom, then, are we to turn? Or are we to admit in despair that there is no tribunal of any sort in England to which we can look to set a wrong right? The Home Office should itself be such a tribunal, but its own conduct is now just one of the questions which has to be judged.

Mr. Gladstone refers to the verdict of the Staffordshire jury, but he is well aware that since that verdict was given many new points have arisen, the most obvious of which is the recurrence of the crimes when Edalji was in gaol. But how weak is this appeal to the chose jugée! When it was persistently urged in the Dreyfus case, what national scorn we showed for so feeble an excuse for not doing justice. It is a singular thing that every point of the Dreyfus case has been reproduced in this humbler drama, the forgeries, the covering of official by official, the reference to the chose jugée. If we judged French Institutions harshly at the time, what are we to think of our own now? But Right prevailed then, even as it will do now, and the only permanent record of the case has been the loss of reputation in the man who mishandled it.

Yours faithfully,
ARTHUR CONAN DOYLE

Regent Hotel, Royal Leamington Spa

To Honour Dorando*

SIR, – May I add a short letter to the description of the race which I have been privileged to give in another column of the *Daily Mail*?

I am sure that no petty personal recompense can in the least console Dorando for the national loss which follows from his disqualification. Yet I am certain that many who saw his splendid effort in the Stadium, an effort which ran him within an inch of his life, would like to feel that he carries away some souvenir from his admirers in England.

I should be very glad to contribute five pounds to such a fund if any of the authorities at the Stadium would consent to organise it.

Yours truly,
ARTHUR CONAN DOYLE

* Italian Olympic Marathon runner who, after leading for most of the race, collapsed shortly before the finish.

"Yeoman Stock"

SIR, – In your report of my remarks at Tunbridge Wells I am made to speak of replanting human stock upon the land. What I said was "yeoman stock."

It seems to me that it would be possible to use the Small Holdings Bill upon a large scale, if it were taken up by some central philanthropic and patriotic agency, such as that established by the late Dr. Barnardo.

The plan would consist of a central agricultural college for training small farmers, their transfer to small farms which had been prepared for them by experts from the same agency, finally the payment for the farm by instalments spread over years. Fifty years of such a system would give us our yeomen back again.

137

Why colonise the ends of the earth when so much of Britain is still uncultivated?

ARTHUR CONAN DOYLE

Windlesham, Crowborough, Sussex

THE TIMES   18 August 1909

England and the Congo

SIR, – We live in the presence of the greatest crime which has ever been committed in the history of the world, and yet we who not only could stop it but who are bound by our sworn oath to stop it do nothing. The thing has been going on for 20 years. What are we waiting for? Our guilt of national acquiescence is only second to that of the gang of cosmopolitan scoundrels who have been actively concerned in turning all Central Africa into a huge slave State, with such attendant horrors as even the dark story of the slave trade has never shown. In the slave trade the victim was of market value, and to that extent was protected from death or mutilation. In this case the State is the owner of all, so that if one be dismembered or shot another is always available.

The Congo Free State (the very name is typical of the smug hypocrisy which deceived the Great Powers into allowing the monster to be born) was created by the Berlin Congress of 1885. One of the articles of that treaty, to which "in the name of Almighty God" we and other Powers have bound ourselves, was that we would undertake "to watch over the preservation of the native races, and the amelioration of the moral and material conditions of their existence." Did those solemn words mean anything? Are they compatible with our standing by year after year seeing these same native races done to death, and never raising an effective hand to help them? Three million of them at a moderate computation have already been ameliorated out of this world. How long more are we to wait?

As I write, my study table is covered with photographs of these unhappy people. They bear the marks of the tortures they have endured. Some have their feet lopped off, some their hands. One is a child, surprisingly beautiful and intelligent even by European standards. His arm has been hacked off. Another with his right foot and left hand missing stares before him with a strange, thoughtful puzzled face. These are the people whom "in the name of Almighty God" we guaranteed. Under each of the mutilated frames might, in all truth, be printed "I was guaranteed by you."

The dreadful story is a commonplace now. It is impossible to deny any part of it. Its authenticity comes from many sources, from missionary reports, Swedish, Belgian, and American, as well as British, from official Consular despatches, from the report of the Belgian Commission of 1905, from the memoirs of returned officers, above all from the incorruptible evidence of the kodak. The story, I say, is a commonplace, but it has been a commonplace for at least 14 years for those who chose to read the evidence. When is something going to be done?

Every day that passes fresh crimes are committed. The rubber has been coming faster than ever to Europe this year, and the rubber can only come through the system, and the system can only be enforced by terror. Consul Thesiger, in his report published this year, shows that the screw is ever tightening, that new tribes are being drawn into the slavery, that they are worked in such a fashion that they have no time to plant their crops, and that a great famine is threatened in the future. That is the last official published report of our representative. And we do nothing.

Last year the business was taken over by Belgium. There were hopes that methods would be changed. But they have not been changed. M. Renkin, the Colonial Minister of Belgium, has frankly said that they would not be changed. He has gone out to the Congo to report. But he is himself an ex-concessionaire who has been a fervent defender of the system in the Parliament. As well send Rockefeller to report on the Standard Oil abuses! Are we children to be deluded by such devices as these? Do we not know the course which events will take? M. Renkin will return about Christmas. Six more months will have been gained for squeezing the country. Then he must not be hurried in his report – six more months for that. Then there is the legislation. Time must be allowed for that. Then legislation must be gradually enforced; and so on and on through the time-honoured round. And all the time more mutilations, more murders, more extortions, in order that a rich King may be richer and a few companies pay 300 per cent. If we wait for any practical results from M. Renkin's visit then we wait, with our eyes open, for at least three more years of this orgy of blood, lust, and greed.

What should be done? The first thing is in a single comprehensive State paper to lay before every civilised Power the evidence which calls for action, and to ask them to convene a European conference for the purpose of taking from Belgium a trust which has been so dreadfully abused, and making such fresh arrangements, either by an international government or by a partition of the State amongst its neighbours, as may give some assurance of just and honest treatment to these unhappy natives. We are told in vague language by Sir Edward Grey that peril lies in the question. Where can that peril be? Who is going to champion the perpetrators of these horrible deeds? Is it Germany, with her traditions of kindly home life? Is it those who are so justly proud of the public and private life of William the Second who will take up the sword for Leopold? Or is it France, the historical home of chivalry? Or the United States, who abhor cruelty and injustice as much as we do ourselves? Where can this bogey lie? If it existed, it would be our duty a hundred-fold to face it. But does it really exist? Would not a frank and self-denying treatment of the case banish it for ever?

That must be the goal of the future – that the Congo passes into more worthy hands. But what about the past? Is there to be no redress for these poor victims? Three millions of them are beyond redress. But what of the butchers and what of their surviving victims? Is there no possible international Court before which these men who have betrayed religion and civilisation can be arraigned? The public conscience cannot be at rest until every one of them, from the schemer at Brussels to the red-handed agent at the spot, has had his deserts. And this same tribunal could surely out of the gorged money bags of the concessionaires force a pension for the thousands and thousands who have been maimed by their representatives and through their deliberate system. Only then, when the victims have been avenged, the survivors compensated, and the land placed under safe permanent rule, can the conscience of Europe be at rest.

Yours faithfully,
ARTHUR CONAN DOYLE

Windlesham, Crowborough, Sussex

THE TIMES   28 August 1909

England and the Congo

SIR, – I do not think that England is likely to be frightened off from doing her duty to the natives of the Congo by the threats of your anonymous Belgian correspondent. As to his general accusations of inaccuracy, I hope within a week or two to have a small book published which will give chapter and verse for every statement I have made. His remarks about the formation of a new Belgian Society for the Protection of the Natives would cause any one to smile who knows the history of the previous bodies of this nature and the results which have sprung from them. I can assure him, finally, that a great surprise is awaiting him and his countrymen if they treat lightly the deep feeling upon the question which is growing up in this country.

Yours truly,
ARTHUR CONAN DOYLE

Windlesham, Crowborough, Sussex, Aug. 25

The Congo Question

Sir, – Some weeks ago you kindly published a letter from me, in which I expressed my opinion that the story of the Congo constituted the greatest crime of which we have any record in history, and my hope that our Government would at last fulfil those solemn pledges to the natives which are incorporated in that Treaty of Berlin by which the vile Congo State was originally created. I remarked in this letter that M. Renkin, the Belgian Colonial Minister, would soon return from his tour of inspection, and that the result of that tour would be certain vague promises of reform which would prolong the present situation from year to year until either the rubber or the natives were exhausted. The trick has been done again and again in Congo history, but there seems to be no limit to the credulity, or rather, perhaps, to the indifference of the Powers.

On this occasion, however, there has been an effrontery in the remarks of the returning official, as reported in the Press, which transcends any of the efforts of his predecessors. It is to be remembered that M. Renkin is himself an ex-director of one of those Congo concessionaire companies which are red to the elbow in the blood of the natives. A recent British Consular report has shown that this very company by the aid of the chicotte and of the hostage house enforces 240 days in the year of forced labour upon its slaves, for which it pays them 6s. 4d. in trade goods per annum. The food of a bought slave would cost many times that sum, so that it may truly be said that the new Belgian slavery is the cheapest to the owner as well as the most cruel to the victim that has ever been devised.

This being M. Renkin's record, no very helpful report could be expected from him. But his actual statements as reported since his return are incredibly perverse. They bear no relation at all to the actual facts of the situation. He says without qualification that there have been no outrages upon the natives. Putting aside missionary reports, Consular reports, Belgian judicial reports, travellers' reports, all confirmed and reconfirmed, there is the terrible evidence of the Commission appointed by King Leopold himself in 1905 to show how shameless is such an assertion. It is only in a country which is kept in the dark by a venal Press that such a statement could be taken seriously. But perhaps M. Renkin means, as Mr. Belloc appears to do by his recent question in Parliament, that the more obvious brutalities, the hand-loppings and shootings, are more or less in abeyance. If Mr. Belloc were deprived of all means of earning a living for himself, if he were set to forced labour for the benefit of another, and cut to the bone with hippopotamus-hide whips to urge him onwards while those whom he loved were shut up in a noisome prison in the power of licentious soldiers, so as to ensure that he did not run away from his servitude, he would find that there were other forms of cruelty besides the bullet and the knife. This, exactly as I describe it, is the normal daily existence of millions of the Congo natives, and I appeal to ex-Consul Casement, to Consul Thesiger, and to Vice-Consuls Armstrong, Mitchell, and Beak whether it is not so. And then in the face of this horror we read M. Renkin's twaddle about teaching the native intensive methods of agriculture, and gradually introducing free trade – a thing which was secured by treaty 24 years ago. But surely this marks the limit. The Government has been awaiting M. Renkin's return and M. Renkin's message. We have now had his message. Is this scandal to drag on for ever, or has the time come when once for all we shall put down our foot and say that we will be true to our pledged word, and that this organised crime must at last come to an end?

Yours faithfully,
ARTHUR CONAN DOYLE

Windlesham, Crowborough, Oct. 2

THE DAILY EXPRESS   8 October 1909

"Belgian Denials"

SIR, – Every friend of the Congo races must thank you for your noble and energetic championship of their cause. After the long night dawn seems to be breaking at last.

Our most urgent need is to put the facts before the public. For this end the dissemination of free literature and the holding of public meetings are essential, but both these methods require money, and the purse of the Congo Reform Association is empty.

Will those who are willing to help a good cause send what they can afford to Mr. Travers Buxton, the honorary treasurer of the association, at Granville House, Arundel-street, W.C.

Only one word would I eliminate from your splendid articles. I am in no sense the originator of this new crusade, but only a late recruit to Mr. Morel's banner.

Yours faithfully,
ARTHUR CONAN DOYLE

Windlesham, Crowborough, Sussex

142

The Congo Question

Sir, – I observe that you deprecate my remark at Newcastle that "it is to the eternal disgrace of England that we have not interfered long ago." The remark is taken from its context, which contains qualifications; but apart from this some justifications for the view may be advanced.

I admit that had we no treaty obligations in the matter your criticism would be justified. But as we are parties to an agreement which in the most solemn manner guarantees the safety of the native races, and as we have stood by with no action save half-hearted remonstrance while these same races have been more than decimated, I contend that it is indeed a disgrace to our country. The vague fear that some European Power might take up the quarrel of King Leopold is not in my opinion a sufficient reason for our being false to our pledges.

In one sense we are more guilty than Belgium, for the facts have been well ventilated here, while they have been studiously concealed from the greater part of the Belgian people.

Yours faithfully,
ARTHUR CONAN DOYLE

Windlesham, Crowborough, Sussex, Nov. 12

The Congo

Sir, – I observe in your note of November 6 upon the Congo question that you state "the Belgian Parliament took over the responsibility for the government of that vast territory only in August last." May I call your attention to the fact that it was in August twelve-month, and upon a promise that there would be immediate ameliorations. Fifteen months have elapsed, and the state of the natives, which has been described by two successive foreign ministers as one of virtual slavery, has in no way been amended.

The following extract from the report of an agent just returned from the Congo, should give Catholic readers an insight into the true state of things out there.

"As I was returning to the steamer a voice from the wood called for help, and there appeared a human being covered with great festering wounds. He was filthy and covered with flies, and he crawled rather than walked with the aid of two sticks. I asked him 'What have you done that you should be so shockingly punished?' The man answered that he was the Catechist of the Catholic mission of Trappists at Bamania, and that he had come to proselytise among the people of the factory. For this the white man at Yele had had him flogged with a whip an inch thick and sharp nails stuck in it. I had the accused agent up. He cynically admitted the deed, and indeed seemed proud of it, but added that the man had stolen two bottles of wine, which the latter energetically denied. The agent was quite pleased at his own behaviour, and indeed he had only followed the example which the directors themselves gave in Bussira. A fierce hatred had raged there for months against the Catholic missions. They used to disturb the divine service by hideous clamour, by firing shots, by obscene cries, and by injuring the people of the mission in every way. Two white officials, friends of the directors, were the ringleaders in this.''

The original with all the names is in my possession, and open to your inspection should you desire it.

And this is the system, or at least some of the smaller fruits of it, which has for so many years been condoned, and defended against the would-be reformers, by the spokesmen of the Catholic Church.

Yours faithfully,
ARTHUR CONAN DOYLE

Windlesham, Crowborough, Sussex, November 12

THE DAILY
GRAPHIC   23 November 1909

The Crime of the Congo

SIR, – I observe in your leading article upon the Congo meeting that you say that we have no reason to doubt M. Renkin's word. Unfortunately a great many of us cannot agree with you there. M. Renkin is an ex-director of one of those concessionaire companies, the atrocious deeds of which have brought the present situation about. As such we cannot regard him as an impartial judge upon this question. He has committed himself since his return to the statement that there are no outrages in the Colony.

On the very boat which brought him back travelled Dr. Dörpinghaus, a German scientific gentleman of irreproachable character, who has submitted from his own personal observation a long list of outrages, many of them occurring during the present year. Letters from the Congo, dated as recently as September

27th, show us, also, from personal observation, that forced labour, kidnapping, chain gangs, and the burning of villages still proceed in their normal fashion.

It is for this reason that we cannot entirely trust the bona fides of M. Renkin, and that we are not surprised to find that the Congo Reform Bill as it now stands will require many modifications before it can even approximately fulfil the provisions of the Treaty of Berlin.

Yours faithfully,
ARTHUR CONAN DOYLE

Windlesham, Crowborough, Sussex. November 20th

THE ECONOMIST   27 November 1909

The Congo Loan

SIR, – In your interesting article on "Proposed Reforms in the Congo" you allude to a grant in aid of £1,320,000. If such were indeed the case, much of the ground would be cut from under the feet of the reformers. But instead of being a Belgian grant in aid, it is a loan which is raised for the colony, the unfortunate natives paying the interest, although an analysis shows that it serves no purpose which could possibly be of any use to the native himself. The incredible meanness of Belgian finance may be gathered from the fact shown in the Budget that the wretched savages, from whose labour the Congo funds are obtained, have to find the money for subsidies to the Heir-Apparent, for the upkeep of museums and conservatories, for the payment of medical schools in Belgium, and a variety of other home purposes. Imagine our taxing the Kaffirs of South Africa for the support of the South Kensington Museum, and for the electric lighting of the Colonial Office. That would be a fair analogy.

Yours truly,
ARTHUR CONAN DOYLE

THE TIMES   3 December 1909

The Congo Reforms

SIR, – As one who has done some work on the question of Congo reform, it was with deep regret that I read your article upon the subject this morning. Perhaps you would have the courtesy to permit me to make a few observations upon it.

The history of our relations with the Congo authorities in the past has been one of flattering hopes and broken promises, and the price of our credulity has been paid not by ourselves, but by the unhappy natives.

Beginning with the Anglo-Congolese Convention of 1881 and the Berlin Treaty of 1883, there has been no connexion between a European pledge and African performance. Again and again we have been deceived. In 1905 there was a promise that the evidence given before the Belgian Commission of Investigation should be published. It has not been published to this day. Finally, on the eve of Belgian annexation, a definite promise was given to the British Government that there would be instant amelioration of the lot of the native. Fifteen months have elapsed, and nothing has been done. The old Congo State in a day, by a stroke of the pen, appropriated the whole vacant lands and produce of the Congo. Surely the new Congo State could within 15 months have done something to change those laws, which had already for many years been debated in the Belgian Chamber, and were, therefore, no new problem to the Government.

With such a record we should be indeed remiss if we did not carefully scrutinize these new arrangements. If we were silent upon them, we might well give the impression that public opinion in Great Britain was satisfied with them, whereas, if we can let it be clearly understood that there are some points which are from our point of view inadmissible, and which would prevent this change from being accepted as a final settlement by this country, we may get them altered. Surely this is a complete justification for our agitation by public meeting and otherwise. What is the use of being silent now, and then being forced to start a fresh agitation after the new proposals are made into law? Now is the time to make our sentiments heard, and so possibly to influence legislation – or at least to preserve our own consistency. The objection to the reforms are only epitomized by your own Correspondent. They are, in a word, the delay in granting that freedom of trade which is not a favour, but a right, the increase in the native army, which has always been a scourge to flog the people; the continuance of forced labour, as shown by the fact that 40 per cent. of the Budget is to come from rubber, copal, &c., paid as taxation; and, finally, the absence of any adequate financial provision for the feeding of the horde who now live upon the people. These are the proposed reforms which we are criticised for not accepting with a silence would would certainly be taken as approval. I hold, on the contrary, that these are the critical weeks in which we must make the Belgians understand that such changes will not serve, and that they must make a clean sweep of all abuses before this country will regard the question as closed.

We have a right, too, to examine the spirit which lies behind these proposals, for in that spirit will they be carried out. Has there been any admission of the monstrous past? On the contrary, M. Renkin's tone has been one of self-congratulation, with a denial of all outrages. On the same steamer in which he returned from the Congo came Dr. Dörpinghaus, an ideal witness, with an appalling list of outrages, many of which he had himself seen, and some of which were of recent date. These were all drawn from a single limited district. On the top of this, Mr. Morrison, whose veracity is guaranteed by the failure of the Kasai Company to establish their libel action against him, wrote to me on September 27 a letter which you were good enough to publish, in which he gave particulars of the slave-raiding round his own mission for the purpose of supplying labour for the Grands Lacs Railway. How then can M. Renkin contend that there are no outrages in the Congo? Had he come back with an admission that the conditions were bad, and had then set to work to try to improve them, he would at once have commanded our sympathy.

Again, I would ask, why is there no question of judicial examination into the past? Baron Walus is in Belgium. He ruled the Congo for many years, during which it was such a murder State as has never been known in the civilised world. His trial and punishment would be some guarantee of the good faith of the Belgian Government. We have tried our great pro-Consuls, our Clives and our Warren Hastings, though it is a desecration to mention them in such a connexion. And the smaller agents in this tragedy, such men as Captain Arnold, condemned to twelve years' penal servitude in the Congo, and yet retaining his commission in Belgium – is there not room there for the Belgian Government to give some proof of the reality of its professions?

I repeat, then, my earnest conviction that the reforms cannot meet the situation, that outside pressure is needed to draw attention to their weakness, and that a benevolent attitude upon our part will indefinitely prolong the evil which we are trying to set right.

Yours faithfully,
ARTHUR CONAN DOYLE

Windlesham, Crowborough, Sussex, Nov. 29

P.S. – I note that your Correspondent has been assured that our opposition may be humanitarian but Germany's is certainly interested. The converse is what is served to German papers. This embroiling of the Great Powers has always been one of the cornerstones of Congo policy.

Yeomanry of the Future
Sir. A. Conan Doyle's plan for Cyclist Cavalry

SIR, – Your interesting article upon the superiority of motor traction over horses for ambulance and commissariat purposes in time of war is very convincing. But I have long held views upon an analogous subject which is suggested by your essay. This is the enormous advantage which would result to the State both in efficacy and in cost by substituting bicycle regiments of mounted riflemen for the Yeomanry cavalry, whose services are confined to the defence of this island.

Were this done, and were the bulk of our artillery drawn (as is the dream of many gunners) by petrol or steam, we should almost eliminate the horse – with the endless worry of buying, tending, and feeding him – from our home military system.

Let me briefly state the case, as far as I understand it, for the bicycle as against the horse in a country which is intersected with a network of roads. Let me premise that the machines which I should recommend would be strong and serviceable, fitted with clips for rifles and a small carrier for essentials. They should have solid but resilient tyres. Each regiment should have its equipment of attendant motors, with full repair shops, cartridge reserves, etc.

ADVANTAGES SUMMARISED.

1. RAPIDITY OF STRIKING. – Here there could be no comparison, and this is the most important of all considerations in the defence of an island from invasion.

If an enemy landed at Dover, a force of cavalry starting from London would arrive at the scene of action – I presume that they find their own way – two, or possibly three, days later, when the enemy is established. A force mounted on bicycles would be there within five hours, while disembarkation might still be proceeding.

2. EFFICIENCY AT THE END OF JOURNEY. – The cavalry is done at the end of a long march. The horse has to be tended and fed. Often his forage has to be brought. All this is surely in favour of the bicycle.

3. PERMANENCY. – The horse may be wounded or killed. The horse may die of fatigue or disease. The bicycle only wants an hour in a repair shop.

4. RADIUS OF ACTION. – Thirty miles or so may be taken as the extreme limit which mounted men can cover in the day and be fit for action at the end of it. Large masses of men could be

moved a hundred miles a day easily upon bicycles. This should mean a great strategical advantage.

5. EXPENSE. – At a wholesale price the bicycle I picture should not exceed £7. It should outlast several £40 horses, besides doing away with forage, stables, etc.

6. TACTICAL ADVANTAGE WHEN IN ACTUAL TOUCH WITH THE ENEMY. – The firing line, when dismounted, is not denuded by one-quarter of the men holding horses. Cyclists charged by cavalry can form their machines at once into a zareba, and fire from behind them.

These reasons, taken together as they bear upon the economy, efficiency, and the large increase of numbers available, seem to me far more powerful than any objections. Of these objections the chief would be that we should no longer have in our Yeomanry a feeder for the Regular cavalry. I am not aware how much it is so now.

Another would be that across the country the cavalry would be more effective.

A third is that on the South Downs or on Salisbury Plain the cavalry would also have a fuller scope. These seem small matters as compared to the advantages which I have indicated.

ARTHUR CONAN DOYLE

Windlesham, Crowborough, Sussex

THE PALL MALL
GAZETTE   6 April 1910

Cavalry Training

SIR, – Might I make a few comments upon your Military Correspondent's article upon the question of Cavalry training, as it is one in which I have long taken a keen interest, and I do most heartily believe, with Mr. Erskine Childers, that we are in imminent danger of losing all the lessons which we purchased so dearly in South Africa?

In the first edition of *The Great Boer War*, which appeared towards the close of 1900, I added a chapter on the military lessons of the war, which was omitted in subsequent editions, not because I felt that my views had been shaken by the expert criticism to which they were subjected, but because each succeeding edition contained so much more narrative that this supplementary chapter was squeezed out. In this essay, with all that I have seen, heard, and read in South Africa fresh in my mind, I expressed some strong opinions, but I venture to say that subsequent events have seemed to justify them. I said, among other things, that there was, outside artillery, only one weapon in the world, the magazine rifle, and that the only place for swords, lances, and revolvers was a museum. I said, also, that good Mounted Riflemen must always dominate Cavalry, and I gave my opinion that the whole Cavalry force with its splendid personnel should at once be rescued from impotence by being rearmed and put on a level with their foes. This was not done at the time, but within a year or eighteen months we had learned our lesson, and the Cavalry had actually returned their arms to store, received their rifles, and become mounted riflemen. I mention this to show that the views I advocate are my own, and that I am not merely repeating Mr. Erskine Childers' argument, though I agree most heartily with all of it.

This was the practical lesson shot into us on the veldt, a land which, when compared to any European country, is a perfect terrain for Cavalry. What has occurred since then to alter it? I claim that everything has been in the direction of enforcing the lesson. The "arme blanche" can never improve, but the rifleman has been reinforced by quicker fire and a lower trajectory. If he dominated in South Africa he has increased his superiority since. And yet our Cavalry, while, it is true, retaining their rifles, have gone back to the sword and lance, with those prehistoric shock traditions which these implements imply. It is, indeed, a sad thing that we should put aside our dearly-won experience, and follow German theorists who have never seen a shot fired in anger.

Your correspondent follows the Cavalry manual in the opinion that a soldier may be trained to be equally expert with sword, lance, and rifle. But the tactics of the shock horseman and of the mounted rifleman are absolutely contradictory, and it is not possible to train a habit of mind to take two irreconcilable shapes. The shock horseman is always looking for good ground and some one to charge. The mounted rifleman is looking for bad ground where he and his horse can both be concealed, with a good fire field. You can have it either way, but you cannot have it both. Which is the better way of extracting the most value from the soldier has surely been shown by all modern warfare, but most of all by the American Civil War and the African War, where men of our own blood, faced with the practical conditions of a long campaign, evolved in each case the same form of mounted soldier. In the past we would have been wiser to study the methods of Americans like Sheridan and Stewart than those of Continental Cavalry. Now that our own African lessons have reinforced those of America, it would indeed be sad if the traditional conservatism of our Cavalry were permitted to overlook them.

Passing from the general to the particular, your correspondent's article seems to me to abound in statements which might be challenged. He goes back to the wars of the eighteenth century for his examples of Cavalry success, but it would be more convincing if he could name any single deed of the Cavalry in South Africa during three years which could not have been done as well by mounted riflemen. It would be easy to give a score of deeds by mounted riflemen which could not possibly have been done by Cavalry.

The Cavalry prejudice is continually evident in your correspondent's remarks. For example, he talks about "lowering the Cavalry to the level of mounted infantry." But why lowering? The object is to produce the more formidable soldier. If, as South Africa showed, the mounted rifleman is so, then it is not to lower, but to raise, the Cavalry when they are converted to that type.

Your correspondent's chief argument is the old one that Cavalry can charge, and that mounted riflemen cannot. Both propositions may be disputed. Neither in the Boer War nor in that of Manchuria has the Cavalry ever shown that they could charge under modern conditions. On the other hand mounted riflemen have charged in the Boer service again and again, and, indeed, the charge on horseback was their normal method of attack during the last year of the war. Your correspondent mentions Potgieter's charge, which was arrested. But he does not mention the Boer charges at Vlakfontein, Tweebusch, or Bakenlaagte, which got home with deadly effects. The mounted riflemen's charge does not depend upon shock, but it is none the less deadly, arresting itself at the last moment for the use of the rifle. Botha at Bakenlaagte stopped his horsemen only thirty yards from the British line, but under a fold of ground, with the result that our force was annihilated. What could sword or lance do more? And is it fair to say that if Cavalry become mounted riflemen they can never hope to charge? I believe the reverse is the fact, and that it is not until they have become mounted riflemen that they will ever be able to play a spirited rôle in modern warfare.

There is no use in parading one thing in peace time and hoping for another in war, in scouring the heaths of Aldershot with swords and lances, but reserving the rifle, and the rifleman's habit of mind for real business. We must be logical and whole-hearted in this matter. The change should be thorough. I will never believe that it has been effected until I see a hundred lightly-equipped men, with rifles slung on their backs, and bandoliers across their chests, riding behind the King's State carriage, in the place of the present picturesque, but mediæval, guard. That will mark the final triumph of the modern type.

Yours faithfully,
ARTHUR CONAN DOYLE

April 5

THE PALL MALL
GAZETTE   13 April 1910

Sir A. Conan Doyle and Cavalry Training

SIR, – I regret if I at all misread your correspondent's letter. It was his use of the word "heresy" in connection with Mr. Erskine Childers's views which gave the impression that his view was an extreme one.

A civilian like myself might indeed feel helpless before the authority of so great a soldier as Sir John French, if it were not that Lord Roberts has declared himself strongly on the side of the rifleman, and against the preparation for shock tactics.

As to the French, Germans, and Austrians, it is they who should be sitting at our feet, not we at theirs. We have had the experience, and it drove a lesson into us. Why should we forget that lesson at the bidding of foreign theorists?

Bakenlaagte must remain a matter of opinion, and personally I do not believe that any cavalrymen could have ridden down such troops as the Buffs and the Scottish Horse, who formed the bulk of Benson's force.

As to Great Britain not producing mounted riflemen, she will certainly never produce them if they are not trained; but surely it is notorious that the regular mounted infantry reached a very high standard in the last year of the African war.

Yours faithfully,
ARTHUR CONAN DOYLE

Windlesham, Crowborough, April 12

THE DAILY EXPRESS   13 April 1910

The Congo Reforms

SIR, – Your readers must bear in mind that so long as in any report of Congo reforms, such a sentence occurs as "Adult natives will be compelled to work," there can be no true reform whatever. That is the touchstone as to whether reform is bogus or genuine.

If the man is compelled to work, then the prison, the chicotte, the hostage-house, and all the old abuses come inevitably as part of the machinery of compulsion. The windows of the Congo are now dressed for European inspection, but the back shop was described only last week by one who has had great experience of it, as being worse than he had ever known it.

ARTHUR CONAN DOYLE

Crowborough, Sussex

The King's Declaration

SIR, – Surely Colonel Sandys and the members of the Protestant Reformation Society should, looking at the matter simply from their own point of view, recognise that the surest way to strengthen any creed is, as the whole history of the world has proved, to persecute it. And it is mere juggling with words to attempt to show that it is anything other than persecution to hold up the Roman Catholic faith to obloquy in the Coronation Oath, while every other creed, Christian or non-Christian, is left unassailed. Is it not a shocking thing that, while Roman Catholic chapels throughout the whole Empire are still draped in black for a deceased Monarch, his successor should be compelled by law to insult the most intimate convictions of these same mourners? And is it not a most narrow and foolish policy, unworthy of this tolerant age, that a young King should be forced to offend the feelings of great numbers of Irishmen, Canadians, and other subjects? I feel sure that, apart from Catholics, the great majority of broadminded thinkers of any or of no denomination in this country are of opinion that the outcry of fanatics should be disregarded, and that all creeds should receive the same courteous and respectful treatment so long as their adherents are members of the common Empire. To bring these mediaeval rancours to an end would indeed be an auspicious opening of a new reign.

Yours faithfully,
ARTHUR CONAN DOYLE

Windlesham, Crowborough, Sussex, May 10

Mr. Housman and the Censor

SIR, – Without touching upon the question of the total abolition of the Censorship, about which some difference of opinion may exist, we would strongly urge that the rejection of Mr. Laurence Housman's play, without reason assigned, shows clearly the imperative advisability that the judgment of the Lord Chamberlain, in his capacity as Censor of plays, should be made subject to appeal.

We are, Sir,
Yours faithfully,

RUDOLPH BESIER   SYDNEY GRUNDY
J. COMYNS CARR   HENRY HAMILTON
R.C. CARTON   ANTHONY HOPE
C. HADDON CHAMBERS   JEROME K. JEROME
HUBERT HENRY DAVIES   W.S. MAUGHAM
A. CONAN DOYLE   LOUIS N. PARKER
H.V. ESMOND   CECIL RALEIGH
JAMES B. FAGAN   ALFRED SUTRO
W.S. GILBERT   I. ZANGWILL

THE DAILY EXPRESS   1 November 1910

Guinea Pig or Man?

SIR, – If Mr. Wall has read Lord Cromer's speech he would see
statistics as to the difference of plague effects among the inoculated
and the normal population in a district of India.

How, then, can he say that Lord Cromer indulges in mere
assertion? Such a statement is characteristic of the anti-human
campaign with which Mr. Wall is associated.

ARTHUR CONAN DOYLE

Crowborough, Sussex

THE TIMES   17 February 1911

Belgium and the Congo

SIR, – I am sure that Congo Reformers as well as others are
prepared to welcome our Belgian guests to England, but it would
be sad indeed if such a visit were made the occasion for any
slackening in our efforts to procure complete justice for the
unfortunate natives of the Congo. It is impossible for us to speak as
if the problem were solved, so long as the Concessionaire
Companies with their villainous records still retain their absolute
monopoly in large sections of the country. Such a monopoly is
inconsistent with that complete freedom of trade which was
guaranteed by the Congress of Berlin in 1887. As to the treatment
of the natives, which was guaranteed by ourselves and the other
signatory Powers, it is difficult to see why any Treaty should ever
in the future be observed when this one has been so openly and
flagrantly broken. We can but hope that at this eleventh hour
Belgium will endeavour to repair the wrong which her citizens
have done, and to make some reparation to their victims by such a
grant in aid as all other European Powers have been constrained
to make in order to administer their tropical possessions. Until

this has been done there must always be reserves in the feeling which many of us would wish to have for our Belgian neighbours.

Yours faithfully,
ARTHUR CONAN DOYLE

Windlesham, Crowborough, Sussex, Feb. 15.

THE BOOKMAN   March 1911

A Warning

SIR, – I should be much indebted to you if you would warn your readers against some swindler who is touring the country and professing to be my representative. He has some story of a school of literature and extracts dollars by a promise of epistolatory lessons. I have heard from at least two people who have received visits from him, one of whom was so deceived that he wrote me a reproachful letter, which drew my attention to the matter.

With apologies for troubling you,

Yours faithfully,
ARTHUR CONAN DOYLE

Windlesham, Crowborough, Sussex, December 30, 1910

THE DAILY EXPRESS   9 March 1911

Great Britain and Belgium

SIR, – In his interesting letter from Brussels your special correspondent says, speaking of the Congo outrages, that "every one here, Clerical, Liberal, and Socialist, absolutely believes them to have been grossly exaggerated."

That the Clericals should profess to believe so is natural enough, since it was this party which for so many years defended, and in some cases actually administered the Leopold regime. That the Socialists think so is inconceivable, since, through their two great spokesmen, Vandervelde and Lorand, they have repeatedly quoted and attacked these same outrages both in the Press and in the Belgian Chamber.

There can, as a matter of fact, be no question of exaggeration so far as the infamies are concerned which Mr. Morel cites in the terrible pages of his *King Leopold's Rule in Africa* or I, on a smaller scale, have compiled in my *Crime of the Congo*. The facts are taken from the judicial proceedings at Boma, from the evidence given before the Belgian Commission of Inquiry, from the admissions in the report of that Commission, from the British consular reports, from the printed accounts of Belgian and Italian officers, and from the personal experiences of numerous missionaries of many faiths and nations.

It is impossible for human imagination to exaggerate the accounts received from these sources.

These evil deeds are quite recent. The evidence of the German scientist, Dr. Dörpinghaus, brings them down to 1908. Since then we have had a change of regime, but the same concessionnaire companies, acting in many cases through the same agents, still retain their monopoly in the old scenes of their misrule.

Until we are quite certain, then, that conditions have indeed utterly changed it would be madness upon our part to do what your correspondent recommends, and to throw away the only weapon which we possess by which we, acting concurrently with the United States, can hope to control the situation.

ARTHUR CONAN DOYLE

Hotel Metropole, W.C.

THE TIMES   11 July 1911

The Prince Henry Tour

SIR, – As a driver in the Prince Henry contest I should welcome the opportunity of acknowledging through your columns the extreme kindness and hospitality which we competitors have received in Germany. That our hosts should endeavour to make things pleasant for us might be taken as a matter of course; but what could not be prearranged or organised is the warm reception which our motors bearing the British flag have received from every class of people along the whole line of a route which extended to nearly 300 miles. Some of this may be discounted as being due to the great personal popularity of Prince Henry, which must cause general sympathy for a contest in which he takes part; but, making every allowance for this, no one can possibly doubt that we received a true message of good will for England. The endless line of students, soldiers, peasants, wine growers of the Rhineland, artisans of Westphalia, agriculturists of the North, all had the same wave and cheer for us as we passed, while the enormous assemblage of children, presage of the great future of Germany made a deep impression upon our minds. The only *contretemps* (and it is one which is worth mentioning in view of the thousand miles of road work awaiting us in Great Britain) arose from ignorance of the fact that even a small bunch of flowers received in the face when you are travelling at high speed may become a dangerous missile. Several nasty blows were received, and one German competitor was so injured in the eye that he will be compelled, as I understand, to retire from the race. This exuberance of welcome is really the only possible criticism which could be made of our perfectly organised excursion. I can only hope that during our British run, which extends from Southampton, through Leamington, Harrogate, Newcastle, Edinburgh, Windermere, Shrewsbury, Chepstow, Cheltenham, and so to London, we can make our German friends feel welcome in the same complete way that they have done for us.

Yours faithfully,
ARTHUR CONAN DOYLE

Norddeutscher Lloyd, Bremen (Dampfer, "Grosser Kurfurst.")

THE BELFAST EVENING
TELEGRAPH   22 September 1911

Conan Doyle and Home Rule
"How I Stand In the Matter"

SIR, – It is true that I have twice contested Parliamentary seats as a Unionist, but on each occasion I very carefully defined my own position as regards Home Rule. That position, which I made stronger in 1905 than I did in 1900, was that Home Rule could only come with time, that it would only be safe with an altered economic condition and a gentler temper among the people, and above all after the local representative institutions already given had been adequately tested.

It seems to me that these conditions have now been fairly well complied with. The land system is in a simpler basis, there is better feeling among representative Nationalists (I admit, of course, the existence still of those fanatics who have stood in the way of their own desires for so many years) and, finally, the local institutions seem to me to have worked as well in Catholic as in Protestant Ireland. So far as being law-abiding citizens goes, England, which is just recovering from a period of absolute anarchy, is not in a position to criticise Ireland, which remained perfectly quiet during the same time.

There are other more general considerations which have, as it seems to me, profoundly altered the whole Irish question. One is the apparently complete success of Home Rule in South Africa. This has had a great influence upon my mind for the animosities in Ireland are tepid compared to the boiling racial passions which existed only ten years ago in Africa. A second is our assurance that Ireland can never break away from the Union, since South Africa

157

showed that every State of the British Empire would unite against any disruption. There are many other considerations which weigh with me, but these are the chief ones.

I think that a solid loyal Ireland is the one thing which the Empire needs to make it impregnable, and I believe that the men of the North will have a patriotism so broad and enlightened that they will understand this, and will sacrifice for the moment their racial and religious feelings in the conviction that by so doing they are truly serving the Empire, and that under any form of rule their character and energy will give them a large share in the government of the nation. They may rest assured that any attempt at religious persecution or financial spoliation would be made impossible (if any one contemplated such a thing) by the burst of indignation which it would produce. There may be an element of risk in Home Rule, but we ran the risk in Canada, and we ran the risk in Africa, so surely we need not fear after two successes to try it once again. I believe that after an experience of a united friendly Ireland nothing would induce the North to go back to the old conditions.

If you care to publish my view, I shall be glad. If not, I shall do so myself, as I owe it to the electors, whom I may have influenced of old, to let them know how I stand in the matter.

Yours faithfully,
ARTHUR CONAN DOYLE

Windlesham, Crowborough, Sessex, Sept. 19, 1911

THE MORNING
POST   28 September 1911

Sir A. Conan Doyle
and Home Rule

SIR, — You were kind enough to refer in a leading article to my views upon the Home Rule question. I am, as you truly say, an Imperialist, and it is as an Imperialist that I have formed these opinions. I am prepared to admit that in South Africa, as you state, there are still racial difficulties and many injustices. The same has, I believe, in the past held good of Canada. Reasoning from these precedents I should expect to find that Home Rule in Ireland would produce a similar crop for many years to come. All this I am prepared to grant, but I think that for Imperial reasons, so long as the flag and the authority of the King can be kept above all such local dissensions, it is better that we should endure them. We are then at least consistent to one fixed principle, viz., that the majority of the people in each white community of the British

Empire should rule themselves. On broad Imperial grounds almost any sacrifice is, as it seems to me, justified in order to attain such a result. No Imperialist can be blind to the evil effects which spring from the disaffection of the Irish both in the United States and in the Colonies. If these, as well as the majority of the actual inhabitants of Ireland, can be thoroughly reconciled to the Flag it is worth a very great deal to the Empire.

Yours, &c.,
ARTHUR CONAN DOYLE

Windlesham, Crowborough, Sussex, Sept. 27

THE SATURDAY
REVIEW   4 November 1911

The Amateur Soldier Again

SIR, – In his review of Mr. Erskine Childers' recent book upon the subject of cavalry tactics, in which he repeats his argument that we should be wiser to learn from our own experience than from German theories, your critic continually quotes an anonymous cavalry officer who deprecates the writer's views. Might I, as a supporter of those views, give an instance on the other side? A distinguished soldier who saw the whole of the African War and won his D.S.O. in the course of it (I enclose his name, but not for publication), was in my study the other day, and seeing Childers' *War and the Arme Blanche* upon my desk, he took it up with the remark, "This is to me an absolutely convincing military treatise". I mention the incident merely to show that to pooh-pooh these views as those of an amateur soldier is not a reasonable attitude. As a matter of fact, though Mr. Childers is technically an amateur, he actually served in Africa and saw a good deal of fighting. No one can read his books without admiring the amount of military reading and thought which goes to the making of them, and they are not to be lightly set aside by mere assertions unaccompanied by argument or proof.

Yours faithfully,
ARTHUR CONAN DOYLE

Windlesham, Crowborough, Sussex

The Amateur Soldier Again

SIR, – I should disregard your correspondent's letter, but he asks me a definite question in it. The particular officer whom I quoted in my former letter as strongly favouring Mr. Childers' views upon cavalry equipment, was a sapper, a corps which has some reputation for intelligence. But I can truthfully say that I can never once remember, in personal conversation with soldiers, meeting one who was not in general agreement with him, and of course Lord Roberts has placed himself on record to the same effect. It is absurd therefore for your correspondent to take the ground that this view is some three-man heresy which can be treated by a few words of clumsy sarcasm.

As to Mr. Childers and myself being novelists, it was not as a novelist that he – nor I may add that I – was in South Africa. The same motives which took us there are influencing us now in our desire that the lesson of the war which cost us so much should not be lightly forgotten.

Yours faithfully,
ARTHUR CONAN DOYLE

Windlesham, Crowborough, Sussex

Marriage Problems

SIR, – I observe that your correspondent Mr. George E. Bell, in his lament over the assumed decay of the British race (an assumption which I believe to be entirely unwarranted), has given as one of the causes: "How about divorce scattering English hearths to the winds?"

Is Mr. Bell aware that the English divorce laws are the most conservative and, from a reformer's point of view, reactionary in Europe – far more so even than the divorce laws of Scotland.

I do not know whether Mr. Bell seriously contends that to hold together for the term of their lives a sane person and a hopeless idiot, an innocent person and a criminal suffering penal servitude, or a normal man or woman and a dipsomaniac partner, is a just proceeding and conducive to the best interests of society. Or does he think that to separate 100,000 of each sex, as has now been done, and to forbid them to marry anyone else is helpful to public morality? If he does not think so, then he should help to bring about reform. If he does think so, then he is only one more proof that theology and reason cannot go together.

ARTHUR CONAN DOYLE
President Divorce Law Reform Union.

Windlesham, Crowborough

THE DAILY MAIL   23 January 1912

Sir A. Conan Doyle on Divorce

SIR, – In answer to Mr. Easter's question in the *Daily Mail*, I did not advocate the compulsory divorce of idiots, criminals, etc. The hardship is that they should not have a divorce if the sane or innocent partner desire it.

Of the hundred thousand of each sex who are now separated by law, and yet forbidden to marry anyone else, the causes of separation are many, but I should think that cruelty and habitual drunkenness predominate. My argument is that the existence of this great number of enforced celibates must have a subversive effect upon public morals, and incidentally a depressing influence upon that dwindling birth-rate which everyone deplores as a national disaster. After a fitting interval the separation should, as I hold, be changed into absolute divorce.

As to theology being the root of all the mischief, that was clearly borne out at the Commission, where the objections to reform were based largely upon theological considerations. We have had a striking object-lesson from India of late as to the folly of founding a practice upon texts. It is stated that a million widows have been consumed in the rite of suttee because the original direction in the sacred books were misread "fire," when it was actually "altar." It is a terrible and apposite example of the danger of allowing sayings uttered in a foreign tongue, under different conditions, in distant lands and far-off days, to hamper our common sense and to throw a blight upon living men and women.

ARTHUR CONAN DOYLE
(Pres. Divorce Law Reform Union.)

Windlesham, Crowborough, Sussex

THE DAILY MAIL   25 January 1912

On Divorce

SIR, – Your correspondent Mr. Bell says, "Had there been no such thing as divorce, there would not have been 100,000 separated couples." Apparently, Mr. Bell is confusing divorce with

161

separation. These separated couples are not people who are divorced, but people who live apart from each other and yet are not allowed to marry anyone else. If their separation were changed to divorce many of them would presumably remarry and form normal healthy households.

ARTHUR CONAN DOYLE

Windlesham, Crowborough

THE DAILY NEWS   5 March 1912

Rubber Atrocities

SIR, – I read in your issue of March 1st the terrible letter of Mr. D. MacCammond upon the Putomayo rubber trade, and I know well that no word of it is exaggerated. There is only one sentence to which I take exception, and that is "Tribes are held in a bondage that is grimmer and far more dreadful than anything which took place in the Congo." That cannot be true, for nothing which the human imagination could conceive could be more dreadful than the deeds of the Congo, and the roasting of the two small Indian boys which your correspondent cites differ only in being on a smaller scale from a great many incidents which one might narrate.

It would be a thousand pities if the presentation of one great wrong was made the occasion for depreciating or lessening our efforts to remedy another even greater one. Let us by all means bring all possible diplomatic pressure to bear upon the Peruvian Government, and let us do all that the utmost rigour of the British law permits to the erring company. It is, however, to be borne in mind that though it is a British company in the sense that is registered in London, it is in truth Peruvian both in its inception, its management, and to an overwhelming extent in the holding of shares. Those British investors who are in the unfortunate position of having put money into it had no possible means of judging from the prospectus what the real nature of the enterprise was or how its working was conducted. So long as they act upon the knowledge now acquired no moral blame can fairly rest upon them.

But the case of the Congo is very different. In Peru we have no direct responsibility. If any outside power has a direct responsibility it is the United States which, by her Monroe Doctrine, has assumed a position of tutelage over the South American countries. In the Congo, however, the call of duty is clear. We have sworn (in company, it is true, of the other great European Powers) that we would jointly guard the natives. The result of our guardianship has been that in more than thirty years this great country has lost

162

at a fair computation about two-thirds of its inhabitants.

An attempt is made now to deal with the subject as if it were concluded. It would be a fatal and an inexcusable error if under such a delusion we were to relax our attitude of criticism and to give away our last lever for amelioration by recognising the Belgian annexation. For the moment things are better. But we have no guarantee that they would remain so if the pressure caused by our non-recognition were removed. On the contrary, no one can read the Rev. J.H. Harris's recent letters after his travels through the country without seeing how delusive are the so-called reforms and how threatening the future.

They have given partial free trade, but with such taxes and restrictions upon the trader that it is practically inoperative. They have announced that they will collect taxes in francs instead of in rubber; but as there are no francs in the greater part of the country, they take the equivalent of francs in rubber, arbitrarily fixed, so that the end is much the same. They are starting vast Government plantations and other schemes which can hardly be run save by forced labour. Finally worst sign of all, they are retaining and restoring many of the old officials, accustomed to outrage and hardened to oppression. If in the face of all these signs we recognise the annexation, it will be to throw away at the last moment all that we have gained during the last ten years of agitation.

I hope that in nothing that I have said I have weakened the case made out by Mr. MacCammond for such action as is possible in the Putomayo district. But it would be a great misfortune if our attention to Peru should in any way relax our vigilance upon the Congo.

ARTHUR CONAN DOYLE

Grand Hotel, Lyndhurst, New Forest, March 3

THE DAILY EXPRESS   26 March 1912

"Peaceful Ireland"

SIR, – I observe that you use the above heading in an ironical sense whenever you have to chronicle any disorder in Ireland. But if the two islands be compared, is it not true in its lost literal sense?

Where in Ireland is there evidence of that syndicalism among men or sex perversion among women which has convulsed this country?

If disorder be an argument against fitness for self-government, then Ireland is surely the fitter of the two.

ARTHUR CONAN DOYLE

Crowborough, Sussex

"Peaceful Ireland"

SIR, – I did not say that Ireland was crimeless, but that her general condition was an object lesson to ourselves.

Mr. Grantham quotes the exceptional case of certain districts in a single county – Galway, if I remember right. Let me in return quote the following news item from a Dublin paper (*Evening Telegraph*, March 22): "A large number of the Irish judges have received white gloves as evidence of a crimeless calendar. Except for the presence of one case of petty larceny, the Lord Chief Justice would have received white gloves at the Cork City Assizes. This is an instructive instance of the state of crime in one of the principal cities of Ireland."

ARTHUR CONAN DOYLE

Crowborough, Sussex.

Home Rule
Letter to R. J. Kelly of Dublin

DEAR SIR, – Very many thanks for your note. I am an Imperialist because I believe the whole to be greater than the part, and I would always willingly sacrifice any part if I thought it to the advantage of the whole. It was the apparent enmity of Ireland to the Empire which held me from Home Rule for many years, and it is still that view which is hardest to overcome.

But I came to understand that these cheers for the enemies of the Empire were symptoms, and not the disease, and that, if you want to remove symptoms, it is not good treatment to continue the cause of them, but rather to alter that, and then the symptoms go of themselves. It seems a simple proposition, but nothing is simple when human prejudice and party politics distort it.

I hope the Nationalists will soon cease to allow their opponents the use of the Union Jack as a symbol. More Irishmen have died for that flag than men of any other race in proportion to numbers. It is the sign of the Empire which Ireland has helped to build, and which, be the local exception what it may, has stood for freedom and progress all the world over. Britain, be the past what it may, has honestly tried to do its best for Ireland for at least one long generation of mankind – the one party by legislation, the other party by endeavouring to restore Ireland's Legislature. Surely the days of bitter feeling are drawing to an end, and the Throne and the Flag should be recognised as they are everywhere recognised in the Empire, as being high above the clouds of political ill-will. It may be objected that it is putting the cart before the horse, but I am convinced that, if the Flag was honoured in Ireland as elsewhere, it would weaken British resistance to Home Rule more than any other cause. Folk do want to be reassured upon this point, that an Irish nation would be a loyal friend and not a scheming enemy. Of course, the whole lesson of history is that it would be so. This has always been the result of past grants of freedom to various portions of the Empire, but people, especially biassed political people, have always some reason why each particular case should be an exception to a general rule.

Yours faithfully,
ARTHUR CONAN DOYLE

Windlesham, Crowborough, Sussex, April 2, 1912

THE DAILY NEWS   20 May 1912

Mr. Shaw and the Titanic

SIR, – I have just been reading the article by Mr. Bernard Shaw upon the loss of the *Titanic*, which appeared in your issue of May 14th. It is written professedly in the interests of truth, and accuses every one around him of lying. Yet I can never remember any production which contained so much that was false within the same compass. How a man could write with such looseness and levity of such an event at such a time passes all comprehension.

Let us take a few of the points. Mr. Shaw wishes – in order to support his perverse thesis, that there was no heroism – to quote figures to show that the women were not given priority in escape. He picks out therefore one single boat, the smallest of all, which was launched and directed under peculiar circumstances, which are now matter for inquiry. Because there were ten men and two women in this boat, therefore there was no heroism or chivalry; and all talk about it is affectation. Yet Mr. Shaw knows as well as I know that if he had taken the very next boat he would have been obliged to admit that there were 65 women out of 70 occupants, and that in nearly all the boats navigation was made difficult by the want of men to do the rowing. Therefore, in order to give a false impression, he has deliberately singled out one boat; although he could not but be aware that it entirely misrepresented the general situation. Is this decent controversy, and has the writer any cause to accuse his contemporaries of misstatement?

His next paragraph is devoted to the attempt to besmirch the conduct of Capt. Smith. He does it by his favourite method of "suggestio falsi" – the false suggestion being that the sympathy shown by the public for Capt. Smith took the shape of condoning Capt. Smith's navigation. Now everyone – including Mr. Bernard Shaw – knows perfectly well that no defence has ever been made of the risk which was run, and that the sympathy was at the spectacle of an old and honoured sailor who has made one terrible mistake, and who deliberately gave his life in reparation, discarding his lifebelt, working to the last for those whom he had unwillingly injured, and finally swimming with a child to a boat into which he himself refused to enter. This is the fact, and Mr. Shaw's assertion that the wreck was hailed as a "triumph of British navigation" only shows – what surely needed no showing – that a phrase stands for more than truth with Mr. Shaw. The same remark applies to his "wrote of him as they would hardly write of Nelson." If Mr. Shaw will show me the work of any responsible journalist in which Capt. Smith is written of in the terms of Nelson, I will gladly send £100 to the Fabian Society.

Mr. Shaw's next suggestion – all the more poisonous because it is not put into so many words – is that the officers did not do their duty. If his vague words mean anything they can only mean this. He quotes as if it were a crime the words of Lowe to Mr. Ismay when he interfered with his boat. I could not imagine a finer example of an officer doing his duty than that a subordinate should dare to speak thus to the managing director of the Line when he thought that he was impeding his life-saving work. The sixth officer went down with the captain, so I presume that even Mr. Shaw could not ask him to do more. Of the other officers I have never heard or read any cause for criticism. Mr. Shaw finds some cause for offence in the fact that one of them discharged his revolver in order to intimidate some foreign emigrants who threatened to rush the boats. The fact and the assertion that these passengers were foreigners came from several eye-witnesses. Does Mr. Shaw think it should have been suppressed? If not what is he scolding about?

Finally, Mr. Shaw tries to defile the beautiful incident of the band by alleging that it was the result of orders issued to avert panic. But if it were, how does that detract either from the wisdom of the orders or from the heroism of the musicians? It was right to avert panic, and it was wonderful that men could be found to do it in such a way.

As to the general accusation that the occasion has been used for the glorification of British qualities, we should indeed be a lost people if we did not honour courage and discipline when we see it in its highest form. That our sympathies extend beyond ourselves is shown by the fact that the conduct of the American male passengers, and very particularly of the much-abused millionaires, has been as warmly eulogised as any single feature in the whole wonderful epic.

But surely it is a pitiful sight to see a man of undoubted genius using his gifts in order to misrepresent and decry his own people, regardless of the fact that his words must add to the grief of those who have already had more than enough to bear.

ARTHUR CONAN DOYLE

May 18

THE DAILY NEWS 25 May 1912

Mr. Shaw and Sir A. Conan Doyle

SIR, – Without continuing a controversy which must be sterile, I would touch on only one point in Mr. Shaw's reply to my letter. He says that I accused him of lying. I have been guilty of no such breach of the amenities of discussion. The worst I think or say of Mr. Shaw is that his many brilliant gifts do not include the power of weighing evidence; nor has he that quality – call it good taste, humanity, or what you will – which prevents a man from needlessly hurting the feelings of others.

ARTHUR CONAN DOYLE

May 23

THE DAILY MAIL 20 June 1912

The Labour Unrest
A Rejoinder to Mr. Wells

SIR, – I have been reading with much interest and some sympathy Mr. Wells's statement as to the labour unrest. In it he adjures every citizen to use his own best thoughts in the matter. Let me record mine for what they are worth.

I never read any contribution of Mr. Wells's to sociology that I do not feel more mentally alive for having done so. His clearness of vision and energy of expression are stimulating. At the same time I usually rise in a dissentient frame of mind, and never more than now. The general impression which he has left with me – I am not talking of these articles alone – is that of a man who, wandering in an orchard, says, "I do not like that fruit tree. Its fruit is not of the best, neither is its shape perfect. Therefore cut it down and let us take our chance of getting a better one." That is not the voice of the genius of the British people. Rather would it say, "I do not like that fruit tree. Let us see how best we can improve it without damage of the trunk. It may be trained to grow as we wish it, but if it be destroyed all the past is wasted and we know not what we may get in the future." This latter is surely the voice of practical wisdom.

In this particular case one is left at the close with the alternative of either letting the tree of State be utterly cut down, or of so altering it that it becomes another sort of tree – such a sort as the world has never seen. But is the crisis so great as this? Is it not rather a phenomenon which has been periodical in our history and which, though I must admit that it is more general, is less intense than on many previous occasions of its appearance? Had Mr. Wells lived in the days of the frame-breaking riots, of the early trade union outrages, before the movement became constitutional, and, above all, of the Chartist riots, he would have seen graver symptoms. And yet in each case the old tree with a little trimming and pruning grew as strong as ever. What is there now which should make us fear a more violent outcome? In the older days everything made for an explosion, since the whole weight of the State was pressing on the safety valve. Now, with an extended franchise, discontent can express itself in votes rather than in action. Those votes may lead to action, but they will do so in a gradual, orderly, and constitutional manner.

I agree with Mr. Wells that the working man has in many trades this excuse for his discontent, that prices have advanced in a greater ratio than wages. The same grievance applies to countless people who are not in the ordinary sense working men – to Government employees, pensioned officers, and others who have small, inelastic incomes, and are at the further disadvantage of having to keep up appearances in order to retain a place in their own class. It is deplorable that it should be so. The cause may or may not be greater output of gold, which has lessened its value as compared to commodities. Can we reduce that output? Such a remedy is unthinkable. Where, then, shall we find one?

Mr. Wells suggests that a cure be found in a commercial partnership between employer and employed. Such an arrangement would be unjust as excluding all those other classes who suffer from the same cause but would not be reached by such a remedy. But the scheme when viewed narrowly is full of flaws. It may well be adopted in a steady-going business which is in the

168

nature of a monopoly, such as a gas company or a railroad. But how about the numerous concerns which have no profits, but only losses? Is the working man to have his full wages, plus a share of the profits when a concern is successful, but when it is unsuccessful his full wages still, while the whole loss falls upon the capitalist? Is that justice? He must surely take the rough with the smooth, and my belief is that the rough would just about equalise the smooth, leaving him nothing whatever. I have no positive statistics at hand, but it is my strong impression that if you pooled all the companies of the last ten years, and wrote off from the profits of the successful ones the dead losses of the failures there would be either no profits left or so little that their division would make no difference to the working man. A man is perhaps unduly influenced by his own personal experience, but I know that I have twice endeavoured to establish businesses, that they have cost me at least twenty thousand pounds, that I have never had a penny of interest from them, that all my interest from other sources never came near my losses, and that any working man who had stood in with me would have been out of pocket. I have no reason to think my experience exceptional. What becomes, then, of the scheme by which the labourer is to share with the capitalist in the products of his labour? It falls to pieces when you try to apply it.

Is there any remedy through Parliament? I do not see how Parliament can affect the large questions of supply and demand which regulate the price of labour. They could pass a Minimum Wage Bill, but if it were unreasonably high it would only have the effect of driving away the trade and turning an inflated wage into no wage at all. One thing Parliament could do. They could rescue the British workman from his present position of being unprotected in his competition against the cheap and sweated labour of the world. In that fact lies, in my opinion, the main reason of the stagnation in the rise of wages. This remedy has been placed before the proletariat by the first statesmen of the age, but they have allowed themselves to be confused by party politics and have rejected it. On their own shoulders lies the weight.

What else can be done? Mr. Wells thinks some solution could be obtained if our party system could be set aside. On this point he seems to me a little querulous. After all, as the Great Duke said, "the King's Government has to be carried on," and it is difficult to see how that could be done by the amorphous debating society of experts which he has outlined. In the competition of two parties to gain the votes of the people lies the surest way of getting the wants of the people attended to. Parliament may, as he says, be blocked by business, but such a measure of devolution as Irish local government must surely have the effect of clearing the ground afterwards for the consideration of internal social reform.

169

Apart from the question of wages, where I see no hope of a rise save through a tariff, I agree with Mr. Wells that much good could be done by measures for the better housing of the poorer classes, especially in the country where the present state of things is a national disaster. When, if ever, the German cloud has been dissipated and we can afford to relax our present high insurance which absorbs so much of our Budget, this should surely be the first care of our rulers. I confess, too, that I am all on the side of land reforms. To my eyes the most beautiful manorial park or the fairest common is less pleasing than the same ground would seem with ten self-supporting farms upon it. We have not room in this little island for such luxuries, delightful as they are.

Mr. Wells is justly severe upon the idle rich, but does he not exaggerate the evils. Surely among the wealthy classes there is now more earnestness and personal service than in those hard-riding, gambling, three-bottle days of which we have read. The working man, as he sees the great motor pass him, knows well that of the thousand pounds which it cost the owner, five hundred or so went in wages straight into the pockets of his comrades. A greater austerity and economy among such owners would surely mean bad times in Coventry, Birmingham, and many another centre. I can see no cure for the labour unrest in such measures as that, but rather a danger of throwing fresh classes out of their employment.

Mr. Wells has indulged in prophecy, so I will venture upon the same very dangerous game. My reading of the future, then, is that this unrest will pass away into a cycle of repose, as every labour unrest has done before. The working man, being educated and intelligent, will realise that, he has many compensations in life. He will remember that at the present moment a good artisan often earns more than a clerk, a shopman, or a curate, and that a highly skilled workman may show a larger income than a member of the learned professions or an officer in the public service. He knows that the market varies with his own gifts, and that with sufficient energy and industry there is no position which he may not attain. I do not believe that there is any immediate danger of Mr. Wells or myself being forced to quit our manuscripts in order to work upon the face of a coal seam, nor do I dread any revolutionary upheaval. The working man will realise that he, like everyone else, is subject to certain communal laws, and that his highest wisdom is to do nothing which may drive trade from the country and so wither the very root of his own branch of it.

ARTHUR CONAN DOYLE

Windlesham, Crowborough

The Empire and the Games

Sir, – We have four years in which to set our house in order before the Berlin Olympic Games. Might I suggest that the most pressing change of all is that we should send in a British Empire team instead of merely a British team? The Americans very wisely and properly send Red Indians, negroes, and even a Hawaian amongst their representatives. We, on the contrary, acquiesce in our white fellow-subjects from the Colonies contending under separate headings. I am sure that if they were approached with tact they would willingly surrender the occasional local honours they may gain in order to form one united team in which Africans, Australians, and Canadians would do their share with men from the Mother Country under one flag and the same insignia. I would go further and see whether among Ceylon or Malay swimmers, Indian runners, and Sikh wrestlers we cannot find winners among the coloured races of the Empire. Such a movement would, I think, be of the highest political importance, for there could not be a finer object lesson of the unity of the Empire than such a team all striving for the victory of the same flag.

Yours sincerely,
ARTHUR CONAN DOYLE

Windlesham, Crowborough, Sussex, July 15

Our Olympic Failure

Sir, – I do not know who "H.A.S." may be, and I am not surprised that he does not sign his name to his letter in your columns. His spirit is that of the Little Englander, and he must broaden it before he can call himself an Imperialist.

If the Americans, who have the colour feeling more than we, can find places in their team for Red Indians, Negroes, and a Hawaian, why should we exclude the pick of 300,000,000 of our fellow subjects? Could anyone conceive a meaner position than to say that the Sikh, the Ghoorka, or the Rajpoot may fight for the Empire in war, but may not play for it in peace?

The Empire would soon be at an end if many Englishmen had the narrow outlook of "H.A.S."

ARTHUR CONAN DOYLE

Princes Hotel, Brighton

THE TIMES   30 July 1912

The Olympic Games

SIR, – All who have our reputation as athletes at heart owe a debt of gratitude to your Correspondent at the Stockholm Games for his very clear and outspoken comments upon the situation. We can now see the causes of past failure. The question is how far they can be removed in the future, and what steps should be taken to that end.

Every one is agreed as to our possessing the material. There remain only two factors – the money and the management.

To make worthy preparation we must have liberal funds. If the public do not provide them, then they can blame no one but themselves for our failures. I think that where the Olympic Council is most open to criticism is that they have not kept sufficiently in touch with the Press and the public, by explaining what had to be done and what was needed to do it. I am sure that with fuller knowledge the public would have responded more fully. Can we not find among our rich men some one who will make the Games his hobby and be the financial father of the team? How could a man spend his money better? But failing that we must all make an effort – and the sooner the better, before we have lost the stimulus which our defeat provides – to secure ample funds for doing everything which money can do to put the flag at the top in Berlin in 1916. I hope that a strong and influential appeal for funds will be made in the immediate future, with some reassuring statement as to how they will be expended. If the public does not respond it will prove that there is no national interest in the Games and that our case is serious. But I am convinced that this is not so, and that the money will be forthcoming.

Having secured a good war-chest, what are the other measures which should be adopted?

1. The first is the formation of a British Empire Team, which you have already discussed, and which seems to have met with general acceptance.

2. Annual, or even bi-annual, games should be held on the Olympic model each year from now to 1916. Every Olympic Stadium event should be contested in these with handsome prizes. They should be held alternately in the provinces and in London.

172

In this way we would thoroughly understand what material was available, and we would accustom our athletes to metre distances, and to the unusual competitions, such as the discus and javelin. I may say here that there is a small society existing, of which I have the honour to be president, called the Field Events Association (Hon. Secretary, F.A.M. Webster, 161A, Strand, W.C.), which endeavours to promote these abnormal events, and which has already obtained very gratifying results.

3. We must bring our full strength into the field. It should be recognised that just as all counties give up their best men for an England match, so Bisley, Wimbledon, or Henley must not detain our Olympic champions. The absence of our tennis players and of our yachts this year was a deplorable thing. There should be such a public spirit over the Games that it would become impossible for any one to throw obstacles in the way of our complete representation. As a mark of such public interest the team should have a public send-off and a public reception upon its return.

4. The team should be brought together into special training quarters for as long a period as possible before the Games, with the best advice always available to help them. At the Games themselves every effort should be made to keep them under the most healthy and comfortable conditions.

5. In every branch of sport some one must be responsible and on the spot to see that our men are fulfilling every condition. Then such fiascos as the two young officers disqualified in the riding would be avoided.

There is, as I understand, to be an important meeting of those interested in the question during the week, and it is to be earnestly hoped that some way will be found by which the central controlling body (who have, I believe, in some things done excellent work with very insufficient means) will be brought into closer touch with public opinion.

Yours faithfully,
ARTHUR CONAN DOYLE

Windlesham, Crowborough, Sussex, July 29

THE TIMES   8 August 1912

Britain and the Olympic Games

SIR, – The debate as to our preparations for the next Olympic Games tends to take the shape of recrimination rather than of construction. Might I appeal to all concerned to let bygones be bygones, and to centre our efforts upon the future? The scoring of debating points over each other only darkens counsel. The chief offender in the past has been the easy-going public, which has not taken an interest until our comparative failure at Stockholm came to waken it out of its indifference. The first step now is that every one should be magnanimous enough to forget any quarrels of the past, to express regret for them, and to unite with the one unselfish ideal of forming the best instrument for the purpose in hand.

I am aware that I speak with no authority upon such a subject, but I have the advantage of complete independence since I do not belong now, and never could in the future, to any governing body, nor have I taken sides in any altercation. Perhaps, then, I may be allowed to make a suggestion as to organisation. It is clear that this matter must be set right and endorsed by Press and public before any appeal for funds upon a large scale will have any chance of success.

The Olympic Association of the past has worked against the great difficulty of public apathy. It has done some particularly good work – especially in the matter of the London Games, which will probably fix the Olympic type for ever. The Council consists of about 50 members, who include the presidents or representatives of nearly every branch of sport. Such a body is, as it seems to me, far too valuable to dissolve, and should always be retained as a final court of appeal in which any matter affecting the general policy of Great Britain towards the Games might be discussed and settled.

It is clear, however, that such a gathering is much too large for executive purposes. The smaller a body the more does each member feel his personal responsibility and the greater the results achieved. The ideal executive committee would, as it seems to me, consist of a nucleus of four or five from the present Olympic Association, with as many more co-opted from outside – not only from the Universities, but from popular athletic bodies throughout the country, and from men of affairs who are outside the ordinary circles of sport. Various committees for finance, training, and other purposes could be formed in such a way, each with wide powers in its own department. Such an arrangement would have the advantage that it could be taken in hand by the Association and put through without delay.

My contention is that if some practical organisation of this sort could be at once formed and gain the general endorsement and confidence of the public, we could then appeal for the large sum which will be needed without any danger of being refused. The public will want to know in advance what it is going to get for its money. If they see a definite practical scheme, and if the names which guarantee it show that the ranks are closed and all are of one mind, we shall have overcome the greatest difficulty which lies between us and Berlin.

Yours faithfully,
ARTHUR CONAN DOYLE

Windlesham, Crowborough, Sussex, Aug. 5

THE DAILY MAIL   2 September 1912

"The Case of Oscar Slater"

SIR, – Since the publication of my brochure on the Oscar Slater case ten days ago I have received numerous letters from correspondents all over the country urging me to use any influence I have in getting the authorities to reconsider the trial.

I trust, therefore, that by pointing out to the British public the possibility and probability of a miscarriage of justice having been perpetrated by the conviction of the man Slater for the murder of Miss Gilchrist I have awakened a more general interest in the case, and, if the British public agree with my views, it is for them to see that the case is reopened.

A. CONAN DOYLE

Windlesham, Crowborough, Sussex

THE SPECTATOR   12 October 1912

The Slater Case

SIR, – Mr. Risk's long letter upon this subject is full of inaccuracies. His idea of argument seems to be simply to make assertions of things which were never proved at the trial, and thus to form a *post-factum* justification of the verdict. His allegation that certain gamblers knew of the existence of Miss Gilchrist's jewels was never even alluded to at the trial, and the police entirely failed to prove that Slater travelled to Liverpool with anything but a Liverpool ticket. As he had previously announced to several people where he was going, it seems highly improbable that he bought a London ticket in order to throw pursuit off his track. As to the assertion that Slater confessed, I am entirely incredulous upon the subject. Slater's words (reported in several forms) seem to me to bear the interpretation that if he were executed it would be the death of his mistress also. The so-called confession was entirely denied by Mr. Spiers, Slater's solicitor, who, not only in public but in the privacy of his own family, asserted his belief in the complete innocence of his client up to the day of his death. Slater also protested his innocence after reaching prison, which is

175

surely incompatible with the idea that he had already made a confession of guilt.

Mr. Risk's logic and temper may be judged by the sentence, "Even if Slater were innocent, . . . Peterhead" (meaning penal servitude) "is the proper place for him." Of course, if that is so there is an end of the discussion. But some of us still retain an old-fashioned prejudice in favour of a man being punished for the crime that he is tried for, and not for the morals of his private life.

I am, Sir, &c.,
ARTHUR CONAN DOYLE

Windlesham, Crowborough, Sussex

THE SPECTATOR   26 October 1912

The Slater Case

SIR, – All this talk on the part of Mr. Risk as to personal knowledge which he has of facts not known to the public and not mentioned at the trial can count for nothing in this controversy, since it cannot be subjected to cross-examination. It is mere *ex parte* statement, and it is obvious that many people have a strong interest in upholding that there has been no miscarriage of justice. Everything outside the facts actually adduced at the trial is really irrelevant.

Mr. Risk returns to the so-called confession. He does not seem to see that the withdrawal of the death sentence is proof positive that in the opinion of those who were in the best position to know the truth no such confession was made. If it had been, nothing could have saved a man who had avowed himself guilty of the vilest and most cowardly murder of modern times. This consideration alone should for ever dispose of this assertion.

To call the legal gentlemen who revised the sentence a court of appeal is a misuse of terms. The question of innocent or guilty was never before them – nor, I believe, within their competence. Their choice lay between two forms of punishment, the graver and the more merciful. That they chose wisely is surely shown by the fact that this agitation still continues, and cannot fail to continue until the reasonable doubts in men's minds are set at rest.

Since there were 20,000 signatures to the appeal for a reprieve, and since this appeal was based upon the unsatisfactory nature of the conviction, I cannot believe that the citizens of Glasgow are so unanimous upon the subject as Mr. Risk would have us believe.

I am, Sir, &c.,
ARTHUR CONAN DOYLE

Windlesham, Crowborough, Sussex

A Channel Tunnel

SIR, – I welcome General Sir R. Talbot's letter dealing with the Channel Tunnel which appeared in your issue to-day. The matter seems to me to be of such importance that I grudge every day that passes without something having been done to bring it to realisation. Built from national funds, it would in peace be a most valuable asset, while in war with any nation but France it would vastly increase our strength both for offensive and defensive purposes. The advantages which I see for a national tunnel are briefly as follows:–

1. If constructed by the nation for anything like the estimate advanced by capable engineers it should be a source of great profit to the country.

2. It should stimulate our trade with the Continent, since bulk need not be broken.

3. It should bring to England very many thousands of Continental travellers every year who are at present deterred by the crossing.

4. Should we ever be forced to send troops to the Continent, it provides a safe line of communications, besides ensuring an unopposed transit.

5. It enables food to be introduced into the country in war time, and would help us to hold out, even after a naval defeat. All the supplies of the Mediterranean are available *via* Marseilles.

6. It passes out some of our exports in war time, and to that extent relieves the Fleet of the duty of convoying them.

These six reasons seem to me to be weighty ones. Against them there is only one that I have ever heard, the fear of invasion. This can of course only mean invasion by France, which cannot surely be regarded as a serious danger, although I admit that every defensive precaution should be taken. As to invasion by any other country it means that they have first to win and to hold both ends of the tunnel. Such a contingency is, I hold, beyond all bounds of common sense.

Yours faithfully,
ARTHUR CONAN DOYLE

Athenæum Club, March 10

Olympic Committee

SIR, – You were good enough to mention my name in connection with your article upon the above, and you will therefore permit me, perhaps, to write a brief reply. Let me make it clear in the first instance that I do this entirely as from myself, and that I have no warrant to speak for anyone else upon the committee.

It is difficult for one who is himself a member of that body to eulogise its constitution; but I would accept the description of it which you have quoted from one of my early letters as being approximately what we have realised. We are fortunate in having the representative of one popular body of sport as chairman. We have business men connected with sport, and we have members who are themselves athletes. It has to be borne in mind that a very great deal of heavy and continuous work has to be done by such a committee. It would be vain to form it by adding to it such names – I quote the first which occurs to me – as Lord Alverstone, Lord Lonsdale, Sir Thomas Lipton, or the like. Senior men whose lives are already filled with pressing duties would find it almost impossible to fulfil the demands which must be made upon a member of the Olympic Committee. There is no doubt that whatever names were selected, other alternative ones could be suggested; but it would make any united national effort impossible if we were to wait for such a heaven-sent committee as would equally commend itself to everyone. The point to be insisted upon at present is that we shall soon have to appeal for funds, without which nothing can be done, and that all unnecessary and premature criticism of the committee may have the effect of reducing the answer to that appeal, and so weakening our position at the Games at Berlin.

As to the question of an American trainer, it has not even been mentioned upon the committee, and all criticism upon the point is meaningless. Individual members of the committee have no doubt made their inquiries in various directions so as to be in a position to say what can be done before it is decided what shall be done. But if prejudice is to be raised before matters have been discussed, far less carried through, it makes a task more difficult which is already quite onerous enough.

I am, etc.,
ARTHUR CONAN DOYLE

Windlesham, Crowborough, Sussex, March 22, 1913

Lord Wolseley

SIR, – I have one or two vivid recollections of the personality and conversation of Lord Wolseley which might furnish a paragraph for his future biographer. He was a man who possessed not only the courage and energy which are the proper qualities of a successful soldier, but a breadth of thought and power of brain which would have brought him to the top in any profession. There was something of the knight errant in his disposition, a real love for perilous deeds, and when he spoke of war and its hazards the whole man seemed to become tense and quivering with a suppressed eagerness. There was nothing small or petty in his nature, and I have heard him speak with enthusiasm of brother generals quite outside that circle of comrades who had shared in his own triumphs. I remember sitting next to him at a very small dinner party upon the evening that the news of the battle of Omdurman came to England. It was during the Salisbury Plain manoeuvres of 1898. As Kitchener's exploit was an actual accomplishment of that which Lord Wolseley, through no fault of his own, had failed to achieve, some reserve in his feelings would have been human and natural. On the contrary, I can never forget the whole-hearted boyish warmth with which he sprang to his feet and drank his first glass of wine (probably his last also, for he was one of the most abstemious of men) to the victor in the great battle which cleared the way to Khartum.

I remember one or two of his sayings which may be of interest. To a direct question from me as to whether he felt any sensation of fear when he was first under fire he answered, "The human mind can only think of one thing at a time. If a young officer is thinking whole-heartedly of his men and how he is to handle them, he cannot possibly think of himself." The conversation having turned to the religious future of Great Britain, he said, "That question was definitely and finally settled 300 years ago. There is no example in history of a nation going back upon a decision of that sort." He carried away from his Crimean campaign a very great esteem for the Russians not only as soldiers but as men. This he said was universal among the troops, and went so far that they were in closer personal sympathy with their enemies than with their allies. He had a keen sense of humour, and could bring out the points of a story. I can never forget one of his anecdotes, which was to the effect that he had taken a notoriously eccentric officer with him to Egypt on a solemn promise that he would restrain his strange sporting propensities and do nothing out of the way. On the first morning in Ismailia the General was disturbed by a great hubbub outside his quarters, and, looking out, saw the officer in question endeavouring to drive up to the door with a camel and a donkey in tandem.

Yours faithfully,
ARTHUR CONAN DOYLE

Athenæum Club, April 1

THE DAILY EXPRESS   19 April 1913

The Channel Tunnel

SIR, – You are good enough to quote my views on the Channel Tunnel. Your readers would find them set forth at some length in the *Fortnightly Review* of February.

It may interest them to know that the cost of such a tunnel has been estimated to be not more than five million pounds, and that three years would see it completed.

Apart from its obvious advantages as a security against starvation in time of war (it would tap the whole Mediterranean basin via Marseilles), it should be a great national asset, for it would encourage Continental traffic, and it would bring very many thousands of tourists to our shores who are at present deterred by the sea voyage.

As to danger of invasion through the tunnel, it seems to me to be a very far-fetched idea. At the same time, it would be easy to allay the fears of nervous people by such measures as engineers can readily suggest for destroying the tunnel in case of need. I think, however, that it is imperative that the undertaking should be under direct national control.

ARTHUR CONAN DOYLE

Windlesham, Crowborough, Sussex

THE TIMES   13 May 1913

Political Prisoners in Portugal

SIR, – Portugal is our ancient ally, and we have given each other many mutual proofs of friendship in peace and in war. We cannot believe, however, that the present Government truly represents Portugal any more than Robespierre and his Jacobins represented France. We have before us cruelty, injustice, want of chivalry, everything which is alien to the real Portuguese nature. In protesting against it we are not wronging our old friend, but rather asking to see that friend's face once more.

No one can read without pain and anger the piteous tale of the thousands of political prisoners who have been held under the most barbarous conditions, some of them not even tried after two years, under a *régime* which supplies no food at all to an untried prisoner. The present condition of the Lisbon prisons seems to have been equalled only by those of Naples in the days of King Bomba. The damp, reeking, vermin-crawling cells are tenanted by men who are either entirely innocent or else are guilty only of being loyal to the *régime* under which they were brought up. Men are flogged – sometimes to death – and no voice can be raised in protest. Surely, Sir, if we have indeed any influence it can never be used in a better cause. But only energetic action can avail. Mere remonstrance has effected nothing.

There is a precedent in the case of Servia. That nation murdered its King and Queen under atrocious circumstances. We showed our sense of the crime by withdrawing our representative. The Portuguese – or a section of them – have also murdered their late King and his son. The present Government have made the deed their own, since public demonstrations have been permitted this very year in Lisbon in honour of the murderers. Why should we not do once more what we did in the case of Servia? It would make the powers that be in Portugal realise as nothing else would do how utterly unworthy they are to belong to the comity of nations. The mere threat of such an action might bring about an amnesty. If not, we can only show our displeasure by refusing to have any dealings with people so devoid of justice and humanity.

Yours faithfully,
ARTHUR CONAN DOYLE

Windlesham, Crowborough, Sussex, May 5

THE DAILY
CHRONICLE   16 May 1913

The Portuguese Prisoners

SIR, – In your issue of yesterday you quote Mr. Swinny upon the state of the Portuguese prisons, and you mention my name as one of those who should respond to his statement. One can only do so by quoting one British witness against another. Mr. Aubrey Bell (correspondent of the *Morning Post*), writing at the end of February of this year, says: "Except for the fact that the convicts in the Penitenciaria now no longer wear the hood, which by all the laws of civilisation should never have been inflicted upon political prisoners, the miserable condition of the Royalist prisoners remains unchanged. Moreover, those benefiting by the reforms do not include the hundreds of Royalists who are not confined in cells but crowded with every kind of criminal in the Limoeiro and other prisons. . . . The remainder of the arrested Royalists are kept for six months, a year, two years without a trial. . . ."

On March 13 of this year the conditions were still the same. An English correspondent, writing from Lisbon says:–

"The treatment of the political prisoners here is still scandalous. I know several men of the poorer classes who have been awaiting trial for over two years, and are now condemned to fifteen years' imprisonment, though there are no proofs against them. All the time they were in prison awaiting trial their families had to supply all their food, the prison authorities giving nothing."

Senhor Osorio, a Republican lawyer, points out on March 12 that, save for the abolition of the hood, the lot of the politicals is unchanged. There is a mass of evidence to the same effect from Portuguese newspapers and from private testimony. Therefore I think it is only reasonable to suppose that Mr. Swinny has been shown what the authorities desired him to see, and that he is quite unwittingly helping to bolster up a most cruel system.

ARTHUR CONAN DOYLE

Windlesham, Crowborough, Sussex, May 15, 1913

THE DAILY EXPRESS   24 May 1913

Olympic Games Lethargy

SIR, – My attention has been called to an article by your correspondent "Orion," in which a number of questions are asked upon points connected with the organisation of the Olympic Games. Most of these questions seem to be addressed to the Olympic Council, and some, I may add, are concerned with matters which have already been fully explained in communications to the Press.

There are a few, however, connected with the genesis of the whole organisation, which I may, perhaps, be better able to answer than any one else, and I can begin by assuring your correspondent that there is no mystery in the matter, and that all the facts are entirely at his disposal.

At the time of the last Olympiad there was, as he recalls, a wide-spread dissatisfaction at the performance of the British team, and at the failure of the Olympic Council to produce a better result – which failure was, in my opinion, largely due to the wretched support which they had received from the public and the Press. However, there was a generally-expressed desire that some change of organisation should be made.

As I was interested in the matter, and had some definite ideas as to the lines the reorganisation should take, I wrote a couple of letters to *The Times* indicating my views. These letters brought me in contact with two members of *The Times* editorial staff. Finally, Lord Northcliffe was interested in my expression of opinion, and he intimated that if I could effect such changes he would support the Olympic movement to the best of his ability.

Let me say at once that it was clearly understood and asserted from the beginning that this arrangement should be national, and that no private interest should in any way be served. All Press communications were to go through a common agency. This condition has been most loyally fulfilled – and, indeed, I think that the first suggestion of it came from Lord Northcliffe himself.

Apart from the help which he could give the cause by public ventilation, Lord Northcliffe came forward also, in a most sportsmanlike manner, with an offer for financial help from his own private purse. No sum was named, but the understanding was that his contribution should bear some relation to the amount subscribed by the public.

As no public subscription has yet been made, it is not possible to give your correspondent the details upon this point which he demands. The reason why the appeal has been delayed is that the state of the money market during the Balkan War made it a very inopportune time to go to the public for funds.

So much for Lord Northcliffe's association with the matter. There remain the questions connected with the formation of the committee.

My draft proposals in *The Times* met with so much general approval, both from individuals and from the Press, that I put myself in communication with the Olympic Council, and inquired how far changes could be carried out on those lines, pointing out that such an organisation was assured of a certain amount of support. The representatives of the council met me in a very courteous and reasonable spirit, but the matter was delicate and complicated, and some months elapsed before all the details were settled.

It was then agreed that, as the public were putting up the money, the public should be represented to the extent of one-half upon the financial committee, which should have an absolute control over the spending of the fund.

The question then arose as to who should form the committee. There was only one body existing which had any legal status in the matter, and that was the council itself. Yet the choice of the public members could not be left to it, otherwise the rearrangement became a farce.

Under these circumstances, the gentlemen who had already interested themselves in the matter, including myself, selected certain names which seemed suitable, and these were submitted to the council for criticism, and, if necessary, for veto. There was no other way in which the matter could be carried through.

The result was the formation of an exceedingly strong committee – if I, who am a temporary member of it, may be allowed to say so. The members representing the public are, as has been already stated, Mr. J.E.K. Studd, who has had great administrative as well as athletic experience; Mr. H.W. Forster, M.P., also an administrator as well as an athlete; Mr. Edgar Mackay, of motor-boat fame, who will act as hon. treasurer; Mr. Bosanquet, who has played for England at cricket; and Mr. Anderson, who was one of the English team at the last Olympiad. To these the council has added Mr. Theodore Cook and Mr. Robertson, both of them ex-Olympians with Mr. Fisher, the hon. secretary of the Amateur Athletic Association, and Mr. Hurd, ex-secretary of the Swimming Association.

These form the Financial Committee, who are responsible for the wise expenditure of the fund. In determining that expenditure they will, of course, be guided by the advice and requirements of the various governing bodies of sport.

I trust that these details may cover the points raised by your correspondent, so far as they come within the events in which I have been concerned. I agree that the public have a right to know every detail when they are asked to subscribe and when the matter is national.

I think, however, that questions should be asked in a less querulous fashion than in this instance, for it is annoying to those who are giving time or money or both to the public service when they receive less than common courtesy in return.

ARTHUR CONAN DOYLE

Windlesham, Crowborough

THE DAILY EXPRESS   5 July 1913

The British Olympic Council

SIR, In answer to the article in to-day's "Express," it must be evident that an ill-timed appeal for funds would be disastrous, since the future success of the British team must depend largely upon the result. The money market is still unfavourable, and there is already one large appeal for what is really a national object before the public.

In the meantime, money is being found for every immediate purpose. Even if the money were in hand, it could not be allotted until the plans of every one of the governing bodies of sport had been examined and reported upon. Thus no time is actually being lost by the British Olympic Council.

I trust that when the appeal does appear we shall have the hearty support of the *Express* and its patriotic readers. We have the men and we have the organisation. All we need now is the money. But that is essential.

ARTHUR CONAN DOYLE

Windlesham, Crowborough, July 4

THE TIMES   14 August 1913

The Channel Tunnel

SIR, – In your issue of to-day Mr. Ronald McNeill describes the project of a Channel tunnel as a "crazy" one. I venture to prophesy that when the thing has been done the verdict of posterity will apply that adjective to the undignified and unjustified fears which have so long stood in the way of a great and beneficent national enterprise.

Mr. McNeill mentions the entente with France and the development of the aeroplane as being the only fresh factors which bear upon the question since it was discarded many years ago. To my mind there are others of greater importance. It is admitted on all hands that the greatest danger which can threaten this country in war is the possible failure and certain diminution of our food supplies. Weighty authorities have stated that a single defeat at sea might entail our absolute surrender. Recent years have seen the development of a new great European navy and of a political situation which might conceivably place it in opposition to our own. An adequate tunnel would certainly lessen the difficulty of our food supplies, since it would place us in communication with the whole Mediterranean basin through Marseilles. Even granting that we held the seas successfully it would to some extent relieve our Navy of that duty of protecting our food cargoes which must take something from its strength. Again, it is possible that circumstances might arise in which British troops would be used on the Continent. If such a situation should unfortunately occur it is difficult to say, considering the possibilities of the submarine, how the transports which would carry them, and which would afterwards form their line of communications, could be safe-guarded. In such an event a tunnel would be a great strategic advantage.

Finally there is the effect upon national wealth, which means national strength. Not only would actual trade gain a great advantage, since merchandise need not break bulk, but we might reasonably hope that a stream of foreign tourists would be directed towards London which would do something to atone for the vast sums which are carried abroad every year by our own people.

As to the dangers involved the idea of the invasion of a great country through a hole in the ground 26 miles long and as many feet broad seems to me to be a most fantastic one. An enemy to use the tunnel has to hold both ends of it. In the unlikely event of a quarrel with France it is surely not difficult to seal up our end. I cannot imagine the circumstances under which any other Power could gain both ends. If such circumstances did arise it would surely mean that tunnel or no tunnel we were beaten to the ground.

At the same time to prevent periodical scares every reasonable military precaution should be taken. The tunnel should open within the lines of an intrenched camp at Dover, and the end of it would be commanded by heavy guns from the heights. Other even more stringent safeguards could readily be devised.

Yours faithfully,
ARTHUR CONAN DOYLE

Windlesham, Crowborough, Sussex, Aug. 12

THE TIMES　　　　27 August 1913

The Olympic Games

SIR, – I have read with great interest Mr. Frederic Harrison's letter upon the Olympic Games. In common with all the world, I have the utmost respect for Mr. Harrison's character and opinions, but I have hopes that there are some aspects of this matter which have escaped his attention or upon which he has been incompletely informed.

In the first place, it is admitted by the Appeal Committee that a hundred thousand pounds is a very large sum, but it is clearly stated that only a portion of it should be allocated to the Olympic Games, and that the fund shall be a nucleus for some such system of universal physical education as would be entirely outside the strictures which Mr. Harrison makes. Such a scheme, with its necessary provision of gymnasia and playing fields for the poor, must, I am sure, have his approval. It is impossible at this early stage to give exact figures, but certainly a good proportion of the fund would be spent in such a fashion.

Let us now come down to the balance which is expended upon the preparation for the Games themselves. Mr. Harrison implies in his letter that the British team would number about a hundred. Three times this estimate would be nearer the mark. He must remember that besides the single events there are many team competitions, football, gymnastics, physical exercises, hockey, rifle and clay-pigeon shooting, rowing, &c. If we make a full entry we must be prepared to look after at least 300 men. Mr. Harrison would admit that these men, who represent their country, should not have the burden of their expenses laid upon their own shoulders. They have to be conveyed to Berlin and back, and they have to be comfortably housed and carefully fed at a time of inflated prices. The sum will not be less than seven or eight thousand pounds for this item alone. How does Mr. Harrison propose to raise this, save by national appeal? Can he suggest any other course?

Mr. Harrison in discussing the general question of preparation for the Games draws a dismal picture of "an army of professional coaches" over-running the country, and of the likely youths being drafted away and maintained by the nation during the long period of training and preparation. I am convinced that those who have the management of the Games in hand would reprobate such a programme as heartily as Mr. Harrison does, and that all his fears upon this head will prove to be baseless. The army of coaches does not and never will exist. The new developments will take the form of providing practice grounds where none now exist (in all London how many places are there where a man could practise throwing a hammer?), in providing places for winter practice, in providing the impedimenta of sport for those who cannot procure them, and, finally, in encouraging every form of sport to adapt its conditions or distances to those which obtain at the Olympic Games. This can only be done by offering special medals or prizes to be competed for at those distances. It may seem that no great expense is involved in these developments. Perhaps not in any single case. But the Olympic Fund will have to meet demands from every part of Great Britain and Ireland, each legitimate in itself, and together making up a considerable sum.

Let us for a moment trace the evolution of that novice concerning whom Mr. Harrison has such misgivings. He is probably unearthed at one of the special novices competitions which give him a chance where he will not be overshadowed by some crack. He would then be watched and reported upon by the officials of his amateur body, which must be affiliated to the Amateur Athletic Association of his country. If he continued to make good he would probably be inspected and advised by the professional coach of his district – one, perhaps, of half a dozen in the country. He would advise the youngster as to form, precisely as an amateur cricketer has always been advised by a professional. If he continued to make progress and made good his claim to represent the country in an Olympic event he would train at the last, as a 'Varsity Blue trains for the boat race, and he would have the advice of the best professional that could be found. At no time save perhaps for the final week would his ordinary work in the world be interfered with, and at no time at all could any direct or indirect remuneration be given to him. What is there in all this which can justify Mr. Frederic Harrison in his lurid picture of athletic degeneration?

If Mr. Harrison's contention was that we should never have gone in for the Olympic Games at all, he might find many to agree with him. But, things being as they are, I would ask him to consider the courses open to us. One is to retire in the face of defeat and to leave the Colonies to put the Union Jack at the top when they can. As a good sportsman I am sure Mr. Frederic Harrison could not tolerate that. A second is to continue with our present haphazard half-hearted methods, and to see ourselves sink lower and lower from that third place which we now occupy. Surely that would not satisfy Mr. Harrison. There only remains one other course of action, and that is to do the thing thoroughly and well, to find out what talent we have, and to bring it to the scratch in the best possible condition. If Mr. Harrison will look at the names of those who have the matter in hand he will, I am sure, admit that they are very capable of devising means to this end, and that such money as is required will be spent wisely and in a manner which will be consistent with the best amateur traditions of this country. What our representatives could do when unaided by adequate national support was shown last year in Stockholm. Surely Mr. Harrison would not wish to see it repeated at Berlin. Can he devise any method to prevent such a misfortune save systematic and painstaking preparation, which in the end must mean money?

Yours faithfully,
ARTHUR CONAN DOYLE

Frinton, Aug. 26

THE TIMES   13 September 1913

The Olympic Games Fund

SIR, – I should like to ask one question and receive a definite reply from all those persons, including Mr. Punch, who are making our

Olympic task more difficult. It is this:– "Are you prepared to stand down from the Berlin Games altogether?" In answering it they would do well to bear three points in mind – that we were defeated at the last Games, that the Games are in Berlin, and that all the chief nations have already announced their intention of seriously competing. If in the face of this they are prepared to stand down, then their attitude is, I admit, perfectly consistent. If they are not, then what is it that they want to do?

Yours faithfully,
ARTHUR CONAN DOYLE

Windlesham, Crowborough, Sussex

THE TIMES   11 October 1913

The Olympic Games Fund

SIR, – The progress of the Olympic Fund is sure and steady, but it must be admitted that it is slow. This is due, in my opinion, to the idea in the minds of the public that the Games are three years distant, so that they dismiss the subject from their immediate attention under the impression that there is plenty of time. But this is a fallacy. Seed-time is rapidly passing. When harvest time comes not all the money in England will buy the crop if it has not been planted now. Three years hence we, like every other nation, will be intensely interested in the great international contest in Berlin. We must see to it now, in this autumn of 1913, that we have not then to look back with bitterness and reflect that our preparations came too late.

Yours faithfully,
ARTHUR CONAN DOYLE

Windlesham, Crowborough, Sussex, Oct. 10

THE STOCK EXCHANGE
CHRISTMAS ANNUAL
1913–14

Some Views on the Olympic Talent Fund

SIR, – Some little time ago certain members of the Olympic Committee, being wearied of the constant misrepresentations in the Press, invited all the sporting journalists of the Metropolis to meet them at a London hotel, there to discuss the question.

Face to face with these gentlemen, many of whom had been severe critics of the Committee and its plans, those plans were expounded both by the Chairman, Mr. Studd, and myself. We

189

received a most courteous hearing and, at the end of our remarks, we asked for criticism. After a long ventilation it was admitted by all those present, including, as I have already said, many constant critics, that the Committee had worked upon the right lines, that they could not have done more than they had done, and that they were deserving of all support. And this, I venture to say, would be the verdict of every other impartial critic in this country if we could meet them face to face.

There has been an immense amount of misapprehension and misrepresentation in the Press, which has had the unhappy effect of diverting subscriptions from the Fund, and so hanging up our essential preparations. We may still send a good team to Berlin, but, do what we may, we can never send so representative or so highly-trained a team as would have been available had we been able to organise during this last year.

It is quite clear that there are three courses which might be adopted towards the Berlin Games. The first is, not to attend them at all. This is surely out of the question! All other sporting nations, including our own Colonies, are not only attending, but are making special efforts to send worthy representatives.

If we stood down now it would certainly and justly cause considerable international ill-feeling.

The second course is to go on depending upon our ordinary sporting organisations and then to make a "whip round" at the last moment, to cover the actual travelling and living expenses of our team. This is exactly what was done at Stockholm last year.

Surely we have not already forgotten the humiliating result and the universal outcry in the Press, that such a failure should not be permitted to occur again!

Some of us, who took those words literally, and set ourselves earnestly to work to try to prevent a recurrence, have found ourselves continually thwarted in our efforts by the very papers which raised such an outcry.

There remains a third course, which is, as I hold, the only possible and reasonable one; this is, to make a serious effort to improve our methods and to win upon our merits. To do this, money and organisation are needed in this as in every other country. £100,000 was stated to be the amount required for complete preparation, but this was admittedly an outside figure, which would enable things to be done on a broad, national basis. With £50,000 half the result could be obtained and a good team put in the field. Even with £25,000 a little could be done. Below that figure adequate preparation is absolutely impossible, a fact which is so appreciated by the Committee that they propose to dissolve unless they are shortly assured that the public will support them to that extent.

People ask: "What is the money for?" The moment you come down to practical details, you appreciate the need for money. The final and essential charge is, of course, the expenses of the team at Berlin. Some £12,000 or £15,000 is needed for that. There is no central training quarters in London. This must be found or created, and the best possible trainers stationed there. Efforts must be made to bring on talent. In the case of the Public Schools good trainers must be sent round to give instruction. Our lads are systematically taught in cricket or football, but have, as a rule, not the least idea how to jump or run scientifically. By the time they reach the Universities they have developed bad habits which they can never shake off. Then there is the finding of talent among the general public. This can only be done by holding numerous local athletic meetings at which there shall be novices' prizes, and where Olympic events may be practised. Special encouragement, in the form of medals or badges, must be offered for all those who approach an Olympic standard. There is hardly a branch of sport in the country which has not approached the Committee, and shown how much its records could be improved by the expenditure of a little money.

The Fund has been attacked from two different sides in the Press, the two contentions being mutually contradictory and equally absurd. On the one hand it is said that the money will be used to encourage professionalism. As the money will be spent under the supervision of the Committee, by the same amateur bodies who at present manage the various branches of sport, and who are responsible for the amateur status of their representatives, I see no cause at all to fear that we will change our traditions in this matter. On the other hand, some of the more democratic papers have attacked the Fund on the ground that it is a snobbish endowment of the richer sportsman. Nothing could be more wrong-headed or perverse than this, for one of the primary objects of the Fund is to put within the reach of the poor amateur those means for athletic training and development which have always been open to the University man.

Such is the situation. It has been stated again and again. The public seem apathetic on the question. Three years hence I believe that they will take a very different view and mourn for the time which we are now wasting. Meanwhile, unless prompt and generous help comes to us, the Committee will have dissolved, and the organisation, which has been laboriously built up during the last year, will have gone to pieces. The next few weeks will decide the matter.

ARTHUR CONAN DOYLE

Crowborough, November 27th, 1913

Divorce Law Reform

Sir, – I thought that I had made it sufficiently plain in my previous answer to Lord Hugh Cecil that it was the general recommendation of the Majority Report of the recent Commission upon the Divorce Laws which I supported. Lord Hugh talks as if some wild, strange thing were proposed, subversive of all the traditions of Christianity. Who would imagine, to read his article, that the changes suggested are already in force in varying degrees in every Protestant country in Europe! I can assure him that nothing revolutionary is involved in our discussion – nothing which has not been tested and approved by communities which are quite as religious and as moral as ourselves.

Lord Hugh blames me for not stating a number of things which it would take a good-sized volume to state – to propose a substitute for the theological foundations of the Christian Church, to elaborate a new moral system, and so forth. I may have my own views upon such matters, but it would be a mere personal intrusion to express them upon such an occasion. I will content myself by saying that if any so-called moral law compels the continued union of a confirmed lunatic with a sane person, or of a helpless woman with a cruel and brutal man, then it becomes an accursed thing though you bolster it with a thousand texts. A sound morality must rest not upon the varying quick-sands of theology, but upon the solid welfare of humanity.

Lord Hugh presses me as to what I would define as chastity and what I would not – what is marriage and what is fornication. I can only answer by taking an illustrative example. A union blessed by the Church, but unaccompanied by love, worldly, heartless, and interested in its essential nature, appears to me as fornication. A union, be it with a deceased wife's sister or with one who has been divorced, or any other in which the Church's ruling differs from that of the British law, is a true marriage so long as it is blessed by an unselfish love. I am as opposed to licence as Lord Hugh can be, but I am also opposed to the continuation of a vast amount of misery, which both commonsense and the experience of other countries have shown to be unnecessary.

What Lord Hugh means when he says that our law of marriage does not coerce anyone I cannot imagine. It seems to me to be on a par with the old dictum of the Church, which delivered a heretic into the civil power with the injunction that there should be no bloodshed, well knowing that he would be burned alive. The whole system rests ultimately upon coercion. Suppose that a man who has been deserted by his wife goes through the form of marriage with a second woman. Would not a policeman appear with a warrant for bigamy, and would not that warrant have the support of the whole forces of the Crown? How can it be said, then, that there is no coercion in our marriage laws?

Lord Hugh in the final passage of his article says: "I think Sir Arthur Conan Doyle will find that the vast majority of the English people are indisposed to depart from the Christian standard." It is one of the curiosities of the theological mind that it can never help begging the question at issue. He says it is the Christian standard. But every Protestant nation in Europe denies this, and has already departed from it in its legislation. A German or Swiss divine would by no means assent to the proposition that such amendments of the law as are recommended by the Majority of the Divorce Commission represent an apostasy from Christianity. Even in Lord Hugh's own Church there is a party which would disagree. In the independent Christian Churches he would find this disagreement widespread, if not unanimous. It is therefore a begging of the question (arguing it merely from the Christian point of view) to say that rigidity in our marriage laws is part of some unalterable standard. As to the views of the vast majority of the English people, I have no doubt myself that they will be on the side of reform, but that can only be shown when an actual Bill is laid before Parliament.

I seem to have done Lord Hugh's argument some injustice when I inferred that he was of the school which opposed the use of chloroform when a text appeared to condemn it. Even now it seems to me to be a fair parallel if we substitute mental for physical pain. But suppose that we grant that the married person having made a contract which is violated by the other partner to it still feels himself or herself to be spiritually bound to observe it at any cost of agony to themselves, what about the children? The wail of the helpless child, who is brought up in an atmosphere of drunkenness, cruelty, and brutality, which the law enforces as its unchangeable environment, is the most powerful voice which can be raised against our present dispensation. Is this vicarious suffering part also of the inviolate Christian standard? Or will healthy commonsense and equity override so senseless a superstition and insist that the crying needs of living people shall take precedence over ancient precepts, many of which we have already recognised as bearing no relevancy to the conditions of modern life.

Yours &c.,

Crowborough, Sussex, Dec. 8   ARTHUR CONAN DOYLE

P.S. – I find that I owe the eminent Scottish Judge, Lord Guthrie, an apology for having confused his biography in my previous article with that of his famous father.

THE TIMES   26 December 1913

The Channel Tunnel

SIR, – The following dialogue which I had recently with a distinguished naval officer of the younger school may seem to bear upon this subject:

Q.–What would be the result if a flotilla of submarines got among a fleet of transports carrying troops?

A.–They would be helpless. They would be destroyed.

Q.–Could submarines be prevented from coming down the North Sea in war time?

A.–I don't see how they could.

Q.–Would a cordon across the Straits of Dover protect transports to the south of that cordon?

A.–Submarines could easily dive under any cordon.

In a word it would be impossible under present conditions to send any expeditionary force abroad without grave risk of appalling disaster. Is this not a sound military argument for a tunnel?

Yours faithfully,
ARTHUR CONAN DOYLE

Windlesham, Crowborough, Sussex, Dec. 23

1914–1918

The Importation of Plumage Prohibition Bill

SIR, – We, the undersigned, have considered the Importation of Plumage Prohibition Bill. We are most heartily in accord with this measure, as we believe that it is the duty of this country to put an end to the traffic in the skins and plumes of wild birds. The evidence is abundantly clear that many rare and beautiful species are being ruthlessly exterminated, and that the trade creates a demand for the plumes of certain birds which these birds only acquire in the breeding season, thus encouraging the horrible and cruel practice of killing parent birds when the young are in the nest. The argument that the trade in prohibited feathers will not be diminished, but simply diverted to the Continent, is, in our opinion, absolutely a false one; on the contrary, we believe that the passage of this Bill will greatly strengthen the hands of the various societies and individuals who are endeavouring to promote prohibition upon the Continent. The Conference which the British Foreign Office are calling in London to consider the question of international action and prohibition has been accepted by nearly all the countries invited to attend, and though the list is not, we understand, complete, the immense majority of all countries, European and American, appears to be in accord with the proposals of the Plumage Bill. In particular, we do not believe that the passage of the Bill will bring about any shortage of work among those employed in the trade. A great part of the work done in connexion with this fancy plumage is performed on the Continent, and the bulk of feather-workers employed in England work, not upon wild bird plumage, but upon ostrich feathers, whose entry will be permitted, and even stimulated, by the provisions of this Bill. Also, in the natural course of things, substitutes and imitations will be found, which will divert to British labour much work that is now done in Paris and Vienna.

We are, Sir, &c.,

RUTLAND.
LEICESTER.
GALWAY.
LILFORD.
E. LYTTELTON.
J.E.C. WELLDON.
HERBERT MAXWELL.
GODFREY BARING.

H.H. JOHNSTON
E.H. SHACKLETON.
ARTHUR CONAN DOYLE.
OWEN SEAMAN.
W.R. OGILVIE-GRANT.
J. ST. LOE STRACHEY.
E.B. WAGGETT.
H. HESKETH-PRICHARD.

"Prophecy – and Finance"

SIR, – I notice that Mr. Charles Duguid regards my prophecy as to the immediate future of the Kent coal enterprise to be unduly optimistic. Only the future can show.

But I would remind him that the pessimistic prophecies of the past – to some of which he has appeared to lend his own high authority – have invariably been falsified. There was no coal in Kent. Coal in Kent could not be won. If coal in Kent were won it would be of poor quality and would find no market – each of these in turn has been disproved. Up to now, at any rate, my own more cheerful outlook has proved to be justified.

Details of finance I must leave to those who are more competent than myself, remarking only that I have seen the property and what has been done upon it, and that it seems to me that it is very extraordinary value for the money expended.

I would repeat, however, what I said in my original article, that the matter is far too great to be influenced by personal prejudices or by narrow questions of detail. If such letters as that of Mr. Charles Duguid, typical as it is of a series which has appeared in various papers, has any effect at all, it would be to seal the financial market, to wreck the present mines, and to ruin the pioneers of a great industry.

Fortunately, this cannot occur, as a stage has been reached when the property has a definite selling value, but experience has shown that these sales can be effected most readily to foreign syndicates, who approach the matter without prejudice. It is this selling of what should be a national birthright to which I called attention in my original article, and I fear that such letters as that of Mr. Charles Duguid can only tend to this deplorable end.

Yours faithfully,
ARTHUR CONAN DOYLE

March 3

Kent Coal

SIR, – I had no intention, when I wrote to you first upon what I regard as an important national matter, of being drawn into a correspondence upon details. When, however, I have lists of questions addressed to me in your columns I have no choice but to answer them or to let them seem to go by default.

In answer, then, to the three queries of your anonymous Canterbury correspondent, I would say:–

1. That it is the present management who negotiate sales to foreigners. Who else could it be?

2. That so far as I understand Mr. Arthur Burr controls the management.

3. That this group of companies has been in existence between six and seven years, so that your correspondent in alluding to fourteen years is confusing them with other companies under different control and with a different objective. The faith of the shareholders in the enterprise has been, and continues to be, so firm that all the heavy, financial calls needful to buy and develop so great an estate have been found from their own pockets, without any appeal to the general public. Much money has, as your correspondent says, been sunk, but since nearly all the shares are at the present moment at a substantial premium none can be said to be lost.

My point still remains untouched: that if unsympathetic comment by men who have never even troubled to go sixty miles to look at the results achieved is allowed to cripple this enterprise, neither Mr. Burr nor any other manager has any choice but to sell it in sections. Experience has shown that these sections are readily bought by foreigners, and thus the British public is frightened out of what I regard as a very valuable heritage.

Let me say, in conclusion, that I know Mr. Arthur Burr very slightly, and that I have only had one conversation with him in my life. My attention was first drawn to him by the extreme virulence of the attacks upon him in the Press. My own experience for what it is worth, is that he has managed this great concern with marked wisdom and foresight in the face of very determined opposition, which has never, save in one instance, come from shareholders, but always from outside critics. I believe that the future will speedily justify both him and those who have supported him.

Yours faithfully,
Arthur Conan Doyle

March 5

THE TIMES   25 March 1914

Nationalists and Exclusion

Sir, – As one who has been converted to Home Rule by Imperial considerations I have never been able to understand why

Southern Home Rulers should refuse to the North the very justice which they have so long demanded for themselves. I believe that the Nationalists would act with great wisdom if they were cordially and generously to agree to the indefinite exclusion of the six more or less Protestant countries. Then they should turn all their energies to making the four-fifths of Ireland which would remain in their hands as loyal to the King and the Empire as all other parts of the British Dominions. When this had been done, and when the Union Jack meant the same north and south of the Boyne, then there would be a beginning of winning the affection and confidence of the missing counties. At present it seems to me that they are trying to reach the end before they have made a beginning.

Yours faithfully,
ARTHUR CONAN DOYLE

Windlesham, Crowborough

THE MORNING POST   4 April 1914

Lord Hugh Cecil and Divorce Law Reform

SIR, – You kindly opened your columns to a debate between Lord Hugh Cecil and myself upon this subject. It is worth noting the sequel. The question was to have come before the House upon Wednesday, but Lord Hugh, despairing apparently of argument, managed to burke the discussion by some Parliamentary trick, which claimed preference for a bogus Bill. This is no doubt a clever device, but it is worth considering what price the Unionist Party pays for Lord Hugh's ingenuity, when one remembers how many voters there are to whom this is a very vital matter, who will bitterly resent its being shelved in so shabby a manner.

Yours, &c.,
ARTHUR CONAN DOYLE

Windlesham, Crowborough, Sussex, April 3

LE TEMPS*   1 May 1914

La "Force Mystérieuse"

SIR, The *Temps* has on two occasions, in its literary chronicle and in an article by M. Paul Souday, called attention to the strange imputations made against Sir Arthur Conan Doyle, in connection with his latest book, *The Poison Belt*, by M.J.H. Rosny, senior, at the beginning of the novel *The Mysterious Force*. While

200

acknowledging the impartiality with which, from the critical point of view, M. Paul Souday has thrown light on certain matters, I venture, as the literary agent of Sir Arthur Conan Doyle, to appeal to your courtesy and beg you to be so good as to reproduce the following letter which Sir Arthur Conan Doyle, as soon as he was informed of the facts, addressed to the French translator of his latest works:

'DEAR MR. LABAT, – I have other things to do in this life than to keep watch on the works of M. Rosny, in order to endeavour to copy them. The first chapters of *The Poison Belt* were written almost a year before the book was finished, before I dispatched the manuscript, and before it began to appear in the *Strand Magazine*. M. Rosny relies on the fact that he had already published at this time two parts of his book; but common sense ought to tell him that even if I had wished to imitate him, it would have been impossible not only to write my story, but also to have the illustrations ready for a similar production, in an interval of two months. My agent, Mr. Watt, and the editors of the *Strand* can testify that they had my manuscript in hand more than two months before its publication. It only remains then for M. Rosny to express his regret for an injurious insinuation which I should not have thought worthy of consideration if it had not been calculated to cause you some uneasiness.

'Believe me, yours sincerely,
'ARTHUR CONAN DOYLE.'

Doyle The Bookman, *June, 1914*

Although Sir Arthur's word needs no confirmation from me or from the proprietors of the *Strand Magazine*, I may add that it is clear, from the verification which I have made of the dates, that the manuscript of the first part of *The Poison Belt* was in my hands about six months before this novel began to appear in the *Strand*.

Thanking you in anticipation,
I am, etc.,

April 28th 1914   A.P. Watt

* Translation from the *Bookman* of June 1914. The original letter from Conan Doyle was as follows:

'CHER MONSIEUR LABAT,
'J'ai autre chose à faire en ce monde que de guetter les œuvres de M. Rosny pour tâcher de les copier. Les premiers chapitres de *The Poison Belt* étaient écrits près d'un an avant que le livre fût terminé, que j'en eusse remis le manuscrit, et qu'il commençat à paraître dans le *Strand Magazine*. M. Rosny se prévaut de ce que lui-même

avait déjà publié à ce moment deux parties de son livre; mais le sens commun devrait lui dire que même si j'avais voulu l'imiter il m'aurait été impossible non seulement d'écrire le mien, mais encore d'avoir eu les illustrations prêtes, pour une publication similaire, à deux mois d'intervalle. Mon agent, M. Watt, et les éditeurs du *Strand* peuvent témoigner qu'ils avaient mon manuscrit en main plus de deux mois avant sa publication. Il ne reste donc plus à M. Rosny qu'à exprimer son regret d'une insinuation injurieuse que je n'aurais pas daigné relever si cela n'avait été de nature à jeter quelque trouble dans votre esprit.

'Croyez-moi sincèrement votre
'ARTHUR CONAN DOYLE'

April 28th 1914

THE TIMES   2 May 1914

"The Poison Belt"

SIR, – Your Paris Correspondent is not clear upon this matter and his paragraph is open to misconstruction. Only two communications passed. The first was from M. Rosny, who, in the preface of a new edition of *La Force Mystérieuse*, suggested that I had received some assistance from his book in writing *The Poison Belt*. The second was a letter from me to my translator M. Labat, published by him in *Le Temps* showing with the corroboration of Mr. Watt, my agent, that my manuscript had been delivered before any of M. Rosny's story had appeared.

Yours faithfully,
ARTHUR CONAN DOYLE

Windlesham, Crowborough, Sussex

THE TIMES   16 July 1914

Irish Compromise
Catholic Counties in Ulster

SIR, – The sands are running low, and every one expresses dismay at the Irish situation, while no one, so far as I can see, builds a bridge which can bring the two parties together. Is it really impossible to suggest a compromise which could be a basis for peace?

The essence of a compromise is that neither party in a dispute should get its full claim. At present the full claim of Ireland is for an unbroken Ireland and of Ulster for an unbroken Ulster. A compromise, therefore, must give Ireland something less than Ireland and Ulster something less than Ulster.

The question, then, resolves itself into how much should be taken from Ulster. It seems to me that the subtraction of the two predominantly Catholic and Celtic counties of Cavan and Monaghan would in any case be greatly to Ulster's advantage. Without such an excision the province would be nearly equally divided between Catholics and Protestants, with the result that political life would be one continual crisis, in which every parochial election would assume the utmost importance as affecting the balance of power. There would be every material for civil strife inside the province itself, which would communicate itself to the rest of the island. It is surely better that Ulster should be compact and comparatively homogeneous than that it should be large and fatally divided within its own borders.

In the giving up of these two counties to Ireland there would appear to be a compromise which might go some way to satisfy reasonable Irish opinion without being absolutely unacceptable to the more moderate men of Ulster. Ulster would still retain two counties, Tyrone and Fermanagh, in which the Catholics are somewhat in a majority, and one, Donegal, which is predominantly Catholic. Therefore, by consenting to such an arrangement the Irish leaders would show generosity, while by refusing it Ulster would appear to be unreasonable and weaken her case before the general public.

Of course such an arrangement should not be hampered by any time-limits. At the same time, every Irishman would hope that the day would speedily come when the tolerance and loyalty of Ireland would be so unquestionable that Ulster's present fears would pass for ever and the island be reunited by the voluntary adhesion of the north-eastern counties.

The only strong objection which I can see to such an arrangement is the financial one. But that can surely be overcome. If Ulster is paying taxes into an Imperial instead of a national fund, then the British Treasury can afford to be more generous with Celtic Ireland. In any case, nothing can be more extravagant than civil war.

Yours faithfully,
ARTHUR CONAN DOYLE

Windlesham, Crowborough, Sussex, July 14

P.S. – Donegal is of course Celtic and Catholic, but its geographical position makes it an integral part of Ulster.

Irish Compromise
Concession as the Alternative
to Force

SIR, – I ventured to suggest in your columns a possible division of Ireland (we would hope a temporary one) which might satisfy moderate and reasonable men of both parties. In such a division I proposed that the counties of Cavan and Monaghan should be taken from Ulster as being proponderantly Catholic and therefore a source of weakness rather than of strength to Ulster. I argued, however, that the isolated position of Donegal made it almost impossible to unite it to Ireland. To this Mr. Hugh Law and Mr. Swift MacNeill take exception. I would remind them, however, first, that if Nationalist Donegal remains with Ulster large numbers of Unionists in Dublin and other parts remain with Ireland; secondly, that in case of a movement within Ulster to reunite her to Ireland it would be much to the advantage of Ireland to have at least one predominantly Catholic county included in Ulster.

The situation is one which must end either in concessions or in violence. The latter can bring nothing but misery and loss to Ireland, and would in all probability leave the question still unsolved. If Ulster be staked off in peace she may some day pull the stakes up of her own free will. But if she has to fight for a separate existence she will be for ever lost to Ireland. The highest service one can do Ireland is to counsel moderation and reasonable concession.

Yours faithfully,
ARTHUR CONAN DOYLE

Windlesham, Crowborough, Sussex

The Oscar Slater Case

SIR, – You were good enough to open your columns to a correspondence upon the subject of the conviction of Oscar Slater, which was effected by a majority of three in a jury of fifteen, under circumstances which caused so high an authority as Sir Herbert Stephen to state in the Press that in his opinion there was hardly a *prima facie* case against the prisoner. The authorities have lately had a belated inquiry into the matter, the man having already served five years. This inquiry was held *in camera* before a single local sheriff, with no oath administered to witnesses. It savoured rather of Russian than of Scottish jurisprudence. The result of this inquiry was a decision that nothing should be done, and the evidence given at it is now published in a White Parliamentary Paper.

I think that no one who has mastered the facts can read this paper without amazement, for it appears to completely cut away point after point which told against Slater at the trial. How the verdict could be that there was no fresh cause for reversing the conviction is incomprehensible. The whole case will, in my opinion, remain immortal in the classics of crime as the supreme example of official incompetence and obstinacy.

The chief witness for Slater (who was in no way represented at the inquiry) was Lieutenant Trench, a well known Glasgow detective. This gentleman could have nothing to gain by testifying for the friendless and penniless prisoner, while, as the result shows, he had everything to lose, since already steps have been taken to punish him for his independence by expelling him from the force. Trench's statement was that *at the time* Lambie, the chief witness against Slater, had twice named another person as the murderer. This was vigorously denied – not, be it remembered, on oath – by several witnesses, but was corroborated to the extent that Cameron, a brother detective, deposed that Trench had recounted the facts to him on or about the day that they were alleged to have occurred. As this cut into the evidence of a chief witness for identity, and, to put it at the lowest, cast a doubt upon it, one would think that this alone would justify the reversal of a sentence which was already so open to criticism.

But this point involves a conflict of evidence. There are two other points which involve no such conflict and are of vital importance.

The original police theory represented Slater as stealing a jewel after the murder and flying. The jewel pawned was shown to be his own. There remained the flight. The Lord Advocate made a great point in his speech of this flight – how Slater, on leaving Glasgow, had taken all pains to cover up his tracks. Yet all the time the Glasgow police held the following telegram from the Chief Detective of Liverpool:– "Only two people came off the Glasgow train. . . . They engaged a bedroom in the North-Western Hotel. The man gave the name of Oscar Slater, Glasgow. . . . The chambermaid had a conversation with the woman, who told her that they were about to sail by the s.s. *Lusitania* for America."

There was, therefore, no concealment of tracks. But the Lord Advocate could not have known this when he laid so much stress upon the point in his speech. "When he arrives in Liverpool," said he, "he does not go to the Cunard office and say, 'I am Oscar

Slater' . . ." There is clear evidence that this is exactly what he *did* do, only it was at the hotel, not the Cunard office. The Lord Advocate could not have known that such a telegram was lying all the time in the archives of the Glasgow police. But who is responsible for the fact that he was so ill instructed? Who withheld this telegram from the Lord Advocate? Is there to be no inquiry on so important a point as that? And is the proof of such a misstatement, an allegation of flight when there was obviously no flight, to have no modifying effect upon the verdict?

It is, of course, true that Slater aboard the ship took the name of Otto Sando. He wished to make a fresh start in America under that name, even as he had taken the name of Anderson when he came to Glasgow. But the clear proof that the change of name was for America, and not to throw off any pursuit from Glasgow, lies in the fact that he signed the Liverpool hotel register with his true name and address, at the moment when, according to the police theories, he should have been most carefully concealing his identity. Could you conceive a murderer flying red-handed with the knowledge that there was pursuit behind him and announcing at the first hotel his name and whence he came?

There are many other points here which are destructive of the case of the Crown, but I will only cite one more. The Lord Advocate built up an elaborate schedule of the movements of the murderer after the crime, which would involve his being "taken by a train to some remote part of the city and then strolling back to his house." By this scheme Slater would reach his rooms about or after 9.30 – the murder was about 7 p.m. Now there comes forward a certain MacBrayne, who knew Slater well by sight, as he supplied him with goods, though he had no personal friendship with him. MacBrayne deposes that on the night of the murder he saw Slater at 8.15 o'clock near his own house. If this time be so, the Lord Advocate's scheme of the movements of the murderer falls to pieces exactly as his theory of the secret flight to Liverpool has fallen to pieces.

And yet the officials say there is no case for a reconsideration of the sentence – and, so far as I can see, the public Press acquiesces in the judgment. Is it possible that they have read the White Paper? If they have, and are conversant with the points of the original trial, they surely cannot leave the matter where it is. Nothing but a fresh trial, with no limitations of secrecy, and all witnesses under oath, can meet the case. Until such a trial is held no man's conscience can be easy upon the subject. I trust, Sir, that you will lend your powerful influence to this end.

I am, Sir, &c.,
ARTHUR CONAN DOYLE

P.S. – When I was in New York last month I received a note from the American solicitor who defended Slater in the extradition proceedings. He assured me that he had never had a doubt as to Slater's complete innocence.

THE FREEMAN'S JOURNAL, DUBLIN

3 August 1914

On Ireland and the Empire

SIR, – The chief point which has divided Protestant Ulster from the rest of Ireland, and which has made many non-Protestant Irishmen lukewarm on the subject of Home Rule, is their contention that Nationalists have never been loyal to the Empire. The Empire is in no sense an English thing. Scotch and Irish have combined in the building of it, and have an equal pride and interest in its immense future. There is no possible reason why a man should not be a loyal Irishman and a loyal Imperialist also. Should this view be generally and heartily accepted in the South and West of Ireland the most serious difficulties which stand in the way of complete Home Rule would vanish in an instant.

If Ireland were alone in the Atlantic she would be at the absolute mercy of any European Power which chose to blockade her. No bravery upon the part of Irishmen could prevent her from being the victim of the Fleet of any one of the Great Powers. Her larger neighbour stands between her and such a disaster, and at her back she has the whole force of the Empire to preserve her from such a menace. Therefore it is right and proper that she should herself be a loyal member of this community apart from any changes which she may reasonably desire in her own methods of government.

There is no doubt that a whole-hearted declaration of loyalty to the common ideal would at the present moment do much to allay the natural fears of Ulster and to strengthen the position of Ireland. Such a chance is unlikely ever to recur. I pray that the Irish leaders may understand its significance, and find themselves in a position to take advantage of it.

Yours faithfully,
ARTHUR CONAN DOYLE

Windlesham, Crowborough, Sussex, August 1st, 1914

Our Latent Forces

SIR, – The future is dark and we do not know that we will not need our last ounce of strength before we are through. We can afford to neglect nothing.

Will you allow me to point out how a reserve force can be formed which will be numerically large and which if it does nothing else can relieve more mobile and trained troops for the fighting line? In a word, the suggestion is to form civilian companies of the National Reserve. There are tens and hundreds of thousands of men in this country from 35 to 55 who are often harder and fitter than their juniors, but for whom no place is found in our scheme of defence. Many of them are good shots, they are longing to help in any possible way, and they would fall into line instantly if they could only see how to do it. They would speedily become capable of guarding railways or buildings, helping to garrison fortresses or performing many other military duties.

If I may quote the example of this little town, we held our first meeting to discuss this on Tuesday, by Wednesday night we had enrolled 120 men, and to-day we start drill and practice at the butts. Many of the men are fine shots and all are exceedingly anxious to be serviceable. It is not possible for them to take on long engagements or to live out in permanent camps, but they could do much useful work and in case of a raid they would do anything. They would form our "Landsturm." But at present there is no organisation into which such men can be fitted. Local effort would rapidly form the various companies, but some method of common action has to be devised.

The obvious danger of such organisation is lest it should divert men from the Territorials or any other more useful branch of the Service. But to recognise the danger is to avoid it. The Reserve company would not go the length of refusing to enlist young men who cannot or will not become Territorials, but it has the constant end before it of encouraging them to go further and preparing them so that if they do join the more active Services they are already partly instructed. I am convinced that if they are properly run these civilian National Reserve companies would be not only of value in themselves but would be a stepping-stone for the younger men to take them into the fighting line.

The official organisations have so much upon them for the moment that the work can only be done by independent local effort. But when the men are there, as in the case of the existing National Reserve, they will command attention and find some means of arming themselves. We have our own record of organisation, and I should be happy to send copies of our method to anyone who may desire to form other centres.

Yours faithfully,
ARTHUR CONAN DOYLE

Windlesham, Crowborough, Sussex, Aug. 6

THE DAILY MAIL   13 August 1914

Civilian National Reserve

SIR, – A movement is on foot by which men who can find no other way of serving their country shall form themselves into local bodies which shall drill and learn to shoot, organising themselves, and forming a reserve without worrying the authorities in any way.

In this small town we have raised 200 such men, who are hard at work drilling and at the butts. We have had 250 applications from other centres for details as to our method of organisation.

I should be happy to send these to anyone who desires it. No one can tell the course of this war nor predict how far in a few months' time the existence of some hundreds of thousands of additional men who have some elementary military training may affect the situation.

ARTHUR CONAN DOYLE

Windlesham, Crowborough, Sussex

THE TIMES   8 September 1914

Submarine Mines

SIR, – Is it really beyond the capacity of our marine architects to devise some sort of steel trident or fork which could be projected into the water in front of the bows of a vessel to explode a contact mine before the prow actually touched it? I understand that a surprisingly small interval of water forms an effective buffer against the shock.

Yours faithfully,
ARTHUR CONAN DOYLE

Windlesham, Crowborough, Sussex, Sept. 6

Lifebelts in Men-of-War

SIR, – Boats are not carried in men-of-war going into action for fear of fire. The result is that in case of disaster the crew has no means of escape. It is sad to read of them throwing floating objects over in the hope of keeping up till they are rescued. Is it really impossible to devise something – if it were only an inflatable rubber belt which they could always wear – that they may have a chance in the water? Now that their consorts are forbidden to stand by, the question becomes an even more pressing one.

ARTHUR CONAN DOYLE

Windlesham, Crowborough, Sussex

THE EVENING STANDARD AND ST. JAMES'S GAZETTE   7 October 1914

Lifebelts for the Navy

SIR, – Your naval correspondent, Commander Jane, took me to task in your columns recently for so unreasonable a demand as that our sailors should be provided with some means of escape from certain death when their ships founder.

I had suggested an inflatable rubber belt. He will be interested to hear that an inflatable rubber collar has actually been adopted, and is, as I understand, now being served out to every sailor.

ARTHUR CONAN DOYLE

Windlesham, Crowborough

THE EASTBOURNE GAZETTE   14 October 1914

Recruiting in Eastbourne

SIR, – Each fresh event, such as the fall of Antwerp, which favours the enemy, means a prolongation of the war, and increases the need that we should be making ample preparations for the future. This means men – and always more men. Has Sussex done her duty in this respect? The verdict of those familiar with the recruiting figures is that the villages have done splendidly and the coast towns very moderately indeed. Can nothing be done to wake up Hastings, Eastbourne, and Brighton? Their contingents as compared to their population are at present far too small. I am not hopeful about public meetings. Too many ladies and too few young men are among the audience. But I think a council of employers and leading citizens will find some methods of improving recruiting. In the last resort it is a matter of public pressure, and it is high time that the young man who could go and will not should feel a cold draught wherever he turns. No day should pass which did not remind him that he was a shirker. This healthy public sentiment fearlessly expressed will do more than public meetings. There may be some cases of injustice, but the times are hard and this must be disregarded.

Yours faithfully,
ARTHUR CONAN DOYLE

22, Grand Parade, Eastbourne

THE DAILY MAIL   29 October 1914

"Danger!"

SIR, – Your anonymous correspondent "H.B." would have been wise to make sure of his facts. The story to which he alludes, "Danger", was written in the spring, published in July, *Strand Magazine*, and consisted of a warning of the growing power of the submarine with its special danger to Great Britain. Events have shown how far such a warning was justified.

ARTHUR CONAN DOYLE

Windlesham, Crowborough

THE TIMES   4 November 1914

Civilian Volunteer Reserves

SIR, – At the beginning of the war various bodies were formed, but on receiving an intimation from the War Office that they were not desired, they remained in a state of suspended animation. Drill and rifle practice are now being resumed. I should be thankful if you would permit me to say that any of those corps which were formed in consequence of my original letters upon the subject should communicate with the secretary of the Central Association of Volunteer Training Corps, Judges' Quadrangle, the Law Courts, W.C. This body has Lord Desborough for chairman and Sir O'Moore Creagh, V.C., as military adviser, with a strong representative committee. By affiliating with this all local corps will be able to form part of one great homogeneous body which should easily number half a million men. Every precaution is taken that the movement should only affect those for whom more active service is an absolute impossibility.

Yours faithfully,
ARTHUR CONAN DOYLE

Windlesham, Crowborough, Sussex

THE TIMES   18 November 1914

Recruiting and Publicity

SIR, – Speaking as one who has had some experience of platform work in connexion with recruiting, I should say that the publication of the details of the defeat of the Prussian Guards with the names of the regiments engaged would be worth a fresh service battalion to each of them. What is the non-conductor which has intervened between the military authorities who call for recruits and the Press Bureau who deprive us of the means of getting them?

Yours faithfully,
ARTHUR CONAN DOYLE

Windlesham, Crowborough, Sussex, Nov. 16

THE CROWBOROUGH
WEEKLY   28 November 1914

Volunteer Training Corps

SIR, – A Volunteer Corps raised from men of non-military age is now enrolled in Crowborough and will soon number 50 men.

What is desired now is that Buxted, Maresfield, Jarvis Brook, Rotherfield and other villages should enrol similar corps, which could all assemble together for route marches or exercises.

The movement is now approved by the War Office, and it is every man's obvious duty to learn his drill and to practise shooting at the nearest miniature range.

If the villages have no drill instructors the Crowborough Corps could, no doubt, set them on the right lines.

Yours &c.,
ARTHUR CONAN DOYLE

Crowborough, 24th November

Sir Roger Casement

SIR, – I am sure that you are wise to use no stronger term than "infatuation" for Sir Roger Casement's journey to Berlin. He was a man of fine character, and that he should in the full possession of his senses act as a traitor to the country which had employed and honoured him is inconceivable to anyone who knew him. He had, it is true a strong prepossession in favour of Germany before the war, but this was due to his belief that she was destined to challenge the Monroe doctrine, which Casement bitterly resented as being the ultimate cause of all that Putumayo barbarism which he had officially to investigate. I may say that I disagreed with him upon this subject, but in all our discussions I have never heard him say a word which was disloyal to Great Britain. He was a sick man, however, worn by tropical hardships, and he complained often of pains in his head. Last May I had letters from him from Ireland which seemed to me so wild that I expressed fears at the time as to the state of his nerves. I have no doubt that he is not in a normal state of mind, and that this unhappy escapade at Berlin is only an evidence of it. On the face of it, would any sane man accept an assurance about Ireland which had obviously been already broken about Belgium?

ARTHUR CONAN DOYLE

Windlesham, Crowborough, Sussex

Volunteer Training Corps

SIR, – The War Office has sanctioned the existence of those volunteer corps which are affiliated to the Central Association. They have accompanied this concession by certain conditions which are not unreasonable. There is one, however, which I earnestly hope that they will modify, as it greatly impairs the value of the movement. By this clause any man of military age who joins a volunteer corps promises in writing to enlist in the Army if called upon to do so. Under the present need for recruits this would make it appear the same thing to a man whether he enlisted in the home force or in the Army, since the first could compulsorily be changed into the second. The result is that such men now serve in neither. There are very many men of military age who are married and in business. Most of them could not possibly join the Regular Army, but would be glad to serve in the home defence force. At present it looks as if a trap were set for them, and so the country loses their services altogether.

On the other hand, I think that an order should be made by which every man of the Volunteer Training Corps comes under military compulsion in case of actual or prospective invasion.

Yours faithfully,
ARTHUR CONAN DOYLE

Windlesham, Crowborough, Sussex, Dec. 1

THE DAILY
CHRONICLE   22 January 1915

Saving Our Seamen

SIR, – No one can read Mr. Wells' article upon "Foresight in War" without feeling that there is indeed a lack of intellectual initiative in our activities.

As an illustration, I should like to quote a question to which I have devoted some attention and correspondence – that of providing life-saving apparatus for our seamen. In the merchant service there must be boat provision for every passenger. Is it not simple common sense, therefore, that in a warship, which is so much more likely to sink, and where the men are so invaluable to the country, the same law should hold good?

I do not write in any censorious spirit, for we must all admit the splendid work that the Admiralty have done, and the enormous demands upon them, but the nation would like to be taken into its confidence in this matter, and to be convinced that everything that can be done is really being done.

At the beginning of the war there was absolutely no provision at all. Now we have got as far as a swimming collar, which is useless in a rough or ice-cold sea. We have seen a certain nameless ship with 800 men upon her decks, all of whom owed their safety to the mere chance of a liner with boats being in the neighbourhood. If that object lesson is not enough to make us deal radically with the subject, what will?

Since I first wrote upon the pressing need for life-saving appliances some months ago, I have been flooded with all sorts of letters from inventors, with different devices. There is no lack of ingenuity and brain power in the country if it be encouraged. Most of these were of the swimming bladder, inflatable waistcoat, or canvas raft varieties. Personally, I am convinced, considering the weather and temperature of the North Sea, that nothing can really meet the case but boats – collapsible, no doubt, but still boats. Let us face the difficulties and see how they may be overcome.

The objections are three – they take up too much room in action, they get destroyed in action, and they are inflammable in action.

We have to remember that our losses in this war have not been in action, but by torpedo and mine, so that none of these objections have any validity at all in nine cases out of ten. With a provision of boats every man of the *Hawke*, *Pathfinder*, *Cressy*, *Hogue*, *Aboukir* and other ships might have been saved, and none of these ships would have suffered in action through having them. It is probable also that the loss of the Formidable would have been much less severe had boats been available.

But let us see whether we cannot meet even the tenth case – the case of the lives which are lost when a ship goes down, as Cradock's squadron did, in action. Is it really impossible to find a method by which all three objections can be met and yet the end attained? In answer I would quote the plan of one of my correspondents, a Mr. Cameron Walker, which seems entirely feasible.

It is that each ship should have at least two large motor boats – also enough collapsible boats for the whole crew, which would be stacked where they would be least in the way. Then if torpedoed we should no longer see the terrible sight of men waiting helplessly for death. But if the ship goes into action, what then? The motor boats would be dropped with two or three men in each, they would tow the line of empty collapsibles, and they would watch the fortunes of their ship from a safe distance ready to come up if needed. Here in a moment we get rid of all the three difficulties which have been such bogies. The motor boats should each have a bow gun to protect their collapsibles against a submarine on the surface. Other craft they must avoid. There are plenty of motor boats to be commandeered at every watering-place and the matter could with good will and energy be speedily put through.

Pray excuse the length of this letter, but the subject is the most pressing one before the public. What would we care for naval losses if we knew that the men were safe? We can spare the ships. We can't spare the men. I earnestly hope that something will be done.

Arthur Conan Doyle

Windlesham, Crowborough, Sussex

Germany's "Policy of Murder"

Sir, – I have just read the very courteous and moderate letter of James O'Donnell Bennett which he has done me the honour to address to me through the press. I should be glad to say a few words of comment upon it.

The letter in question is a commentary upon an article of mine in the *Daily Chronicle*, entitled "A Policy of Murder." Some of my statements Mr. Bennett traverses, while others he leaves untouched, from which I may fairly conclude that he cannot shake them.

My first point was mine laying in open waters by the Germans, which was commenced on the very first day of the war by the *Königin Luise*, which was caught and sunk in the act. It was repeated later to the north of Ireland, and it is common knowledge that it was only a warning from a British warship which prevented the *Olympic* running into the mine field with all her passengers, American as well as British.

When a neutral loses his life by such practices, as so many Danes, Dutch, and Norwegians have done, what is it but murder?

A second is the bombarding by sea or by air of unfortified towns. It is known as well in Germany as it is here that Yarmouth, Whitby, and Scarborough are entirely open towns, while Hartlepool has one very feeble battery. Let us suppose that this battery justifies the enemy in firing, not at it, but into the crowded town, and killing or wounding some hundreds of civilians, including thirty-eight children, with only seven soldiers among the victims. Even if we pass this, what can we possibly say in extenuation of Scarborough, Whitby, and Yarmouth? The cowardly Zeppelin which attacked Yarmouth dropped bombs also upon little villages around it and killed five civilians. If this is not murder, what name shall we give it? It is not war, for it is contrary to the laws of it.

Mr. Bennett says the British themselves dropped bombs on Düsseldorf. Exactly! I would not wish a better illustration. Our aviators went to Düsseldorf as they went to Friedrichshafen, and in each case made straight for their strategic aim, the sheds of airships, which, it is admitted, they injured. It is not alleged that there was ever any promiscuous dropping of bombs. Had we adopted German tactics, our bombs would have been dropped in the crowded streets of Cologne and Frankfurt, which were equally accessible.

Mr. Bennett resents my accusation of constant lying applied to the German press. Is it not the German press which described Yarmouth, Scarborough, and Whitby as fortresses? What word save lying can apply to that? Is it not the German press at the present instant that is pretending that we lost a large cruiser and several smaller boats in the sea fight of last week, in which we sustained no losses at all? Lying is an ugly word, but I know no other for the statements which I continually read in the German press.

We now come to the centre of the matter – the French and Belgian atrocities. Mr. Bennett endeavours to mitigate these by stating – and I have no doubt the statement is true – that there are many kindhearted men among the Germans, and that occasionally they treat the invaded people kindly and form friendships with them. I do not believe the German people are cruel, but I am convinced that the Prussian military system is and always has been cruel, and that they have now moulded all the rest of Germany to their own image.

Mr. Bennett, though very incredulous of German atrocities, seems to give complete credence to tales of civilian Belgians firing upon troops. It was originally asserted that they gouged out the eyes of the German wounded, but the search for evidence ended in the declaration from the head doctor at Aix-la-Chapelle that no such case had ever been seen. I believe the Belgian Government made every effort to get arms away from the civil population, and though I will not go so far as to say with some apologists that there never was a single shot fired by a franc-tireur, I think there is a mass of evidence to show that such attacks were few and rare. On the other hand, it is common knowledge that great numbers of Belgian villages have been destroyed, that very many men, women, and children have been murdered, and that the utmost licence has been practised by the soldiery.

Mr. Bennett must be aware that names, dates, and places are given with infinite exactness by the report of the Belgian Commission, while the fact that they exonerate the Germans at some places must make the evidence more convincing in others. The fact that the invaders saved the Town Hall at Louvain was surely very small consolation to the inhabitants when, even by Mr. Bennett's estimate, a seventh of their town had been given to the flames. These outrages would be bad enough anywhere, but are surely most dreadful when one reflects that Germany was under a solemn treaty promise to protect the country which she was so maltreating.

Mr. Bennett seems to think the Germans acted better in France than in Belgium. I have the report of the French Commission before me as I write. It is the same monotonous recital of outrages as the Belgian, with every detail given in support. From Senlis to Dinant is a long chain of barbarous deeds. I learn that a similar list of crimes has been compiled by Russian authorities in Poland. Can Mr. Bennett believe that all these official documents are "lies, lies, lies"? Or is it not more probable that the view held by all the Allies is correct, and that it is part of the Prussian conception of war to cow the civilian population to such an extent that they will be unresisting instruments in their hands?

Prof. Bedier has published a series of extracts from the diaries of German soldiers as to their doings. They are gruesome reading. Here is one which will interest Mr. Bennett, because he appears to admire the restraint with which the Germans only burned the third and fifth house along the street at Dinant. This refers to a village just north of Dinant and was written by Private Philip of Kamenz, Saxony, First Battalion, 178th Infantry:

"At the entrance of the village were about fifty villagers, shot for having treacherously fired upon our troops during the night. Many others were shot, so that we counted over two hundred. Women and children, with lamps in their hands, had to witness the terrible sight. We ate our rice among the corpses."

The next diary has the entry:

"Langeviller, Aug. 22, – Village destroyed by the Eleventh Pioneer Battalion; three women hanged on trees."

Says Private Schlauter of the Third Battery, Fourth Field Artillery of the Guard:

"Of the inhabitants, 200 were shot. Those who survived the volley were requisitioned as grave diggers. The women were a sight, but it cannot be helped."

Yet again:

"We thus destroyed eight houses with their inhabitants. In one alone two men with their wives and a girl of 18 were killed with the bayonet. It went to my heart to see the girl killed – she had such an innocent look – but there was nothing to be done with the excited crowd, for they were not men, but beasts."

Now, Mr. Bennett, are these things really "lies, lies, lies"? Or am I justified in saying there has been a policy of murder all along the line, and that there have been no such doings in Europe since the bad old days? If still in doubt, I earnestly beg you to read the

218

evidence of the French and Belgian Commissions, though I fear they will be inaccessible to you in Metz.

Yours,
ARTHUR CONAN DOYLE

Crowborough, Feb. 2, 1915

THE TIMES   13 February 1915

Volunteer Uniforms

SIR, – Your Parliamentary Summary says that "Mr. Tennant was severe upon the advocates for uniforms for Volunteer Corps." This is a misconception of his remarks. He was severe upon young men who should be at the front wearing such uniforms. The Volunteer corps must have uniforms or they will be outside all military law in carrying out the duties which they hope may be assigned to them.

Yours faithfully,
ARTHUR CONAN DOYLE

Windlesham, Crowborough, Sussex, Feb. 11

THE TIMES   13 April 1915

The Treatment of Prisoners

SIR, – It is difficult to know how to act in the case of these European Red Indians who torture their prisoners. It is clear that we cannot retaliate by spitting on, kicking, beating, starving, or freezing the Germans who are in our power. All appeals to good feeling are unavailing, for the average German has no more understanding of chivalry than a cow has of mathematics. He is honestly unable to understand our attitude when we speak kindly of Von Muller, Weddigen, or any of our opponents who have shown some approach to decency. His papers ascribe it partly to sentimentality and partly to hypocrisy. I have no doubt that when German aeroplanes drove away our boats while we were endeavouring to pick up the survivors of the *Blücher* they were really unable to conceive what it was that we were trying to do.

It is worth noting, since they endeavour to excuse their barbarity by saying that it is a retaliation for our naval blockade, that they acted in exactly the same fashion to our prisoners before this maritime policy had been declared. The narrative of the British Red Cross doctors who were taken in Belgium shows that they endured a similar inhuman persecution. If there is no retaliation which we as a nation can employ there is at least one line of action which might be taken. That is to print Major Vandeleur's account with the American official reports, and such documents as the narrative in the Dutch paper *Tyd* of the torture of three wounded British prisoners in a frontier station in October. This paper should be officially sent, not only to all neutral countries, but it should be circulated among our soldiers in France. No man fights the worse for having his soul aflame with righteous anger, so we should use the weapon which the enemy has put into our hands. It will teach our men, also, if any of them still need the lesson, that it is far better to die upon the field than to trust to the humanity of a German victor. If our enemy is unchivalrous he is at least intensely practical, and if he realises that we are gaining any military advantage from his misdeeds he may, perhaps, reconsider, not their morality, but their wisdom.

Yours faithfully,
ARTHUR CONAN DOYLE

Royal Pavilion Hotel, Folkestone, April 11

THE TIMES　　　　　　　　　　5 May 1915

Advertisements Against Drink

SIR, – The Government has demonstrated the power of advertisement in the raising of a great Army. It is really the result of constant suggestion, which ends by causing an atmosphere and a tendency. Why should the same thing not be done in the fight against drink? If the walls of our dockyards and factories were covered with well-worded appeals, and if the worker could not enter a public house without passing a placard which reminded him of his duty, it would surely produce some effect. If he read, "Drink to you means death to our soldiers," or "They give up their lives for you – won't you give up your drink for them?" or "The sober workman fights for Britain – the drunk workman fights for Germany" it would surely move them. Or the appeal might be put on a wider, more general basis. "You will be happier without it. You will be healthier without it. You will be richer without it. Sign off for the war." The whisky sellers know the power of suggestion, as our hoardings testify. Why should it not be used against them?

Yours faithfully,
A. CONAN DOYLE

The Hotel Metropole, W.C., May 3

Home Guards

SIR, – As a constant reader of your valuable weekly, I have been much interested in your consistent advocacy of the Volunteer movement, and knowing the practical interest you take in this movement I crave your indulgence in airing the following points. (1) Is it your view that the brassard is a necessary part of the uniform? (2) Is it with the sanction of the War Office that a corps of the Volunteer Defence Force wears all or most of the distinctive marks of rank used by the Regular Forces – *e.g.* chevrons on the upper arm in varied numbers, as also Sam Browne belts, &c.? (3) Would it not be within the purview of practical politics that the Deputy-Lieutenant of a county should be entrusted with the care of organising the various units of the force? The first of these questions is prompted by the inquiries of various members of the force, and by the editorial reply to a letter signed by "W.W.S." in which you apparently suggest the brassard as an *alternative* to the regulation uniform as authorised. The third question arises from the fact that the Lord-Lieutenant of a certain county within one thousand miles of the Metropolis sneers at and despises the efforts put forward by hundreds of eager and patriotic people under his jurisdiction. In addition, there is a sensible growth of opinion among committeemen in the provincial districts that the Central Association is becoming less and less interested in the Volunteer movement outside the Metropolis and its immediate neighbourhood; if true, and I am unable to vouch for it, I consider such action deplorable, and partaking of the want of energy and keeness displayed by a section of the public in this critical period of our national life.

I am, Sir, &c.,
A.C.D.

[(1) The brassard must be regarded as a necessary part of the uniform. The Government issue it as the distinguishing mark required by the Hague Convention to confer the full rights of combatants. The uniform is no doubt also a sufficiently distinguishing mark to satisfy the Hague Convention. The Government, however, hold that, as not all corps can afford to buy uniforms, they must maintain the brassard. (2) We cannot say whether or not the corps in question breaks the War Office rules. (3) Deputy-Lieutenants could not be better employed. Our correspondent may reassure himself as to the risk of the Central Association's turning into a London Committee. There is no ground for any such rumours. The Central is quite as fully occupied with, and quite as deeply interested in, the promotion of the best interests of the provincial corps as it is in those of London.

ED. Spectator.]

THE TIMES 27 July 1915

The Use of Armour

SIR, – As an advocate of armour in modern warfare for the last 25 years, I am interested to see a column of *The Times* devoted to the subject. When Ned Kelly, the bushranger, walked unhurt before the rifles of the police clad in his own hand-made armour he was an object-lesson to the world. If the outlaw could to it, why not the soldier? Such actions as that of May 9, where several brigades lost nearly half their numbers in endeavouring to rush over the 300 yards which separated us from the German trenches, must make it clear that it is absolutely impossible for unprotected troops to pass over a zone which is swept by machine guns. Therefore you must either for ever abandon such attacks or you must find artificial protection for the men. It has always seemed to me extraordinary that the innumerable cases where a Bible, a cigarette case, a watch, or some other chance article has saved a man's life have not set us scheming so as to do systematically what has so often been the result of a happy chance. Your correspondents have mentioned the objection that any protection may itself be broken, and that the splinters of it may aggravate the wound. One answer to that would be to arm only those points where the wound would in any case be mortal. These points are really very few and no great weight of metal would be needed to protect them. As a man faces a hostile rifle his forehead and his heart are the only points presented which are certainly vital. The former would be protected by such a helmet as the French have now evolved. The second should be covered by a curved plate of highly-tempered steel which need not be more than a foot in diameter. With this simple and light equipment the two centres of life are safe. The remaining dangers to life are the severance of a large artery or a wound of the abdomen. The former is not common from a rifle bullet and cannot be guarded against without complete armour, which is out of the question. The latter is no longer a certain death wound, thanks to the advances of surgery, but a third curve of steel strapped across from the border of the ribs to the crest of the hip bones would afford protection.

With these three precautions the death-rate should be greatly reduced from rifle and machine-gun fire, as also from shrapnel. Nothing, of course, will avail against a direct shell burst. But granting that the individual life would be saved this does not bear upon the capture of a position since so many would fall wounded that the weight of the attack would be spent before the stormers reached the trenches. For this armour which will give complete protection is needed, and since, as your correspondents have shown, the weight of this is more than a man can readily carry, it must be pushed in front upon wheels. I picture a great number of plates, held together like the shields of the Roman tortoise, and pushed by the men who crouch behind them. When one is disabled it can be readily dropped and the gap closed. Others are fixed sideways upon their wheels and are used upon the flank of the advance to prevent an enfilading fire. There is not one tortoise, which would attract a concentrated fire of artillery, but each company or platoon forms its own. These numerous armour-plated bodies rush with small loss over the space which has already been cleared as far as possible of obstacles, and so have some chance of reaching the enemy's line, not as an exhausted fragment but as a vigorous storming party with numbers intact. Such apparatus would not necessitate a great addition to the impedimenta of an army. It would be a separate item, like the pontoons or the siege train, only to be brought up on special occasions to the point where it is needed for an assault. The vital body-plates, however, should be used in the every-day equipment of a fighting soldier.

Yours faithfully,
ARTHUR CONAN DOYLE

Windlesham, Crowborough, Sussex, July 26

THE DAILY
CHRONICLE   23 August 1915

Compulsory National Service

SIR, – I have always been an opponent of compulsion in military service, and everything which has happened in this war has strengthened my convictions; but at the same time I feel that there is some room for compromise between the two parties who now divide the nation. Each must in reason make some concession to the other. The most determined advocate for compulsion must admit that it is a very serious and deplorable thing that the nation, now more united than it has ever been in the whole course of history, should be divided, and the hands of the small disloyal faction should be strengthened. On the other hand, the convinced anti-compulsionist is bound to acknowledge that there are some monstrous anomalies in the present system, and that on the face of it it is not right that a man of 40 with a family should be fighting in

Flanders while youngsters of 23 are riding motor-bicycles (I have only to raise my eyes to see them) up and down the Eastbourne Parade. If these two concessions be made by either party, there would seem to be some room for a compromise, which like all compromises would offend the stalwarts on both sides, but might preserve the national unity.

One of the chief objections to national service at the present moment is, as it seems to me, that the addition to our forces would be a very small one as compared to the risk and hubbub which would follow. What are the classes from which we should gather these new men? It would be madness to touch any man who is engaged upon productive work. Already our trade is greatly disorganised by the number of men withdrawn. All trade is inter-dependent, and a shortage in one direction holds up in most unexpected ways other branches. The machine already creaks and strains. Yet upon this productive trade the finance of the country, which is as vital to the Allies as to ourselves, is resting. To withdraw a man from his work on the chance that he may six months hence be useful as a soldier when he is certainly of the greatest use to the country at the present instant would be unthinkable. Thus all the great trades, not only those directly concerned with war, such as miners, engineers, metal workers, railway men, transport workers, cloth and leather workers, and shipbuilders, but also those which produce articles which we can export, or which prevent corresponding indispensable articles from being imported, are already serving their country in the most efficient way. To recruit them would be to weaken our power.

But when this huge mass of labour has been taken out of our calculations, how much remains? Is there really so much that it is worth while to turn the country upside down in order to get it? There are the distributors of wealth and the agricultural population. Among the former we should include all the shopmen and clerks. In the case of the shopmen it is difficult to understand how any able-bodied man can in these days find himself behind a counter without having an irresistible impulse to vault over it and plunge into the great adventure. His work could certainly be done by women. The same applies to men-waiters and men-servants generally, but in a less degree to clerks, for very often they are an essential part of the business to which they belong, with special knowledge, so that the money-earning power of the firm, and therefore of the country, depends upon them. In the case of the farmers' sons and agricultural labourers generally, now that the production of foodstuffs is recognised as a most essential factor in the problem, it is a question how many of them could be withdrawn without weakening our position. There remain the students, the schoolmasters, the members of the learned or artistic professions, the police, the men in municipal employ, and finally a small but highly objectionable body who from laziness or want of spirit are real shirkers.

These are the men from whom we must draw, and save in the case of the actual shirkers one cannot draw wholesale and indiscriminately. The population is already somewhat depleted. Is it worth while to split the nation from top to bottom in order to bring all these people into the net, when it is doubtful whether it would be wise to use a considerable portion of them when you have got them? Could some process of selection not be devised which would be founded upon a democratic basis and would treat individual cases in a way which would be more drastic than anything we have at present, while it would be less offensive to the working classes than a general law of compulsion? We are all agreed that there are men – many men – about who ought to go. Can we not make them go without any great national schism? I venture to suggest a method by which it could be done.

In every parish or group of parishes a Recruiting Committee should be chosen out of some popularly elected body, such as the parish or district council. The names of men who should go to the front should be submitted to this body – every patriotic citizen would be ready to furnish them, and the committee should have legal powers of compelling the presence of the individual before them. He should be asked why he has not done his apparent duty. Should he say that his employer has prevented him the employer should in turn be summoned. If it be found that there is no valid reason why the man should not go, the chairman would then address him in this fashion: "We have no legal power to send you to the front. We are, however, strongly of opinion that you are not doing your duty, and we therefore give you ten days in which to settle your affairs and to enlist. If, at the end of that time, we have not proof that you have done so we shall be compelled to print your name in the blacklist of those who have failed their country during the crisis. The list will hang outside the parish church and outside the public buildings of this parish." A similar speech would be made to the employer who held back his men, and his business would certainly not be improved by the appearance of his name in such a list. I am of opinion that in the case both of master and of man such a proceeding would have the desired effect.

No doubt such a solution would be called "worrying the individual" and "putting undue pressure upon individuals" by those who wish the pressure to be equally distributed. But is it not perfectly just that the individual should be worried and have pressure put on him so long as he is the right man to press? If he clears himself before his parish tribunal there is an end of the matter. If he does not, then he should either do his duty or stand disgraced. The old Anglo-Saxons had a custom of proclaiming a man "niddering" or worthless when he shirked his public duties. What I suggest would really be a reversion to an old and reasonable law.

The advantages of such a scheme are that it would entail a minimum of legislation. Statutory powers to enforce attendance by the local committee and a protection against libel actions – that is all. What are the objections? It may be argued that the man would still refuse to serve. If he did so I cannot imagine that a man so callous on a point of honour would ever make a good soldier.

I must apologise, sir, for the length of this letter, but I feel that the question is an exceedingly important and dangerous one. If it were unwisely handled it might have the most serious effects. The issue is confused by appeals to us on the ground of economy, but these seem to me to have little relevancy since the large force already enlisted have their contract, which we cannot break, so that any lower scale of pay could only apply to the new recruits. The best we can hope is that some ground of compromise – either this or a better one – may be found between the two parties, so that we may get the best fighting strength out of our people, and make sure that every man is doing his duty without those methods of compulsion which have always been foreign to our system, and which might provoke a most dangerous spirit in the country.

ARTHUR CONAN DOYLE

Aug. 21, 1915

THE TIMES   15 October 1915

Reprisal

SIR, – Surely it is time that these German murders by Zeppelin should be dealt with more firmly. It seems to me that there should be no great difficulty in the matter. If a small avenging squadron of swift British aeroplanes were stationed in Eastern France, and if it were announced by the Government that every raid upon an open town in Great Britain would automatically and remorselessly cause three similar raids on German towns, we should soon bring them to reason. I can well imagine that our airmen would find such work repugnant, but they must bear in mind that women and children have for a long time been sacrificed over here, that all forbearance has been shown, and that no other methods but those of reprisal offer any assurance that we can save civilians from these murderous outrages.

Yours faithfully,
ARTHUR CONAN DOYLE

The Hôtel Métropole, W.C., Oct. 14

THE TIMES   18 October 1915

The Policy of Air Raid Reprisals

SIR, – There are few men for whose opinion I have more respect than that of Sir Edward Clarke. Moreover, I am perfectly prepared to admit that in the abstract he is right. I have already shown that I though so by mentioning in my original letter the repugnance with which such a task would be undertaken. But there are times when clean-handedness becomes a vicarious virtue by which other people suffer. So it is in the case of the use of gas, which in itself is abominable, and yet cannot be avoided out of justice to our own men who suffer by its use from the enemy. If by laying certain towns in Germany in ruins we can have reasonable hopes that we can save our own civilians we are, in my opinion, fully justified in so doing. It appears to me to be an abuse of words to call such a proceeding murder, when it is in answer to murder in the past, and a preventive to murder in the future. We have without protest allowed the French aviators to make a raid upon Karlsruhe and Stuttgart, the latter being officially announced as a reprisal for raids on open towns in France and Britain. Coming, as it did, immediately after the first raid on London, it was accepted as an answer to that outrage. It is, it must be admitted, dirty work at the best, however necessary it may be, but the dirtiest work of all would be to permit our Ally to do it in our name whilst we explained to the world that it was a thing to which we could not condescend, and that the enemy might work their will upon our unfortunate civilians without any fear for their own.

Yours faithfully,
ARTHUR CONAN DOYLE

Windlesham, Crowborough, Sussex, Oct. 16

THE SPECTATOR   13 November 1915

The Use of the Volunteers

SIR, – There are now some three hundred thousand Volunteers in the country, most of whom can claim to be trained men. General O'Moore Creagh, who has inspected many of them, has stated that the older regiments compare favourably with the Territorials at the outbreak of the war. The question now rises how these men can be used. The State, on the one hand, declares that it needs men. The Volunteers, on the other hand, are most zealous in their desire to be of use. Surely, then, some practical plan can be devised.

It must be admitted, however, that it is not an easy problem. The more closely one examines it, and the more one is familiar with the material of which the Volunteer Force is composed, the more one realises the difficulty. That material is such that to call it all out simultaneously would be to inflict a severe blow to the trade of the country. Nothing but a great emergency, such as an invasion, could justify such a measure. Short of that, the force can only be used in relays, each detachment serving for a certain period and then being relieved by another.

How, then, can they serve? It is usual to say that they could guard prisoners, railways, and posts of various sorts. But work of this kind is already being done by the National Reserve, who are themselves men of some age. Then, again, if the Volunteers are to be split up into small detachments all over the country, it will be impossible to train them into efficient fighting units. The only way to do this would be to have a central permanent camp from which all detachments are sent and to which all detachments return. Then the Volunteers might provide scattered posts and yet preserve their efficiency as trained infantry.

But a considerable force like the Volunteers is not formed for the sole purpose of forming posts. What more can it do, and how can it do it? There is nothing, as it seems to me, that the Volunteer infantry is so fitted for as for the garrisoning of fortresses. It is work which makes no extreme call upon a man's activity or endurance, while no call could be too extreme for the solidity and fidelity of the Volunteers. We will suppose that sixty thousand infantry would serve to garrison the chief fortresses – Dover, Portsmouth, Plymouth, &c. These men might be supplied upon terms of service in which each regiment took its turn of duty every fourth month. With an effort, and at a cost of considerable personal sacrifice, I am convinced that the average Volunteer could get away for one month in four. The authorities might use a regiment or two in each fortress as a start until they had proved their military qualities. In this way a considerable help could be rendered at once by the Volunteers. Later, when our lines of communication become longer on the Continent, I am sure that a large contingent of Volunteers would be available for holding them.

I am, Sir, &c.,
ARTHUR CONAN DOYLE

Windlesham, Crowborough, Sussex

A Preventive of Air Raids

SIR, – It is continually asserted in Continental papers, and it is inherently probable, that the Germans are preparing fresh Zeppelin raids upon London on a larger scale than before. It becomes a very serious question how we should meet this menace.

All attempts to defeat a raid at London itself are, as it seems to me, open to very grave objections. To bring down a blazing Zeppelin with its cargo of explosives on to the roofs of a great city would probably be as dangerous a thing as to endure its bombardment. It might fall where it would produce no harm, but it is equally possible that it might descend on a crowded quarter and cause some great catastrophe. On the other hand, when once a Zeppelin has started upon its way it is very difficult to see how it can be intercepted and stopped before it reaches its destination. We have, I fear, to face the fact that we can neither stop their coming nor deal with them with any certainty when they have gone.

There remains one other course – but it is a very effective one. It is to stop the attempt by showing that you can and will retaliate. The German airship coming from the eastern part of Belgium has to travel at least 200 miles each way upon its mission. Had we an aviation centre near Nancy we should be very much nearer than that to great German centres of population. The distance from there to Wiesbaden would be 100 miles, to Bonn 130, to Frankfurt 140, to Coblentz 120, to Cologne 150. If, then, London is vulnerable, these are very much more so. Without any delay we should establish such an aviation centre, defend it with numbers of the best aircraft guns against the persistent attempts which will be made to destroy it, and announce to the German Government through the American Embassy at Berlin that we can tolerate no more outrages upon our civilian population, and that any further raids will be followed by immediate reprisals.

If such a policy were at once put in force it might act as a preventive – which is better than vengeance. But if it must be vengeance, then the blood is on the head of those who with their eyes open have provoked it. The whole world has been a witness to our patience. But for the sake of our own women and children the time has come when these murders must be stopped. If their civilians die as a consequence of the deliberate actions of their fellow-countrymen, then it is they and not we who have doomed them. There should be no limit to the bombardment of these towns. We should go on and on until we have a formal promise that this form of warfare shall stop. The Hun is only formidable when he thinks that he can be frightful with impunity. "Blood and Iron" is his doctrine so long as it is his iron and some one else's blood. When the French began to retaliate at Karlsruhe and Heidelberg several German journals at once announced that such warfare was inhuman, and it has as a matter of fact been discontinued – for France.

It is eminently a subject for ventilation, for it is clear that the Government cannot act in advance of public opinion, or pledge themselves to a course of action which the public might repudiate. The danger is a very pressing one and this is the only way to meet it. If there were a general concurrence upon the subject in the Press the authorities would feel strengthened in any action they might take. If we move quickly we may be in time for prevention. If we delay only vengeance may be left.

Yours faithfully,
ARTHUR CONAN DOYLE

Windlesham, Crowborough, Sussex, Jan. 15

THE DAILY
CHRONICLE

21 January 1916

Mr. Wells's Prophecy

SIR, – I have read with interest and admiration Mr. Wells's article dealing with the probable course of the war. I think, however, that he dismisses much too easily the idea that the war may be ended by the absolute defeat of the Germans on the field. Bloch was a far-sighted thinker. He saw clearly the war of trenches. But he did not see the power of modern guns and of high explosive shells. Had he done so he might have hedged a little in his conclusions. Both the British and the French at the end of September were very nearly through. Their resources by the spring, both in men and in shells, will have greatly increased. They will also have the valuable experience of these partial victories to guide them. Above all, they may have evolved protective devices by which the assailants may get to close grips without undue loss. Our failure to do this has been one of our blots upon the management of the war. Almost from the beginning it has been under discussion. Yet, now in the 18th month a Canadian Colonel writes to me: "We have now at last got about 50 helmets to the regiment. How many lives would have been saved had we had these earlier?"

If Bloch's trenches have proved themselves to be formidable they may, on the other hand, be recognised later as being the most dangerous military formation ever adopted by an army. If by a sudden concentration they could be broken, and a mobile force got through the gap, it would not be a case of capturing cannon by the tens or by the hundreds, but possibly of seizing every heavy gun along the whole front. By a single movement you outflank everything and make every position untenable. Bloch holds the field for the moment, but it may be that his view will go down in military history as an exposed fallacy. I for one refuse to accept the dismal and enervating doctrine that this war can only come to an end through the inglorious methods of exhaustion.

ARTHUR CONAN DOYLE

Windlesham, Crowborough, Sussex

THE TIMES   22 January 1916

Air Raid Reprisals

SIR, – Sir Edward Clarke characterises the suggestion that we should retaliate as "monstrous," but this seems a harsh term to apply to a policy which has actually been adopted with success by our Allies. Sir Edward is surely guilty of a flaw in logic when he argues that because German raids are admittedly useless and serve no military purpose, therefore a return raid would be open to the same objection. The purpose of raid No. 2 is to prevent a repetition of raid No. 1 and so to save the lives of our civilians. That is a very definite object and I can see no other sure way of attaining it.

We should guard ourselves carefully against the possibility of our action being put in the same category as that of our enemy. If the Government thought fit to send such a warning as I have suggested it would no doubt begin by a repudiation of such methods of warfare as murderous and against the rules of The Hague Conventions. It would then specify the number of times on which we had endured such attacks, with a list of the unfortified places and exact figures as to the numbers of civilians murdered. The document would end with an announcement of our determination to retaliate in case of further attack, fortified by the assurance that the means had been already prepared. Such a document would put us right with the public opinion of the world, and would also perhaps bring home to the Germans what, as Sir Edward says, has never been understood by them, the vile methods that their rulers have adopted, and the contempt which they have universally earned.

Yours faithfully,
ARTHUR CONAN DOYLE

Windlesham, Crowborough, Sussex

Murder Deliberate

SIR, – When Sir Evelyn Wood states that reprisals would be useless in the case of the Germans he really contradicts their own *Kriegsbuch*, which asserts in so many words that their proceedings towards their enemy shall always be regulated by the power which that enemy has of retaliation. Sir Evelyn quotes General Marmont in support of his argument, but Marmont was not speaking of entirely new developments of warfare. Within the last year Marmont's countrymen have used retaliation in the case of the ill-treatment of prisoners with the best possible results. Some of these days there may be a great catastrophe, and then it will be too late for anything but revenge. I claim that this catastrophe may be averted by a public declaration of our intention to hit back, coupled by such preparations as will show that we can do what we threaten. Sir Evelyn argues, with extraordinary charity, that the Germans are really trying to hit legitimate marks and that the slaughter of civilians is an unintentional by-product in the operation. How, then, would he explain the case of the *Franz Fischer*, where the Zeppelin settled down upon an unoffending little boat, sank her, and drowned 13 of the crew? How can anyone doubt after that incident that the murder of civilians is deliberate?

Yours faithfully,
ARTHUR CONAN DOYLE

Windlesham, Crowborough, Sussex, Feb. 5

Reprisals

SIR, – I am entirely in accord with the *Saturday Review* in its policy that reprisals should be threatened and, if necessary, instituted against German cities as a preventive to the hostile air raids. Critics of this measure may well be adjured to live up to their own maxim and to "play the game". It is not playing the game to mis-state a case because you happen to disagree with it. The worthy Bishops, Lord Buckmaster, Colonel Jackson, and other opponents of the measure have all insisted that its object is to kill women and children. This is nonsense. The object is to *prevent* women and children being killed. We have now had some thirty odd raids on England, and many hundreds of civilians have been killed. No method has been found of stopping it. It is my belief that if, after the first raid, we had solemnly protested to the whole world against so inhuman a form of warfare and given due notice that, much as we loathed it, we should be compelled in self-protection to use the same means, we might never have had a second. Thus very many of our women and children would have been saved. Even now it is not too late, for raids on a larger scale will come if we give the Germans the idea that we cannot hit back. Our restraint is, of course, ascribed by them to inability, for they could not conceive of the existence of people who, having the power to hit out in the defence of their own civilians, would refrain on account of a kind of inverted muddle-headed chivalry from doing so.

Again, we have never suggested that civilians should in any case be our mark. The proposal is that we attack Cologne, Coblentz, and the other Rhine towns, most of which are actual fortresses and all of them places on the lines of communications with railways and bridges of strategic importance. If, however, in these military operations civilians get hurt, the Germans will realise what we feel and will probably reconsider their murderous tactics. If for want of taking so obvious a precaution the raids continue, and our civilians suffer, I consider that a direct responsibility rests on all those who have discouraged our adopting the only course which seems likely to influence the enemy.

The argument that the aeroplanes are needed elsewhere will not bear examination. We have great numbers of planes for home defence. The best defence is a strong attack, and some at least of these planes could be used.

Yours faithfully,
ARTHUR CONAN DOYLE

Windlesham, Crowborough, Sussex, 21 February 1916

Where is the Soul during Unconsciousness?

SIR, –I have had my attention drawn rather strongly to this point by two instances of recent occurrence, one personal and the other in my family.

The first and slighter of the two occurred to myself. A fortnight ago I had laughing gas at the dentist's. I was taken there inside a cab, my wife and two little boys being with me. The cab drove on while I was being operated upon. While under the gas I was intensely conscious that I had returned to the moving cab, and that I could very vividly see the occupants, while well aware that they could not see me. This, of course, might be subjective

233

entirely, but the impression was very clear.

The second incident is more convincing. My son Adrian, aged five, was grievously ill of pneumonia, and was lying half comatose with a temperature of 105°. My wife, who was nursing him, left him for a moment and went to fetch something from the nursery, two rooms away. The elder boy, Denis, was standing on a chair, and on getting down he trod upon some tin soldiers on the ground. My wife, anxious not to leave the invalid too long, hurried into the sick room. The child opened his eyes and said, "Naughty Denis, breaking my soldiers!"

He had never spoken of soldiers during five days of illness, so that the remark was beyond the reach of coincidence. Nor was it thought-transference from my wife's brain, as she is clear that she was thinking only of the invalid. I can only explain it by the supposition, which can be supported by a volume of evidence, that the soul can be, and probably is always, out of the body at such times, and that occasionally under rare conditions which we have not yet been able to define, it can convey to the body the observations which it has made during its independent flight.

Such conditions must have existed in the classic case of Sir Rider Haggard. It will be remembered that he wrote a letter to *The Times* some years ago giving the circumstances in detail. He had lost a favourite dog. In his sleep he saw it lying near a certain point of the railway. Upon searching it was actually found there. There was no particular reason why this point should have suggested itself to him, more than any other in the neighbourhood.

Another classic case is that of the Red Barn murder in the eighteenth century. In this case the mother dreamed three times that she saw the corpse of her daughter hidden in a certain loft. The loft was examined and the corpse was found. There are a great number of such cases on record. They are all readily explained on the supposition that the soul drifts out like a captive balloon, attached always by some filament which draws it back in an instant to its body. There is nothing supernatural in such a supposition. It is only the unfolding of a fresh law in a region which is still but little known. There is apparently a "switch-off" between the body life and the extra-body life. Should the switch for any reason hang fire, then we have memory of one carried into the other.

The matter is of profound religious significance. There is, as it seems to me, something very surprising in the limited interest which the churches take in psychical research. It is a subject which cuts at the very root of their existence. It is the one way of demonstrating the independent action of soul, and therefore, to put it at the lowest, the *possibility* of its existence apart from bodily organs. If the balloon can really drift forth upon a filament and retain its own individuality, then it is no great further step to say that when the filament snaps the balloon is still self-sufficient. A fresh unfolding of knowledge – and each such unfolding is in truth a renewed divine revelation – has given us reassurances. Myers, Gurney and Hodgson are messengers of truth from the Beyond as surely as Isaiah or Amos, but, British fashion, they speak coldly and clearly with none of the passion and declamation of the East. Their message has fallen on many ears and strengthened many spirits, but it has never, as it seems to me, had the direct religious effect which one might have expected. Personally I know no single argument which is not in favour of the extinction of our individuality at death, save only the facts of psychic research. But these are so strong that they must outweigh all others, as the positive must always outweigh the negative. A hundred who have examined and tested and seen must always be more convincing than a million who disagree without investigation.

Yours faithfully,
ARTHUR CONAN DOYLE

Windlesham, Crowborough, Sussex. February 28th, 1916

THE TIMES   20 March 1916

An Opportunity Missed

SIR, – It is exasperating to see the Volunteers drilling assiduously night after night while the married Derby recruits take no pains to get on with their training. Had a connexion been formed between them when it was first suggested, these men would have already been well advanced in their education. Such a connexion can only come from an actual War Office order to the effect that men who have had no training will be called earlier than those who can show the certificate of a Volunteer commandant that they are well up in squad, platoon, and company drill. With five nights' hard work each week and a route march on Sundays I believe that it would be possible to bring the men along to the last stage of their training without separating them at all from their families and business. It would be very hard work, no doubt, but as an alternative to being called up at an early date it would, I am sure, be cheerfully accepted. Could not this be done whilst the unmarried men are being finally collected?

As to the value of the Volunteer instructors, I can speak only from personal experience of one platoon, but I know that every man of that unit who has found his way into the Army has won his non-commissioned stripes with very little delay. Considering that many of us have put in 250 drills, both officers and men should know their work within the limits of their facilities.

Yours faithfully,
ARTHUR CONAN DOYLE

Windlesham, Crowborough, Sussex, March 18

THE DAILY
CHRONICLE   2 May 1916

The Surrender of Kut

SIR, – It is to be hoped that the surrender at Kut will be viewed with a proper sense of proportion by the public. The number of men involved is probably far less than a single day's losses for the Germans in an active day upon the Verdun front. They were not wasted, but have done their bit in the general strategy of the war. Their presence has attracted an ever increasing number of the Turks, and thus helped to ease the pressure both upon Egypt and upon the Russians. It is to be expected that the continued presence of General Lake's army to the south of Bagdad will still have this effect.

There is nothing more pernicious than the clamour which breaks out when a bold venture has been made and has failed. Such criticism if taken seriously would kill all initiative and would condemn some of the most brilliant feats in history. What would some of our squealers have said to Napoleon's venture when, with the British holding the seas, he took an army from Marseilles to Egypt? Or to take a more recent example what would they have said to the British Cavalry which, after Tel-el-Kebir pushed on unsupported to Cairo? These are the risks of war, and to discourage them by crying out when they miscarry is to strike at the very roots of successful soldiering. We have failed at Gallipoli, but it was a fair risk and well worth taking. We have failed for the moment at Bagdad. Let us try and try again until the day comes when we do not fail. There lies the road to victory.

But, above all, let us keep united. These perpetual squabbles make a man's heart sick. Can anybody be so mad as to suppose that the Cabinet does not want to win the war? Or can anybody deny that they are of a high average order of intellect and character, with full knowledge of the facts, and with the best expert advice to guide them? Or, again, can anybody suggest any other Government, save a coalition, which would not breed instant internal trouble? Since all these things are obviously true, what is the sense of all this captious and bitter criticism? That suggestions should be offered or methods recommended is

236

reasonable enough. But there are papers and there are public men whose utterances are sheer vituperation. What can be gained by that? Our Government is fighting the German Government. In what possible way can it be helpful that their own people should snipe at them while they fight.

There was a time when a bulldog was our national type. So it is still when you get down to the real nation, for the nation, though liable to partial and temporary deception, is as sound as ever it was. But if we were to judge it by some of its Press and some of its public men we should have to drop the bulldog, and take a basketful of puppies, all whining and yelping together, as a more appropriate national symbol. But this is surely all on the surface. Let us bite hard, hang on, and keep silent. That was the way of our fathers, and it lies deep in our blood.

ARTHUR CONAN DOYLE

Portman Lodge, Bournemouth, April 29, 1916

THE DAILY
CHRONICLE   9 May 1916

Justice in Ireland

SIR, – Many will agree with you in your wise remarks as to the danger of creating political martyrs in Ireland. On the other hand you must admit that there have been many cold-blooded murders, and that unless these are sternly punished justice would become a farce. What about the poor old veterans who were shot down without warning before they had ever heard of a revolt? What of the unarmed officers shot in the streets of Dublin? What of the kindly policeman murdered outside the Castle Gate, or the convalescent soldiers killed while pleading for others, or the cabman shot in cold blood outside the Shelbourne Hotel? No pains can be too great to ensure the punishment of the men who did such deeds, but they should be tried not for rebellion, which might put a halo round their memories, but for most cowardly murder.

A. CONAN DOYLE

Windlesham, Crowborough, May 6, 1916

LIGHT   13 May 1916

Where is the Soul during Unconsciousness?

SIR, – I must write again under the above heading in order to thank the numerous correspondents who have thrown various lights upon the question which I raised. Besides the letters in *Light* I have received many private instances, and another correspondence has treated the matter in a well-known London weekly paper (*T.P.'s Weekly*). The result is a mass of definite testimony which I may elaborate into a longer article where I might have space to dissect the evidence and draw some general conclusions.

Miss Lilian Whiting and one or two other correspondents dissent from my view that the soul or spirit at such a time is floating from the body like a captive balloon on a psychic rope by which it can be drawn instantaneously back. They prefer the view that we have a natural spirit vision which is all-embracing and is only clogged by the body. Since, however, in all the cases cited the result is definite in time and place, and since it does not include a general view of everything but only of one particular thing, I still hold that the floating forth of a sensitive organism which is limited in its perception is the presumption which comes nearest to an explanation of the facts.

The instances are so numerous, so well attested, and so utterly beyond the reach of coincidence that one marvels that any man calling himself a scientist could dismiss them as unworthy of scientific consideration. Such scientists, having formed an *a priori* conception of the universe, simply ignore the plain facts which stand in the way of their hypothesis. One marvels that minds so acute within their own limitations should be so slovenly and illogical outside of them. One cannot forget the famous dictum of Huxley after hearing or reading some inanities of a séance room. "If they are true," said he, "they interest me no more than the gossip of curates in a cathedral city." This was a man who had made his name by a careful classification of crayfish and jellies. Yet he dismissed a whole new order of beings because the particular mental phenomena which he first encountered were not up to his preconceived ideas of what they should be. It would be as reasonable for a recluse coming out into the world to abjure the whole human race because the first gutter-snipe whom he encountered made a bad impression on him. Science (so-called) denied mesmerism for a century. Then it renamed it "hypnotism" and adopted it. Some day, no doubt, it will find a new name for the various psychic phenomena which are now under discussion, and will then find itself in complete agreement.

Yours, &c.,
ARTHUR CONAN DOYLE

Windlesham, Crowborough, April 30th, 1916

238

The Channel Tunnel Scheme

SIR, – Nations are supposed to pay for their sins, but they pay an even higher price for their stupidities. And we deserve to pay it, for we have been very stupid, and have allowed ourselves to be frightened off from doing what was clearly to our advantage by the most absurd bogies, such as that we would be invaded through a rabbit burrow in the ground 26 miles long. I do not think national folly could rise higher than that. From the time that war with Germany became more probable, after Agadir, I sent three separate minutes to the War Office, the Admiralty, and the Council of National Defence, pointing out how essential a tunnel was for our campaign. I foretold submarine danger, and showed how a tunnel would meet it. I pointed out that our line of communications would be safe in all weather, that the ships would be spared for other work, and the convoying warships released. Our present shortage of tonnage is partly due to this cause. I wonder how many tens of millions of pounds would have been saved if these views had met with a sympathetic consideration from any of the three bodies to which I sent them, always presuming that there was time to drive the tunnel through before war broke out. Now that it is clear that a whiff of poison gas down the tunnel would destroy any army within it, we will hope that all the absurd nightmares will die away, and that after the war we shall bring sanity to bear upon this question.

ARTHUR CONAN DOYLE

Body Armour or Shields

SIR, – It is a year now since you were good enough to allow me to express some views about body armour in your columns. Since then, so far as I know, nothing has been done, but now we have got so far that the Minister of War admits that something of the kind may some day come along. To me it seems the most important question of any, and I earnestly hope that you will use your influence to keep it before the notice of the authorities.

Upon July 1 several of our divisions were stopped by machine-gun fire. Their losses were exceedingly heavy, but hardly any of them were from high explosives. The distance to traverse was only about 250 yards. The problem, therefore, is to render a body of men reasonably immune to bullets fired at that range. The German first-line trenches were thinly held, so that once across the open our infantry would have had no difficulty whatever.

Now, Sir, I venture to say that if three intelligent metal-workers were put together in consultation they would in a few days produce a shield which would take the greater part of those men safely across. We have definite facts to go upon. A shield of steel of $7/16$ of an inch will stop a point-blank bullet. Far more will it stop one which strikes it obliquely. Suppose such a shield fashioned like that of a Roman soldier, 2ft. broad and 3ft. deep. Admittedly it is heavy – well over 30lb. in weight. What then? The man has not far to go, and he has the whole day before him. A mile in a day is good progress as modern battles go. What does it matter, then, if he carries a heavy shield to cover him?

Suppose that the first line of stormers carried such shields. Their only other armament, besides their helmets, should be a bag of bombs. With these they clear up the machine-guns. The second wave of attack with rifles, and possibly without shields, then comes along, occupies and cleans up the trench, while the heavily armed infantry, after a rest, advance upon the next one. Men would, of course, be hit about the legs and arms, and high explosives would claim their victims, but I venture to say that we should not again see British divisions held up by machine-guns and shrapnel. Why can it not be tried at once? Nothing elaborate is needed. Only so many sheets of steel cut to size and furnished with a double thong for arm-grip. Shields are evidently better than body armour, since they can be turned in any direction, or form a screen for a sniper or for a wounded man.

The present private contrivances seem inadequate, and I can well understand that those who could afford to buy them would shrink from using a protection which their comrades did not possess. Yet I have seen letters in which men have declared that they owed their lives to these primitive shields. Let the experiment be made of arming a whole battalion with proper ones – and, above all, let it be done at once. Then at last the attack will be on a level with the defence.

Yours faithfully,
ARTHUR CONAN DOYLE

Windlesham, Crowborough, Sussex, July 25

Volunteers and Their Uniform

SIR, – It is difficult to imagine that this discussion about changing the Volunteer uniform to khaki is intended seriously. Why should we change our uniforms when we have only, at considerable cost, succeeded in clothing ourselves? And why should we abandon what is associated with all our honourable work? I am convinced that such an idea would be most unpopular with the force.

Yours, &c.;
ARTHUR CONAN DOYLE

Windlesham, Crowborough, Sussex. 22nd July 1916

THE TIMES   4 August 1916

Body Shields Again

SIR, – Among a number of letters which have reached me upon this subject there is one from an officer of experience, who says, "In the course of numerous discussions I have never once met an officer who did not think some attempt should be made to produce shields." Surely a universal demand of this sort can be met by an inventive engineering community like ours. The crudest plate slung by a thong round a man's neck would be better than nothing at all. Let us produce something for use at once and improve upon it at our leisure. If we had put half the energy into this matter which was shown in our provision of poison-helmets the question would have been solved. On the solution depends not only the saving of life, but, what is even more important, the winning of battles. Take our stormers safely across No Man's Land and the rest is simple.

Mr. Woodward writes to point out that I underrated the weight. No doubt I did so; but my statement was not meant to be a precise one, as, so long as we can get a bullet-stopping shield which a man can carry, the exact weight is immaterial. Indeed, there is a positive advantage in weight, since the impact on a light shield would give a shock to the man behind it, while a heavy shield absorbs it. I am informed that by adding certain elements to the steel a lesser thickness will serve, and the length which I gave (3 feet) could be diminished without exposing the vital parts. Suppose we put the final weight of the shield as high as 80lb.; if the man had no other equipment save his helmet and his bag of bombs, it would still be well within his power to carry it. Formations would soon be devised by which men could lock shields and obtain flank protection.

Colonel Newell points out the difficulty of carrying up such weighty articles. I presume that they would be taken up in motor lorries in the same way as our heavy projectiles. If the shields are provided, I am certain that our very excellent supply service will get them to the front. The essential thing now is to get to the end of the talk and to actually do something to enable our men to face the machine-guns.

Yours faithfully,
ARTHUR CONAN DOYLE

Windlesham, Crowborough, Sussex, July 31

THE OBSERVER   20 August 1916

Body Shields

SIR, – Lord Sydenham has stated to your representative that he can see no military advantage in shielding the heart. The statement is so strange that surely it has arisen from some misunderstanding. Is not the preservation of the soldier's life a military advantage? Again and again in our recent fighting local victory has been changed into local defeat because our men, having reached their objective, were too weak to hold it on account of their losses in the advance. As to the possibility of the man going on fighting after receiving a blow on his heart shield (which is perhaps what Lord Sydenham had in his mind), let me quote the following experience as narrated by a sergeant:–

"As we turned the corner we saw a German lying round the end of a wall. He had got a machine gun. He turned this damned thing on me and got me on the foot. It didn't stop me, but as I was getting near him I felt two kicks over the heart. I didn't wait to see what had happened but bayoneted him. I sat down to see what was the damage. My foot was pretty bad, but when I looked at my left-hand breast pocket I saw two holes in it. I opened my pocket and found that the two bullets had gone through my metal shaving mirror, my pocket case, and had nosed their way into a book I was carrying."

In this case the sergeant was only incapacitated by his foot wound, and could have gone on with his platoon in spite of two bullets over his heart. Was this no military advantage? And is it not possible to give artificial protection which will be as effective as a mirror and a book? In this case the shots were at point blank range, and therefore very much more powerful than the average of those which sweep across No Man's Land with such fatal effect.

I am not, of course, arguing that only heart shields should be used. I am convinced that we can do better. But I am endeavouring to show that Lord Sydenham's reported objection to the heart shield is in opposition to the facts.

Yours faithfully,
ARTHUR CONAN DOYLE

Aug. 13

THE TIMES   4 September 1916

The Somme Films

SIR, – Surely the Dean of Durham's view is a very odd one and will not be shared by many of his fellow-countrymen. How can we learn to understand and sympathise with the glorious achievements and sacrifices of our soldiers so well as when we actually see them in action before our eyes? The film is a monument to their devotion. The theatre is filled constantly with the relatives of the men portrayed, and I do not think that they feel that there is any desecration in the performance. There is, however, one very obvious omission. The name and possibly the portrait of the brave operator who risked his life to secure this invaluable national possession should certainly be flashed upon the screen.

Yours faithfully,
ARTHUR CONAN DOYLE

Windlesham, Crowborough, Sussex, Sept. 1

THE TIMES   11 October 1916

General von Arnim's Report

SIR, – We have good reason to congratulate ourselves upon the opinions expressed in the intercepted report of General von Arnim, upon the British infantry, the British artillery, and the British aircraft. As these views were formed at the end of July they are probably held even more strongly after our victories of August and September. It seems to me, however, that the most suggestive point about the Prussian general's remarks has received less attention than it deserves. This consists in the general tendency to substitute British for German methods, showing that as in commercial and marine matters, so even in that military art which was his special study, the German is by nature a copyist rather than a creator. He creates only when he descends into those

243

regions where he is safe from competition. It is very heartening to our nation and very complimentary to those who order our military affairs to find that one single report should touch upon so many details in which we are admitted to be in front.

To take examples – in one part of the report he recommends the British boot and puttee, in another he holds the British care of the rifle up for imitation, in another he pleads for the light machine-guns with which we have long been provided, in another he recommends the cultivation of individual self-reliance, which has always been the British theory as opposed to blind discipline, in another he recommends helmets, which have long been used by our soldiers, but have not yet reached the German infantry, as all who have seen the Somme pictures can testify.

It is exceedingly gratifying to find upon his own admission that we have out-thought our enemy as well as out-fought him. The fresh chapter opened in warfare by the tanks will furnish an even clearer illustration of the fact. We may be sure from our experience in other departments of life that the Germans will at once copy – and copy very well. It is for us to use the time while they are occupying to make our new models, and so always be ahead. Above all, it is for us to add to our advantages those protective devices, whether shields or armour, which seem to me to be the most vital problem of all. To say that we can protect our soldiers' heads but cannot protect their chests is an impossible position.

Yours faithfully,
Arthur Conan Doyle

Windlesham, Crowborough, Sussex

THE FREEMAN'S JOURNAL
DUBLIN   31 October 1916

Ireland and the War

Sir, – I do not think that Irishmen in Ireland appreciate the consternation and shame which is felt by men of Irish blood throughout the Empire at the present shocking state of affairs, where, on account of politics gone mad, the Irish Divisions are left without recruits in the face of the enemy. Politics can wait, but war cannot wait, and the events of the next few months will determine the position which Ireland will hold in the future, both in the Empire and in the estimation of civilised Europe. Already Irishmen have been found so wanting in all sense of proportion that on account of a National grievance which was in a fair way of being remedied they have fought as the allies of the Turk, the

Bulgar, and the Prussian. If they have no loyalty to the British Empire surely the spectacle of the martyrdom of Belgium and the mutilation of France should move the heart of a generous nation. I still feel that it must do so, and that the present hideous apathy will pass. Ireland, pouring its produce into Britain and growing rich by its sale, while refusing all the common duties of manhood, is surely a most unlovely spectacle. If Irishmen do indeed desire Home Rule then is it not clear that it is madness to turn their friends over here into enemies, and to bitterly affront so many who have worked for their cause in the past. Ireland is in imminent danger of losing not only the fruits of the last thirty years of political work, but her honour as well.

Yours faithfully,
ARTHUR CONAN DOYLE

Windlesham, Crowborough, Sussex, Oct. 29th

THE TIMES   6 February 1917

Soldiers in London

SIR, – Is it not possible in any way to hold in check the vile women who at present prey upon and poison our soldiers in London? A friend of mine who is a Special Constable in a harlot-haunted district has described to me how these harpies carry off the lonely soldiers to their rooms, make them drunk often with the vile liquor which they keep there, and finally inoculate them, as likely as not, with one or other of those diseases which, thanks to the agitation of well-meaning fools, have had free trade granted to them amongst us. Our present policy is to shut the museums – the most pitiful economy ever effected by a great nation – but to keep open the brothels. The lad from over the seas who has for the first and perhaps for the last time in his life, a few clear days in the great centre of his race, cannot carry away any recollections of its treasures of art and antiquity, but is forced into contact with what is least reputable in our metropolitan life. All honour to the Union Jack Club, the Y.M.C.A., and all the other associations which try to mitigate this state of affairs, but it is a case for general legislation and not for sporadic individual effort. It will be a poor return for what our Colonies have done for us if we return their splendid lads the worse in body and in soul.

Yours faithfully,
ARTHUR CONAN DOYLE

Windlesham, Crowborough, Sussex

"Spookery"

SIR, – Does Mr. Kipling Common show either wit or reason in heading his comments upon spiritualism in a letter to the *Daily Mail* as above?

Whatever his personal opinion may be he must be aware, if he has made the most superficial examination of the subject, that the conviction of the continuity of the individual and of the possibility of communication has been forced upon a great many minds of the first order by a careful and prolonged study of the evidence.

Men of the highest character not only in this country but in America, France, Germany, Russia, and Italy have confirmed each other's observations, and many a materialist has for the first time received a broader philosophy of the universe by way of psychical research. Some arrive at such results by faith, but as there are many faiths summoning one in various directions, one finds it hard to know which to follow, unless one is self-complacent enough to believe that one chanced to be born in the right one.

Personally I know of no valid argument for life beyond the grave – the whole analogy of Nature seems against it – save only in the experiences attained by psychical study. The calling of such study by foolish or vulgar means is not really helpful.

ARTHUR CONAN DOYLE

Windlesham, Crowborough, Sussex

Soldiers in London

SIR, – The letters which pour in upon me testify to the fact that the conscience of England is aroused over the shocking state of affairs that has arisen. The conscience of England may well be aroused. Presently she may stand at the bar before the sister nations, who will ask her, "How have you cared for the boys who were sent to help you?" It will not be easy to find a reply. If we answer, as the Bishop of London has done, that some of them were themselves "looking for trouble," that will not, I think, condone the fact that all of them were placed under conditions of provocation which no men should be asked to endure. "The pavement outside is blocked by the women lying in wait; they push open the windows in broad daylight and try to call the men out – they even force their way inside. The police seem powerless though there are plenty of them about." What can we say to the Colonies when we are reproached for such a state of things as that? We can only make the miserable reply that our own youth has been sacrificed as freely and as needlessly as theirs.

With all possible respect to the Bishop of London, I am of opinion that his suggestion of making venereal disease a military offence would be most dangerous in practice. The man would naturally conceal his condition; he would get worse from want of treatment, and would end by total disablement. In the case of the man I can only suggest that the exhibition to him during his training of a few medical pictures depicting the exact effects of advanced venereal disease would have a distinctly chastening effect. I am clear also that the act of a man who, knowing that he has such a disease upon him, risks the spread of the infection should be made criminal and heavily punished.

The case of the women is different. I cannot clearly follow the Bishop when he uses the word "Christian" in order to support one form of coercion as against another. It does not appear to me to be relevant, and it complicates what is already sufficiently complex. Strictly speaking, one might say that it was not Christian to turn the women out of the warm, well-lit halls into the winter streets. Many of us have our doubts how far moving the women from one point to another can have any effect save that of contaminating new areas. As to the alleged total failure of concentration it is remarkable that nearly all Continental countries (Christian nations, by the way) continue to use the system. I think that it would be fairer to say that it has partially failed, and that this failure is due to venal police and lax administration. I can never believe that a disease, moral or physical, which is quarantined, or even partially quarantined, is not more wisely treated than a disease which is allowed to spread without a check.

But the present condition needs a more speedy and drastic remedy. These women are the enemies of the country. They should be treated as such. A short Bill should be passed empowering the police to intern all notorious prostitutes in the whole country, together with brothel keepers, until six months after the end of the war. All women found to be dangerous should be sent to join them. They should be given useful national work to do, well paid, kindly treated, but subjected to firm discipline at the hands of a female staff. So a curse might be changed, for a time at least, to a blessing, the streets of London would be purified, and our conscience would be clear in that we had done our utmost. "I was ready to give his body for the King, but I am giving his soul as well," cried an agonised mother. We cannot let such words be said in vain.

Yours faithfully,
ARTHUR CONAN DOYLE

Windlesham, Crowborough, Sussex, Feb. 8

Soldiers in London

SIR, – The pronouncement of the Executive Committee of the National Council for Combating Venereal Diseases seems to me to be founded upon some misapprehension. A policy cannot have failed which has never been tried, and the complete separation of prostitutes from the rest of the population for a considerable period of time has never been attempted here, nor, so far as I am aware, elsewhere. By the word "internment" I did not mean mere segregation, but that they should be confined in camps or settlements where they could do honest national work under good conditions, without danger of their spreading either moral or physical contagion. It is a time for swift and radical measures. While we write and talk the poison works.

Yours faithfully,
ARTHUR CONAN DOYLE

Windlesham, Crowborough, Sussex, Feb. 15

"The British Campaign in France"

SIR, – Some unknown friend has been good enough to send me a copy of your paper with a leader upon my recent volume bearing the title *The British Campaign in France*. It is not for me to dispute your critical verdict, save that I may claim that the contents are all drawn from actual documents. There are two points, however, on which I would say a word. Your critic complains that I have not said more about the other nations engaged. This was really precluded by the scope of my book, as expressed in the title, nor had I the particular information which I possessed about the British Army. The second point is that he smiles good-humouredly at my having written about *The Great Boer War*. He misses the point that there was a previous Boer war in 1881, and that I had to differentiate between the two.

ARTHUR CONAN DOYLE

Windlesham, Crowborough, Sussex

Supremacy of the British Soldier

SIR, – It may be of interest to remind your readers how completely, judged by every test, the British soldiers have mastered the German during the war.

After the foolish gibe of the Emperor, and the constant sneers of the German Press, which made merry for so long over our attempts to raise an army, it is instructive to get down to the actual figures, which would be infinitely more favourable if it were not for the losses in the first week of actual fighting, when we were in the presence of forces which outnumbered us by five to one.

In prisoners we have at least double, the British prisoners in Germany being about 34,000 in number, while we have close upon 70,000 Germans. Only during the Mons retreat have the Germans taken any considerable number of prisoners from us. Our losses during that week came to nearly 15,000 men.

On the other hand, on the Marne, at Loos, again and again at the Somme, on the Ancre, and now at Arras and the Vimy Ridge, we have made captures which run into thousands.

The comparison of captured guns is even more remarkable. Our losses during the Mons retreat may be put at about 60, the great majority of which were at the glorious defeat of Le Cateau. Afterwards, the guns which we have lost could be counted upon the fingers of one's hands. There were two at the La Bassée action in October 1914, four heavy guns in the poison gas action of April 23, 1915, and possibly one or two at different times, but the total certainly could not exceed 70.

Against this, we have up to date taken about 200 in the present fighting, and 140 in the fighting on the Somme. Eight were taken in the Battery L action and four by the cavalry next day. Six were taken by the Lincolns on September 9, and about a dozen others, mostly disabled, during the Marne retreat. Twenty-one were taken at Loos.

Altogether, our total amounts approximately to 400 guns, as against 70 which we have lost.

It would be well if some prominence could be given to such figures in those little neutral countries where it is not yet understood that the German soldier has found his master. The superstition of Prussian supremacy never rested upon any very firm basis, and now it has been destroyed for ever.

Giving our enemies credit for all the military virtues which they undoubtedly possess, it has none the less been clearly shown that

brave slaves led by clever fiends can and will be beaten by freemen
led by gentlemen.

ARTHUR CONAN DOYLE

Windlesham, Crowborough, Sussex April 18, 1917

THE DAILY CHRONICLE   2 May 1917

The Submarine Menace

SIR, – While it is dangerous to raise false hopes, we must not lose
sight entirely of certain factors which should be weighed before we
judge the exact menace conveyed by the recent figures of
mercantile sinkings.

At the best it is certainly bad enough, but we need not take it for
worse than it is. If the number of victims had increased by some
gradual progression we should have more cause for alarm, but the
fact that they have exactly doubled in one week, and that the fights
with submarines should rise from 13 to 26 in the same week,
proves clearly, I think, that twice the number of raiders were at
work. Since they could not have doubled their fleet so suddenly
this can only mean that their relay squadron is out working with
the one which in ordinary course it would relieve.

The object of getting present results at the expense of future
ones is, of course, to make a good showing before May 1, and so
persuade their dupes that the end of the war is at hand. If my
supposition is correct the high figures should soon be succeeded by
abnormally low ones, which would restore the average.

It seems to me that nothing could be more encouraging for the
Germans than the tone of some of our public men.

ARTHUR CONAN DOYLE

Windlesham, Crowborough, Sussex, April 29, 1917

THE PALL MALL
GAZETTE   11 June 1917

Father Vaughan and Spiritualism

SIR, – Father Vaughan should learn by the history of his own
order, which has often been unjustly attacked, to be more
moderate in his censures upon others.

His article in your columns upon Spiritism displays all the
intolerance and the persecuting spirit of the Inquisition. "So it is
that I declare we must sweep the country clear of these

250

charlatans." In using these words he is evidently not referring to fraudulent mediums, especially as the sentence continues with a thinly veiled allusion to Sir Oliver Lodge. If Father Vaughan confined himself to fraudulent mediums he would have both the existing laws of England and all decent spiritualists upon his side, for they have always been the curse of the movement.

The whole context shows, however, that what he desires to forcibly attack is everyone who believes what few who have really studied the evidence have failed to believe – first, that the dead survive even as we knew them; secondly, that reverent communication with them is not absolutely impossible; and, thirdly, that many people have been confirmed in or converted to the belief in a future life by such experience, and have thus attained great spiritual good from it. Indeed, it may be said that the only valid answer to materialism lies in the phenomena of spiritualism.

I can assure Father Vaughan that the people who believe this are as good and earnest as he is himself, and very much more openminded and charitable. When he talks of persecuting them for their beliefs and springcleaning them out of England he is using language which was sinister in the fifteenth century, but is out of place in the twentieth.

ARTHUR CONAN DOYLE

Windlesham, Crowborough, Sussex

THE BELFAST EVENING TELEGRAPH
17 July 1917

Record of Sinn Feinism

SIR, – The record of the Sinn Fein party during the few years of its existence is a remarkable one.

It has brought about the destruction of part of its own capital city.

It has driven a wedge through the solid South.

It has immensely strengthened the position of the North, by justifying all its fears, and,

It has, so far as it could, thrown away the fruits of fifty years of patient Constitutional reform.

It only remains for it now to open a civil war against a perfectly united Empire which has shown that it can put five million men in the field, and would do so again before it would consent to having a foreign republic between it and the oceans of the world. When it has achieved this result its cycle of insanity will be complete. Meanwhile I would ask whether any British party has ever in the whole course of history injured Ireland so much in so short a time.

A. CONAN DOYLE

The British Campaign of 1915

SIR, – Your reviewer in his courteous review of my "1915" volume remarks that I see the trees more clearly than the wood, or, in other words, detail more clearly than large effects. It is very possible that he is right. I would point out, however, as an example of the same tendency that he has devoted an appreciable part of his review to my use of the word "mutual" but has omitted to notice that I am the first writer who, with no official aid of any kind, has discerned and set forth in its battalions, brigades, divisions, and corps the British battle line in two of the greatest battles we have ever fought.

Yours faithfully,
ARTHUR CONAN DOYLE

Windlesham, Crowborough, Sussex

British Wives of Germans

SIR, – As president of the Divorce Law Reform Association, I receive numerous letters from various victims of those abuses of British law which were so roundly condemned by a Royal Commission, but have not yet been amended. There is a movement afoot at last which will, I hope, meet the favourable consideration of the Government, to turn all the present separations into divorces. It is surely obvious, apart from humanitarian considerations, that to sterilize an appreciable part of our people when there are such gaps in our numbers is a national folly. There is another class of sufferer, however, for whom I would plead, and whose case should receive instant attention. These are the British wives of German husbands, who should, if they desire it, receive their release from a position which is terrible and unnatural. One of these writes: "Although away from me he cannot refrain from sending insulting messages in respect of my nationality. I am married according to English law, but not, owing to his deception, according to German law." Another writes: – "If we could only escape from this detestable and unnatural position of alien enemy, which at times is literally unbearable!" Surely the bitter cry of these poor women should be heard in high places. No doubt some retaliation would be expected from the Germans, but if a German husband had such feelings towards his British wife in Germany that he desired to divorce her, it is all to the good that he should do so. The difficulty in this, as in all other cases of divorce, is that the sufferers are a small minority, and if the majority have not the imagination to understand, and the charity to help their pitiful condition, their situation is indeed hopeless.

Yours faithfully,
ARTHUR CONAN DOYLE

Windlesham, Crowborough, Sussex, Aug. 21

THE TIMES   28 August 1917

British Wives of Germans

SIR, – The argument of "American Woman" that there should be no divorce for the British woman married to a German because the parties have vowed fidelity to each other would be valid if no such thing as divorce existed. Since, however, the civil code of every civilised nation recognises that circumstances may arise which dissolve the contract, we have to determine whether the fact that these women have been placed in so terrible and unnatural a position, mated with the enemy and alienated among their own kind, is not a good reason for such dissolution.

Yours faithfully,
ARTHUR CONAN DOYLE

Windlesham, Crowborough, Sussex, Aug. 25

THE TIMES   8 September 1917

Divorce and Separation

SIR, – Dr. Johnson has said that the most vexatious of controversialists is the man who on being told that there is no fruit in the orchard proves that there are actually five apples. Professor Whitney contradicts my statement that we have the least liberal divorce laws in the world, and states that there is no divorce in Italy or in certain Roman Catholic provinces, and that in Austria it only applies to non-Catholics. It is notorious that divorce is against the tradition of the Roman Catholic Church, and that in legislatures which are predominantly Roman Catholic there are no facilites for divorce. My point, however, remains untouched, which is that Lord Halifax has implied that no truly Christian nation could have those more liberal divorce laws for which we are agitating, and that he therefore rules out from true Christianity all the nations of the world, with the insignificant exceptions mentioned by Professor Whitney. This seems to me to be the height of spiritual arrogance. Putting Italy to one side, would Professor Whitney seriously put forward the examples of Austria and of French Canada as those which Great Britain, the mother of liberty and progress, should choose as her models?

Yours faithfully,
ARTHUR CONAN DOYLE (President of
the Divorce Law Reform Union).

Windlesham, Crowborough, Sussex, Sept. 6

THE EMPIRE NEWS 16 September 1917

Marriage Cruelties

SIR, – I am as anxious as any theologian that those whom God has placed together in marriage should remain together, but I cannot admit that God has ever placed together the drunken, the cruel, the insane, and the other dreadful couples who inflict misery not only upon each other but notably upon their children, and to some extent upon everyone around them.

To quote what someone said at the Council of Trent in the year 1545 is a very poor consolation to some man whose wife is hopelessly insane and who is condemned to life-long loneliness, or to some woman who is being slowly done to death by a brutal husband.

A Bill now under consideration by a committee of members of both Houses of Parliament provides that after three years of judicial separation the order shall have the same effect and force as a decree absolute of divorce.

I hope it will have the favourable support of the Government.

ARTHUR CONAN DOYLE

THE SPECTATOR 20 October 1917

Divorce and Separation

SIR, – We of the Divorce Law Reform Union earnestly hope that we may have the support of the *Spectator* in our efforts to improve the shocking state of things which now exists in this country. The evidence given at the very powerful Commission which sat for two years under the presidency of the late Lord Gorell convinced the great majority of the members – all of them, in fact, who had no ecclesiastical associations – that a drastic change was needed. Five years, however, have elapsed since that admirable Report was presented, but nothing has been done. One would ask what is the use of appointing expensive and representative Commissions if their conclusions are destined for the pigeon-hole or for the waste-paper basket. The particular measure proposed is that all separations of three years' standing should be turned into divorces. If this should result in setting free all the folk who are at present neither married nor single, and if a good proportion of them remarried and had families, it is no exaggeration to say that the single measure would go far to make up for the whole wastage of the war. Our dead can hardly be more than one hundred and fifty thousand, and there are far more than that number of potential couples who are at present sterilized by our senseless law. If the Church should resolve not to solemnise such marriages, it is of course within its rights in refusing; but it goes beyond its rights, and is guilty of pure intolerance and tyranny, when it prevents those who have no conscientious scruples upon the subject from contracting civil marriages. The record of the Church during the war has not been an heroic one, but it will inflict a deep injury upon the country if it stands in the way of that increase of population upon which in years to come the balance of power in Europe may depend.

I am, Sir, &c.,
ARTHUR CONAN DOYLE
(President of the Divorce Law Reform Union).

Windlesham, Crowborough

THE DAILY EXPRESS   2 November 1917

The Naked Truth

SIR, – In reply to your correspondent's question, the reason why spirits wear robes is that modesty does not cease with this life. Has it ever been the custom for any of the Churches to describe the angels as nude?

ARTHUR CONAN DOYLE

Crowborough, Sussex, Oct. 31

THE TIMES   26 December 1917

The Uses of Hatred

SIR, – I had occasion recently to talk with a British officer who had endured captivity in Germany. With a voice which was husky with passion, trembling with the violence of his own feelings, he told me what he and his comrades had gone through. I had read such things in cold print, but to hear them from one who had seen and felt them had an indescribable effect. I was trembling as he was before he had finished.

This officer, of senior regimental rank, a man of dignity and refinement, was taken wounded at the end of 1914. With his comrades in captivity he was starved during the long two days' journey from the front to his prison. At one spot, he thinks that it was Cologne, a soup canteen upon wheels was rolled up to their compartment in order to mock them. Still starving and suffering tortures from their wounds, they reached the town of their captivity. Weak, shaken, and unnerved, they assembled outside the station, hardly able to stand after their dreadful journey. What ensued can only be described in his own forcible words. "They kicked our behinds all the way up the street. There was not one of us who had not his behind kicked." These were British officers, honourable gentlemen, many of them wounded, now helpless under circumstances which have in all ages appealed to the chivalry of the captors. And we, when a German flier is caught red-handed with his apparatus ready for the murder of the civilians of London, hurry him away that he may have a hot supper.

This officer was, as I was told by a third party, a witness of the dreadful incident of the burning hut. One of the huts in the prison camp took fire. It was night, and the door had been locked on the outside. The key could not be found. One of the inmates, a sailor, tried to get out through the narrow window. The sentry of the hut rushed forward. The prisoners who were spectators thought that he was about to draw the man through. What he actually did was to pass his bayonet through the sailor's throat. I am told that the horrified onlookers dropped on their knees, men of all the Allied countries, and swore to God that so long as they lived they would never show mercy to any man of German blood. Can we blame them? Would we not have felt the same?

Why should we recall these incidents? It is because Hate has its uses in war, as the Germans have long discovered. It steels the mind and sets the resolution as no other emotion can do. So much do they feel this that the Germans are constrained to invent all sorts of reasons for hatred against us, who have in truth never injured them in any way save that history and geography both place us between them and their ambitions. To nourish hatred they invent every lie against us, and so they attain a certain national solidity. We have the true reasons for this emotion, we have suffered incredible things from a foe who is void of all chivalry and humanity. Yet though we have this material we do little to use it and to spread it. How powerful it is can best be told by looking into our own hearts. Many of us could conceive of a peace which included some compromise upon frontiers, so long as

Belgium was intact. Many also would be content to sacrifice Russia, if she persisted in her treason. But not one who knows the facts but would fight to the last gasp in order to ensure stern justice being done to the murderers of our women and to the men who tortured our helpless prisoners.

What then should we do? We should have a statement drawn up, not coldly official but humanly moving, signed by the officers who saw and endured these things. This document should be translated into German and put under the nose of every prisoner in England, that they may at least appreciate the contrast in the culture of the two countries. At present we are so pedantically correct in our treatment of these prisoners that when at an earlier stage of the war I made the suggestion that we place a copy of *J'accuse* in every prison, it was refused on the grounds that it was against international law to proselytise prisoners. This was about the time when Casement and the Germans were trying to starve the Irish prisoners into enlistment against Great Britain.

This statement should be served out broadcast in our munition shops and among our troops.

The munition workers have many small vexations to endure, and their nerves get sadly frayed. They need strong elemental emotions to carry them on. Let pictures be made of these and other incidents. Let them be hung in every shop. Let them be distributed thickly in the Sinn Fein districts of Ireland, and in the hotbeds of Socialism and Pacifism in England and Scotland. The Irishman has always been a man of chivalrous nature, and I cannot believe that even the wrongheaded Sinn Feiner has got down to the level of his allies of Prussia and Turkey. Let his eyes rest upon the work of his friends and perhaps he will realise more clearly how he stands, and the position which he has taken up in the world's fight for freedom. The bestiality of the German nation has given us a driving power which we are not using, and which would be very valuable in this stage of the war. Scatter the facts. Put them in red-hot fashion. Do not preach to the solid South, who need no conversion, but spread the propaganda wherever there are signs of enemy intrigues, on the Tyne, the Clyde, in the Midlands, above all in Ireland and in French Canada. Let us pay no attention to platitudinous Bishops or gloomy Deans, or any other superior people who preach against retaliation or whole-hearted warfare. We have to win, and we can only win by keeping up the spirit and resolution of our own people.

Yours faithfully,
ARTHUR CONAN DOYLE

Windlesham, Crowborough, Sussex

"The Uses of Hatred"

SIR, – I have the utmost respect for the Bishop of Winchester, but when he talks of hating the sin but not hating the sinner he gets into a metaphysical region which, to me at least, has no relation to fact. When I hear of a German kicking a wounded British soldier, it is not the kicking that I hate, but it is the German, and it is my hatred of that man, and my hope of punishing him and his fellows, which help me in my will to conquer. I claim that it would have that effect on any Briton, and that it is a driving force which we do not sufficiently use, because we do not disseminate the facts in a way which really reaches the people.

The Bishop uses the well-worn argument that, because the Germans have done this, and because we condemn German mentality, therefore we are debarred from doing it. This argument was raised over poison gas, and if it had prevailed we should now be at a vast military disadvantage. It was used again over retaliation for air raids, when the Bishops took upon themselves the responsibility of pronouncing against reprisals, and so hampered military action until the logic of events showed that the only possible defence was an attack. Now we have this argument put forward once more. The only answer is that it is certainly wrong to initiate such methods, but that if the enemy uses them, and they are of military value, then we must either follow his example or the cause of freedom and progress will be brought to ruin. Let the sin rest with him who made it needful. To quote Christ's words upon a question of how to conduct a war can lead to no useful purpose. If we had taken isolated texts in a literal fashion and "turned the other cheek," it is obvious that the Empire of the Hohenzollerns would now have covered Europe, and that the teachings of Christ would have been superseded by those of Nietzsche.

I have been asked in a hundred letters what steps I should recommend. I think they are perfectly simple. I do not believe in pamphlets, because the prejudiced man never even opens them. I do believe in placards and pictures, because one cannot help seeing them. I think, therefore, that a short, clear, human statement should be drawn up, fringed by pictures of the incidents I have related and of other similar atrocities. There is no lack of material. The tone of the address should vary according to the audience addressed. The munition workers should be told that their fellow-countrymen understand, and have sympathy with their long hours, their hard work, the petty discomforts and vexations which they have to bear. Their attention should be called, however, to what others have endured, as shown in these pictures, and to these visible proofs of what the system is against which they are working. The same address would appeal to the coalminers. To the Irish, on the other hand, there should be a hearty appeal to their native chivalry, with some lines from Cardinal Mercier and a picture or two of what Belgian priests have had to endure. Thus each man should be helped to see the question from his own standpoint. All this is, of course, well within the scope and powers of our present War Aims and Propaganda Committees. I have had numerous offers of cheques to carry the matter out as a private enterprise. The officials have powers of distribution which no private individuals could possibly organise, and distribution is the all-important item. I think, therefore, that it should be left in their hands, and I can only earnestly hope that some good may come from it without unnecessary delay.

Yours faithfully,
ARTHUR CONAN DOYLE

Windlesham, Crowborough, Sussex

THE TIMES   16 January 1918

Records of German Crime

SIR, – The Dean of Manchester speaks of "implacable hatred" and "invincible resolve" as if they represented alternative courses. My whole point was that hatred, or, if my critics prefer it, righteous wrath, is the means to attain invincible resolve, and it is as such that I have recommended it. Luke-warm feelings can give only half-hearted results. If our workers could actually see the vile things which have been perpetrated upon our people they would be filled by such feelings, call them what you may, that they would work with redoubled heart and vigour. Since they cannot see them they should be brought home to them in every way, verbal or pictorial, that is possible. I cannot understand how it is that revered ecclesiastics go out of their way to reprove me for what they judge, rightly or wrongly, to be an excess of anti-German feeling upon my part, while they have not a word of public reprobation for those of their own number who have depressed the national spirit or hampered military counsels by their published utterances.

Yours faithfully,
ARTHUR CONAN DOYLE

Windlesham, Crowborough, Sussex, Jan. 14

1918–1930

The Maintenance of "Light"

SIR, – I beg to subscribe my annual donation of £10 to *Light*. Should there be a deficit I should always be ready to join with others in defraying it. Riches are no doubt enervating either for an individual or for a cause, but you are in a position, I consider, not to beg for but to demand a sufficiency, in the spirit in which St. Paul demanded the needful money for himself and his propaganda from the early Churches. You represent the most living religious cause now existing upon earth, the only conclusive answer against materialism, and to let your work languish for want of funds is unthinkable.

Yours faithfully,
ARTHUR CONAN DOYLE

Windlesham, Crowborough, Sussex. January 16th, 1918

The Synod and Divorce

SIR, – Since my name seems to have been freely used at the Church meeting at Eastbourne I should be glad of the opportunity to say a few words in reply to the flood of misrepresentation which seems to have carried the audience off their feet. The concrete fact which has to be borne in mind is that there are admittedly some hundreds of thousands of separated people in this country, that their existence is a scandal and a danger, and that some plan must be found for dealing with such a situation; that consideration alone should have brought some common-sense into that atmosphere of intolerance and prejudice. Anyone who desires to form an honest opinion upon this matter has to ask himself the following questions:–

1.–Is it right that divorce should be possible for the rich and impossible for the poor? That is notoriously the case at present. £200 is the average cost of an ordinary divorce suit.

2.–Is it right that the law should be different for men and women – that a woman is cast off for one offence, and that a man may have a fresh mistress every week so long as he abstains from cruelty to his wife?

3.–Is it right that a man may desert a woman and make a new life for himself in some far country, and that the deserted woman shall still be tied to him indefinitely?

4.—Is it right that a man or woman who is wedded to one who is hopelessly insane shall be single all their lives? This insanity may be dipsomania, which is the foulest of all insanities.

5.—Above all, the most pressing of all, is it right that a vast number of people should be separated by the Courts, or by legal agreement, from their spouses, but should be unable to form fresh families? This truly infernal arrangement, which is largely due to ecclesiastical bigotry, has affected some 200,000 people who have passed through the Courts, and an unknown but very large number who have shrunk from the horrors of publicity and have, by mutual consent or by a private agreement, separated from each other. In the case of the first category, the judgment of the Courts has shown that there were serious causes why they should not live together – causes which in many cases would have entailed proper divorce had there been funds to deal with the matter in a divorce Court. In the second category, there should certainly, in my opinion, be a legal inquiry and judgment before divorce is given – a course which must prevent any of those pernicious results about which so much was talked by the speakers at the Church meeting.

It should be explained in this connection that the document quoted from as being a draft Bill was really a mere skeleton draft upon which the Parliamentary Committee were to work before laying the matter before Government. It by no means represents the views of the reformers or the final form which the Bill would take, and it is without all those precautions and guarantees which would naturally be included. Its finding its way in so premature a shape into the Press was entirely due to a mistake upon the part of a member of the Parliamentary Committee. Is it not perfectly clear that by this separation system there are large numbers of people who are a misery to themselves and a danger to everyone around them; for if they cannot found families they can and do break them up. We have lost not less than 150,000 killed in this war. That is a conservative estimate. We are in bitter need of increased population. Surely it does not need to be proved that if you enable a large number of people to re-marry who cannot marry at present you are helping the future population of this country.

All the inanities of Mr. W. Petrie about "Sherlock Holmes" cannot conceal the fact. The proposal may seem to Archdeacon Hoskyns to be a very German one, but if he were more conversant with the subject he would know that it corresponds not only with the law of Germany, but with that of Norway, Sweden, Denmark, Holland, our Australian Colonies, and practically every Protestant country in the world. Indeed our law on divorce is more reactionary than that of several Roman Catholic countries, such as Belgium and Bavaria.

The Church of England has a very bad record for the war. By the Church I do not mean individual clergymen, who have often been heroic, but I mean the official organisation. They made themselves a privileged class and escaped conscription; they gave no clear lead upon temperance; their words and deeds have been continually half-hearted. If on the top of this they mar the chance which the nation has of adopting sane divorce laws, and so restoring some of its lost population, they will surely break the patience of the people, and widen the chasm which already exists between them and the true living England.

Yours, &c.,
ARTHUR CONAN DOYLE

Windlesham, Crowborough, 6th February

THE DAILY
CHRONICLE   11 February 1918

The Cheriton Dug-out

SIR, – Under the heading "Two Wartime Ghosts become Casualties" you state on the authority of Mr. Cunningham Craig that the curious phenomena at Cheriton were due to the "emission of natural gas." May I say that such an explanation is the height of absurdity to anyone who has weighed the evidence? We have at least seven witnesses to the levitation of heavy objects, including brick bats, chairs and crowbars, while I have myself seen the chunks which were hit out of the new brickwork by the impact of heavy missiles. It takes credulity, indeed, to believe that all this is due to the emission of natural gas.

There have been many instances recorded of the appearance of Poltergeists or mischievous spirits, the instances being in close agreement as to phenomena, so that the Cheriton occurrence is not to be looked upon as an entirely isolated fact, but rather as a confirmation of many previous instances.

ARTHUR CONAN DOYLE

Windlesham, Crowborough, Sussex, Feb. 8

THE TIMES   16 March 1918

Hospital Ships

SIR, – Can anyone explain why our hospital ships continue to make floating targets of themselves by carrying rows of lights when they know that the enemy are lying in wait for them? And can anyone explain why we have not 20 German officers in each ship on the distinct understanding that in case of accident they shall be the last to leave her? And can anyone say why every ship returning across the Atlantic does not take a full human cargo of the interned Germans, so that these useless mouths may be fed over yonder? And can anyone explain why the policy of putting pickets of German prisoners all over London on raid nights is only now being discussed, when it has been perfectly obvious ever since the Germans put our prisoners in Karlsruhe? There may be some reasonable answers to all these questions, but to the bystander they are absolutely unintelligble.

Yours faithfully,
ARTHUR CONAN DOYLE

Windlesham, Crowborough, Sussex

THE DAILY
CHRONICLE   18 April 1918

Ireland & Conscription

SIR, – I am in hearty sympathy with your views upon this question. I do not suppose that anyone has written more strongly than I have done in the Irish Press upon the sad failure of so many Irishmen to rise to this European crisis, but none the less my heart sank, for the first time in this war when I saw what the Government proposed to do. They have acted so wisely up to now that it seems the more terrible that they should make so fatal a mistake at this all-important moment.

Consider the series of impossibilities. Suppose that in face of every sort of riot and uproar they obtained the men, how could they make them take the oath of allegiance? And if they took the oath how could they make them train? And if they trained how could they make them fight? What would be the feelings of a British division which had such troops upon its flanks? What would be our own feelings if half a dozen divisions, rotten with Sinn Fein, were now in our battle line? Is it not clear that it might lead to serious military disaster, as it has so often done with the disaffected troops of Austria? Would not the sane General say that he would rather have half the troops, but know that he can rely upon them? And yet it is to attain such an end as this that we are venturing upon this desperate path.

Surely there is an honourable alternative for the Government. Let them frankly say that after the eloquent speech of Mr. Devlin, and the way in which it was received by the party, and also in deference to the expressed desire of the Irish officers who have donned the King's uniform, the Home Rule Bill will be passed at once without conditions, and the rest left to the sense of chivalry of the Irish people. The rights of Ulster should be conserved to the point of making the Irish Constitution such as will readily fit hereafter into a federal system.

If this or some other similar solution is not found we shall find ourselves landed in a sordid guerilla war in the West, as well as the vital contest in Flanders.

ARTHUR CONAN DOYLE

Windlesham, Crowborough, Sussex, April 16, 1918

THE TIMES   27 May 1918

The Outrage on the Hospitals

SIR, – I am in full agreement with Lord Denbigh that it is our own nerveless policy which exposes us to the outrages of the Huns. They will do what they think they can do with impunity, and they will avoid that which entails punishment. When Miss Cavell was shot we should at once have shot our three leading prisoners. When Captain Fryatt was murdered we should have executed two submarine captains. These are the arguments which the German mentality can understand. Two years ago you allowed me to plead in your columns for the bombing of the Rhine towns, and now, when at last it is partly done, we at once hear the cry for a truce in such warfare – the very result which I had predicted. But alas for the two wasted years! Now we have to deal with the bombing of hospitals. German prisoners should at once be picketed among the tents, and the airmen captured should be shot, with a notice that such will be the fate of all airmen who are captured in such attempts. We have law and justice on our side. If they attempt a reprisal, then our own counter-reprisals must be sharp, stern, and relentless. If we are to have war to the knife, then let it at least be equal for both parties.

Yours faithfully,
ARTHUR CONAN DOYLE

Windlesham, Crowborough, Sussex, May 24

THE TIMES   28 June 1918

The Case of our Prisoners

SIR, – Von Kühlmann has thrown out suggestions as to a peace conference. This is, of course, entirely out of the question in the present indeterminate state of the war. None the less, does it not give an opening for an official statement from our Government, which could formally say that no discussion is possible between the nations (even if the larger matters could be settled) until the crimes inflicted upon our prisoners, and upon our wounded deliberately bombed in hospitals, had been admitted and expiated? This would bring the question strongly to the front, and possibly improve matters in the future, even if we got no satisfaction for the past. I really think that the greater part of the German nation have no notion of our feelings upon this subject.

Yours faithfully,
ARTHUR CONAN DOYLE

Windlesham, Crowborough, Sussex, June 25

THE FINANCIAL
NEWS   16 July 1918

Thyssen's Revelations

SIR, – The public owe you a debt of gratitude for publishing an important document like Thyssen's pamphlet, which has aroused great interest in America, but has never, so far as I know, appeared in our press. It is to be hoped that our propagandists will ensure that the assertions made therein be widely circulated in India, so that our fellow-citizens in that country may realise the fate from which they have been saved by the armies of the Allies. Their utter ruin and enslavement would, as is clearly shown, have been the first fruits of victory for the Kaiser.

Yours faithfully,
A. CONAN DOYLE

Windlesham, Crowborough, Sussex, July 12

THE TIMES   8 October 1918

Our Prisoners

SIR, – Why are we so mealy-mouthed with these barbarians, who are sensitive to no appeal save that of fear? Why do we not officially state that every man, up to the Kaiser, shall be tried for his life in return for the murder of our prisoners? Why do we not say, also, that we will meet no German representative for any purpose until the matter has been set absolutely right? Our inexplicable silence makes them think that we are indifferent. Let our threat be for all the world to hear, not whispered to officials at a conference. Then we shall get redress.

Yours faithfully,
ARTHUR CONAN DOYLE

Windlesham, Crowborough, Sussex, Oct. 6

THE TIMES   12 November 1918

The German Criminals

SIR, – The next scene in the world-drama will be a general exodus of all the men who may be wanted over the frontiers of Denmark, Holland, or Switzerland. Would it not be as well for the Allies to lose no time in warning these neutrals to be careful whom they may accept as guests, since we shall certainly not recognise any rights of asylum for those whom we regard as murderers? Such an announcement might be unprecedented, but so are the times.

Yours faithfully,
ARTHUR CONAN DOYLE

Windlesham, Crowborough, Sussex, Nov. 9

THE DAILY
MAIL   15 November 1918

Divorce and the Bishops

SIR, – The bishops have lived up to the highest tradition of their order by killing the Bill by which five years' desertion becomes a cause for divorce. Their votes will take their place in history beside those which they recorded against the Reform Bill of 1832, against Catholic emancipation, against the removal of the civil liabilities of the Jews, and against free education.

The unfortunate people affected are a small minority, but there is a side to the question which may affect us all. Many of these people are desperate at the injustice done them since the Royal Commission reported in their favour. They form a class who are filled with a most justifiable hatred of the law and of established institutions. Whether it is wise in these perilous days to allow such a class to continue to nurse a grievance which embitters their whole lives is a question which concerns the public very closely.

As to the Church itself, their record in this and other matters will soon come up for national judgment.

ARTHUR CONAN DOYLE, President
Divorce Law Reform Union

Windlesham, Crowborough, Sussex

269

THE JOURNAL OF
THE SOCIETY FOR
PSYCHICAL RESEARCH   January 1919

A Prophecy

MADAM, – On the morning of April 4th, 1917, I woke up with
a strong feeling that information of importance had been conveyed
to me in my sleep. I had a feeling also that it was of a consoling
nature. I could only remember one word, however, Piave. It rang
in my head. Piave! Piave! It was as though it were some keyword,
and if I could retain that, I should have the essence of the message.

No doubt in my reading I must have seen the word, and on my
visit to the Italian front I had actually passed over the river, but I
had retained the names of none of the many streams, save only the
Isonzo, upon which the war was at that time being waged. Thus
Piave conveyed nothing to my mind. I was so impressed, however,
that I went at once into my study and looked up the index of my
Atlas. By this reference I discovered that the name was that of a
river about fifty miles in the rear of the Italian front, which was at
that time victoriously advancing. I could imagine few more
unlikely things than that the war would be transferred to the
Piave. None the less I was so impressed by my dream that I drew
up a paper at once, under the date April 4, 1917, in which I stated
that I knew some great event of the war would centre on the Piave.
This was witnessed that morning by two witnesses. In view of my
feeling of elation on waking I took it that this event would be
favourable, tho' how a favourable event could occur fifty miles in
the rear was more than I could understand.

It is a matter of history how six months later the Italian army
was driven from its positions. Whilst it was in retreat I sent a
sealed envelope to the S.P.R. with an account of my dream. The
army crossed several points, such as the Tagliamento, where a
stand seemed probable, and halted eventually upon the line of the
Piave, which had been said to be untenable, since it was
commanded from the left rear. They were still there in February,
1918, when I was writing my *New Revelation*. In describing the
incident I said, "If nothing more should occur the reference to the
name has been fully justified, presuming that some friend in the
beyond was forecasting the coming events of the war. I have still a
hope, however, that more was meant, and that some crowning
victory of the Allies at this spot may justify still further the strange
way in which the name was conveyed to my mind." This sentence
appeared in print in April, 1918.

It will be recalled that it was on June 17th, 1918, that the first
battle of the Piave was fought. It was not a great victory, but it was

a victory, and it is noteworthy that this date marked the whole turning point of the war. Up to then the Allies had in this year sustained three severe defeats, that of the second Somme battle, the battle of the Lys, and the second Aisne battle. On June 17th their prospects were very black. From the day of the Piave battle they never looked back again, and on every front they had an uninterrupted record of victory, culminating, in the case of the Italians, in the second Piave battle, which was the most decisive in the war. Thus in conveying the name "Piave" my comforter had given me the keyname which would unlock the whole situation.

Now how could this be accounted for by coincidence? That is unthinkable. Even if my subconscious self had known there was a river called the Piave, that would not have shifted the Italian army back to it. Was it then telepathy? But no one in the world could have conjectured such a series of events. What then was it? I claim that the only possible explanation is that my friends on the other side, knowing how much I worried over the situation, were giving me comfort and knowledge. The ordinary spirit has, so far as my reading and experience teached me, only a very limited and uncertain gift of prophecy. Therefore I have some reason to hope that my information came from a high source. Why I should have been so privileged above others is the one point which is beyond my conjecture.

ARTHUR CONAN DOYLE

Windlesham, Crowborough,
Sussex, November, 1918.

[*The sealed letter to which Sir Arthur Conan Doyle refers above was received by the Secretary of the Society for Psychical Research on November 7, 1917, with a covering note asking that it should be opened only at the writer's request. This letter was opened and read on November 20, 1918. It ran as follows:*]

WINDLESHAM, CROWBOROUGH,
SUSSEX, November 4, 1917.

In the early summer of 1917 I woke from sleep with the word Piave in my head, as the culmination of some dream of which I could remember nothing. I had no remembrance of the word, but thought vaguely it was a place. The index of an atlas showed me that it was a river some distance behind the Italian front. I drew the attention of my wife and brother-in-law to it that morning, and said something would surely occur there. Afterwards the Italians advanced and Piave seemed far in the rear. Now the tide has turned, tho' I have not yet seen the line of the Piave mentioned. It is always the Tagliamento. Still it is worth chronicling and putting into neutral hands.

A. CONAN DOYLE

The New Spiritualism

SIR, – I notice that Mr. Clodd laments my inability to grasp the principles of scientific investigation. It is very deplorable, but since I err with Lodge and Wallace, Flammarion and Lombroso, Richet and James, Meyers and Crookes, I am still unabashed, even before the censure of Mr. Clodd.

As to Colonel Warren's rather crude tests, he knows perfectly well that if a script purporting to be the end of Edwin Drood was to appear he would be the first to reject it as spurious. As to messages from ships, if he were better read on the subject, he would know that such details have been recorded. To take the most obvious example, there is a whole book called *Has W.T. Stead returned?* by James Coates, published in 1913 by Fowler and Co., which gives various accounts of the sinking of the "Titanic" and his death by drowning. The evidence is enormous and convincing, as I can say after thirty-two years of study. What is lacking is earnestness and industry on the part of inquirers, who expect everything to be brought to them, instead of going forth to seek it.

Yours, &c.,
ARTHUR CONAN DOYLE

Windlesham, Crowborough, Sussex

The Epsom Incident

SIR, – If a dock strike is the only reason why the Canadians have been disappointed in their transport, would it not be possible to call for volunteers from among them to do the work of the dockers? Such a course of action would at least assure them that everything possible was being done. It is very painful to those who admire the Canadians to see them spoiling their good name at the last moment. It is only fair to ask, however, whether some of the blame does not lie with want of tact or want of hospitality in these different centres. I have had considerable experience of Canadian troops, having had a whole division encamped for a year close to my house, and having had 700 officers under my own roof, and I can testify that no men could have behaved better, and that they were regretted in this village when they left us.

Yours faithfully,
A. Conan Doyle

Windlesham, Crowborough, Sussex

THE TIMES　　　　　9 July 1919

Profiteering

Sir, – Unless something is done quickly, and done thoroughly, to check rising prices of the necessaries of life, there will be violence in this country. Man must live, and these wicked prices are making it a hard matter.

What are our rulers about, and why are they tacitly protecting a handful of profiteers to the danger of the nation? The men who are making fortunes out of the needs of the people are not very numerous, they are not difficult to find, a very little examination would establish their guilt, and if there is no law adequately to punish them, then it is a reproach to our law-makers that such a law should not exist. Let it be passed and most rigorously enacted. A dozen cases of extreme punishment would work a wondrous change.

I will take an illustration of the present monstrous condition of affairs. I have some first-hand evidence of the condition of that market-garden industry which supplies London with most of its vegetables. The cabbage or lettuce which is bought from the market gardener (who conveys it to Covent Garden) at 1d. or 1½d., is sold in the shops at an average of from 8d. to 1s. Occasionally it passes 1s., for there is no limit to the conscienceless greed. Now only two people have handled that vegetable since the grower received his very reasonable price, which would be lower were it not that every expense which he bears, from his labour to his petrol, has greatly increased. He is guiltless in the matter. The guilt lies between the wholesale dealer who buys the consignment at 3 or 4 o'clock in the morning at Covent Garden or other market, and the retailer who comes to buy it from the wholesale dealer at some later hour. Between them, although they do nothing but handle what others by their work and care have produced, they increase the price at least four – and often six or eight-fold.

The worst case seems to be the wholesale dealer, because as he is handling very large quantities, and only has them for a few hours, one would expect that some very trifling charge upon each vegetable would still give him a considerable profit. Far, however, from his charge being trifling, he gets more, and often much more,

273

on each cabbage or lettuce than the original grower who has taken all the risk and shown all the skill. What the wholesale dealer buys at 1d. or 1½d. he passes on again at 3d. or 4d. That, as it seems to me, is the root of the evil. The shopkeeper may be, and often is, a criminal also in this matter, but at least he does take some risk with a perishable stock and an uncertain demand. But for these huge profits of the middlemen, who must all be on the way to great wealth, there can be no excuse whatever. If they plead that their expenses at Covent Garden cause this inflation, then Covent Garden should itself be abolished and a Government market established. Government has many men available from the Army supply services who are quite competent to handle large commercial matters. I suggest that by the use of such men the middleman's absence in gaol might be successfully tided over, and a better system inaugurated. A few clean-run British officers with plenary powers would very soon set things right.

Meanwhile three matters press. The first is to decree heavy punishment for anyone who destroys food, as is done in some cases in order to keep up prices. A second is to punish in the same way anyone who sets up any impediment to the circulation of marketable goods. Attempts at reform have sometimes been discouraged by the complete disappearance of the goods concerned, and the public is tempted to say, "There is the consequence of interfering with supply and demand." It is much more likely to be the consequence of interference with illicit profits, and an attempt to bully the public into tamely submitting to extortion. The third and most important thing is to define what is a fair profit in the case both of middleman and retailer, and to clap the offenders into gaol. The recent fines of a few shillings are rather an incentive to crime than a deterrent.

Yours faithfully,
ARTHUR CONAN DOYLE

Windlesham, Crowborough, Sussex

COMMON SENSE   12 July 1919

Modern Miracles – Reply to
Jerome K. Jerome

SIR, – Mr. Jerome K. Jerome appeals to me to answer some questions about spiritualism, propounded in your columns. This I am happy to do, although I am bound to say that if he had read, even superficially, upon the subject he would not have needed to ask them.

1. Why is a medium bound in a physical phenomenon seance?

Because otherwise the sceptics would declare that he himself produced the results. In some cases he has been put in a locked cage for the same reason.

2. Why in the dark?

Because experience has shown that the results are better in the dark. It would be more convenient if this were not so. It would also be more convenient if photographs could be developed outside a dark room. In each case physical law is the obstacle.

3. Why a tambourine?

It is the only instrument which shows by its rattle where it is in a dark room. A luminous cross is equally good and is now occasionally used.

4. Why such puerile messages?

Death alters nothing, and we find every grade of intelligence upon the further side from a sprite to an archangel. We get what we deserve. If Mr. Jerome would come to me and examine the 120 books upon this subject which form my reference library he would find that the tone of the communications is by no means so low as he thinks. Some of them are as high as mortal brain can follow.

Mr. Jerome complains that the raps at Hydesville did not disclose something wonderful. I think that when they disclosed intelligence separated from ordinary matter they *did* disclose something wonderful – the most wonderful thing that our age has known. I agree that many of the manifestations seem puerile, but if one looks behind them at the force which produces them they cease to be puerile, but form the starting point of a chain of thought and experiment which is all-important. The appeal was made to a coarse-minded and materialistic generation, and it was just such crude phenomena that were needed to shake them out of their complacency. It would have seemed better to us if an archangel had appeared in Trafalgar Square, but I suppose the problem was made more obscure so that we should have the merit of using our wits and our patience.

Mr. Jerome compares the modern miracles with those of the New Testament. They are, I think, the same. Save for the raising of the dead I cannot recall any miracle in the New Testament which has not been claimed, upon good authority, as having occurred in the experience of spiritualists.

I have myself experienced the rushing wind, the tongues of fire, and the direct voice. As to our modern miracles being funny and those of the Testament free from this taint, it all depends upon the spirit in which an incident is described. I have no doubt that if a cynical press man had told the story of the loaves and fishes or of the Gadarene swine he could have made it very funny, but that does not really dispose of the matter.

I cannot cover all the ground here, but I have done so in my

New Revelation, and would be glad to send Mr. Jerome a copy. I care nothing about proselytising, but if I could give so old a friend the joy which this knowledge brings with it I should spare no pains to do so.

Yours faithfully,
ARTHUR CONAN DOYLE

Windlesham, Crowbrough, Sussex. July 4

THE TIMES   12 July 1919

The Vegetable Market

SIR, – My figures were, as stated in my previous letter, taken from a first-hand source. The garden in question is, I believe, somewhat beyond the 20 miles radius, though I do not understand why this should make any difference, since the produce is delivered by the grower. I have asked the firm in question to corroborate to you direct, but the use of names is difficult, as the wholesaler has considerable powers of injuring the producer. I repeat with confidence that the price received by the market gardener is from a penny to three-halfpence in the case of cabbages and lettuces, and every householder knows that they are exposed for sale at eightpence or upwards in the shops. The guilt lies between two individuals, the wholesaler and the retailer, and the proportion of their gains is roughly as stated in my previous letter.

Mr. Ravenhill has given a double list of the wholesale selling price and the retail selling price. It avoids the price which has been paid by the wholesaler to the producer, which is the real crux of the matter. But taking the figures as they stand they are of no practical value, for anyone who tries will find it quite impossible to buy the vegetables in the shops at the prices which are quoted on the authority of the President of the London and Home Counties Retailers' Federation. It is a mere mockery to have cabbages listed at fourpence to fourpence-half-penny when all the world knows that they cannot be actually bought at that figure. A hotel proprietor buying wholesale for a large establishment assures me that he could not get one under sixpence. If these so-called "official" prices were really official and compulsory, then few retailers in London could escape prosecution.

Yours faithfully,
ARTHUR CONAN DOYLE

July 9

Growers, Sellers, and the State

Sir, – Perhaps you will kindly allow me to say one more word upon this subject. I have nothing to withdraw, and a good deal to add. The profiteers in the wholesale trade endeavour to throw dust in our eyes by claiming that they work upon commission. As a matter of fact they seem to work both ways, as suits them best. But a commission may be as onerous as a direct payment, and it avoids any tiniest element of risk. In a bill which lies before me (it is from Spitalfields Market, but it is a system, not of locality, which I am attacking), the small grower has been charged 40 per cent, commission, so that where his bundle of rhubarb realised 5s. he received 3s. Out of this 3s. he has to pay his rent, his labour, his expenses, while the man who has done nothing at all, save hand the goods across, gets nearly the same remuneration. I can forward this document for your inspection, but these middlemen appear to be bullies, and it is not safe for the producer to cross them. "We might as well shut down our gardens at once," says one of my informants.

In the list of prices given by Mr. Ravenhill one can only wonder at his moderation, for since it has no connexion with actual shop prices he might have adopted any scale. A lady with a small income, and her breadwinner killed in the war, writes to me from Ladbroke-street: – "I cannot get a cabbage under from 8d. to 1s., and the smallest cauliflowers are 1s." The date of the letter is July 11. It was on the same date that the hotelkeeper informed me that he could not get cabbages in wholesale lots under 6d. And yet we have Messrs. Ridley, Bradnum, Lewis, Mason, and the other leaders of the trade assuring the public that they are "highly indignant" with me for exposing these facts. Unless these gentlemen get to work and reform their rotten trade they may find that the public is "highly indignant" with them.

The State is, I am convinced, incurring a grave danger by its complacence towards wholesale profiteers, and towards the voracious retailers who are making fortunes by starving their fellow countrymen. I have always been an optimist during the war, as my numerous letters in your columns will testify, but there are some signs now which overshadow me. One patriotic Socialist desired to bring the question of profiteering before a democratic meeting, and was earnestly persuaded not to do so. "If the price of things only keeps the present level until the winter the chance we have been waiting for for 50 years has come," so said the more extreme man, who wished nothing done to restrain the profiteers.

And we are courting these dangers, which may undo our victory in the field, for the sake of allowing a handful of men to intervene for their own illicit gain between the man who grows the food and the man who eats it. Immediate and drastic legislation is imperatively called for.

Yours faithfully,
Arthur Conan Doyle

Windlesham, Crowborough, Sussex, July 15

COMMON SENSE   16 August 1919

Mr. Jerome and Spirits

Sir, – As Mr. Jerome K. Jerome has had his second innings, perhaps you will kindly allow me to be upon equal terms with him. I note from his remarks that he is sceptical about the facts of the physical phenomena of Spiritualism. But from every word of his article it is evident that he has never examined these alleged facts, and that apart from my own short epitome of the subject, which he has read in the interval between articles, he has no acquaintance with the evidence. Under these circumstances, what is his dissent worth? Clever man as he is, it is not the same weight as the opinion of the first man you meet in the street, if that man has chanced to have real knowledge of what has occurred. To put it in a definite form, has he carefully read Sir William Crookes' laboratory experiments as described by himself from 1871 to 1873? Has he read the researches of Dr. Crawford, of Belfast, set forth in two books between 1915 and 1919? Has he read Professor Geley's recent experiments, which were checked by a hundred French scientists of various types? Has he read the work of Professor Schrenck-Notzing, the German inquirer? Has he seen the books of the famous Professor Lombroso and the record of his twenty years' work? All these works have been accompanied by photographs. Does he accuse all these distinguished scientists of faking these photographs, without the faintest personal object, and indeed with risk of incurring professional ruin? If he has not consulted these authorities then he has no right to assume so intolerant an attitude, and to jeer at those who have. If, on the other hand, he has consulted those authorities, and is still a sceptic, then his mental attitude is beyond my comprehension. It seems to me that the maddest theory ever invented by the human brain is that for seventy years a great number of people in many varying countries have all been claiming to have certain personal experiences, often seen by many at one time, and that the whole thing originates in colossal stupidity or impish mischief. Can

278

anyone really continue to hold such a theory as that? I notice that opponents of the movement are more and more being pushed away from it, and are adopting the alternative, but contradictory ground, that such knowledge is illicit.

In quoting some small instances of abnormal happenings given in my book, Mr. Jerome entirely misrepresents them, and shows that extraordinary inaccuracy which seems inseparable from every controversialist who attacks Spiritualism. For example, in the case of the lady who wrote automatically about the terrible nature of the *Lusitania* disaster, Mr. Jerome suppresses the fact that it was at a time when we had every reason to believe that there was no loss of life. That is, of course, the whole point of the story. Again, in describing my Piave dream, he does not mention that I had never at that time consciously heard of the Piave, and that it was not within the war zone when I recorded the dream. This, again, is the whole point of the anecdote. As to the argument that three cool-headed and responsible men of the world like Lord Adair, Lord Seaton and Captain Wynne are to be disbelieved as witnesses to a fact which all three have seen – namely, the levitation of Mr. Home – because false witnesses swore away the lives of witches in the Middle Ages, I can hardly believe that Mr. Jerome would seriously uphold it. I am fairly well acquainted with the history of witchcraft, and the main characteristics of the old trials were the illiteracy and general independability of the witnesses.

Mr. Jerome is very anxious to know what is our "new religion." I think he will find something very like it if he goes back nineteen hundred years and studies the Christianity of Christ. There he will read of those same signs and wonders which we call "phenomena," there he will read of the discerning of spirits which we call "clairvoyance," and there also he will read of a good deal of ridicule and misrepresentation which did not prevent the new movement from conquering the world, even as this, its successor, is bound to do. This time, however, we must see to it that the sacred fire is not smothered by formalism and the intrusion of materialism. I agree with Mr. Jerome that we have lived to see some very terrible phases of human history. At the same time, I am convinced that anything more unselfish and noble than the conduct of the British Empire as a whole, and of Britons as individuals, during the last five years, has never been known. It is true that the present and future may not be at so high a level, but at least in the wartime the nation has risen with hardly an exception to an extraordinary point of moral grandeur. Personally, I do not at all take the view that Christ was one who would stand by and see cruelty or oppression without interference; but I prefer to believe that had He been amongst us, He would have been the first

279

to risk a second martyrdom in the cause of justice and freedom. He would have done His part in the scourging of the Germans out of Belgium as whole-heartedly as He scourged the tradespeople out of the Temple. I cannot accept the watery, cold-blooded, unpractical reading which some have given to His character. However, I have said enough, and must not lay any greater burden upon your hospitable columns.

Yours, etc.,
A. CONAN DOYLE

Crowborough, August 11

THE EVENING
STANDARD   6 November 1919

Spiritualism's Peril

SIR, – I understand from your columns that Mr. Magee has challenged me to produce Mr. Forbes Winslow's letter in which he disclaimed his previous views upon spiritualism, especially as regards lunacy.

I therefore enclose the essential part of the letter, written in 1912. The allegations quoted by Mr. Magee were made in 1877. The original can be seen at the office of "Two Worlds," 18, Corporation-street, Manchester. It was written in answer to a direct question on the subject from the late J.J. Morse.

I trust that Mr. Magee will apologise, and that he will forward the address of the priest who is alleged to have offered £50 for the production of this document. We may hope that we have now heard the last of the mythical 10,000 lunatics.

Yours faithfully,
ARTHUR CONAN DOYLE

THE DAILY
MAIL   16 December 1919

Woman "Spirit" Painter

Sir A. Conan Doyle and Mrs. Spencer

SIR, – In the early days of this movement it was foretold by Mrs. de Morgan and others that the line of advance would be from the crude material phenomena, common in these days to the finer and more intellectual proofs which the human race would become

280

more fitted to receive. This prophecy has, in the course of the last fifty years, been amply justified. The spirit rap, levitations, and even materialisations have become far less common. The evidence in these directions has been given, and this stage appears to be closing down. On the other hand, we have never before had such an outburst of the finer phases of spirit intervention, of spirit photography, of inspirational addresses, writings, and paintings, and very especially of that clairvoyance or "discerning of spirits" which Saint Paul counted among the most valuable of spiritual gifts.

In writing this letter my object was, however, to point out some of the more intellectual proofs of spirit intervention which may appeal to those minds which recoil from grosser manifestations, only justifed by the necessities of the material age in which we live. Of written inspiration much might be said, for no philosophy that has appeared has such a literature as has grown round spiritualism. To those who imagine that the inspirational messages are of small intellectual value I would name only two recent books: *Claude's Second Book* (Methuen) and *Letters from the Other Side* (Watkins), which contain the very essence of spiritual knowledge, and, incidentally, a good deal of prophesy, in the case of the latter book, which has been literally fulfilled since the time the messages were taken. If those two books are not indeed inspired, then what are we to think of the transcendent intellectual qualities of those two ladies whose hands were used to produce the script?

It is, however, to inspirational painting which I would especially refer, because when a masterpiece is produced by one who has no technical skill, and when it is exposed for all to behold, the most sceptical must admit that there is something there beyond their ken. Some publicity has been given recently to the symbolic drawings of Mr. Charles Horsfall, and after inspecting them I am certainly of opinion that they are indeed truly inspirational in their origin and profound in their meaning.

I could, however, appreciate the position of those who have no turn for mysticism and who do not understand that there are some subjects so complex that they cannot be treated in a pictorial but only in a diagrammatic fashion.

To these people I would recommend an inspection of the head of Christ now exhibited at the Walker Gallery in New Bond street. This picture is, in my opinion, the very finest head of the Founder of Christianity that has ever been conceived, and I can well understand the action of a great painter in Paris who, when he saw the companion full-face drawing, fell instantly upon his knees.

It is, indeed, a most marvellous production, with all that inner soul which is so lacking in the old masters, whose Christs and

Virgins appear to me to be very often the quaintesence of materialism and vulgarity.

Yet this wonderful work was done in a few hours by a lady who, as I am assured by her family, has no power of artistic expression when in her normal condition. It is a supreme example of the working of spiritual intelligence through a material mortal frame.

ARTHUR CONAN DOYLE

Windlesham, Crowborough, Sussex, Dec. 13

THE TIMES   30 December 1919

"A Disclaimer"

SIR, – In answer to the Hon. Major Victor Spencer's letter in your columns, may I disclaim having ever mentioned Mrs. Spencer's name at any time in connexion with psychic phenomena. A reference to the original published correspondence will show that it was her own family who mentioned her name, and that it was a close relation who said, "Mrs. Spencer has strong psychic power," and also asserted in one picture that it was done upside down. "When she had finished she wondered what on earth she had done. It was only on turning it upside down that a perfect head of Christ appeared." I enclose the cutting with marked passages to prove my assertion.

Major Spencer is, of course, entitled to have his own views upon psychic matters and their value, but the tide of events is, I think, against him.

Yours faithfully,
ARTHUR CONAN DOYLE

Windlesham, Crowborough, Sussex, Dec. 29

THE WORLD OF TRADE,
FRANKFURT   15 January 1920

British Attitudes towards Germany

SIR, – I have no ill feeling against you, but we have suffered so heavily in this country from the policy of your rulers, which has never been in any way apologised for or atoned for by your people, that we all have a horror of Germany and all things connected with it. Hardly a family in the land has escaped loss, rich or poor, and all because we were placed in the dilemma of either incurring these losses, or forfeiting our nation's honour for ever by breaking our solemn promise to defend Belgium. We chose the path of honour and duty but it has cost us dear and we have no love for those who, as Prince Lichnowsky's report shows, forced us into such a position against every effort our Statesmen could make. That will be the feeling of all this generation of Britons, but a full admission of error and expression of sorrow may at last bring an appeasement.

yours sincerely
ARTHUR CONAN DOYLE

Windlesham, Crowborough, Sussex, Dec. 9 1919

THE SOUTHPORT
VISITER   22 January 1920

Spiritualism and the Church

SIR, – I observe that one of my reverend critics, who seem certainly to have inherited the spiritual gift of prophecy, since they attacked me before knowing what I would say, has repeated the ancient discredited story about American lunacy asylums being filled by Spiritualists. There is not a word of truth in this. The only statistics which I have been able to find are collected by a Dr. Eugene Crowell, who examined the asylums of New England, where Spiritualism is very common, and who found, out of 16,000 lunatics, four Spiritualists – and, I regret to say, 222 clergymen. The myth began with a statement in 1876 by the late Dr. Forbes Winslow, which he retracted in after life, when he was himself a Spiritualist. I have a copy of this retraction in my possession. As to the statements of the other clerics that irreverence is shown to God or Christ by Spiritualists, it is typical of the ignorance of the subject shown by so many of these gentlemen, whose job it is, as the Rev. Vale Owen said, to be well informed about it. True Spiritualism belongs to no creed, but it is the root fact of all religion, and can be equally professed by an Anglican, a Roman Catholic, a Nonconformist, or even a Unitarian. It is only with the materialist that no compromise can be made, for our views are diametrically opposed.

Yours etc.,
ARTHUR CONAN DOYLE

Hotel Metropole, Blackpool, January 20th

THE TIMES   6 February 1920

The German Criminals

SIR, – If the war had gone against us, and part of the German peace terms had been that Haig, Beatty, Jellicoe, and some hundred others should be delivered up to be tried upon some points which appeared to us to be inadequate, we should certainly feel an enduring resentment. We can therefore understand the feelings of the ill-informed German public. It is the first duty of a wise diplomacy to avoid enduring resentments, and therefore we should endeavour to find some means for alleviating the situation, so long as justice does not suffer.

Might I suggest that the German face would be saved, and no real harm done, if they were asked to provide a Judge, or possibly two Judges, for the tribunal? If it could be so arranged that these Judges were drawn from the non-Junker class, then it is possible that they would concur with much that has to be done. But at the worst, where the Allied Judges were unanimous their presence would do no harm, while where there was difference of opinion it would tip the scale in favour of the prisoner. In every way, as it seems to me, we should now work for a peaceful Europe, which offers the only hope for financial stability.

Yours faithfully,
ARTHUR CONAN DOYLE

Windlesham, Crowborough, Sussex, Feb. 5

THE SOUTHPORT
VISITER   12 February 1920

Spiritualism and Insanity

SIR, – I must apologise for leaving Father Thurston's letter unanswered. When I wrote before, I was far from home, and had to trust to my memory. This has not entirely betrayed me, but it has confused two sets of figures, each of which is excellent for my purpose. The first set is that of Dr. Crowall, correctly quoted by Father Thurston, showing that out of 32,313 male patients 215 were clergymen, while the total male and female Spiritualists under treatment were 45. There is no reason at all to think that the word Spiritualists was confined only to mediums. This is shown by the result obtained by the *British Medical Journal* Inquiry, as stated on February 13th, 1879. It stated "We have been at the pains to turn over a file of last year's reports of American State Asylums. In these reports appear the tables of assigned causes of insanity among the inmates, 14,550 in number. The only cases attributed to Spiritualism are four." The journal adds "We have before us the 62nd report of last year of the Commissioners of Lunacy, and not one single case due to Spiritualism is there recorded."

It should be added that there has notoriously been a great increase of Spiritualism in this country since the war began, and yet there has been a considerable drop in the lunacy statistics. The report of January 1st, 1919, showed a decrease of nearly 10 per cent. over the similar report of 1918.

Those facts have been frequently pointed out, and the excuse of ignorance when these misrepresentations are made, can not be much longer maintained.

Yours, etc.

Arthur Conan Doyle

Windlesham, Crowborough, Sussex. February 10th

THE SOUTHPORT
VISITER
2 March 1920

Spiritualism and Insanity

Sir, – I willingly acknowledge the moderation of Father Thurston's letter. The fact is that when the strong wine of religious emotion comes to a neurotic it matters little what sect he or she may belong to, and we may all live in glass houses in this respect. The Catholic neurotic expecting stigmata, the Puritan brooding over predestination or, if you will, the Spiritualist indulging in an excess of occult investigation, are all in that unhealthy condition which over-indulgence in any line of thought may induce. I have, however, quoted figures and authorities which have, I hope, convinced your readers that Spiritualism can stand an investigation of this sort as well, to put it at the lowest, as any other cult.

Yours, etc.,

A. Conan Doyle

Windlesham, Crowborough, Sussex

JOHN O' LONDON'S
WEEKLY
27 March 1920

Mrs. Piper's Credibility

Sir, – It is amusing to notice that so mild a phrase as "specious misrepresentation" arouses Mr. Clodd's anger. He is himself the most ill-mannered of controversialists. Everyone opposed to him becomes at once a "hussy," an "impostor," or a purveyor of "nauseous drivel." He has been known to put Dr. Crawford's D.Sc. in quotation marks, and to add, after an allusion to Sir

Oliver Lodge and myself, "Knighthoods are cheap." And now he squeals at a very mild rap. It is truly comic.

Yours, etc.,
ARTHUR CONAN DOYLE

THE TIMES   30 March 1920

Divorce Law

SIR, – The excesses of some few States in the American Union have been used too long as a bogy to prevent a reasonable measure of divorce reform from being passed in England. *In medio tutissimus,* and because Nevada is too advanced is no reason why England should be behind every Protestant country in the world. It is to Holland and to the Scandinavian States rather than to America that English reformers look for their models. If, after the successful debate and vote of the House of Lords, the cup is now dashed from the lips of so many sufferers, it will indeed be a national tragedy. It is not generally appreciated that if the great numbers of both sexes now sterilized by separation were allowed freedom to marry, the results in population would in a very few generations compensate for all the losses in the war, while the happiness and general morality of the community would be greatly increased.

Yours faithfully,
ARTHUR CONAN DOYLE,
President,
Divorce Law Reform Union.

Windlesham, Crowborough, Sussex, March 29

THE EVENING CHRONICLE,
NEWCASTLE-UPON-TYNE   15 June 1920

The Fighting Spirit

Letter to "Jimmy" Lowes

DEAR MR. LOWES, – I have now read your little book, and enjoyed every page of it. I hope you will have gentle and happy later years to make up for all the turbulence. Your life is the kind of thing we writers can only imagine and make stories out of.

I think that all of us who, by example or by word or by pen, did anything during the last thirty years to keep the fighting spirit alive in this country "builded better than we knew," for it was invaluable when it came to the great crisis of the world's history. One of the best things it did was to spread to France, and I am sure it made the Frenchman of 1914 a very different man from him of

1870, as the Germans were bound to admit. It is not only the self-respect that a man gains if he knows he can hold his own, but a whole country gains in self-respect and confidence when it knows that its picked lads can hold their own with those of other lands. I reckon that Carpentier had more to do with winning the war than any single Frenchman, except, perhaps, the Generals – perhaps more than they. You've done your part in the same way, and I have always been proud to think my *Rodney Stone* had, as I am told, a marked effect upon the revival of boxing in the country.

With best wishes,
Yours sincerely,
Arthur Conan Doyle

Windlesham, Crowborough, Sussex

THE TIMES   29 July 1920

Propaganda in India

Sir, – It is notorious that our propaganda system has always been our weakest point. In the South African War the European nations hardly realised that Great Britain had any case at all until the war was far advanced. In the recent world-conflict our propaganda were also sadly deficient until towards the close they came into the masterful hands of Lord Northcliffe, who brought them to a high point of efficiency, which had a direct effect upon the result. We are always too slow in getting to work. The Bolshevist designs upon India are not to be looked upon as the invasion of an army. They rather suggest the comparison of a creeping prairie fire which feeds upon what it finds. To fight such a fire the true method is to clear the ground in front of it, so that nothing combustible may be left on which it can be nourished. To this end a thorough propaganda should be instituted in the native languages of India which should set forth simply and truly the horrors which have come upon every country to which this accursed thing has spread. The outrages upon Tartars and Mahomedan communities might be given in detail, and a picture drawn of the contrast between the settled order of British rule and the chaos and ruin which would devastate the peninsula if such doctrines were reduced to practice. A comparatively small sum spent judiciously in this fashion might save great mischief in the future. The great danger is that the fire will already have leaped across before the ground has been cleared.

Yours faithfully,
Grosvenor Hotel, S.W.1., July 28   Arthur Conan Doyle

Sir Arthur Conan Doyle's Tour

MY DEAR EDITOR, – Just reaching Bombay. We have had the hottest voyage on record – so I am told. It certainly was very warm in the Red Sea. I gave a lecture on our truths to the first-class passengers south of Crete, and another to the second-class in the Red Sea, and there has been, as you may think, much discussion, mostly good-humoured and intelligent. I don't suppose there have ever been so many Spiritualists on one ship before, for the number convinced is many and the earnest enquirers even more. If I had no further experience, my journey is amply justified, for a big ship is like a seed pod, and the seeds scatter over all the world; also they are a picked lot of people. There is no lantern, but I show psychic photos at ten each morning, explaining the philosophy of it, and I generally have as many auditors as I can handle. The Parsees are particularly interested, and a good deal more intelligent than some of our home critics. I understand that they have all accepted our position. I have also Buddhists and Mahomedans in my little class. They have the phenomena as we have, but they are done as wonders by the fakirs, and have not been worked out scientifically or in a philosophical way.

Yours always,
A. CONAN DOYLE

September 1st

The Character of D.D. Home

SIR, – My attention has only just been called to an anonymous attack (for I presume that "John Doe" is a nom-de-plome) upon the character of Mr. D.D. Home. As Home is not in this world to answer posthumous slanders, and as I happen to know something of the facts, perhaps you will allow me the right of reply. The reason that I know something about it is that I have recently edited a new edition of Home's life, and while doing so perused all the papers I could get connected with the Lyons case. An account of it, with all the prosecutor's statement of claim and the letters of Mrs. Lyon, were published by Home himself in the second volume of his experiences, which would be a remarkable thing for a guilty man to do.

One single test will show how completely his character survived this attack upon it. Home was a man of much charm of manner. The result was that he had many friends among men of unquestionable honour and probity. Among these were Bulwer Lytton, Lord Dunraven, his son, Lord Adair, Lord Lindsay, Robert Chambers, (the publisher), Samuel Carter Bull (editor of the *Art Journal*), and so many others that I could fill a column with them. I defy your correspondent to show that one of these friends, who knew the whole facts, deserted Mr. Home after this trial. On the contrary, their intimacy seems to have grown, and in 1868, two years later, Home was on Christian name terms with the noblemen I have named. How could this be, if he had, as Mrs. Lyon contended and Judge Gifford alleged, done a dishonourable fraud? This particular judge was a materialistic philosopher of pronounced views, and his opinion upon mediumship, of which he knew nothing, is no more unfavourable than his opinion upon orthodox divinity would have been. To quote him against Home is like quoting a Roman tribune's opinion of an early Christian. In each case the defendant was likely to get little sympathy.

Your correspondent weights the scale against Home by simply taking as true all that Mrs. Lyon said, and ignoring all that Home said in refutation. He has omitted the fact that the judge decreed that Mrs. Lyon was guilty of gross perjury. This declaration he made when Mrs. Lyon attempted to drag Mr. Wilkinson, Home's lawyer, into the case. As a matter of fact, it was shown perfectly clearly that both Carter Hall, representing Home, as a friend, and Wilkinson, representing him as a solicitor, had implored Mrs. Lyon not to make such provisions, and to bear in mind the claims of her own family. To this she had answered that she had no near relatives, and that her mind was made up. She was a half-mad woman, who had a craze for making wills and then revoking them. In this case she had tied herself up so in the original deed that she could not revoke it, and the only possible way in which she could get out of it was by pretending that it was caused by undue influence. There was not a tittle of evidence for this beyond her own word, and as £35,000 was at stake, and she was pronounced to be a perjurer by the judge, it is not a very solid thing upon which to defame the character of a man who had never in his life taken money from anyone for spiritual services. Why should he begin to do so with this woman? Is it not evident that she was lying. That was certainly the view taken by Home's friends, and I cordially endorse it. I think that he acted with propriety and delicacy in very difficult circumstances, and if Mr. Doe, in attacking spiritualism, has to go back to the year 1868 for so weak a case as this, then his supply of situations is not a very formidable one.

Apart from the case of Mr. Home, your anonymous correspondent begins his letter by the statement that "most of the mediums upon whom my belief and proofs depend have either done time or admittedly should have been convicted of fraud quite frequently." It would take Mr. Hughes to furnish an adequate denial of so false a statement as that. The mediums upon whom I have most depended have been amateurs, who have never taken a shilling in their lives, men like Evan Powell, Sloane, Phoenix, and others. It is an example of the reckless slanders and falsehoods with which our cause is assailed.

ARTHUR CONAN DOYLE

THE INTERNATIONAL
PSYCHIC GAZETTE   January 1921

Wake up, Australia!

To the Editor of the *International Psychic Gazette*

MY DEAR LEWIS, – Just a line to show you that I am not done for, in spite of some ups and downs over here! The ups are permanent and the downs temporary, so all is well. Amid the former are my full audiences, their sympathy and acquiescence, and the large amount of interest and consolation which has come with my mission. Of that I have ample proofs. Amid the downs are a Press boycott here, caused partly by ignorant want of proportion, and partly by moral cowardice and fear of finding later that they have backed the wrong horse, or even given the wrong horse fair-play. They are very backward and far behind countries, like Iceland or Denmark, in the knowledge of what has been done. They are still in the stage when folk imagine it's all a sort of three-card trick, and that a clever conjurer could suddenly cry "Hey, Presto!" and in a moment put Crookes and Lombroso and Lodge and all the poor simpletons into their places! It would be comic if it were not so sad. They are dear folk, these Australians – kind, hospitable, straight – but Lord! they do want spirituality and dynamiting out of their grooves of thought. They are where England was before the war. But the tidal wave will strike them – perhaps is striking them. They are actually in the stage when meetings of business men are held at lunch hour to pray that I may be confounded! They prayed when I was on the seas – the Presbyterians did – that I might not reach the country! It was rather near murder, if they really thought their rotten prayers would avail. The result was that we had an excellent voyage!

Well, goodbye. I open in Sydney presently and will have a very lively time by all account. I hope so. It's the unliveliness, the spiritual deadness of this place, which gets on my nerves. It's a great country and worth helping.

Yours very sincerely,
A. CONAN DOYLE

The Grand Hotel, Melbourne. November 3, 1920

LIGHT   18 June 1921

Fairy Photographs

SIR, – In a recent article Mr. Patrick declares that the photographs of fairies, published in the *Strand*, are clumsy fakes. These photos have been enlarged and also examined in the negatives by some of the most competent professional photographers in England, who could find no flaw. Mr. Patrick has not even asked to see the negatives, although Mr. Gardner has held them at the disposal of any inquirer. His criticism is therefore worthless save as a monumental example of the irresponsibility and slovenly looseness with which he and his colleague Mr. Whately Smith have approached an important subject.

Yours &c.,
A. CONAN DOYLE

Windlesham, Crowborough

THE FREEMAN'S JOURNAL,
DUBLIN   27 June 1921

A Voice from the Grave

SIR, – At a moment when the King's words of peace are resounding through Ireland might I ask you to republish the letter which I received shortly before his heroic death from Major Willie Redmond. Surely that name deserves some consideration in the councils of Ireland. He says, writing on December 16, 1916:–

"There are a great many Irishmen to-day who feel that out of this war we should try to build up a new Ireland. The trouble is that men are so timid in meeting each other half way. It would be a fine memorial to the men who have died so splendidly if we could, over their graves, build up a bridge between the North and the South. I have been thinking a lot about this lately – no one could help doing so when one finds that the two sections from Ireland are actually side by side, holding the trenches. Had poor Kettle lived he would have given the world a wonderful account of things out here. I saw a good deal of Kettle and we had many talks of the

291

unity we both hoped would come out of this war. I have been an extreme Nationalist all my life, and if others as extreme on the other side will only come half way we shall be able to hit upon a plan to satisfy the Irish sentiment and the Imperial sentiment at one and the same time."

It is now or never. Forgive, forget, and start again or miss the chance and have Ireland for another generation a land where, as Lord Dosart said, "no man or woman can be happy." I pray that you will use your great influence for peace.

Yours faithfully,
ARTHUR CONAN DOYLE

Windlesham, Crowborough, Sussex, June 26

THE TIMES 29 June 1921

The King's Speech

SIR, – One would not venture to suggest that which is obvious, if it were not that experience shows how often the obvious is missed. Let us hope, then, that the King's Irish Speech – the most perfect little gem of oratory that this generation has known – will be printed broadcast upon every hoarding in the South and West of Ireland. Let the people see and read it.

Yours faithfully,
ARTHUR CONAN DOYLE

Windlesham, Crowborough, Sussex

THE TIMES 9 September 1921

Irish Separatism

SIR, – I do not think that it has been brought home to the Irishman that in case the separation proposition was adopted he would himself be a foreigner within that British Empire which Irish soldiers and Irish Colonists have helped to build. His status in Australia or Canada would be that of the Russian or the Slovak – a foreign immigrant, who was there on sufferance. It would equally affect his status within Great Britain, where new-comers at any rate would have to be nationalised and renounce their mother country before they could have the vote. I am sure that there are many of us who are of Irish extraction, and who have supported Home Rule, who would view with horror such a position. Might I suggest that a petition be drawn up expressing these sentiments, that it be signed by men and women of Irish extraction who have

supported the Home Rule cause, and that it be then forwarded
either to Mr. de Valera or to the Speaker of Dail Eireann?

Yours faithfully,

ARTHUR CONAN DOYLE

Windlesham, Crowborough, Sept. 8

THE EVENING
STANDARD   14 September 1921

Sir Conan Doyle's Book*

SIR, – I do not complain of Mr. McCabe's inaccuracies, because it
is understood beforehand that whatever conflicts with his
conviction that we wind up in the dustbin is not likely to receive
much toleration at his hands.

But I would implore him to be more careful with Mark Twain.
Mark Twain's remark was that instead of turning the other cheek
he returned the other's cheek. This is witty, but Mr. McCabe
reproduces it: "When a man hits you on one cheek you return his
cheek," which is senseless. He should not tamper with the classics.

As to the rest of Mr. McCabe's slashing review, I will favour
him with one more instance of my mental degeneration by quoting
the comment of a wise old Chinese control in a similar muse: "He
good man but foolish man. Plenty time. He learn better."

ARTHUR CONAN DOYLE

* *The Wanderings of a Spiritualist*, reviewed by Joseph McCabe, 13
September 1921.

THE TIMES LITERARY
SUPPLEMENT   29 September 1921

Darkey of Christchurch*

SIR, – Without entering into the polemics of spiritualism – a
subject upon which no conclusions can be reached save by
personal experiment – I would wish to say a word about Darkey,
the Christchurch Terrier, which barks out the answer to
questions. Hundreds of people have tested this dog's powers and a
considerable sum was raised for war charities by their exhibition.
A committee of three, Mr. Poynton a well-known magistrate being
one, investigated and reported, declaring that they could find no
evidence of a trick and that 90 per cent. of the questions were
correctly answered. I was unable to get equally good results
myself, though what I did get was remarkable so far as it went. As
to alleged clairvoyant powers I preferred to think, as stated in my

book, that thought transference was a more normal explanation. Your critic quotes this as an example of my "strange credulity." I should say it was "strange incredulity," which in this, as in other cases, refused to face well-attested facts.

Yours faithfully,
A. CONAN DOYLE

Windlesham, Crowborough, Sussex

* In reply to a review of *The Wanderings of a Spiritualist*.

THE YORKSHIRE
WEEKLY POST   8 October 1921

Psychic Photographs

SIR, – In your courteous review of my book *Wanderings of a Spiritualist* – which by the way costs 12s 6d. not 18s. as marked in your paper – your reviewer comments upon my refusal to produce negatives for the Auckland photographers and adds "Is it to be assumed that this is the end of the matter?"

It is evident that I could not carry negatives which did not belong to me all round the world, but the objection is removed now that I am home again, and I will gladly assist your critic or any other competent observer to apply in the proper quarter for a sight of any of these negatives.

The fairy negatives are kept by Mr. E.L. Gardner, 5, Craven Road, Harlesden, N.W., who has had them inspected by several of the first authorities in England, who have found no flaw in them. When one considers that these are the first photographs which these children ever took in their lives it is impossible to conceive that they are capable of technical manipulation which would deceive experts.

As regards purely psychic or spirit pictures a large selection – some of which I hope to exhibit shortly in Leeds – are in the hands of Mr. F. Barlow, Bryntirion, Springfield Road, Moseley, Birmingham, who would also, I am sure, assist any honest critic by allowing him access to negatives.

The matter is complicated by the absolute ignorance of the average photographer as to psychic science, or the results of the accumulated experience since the historic day in 1861, when Mumler of Boston received the first extra upon a plate. What can you do with men who have never heard of psychographs, and do not know what you mean when you talk about matters which are at the very root of the subject? A psychograph is a picture which produces a photographic effect without having been exposed to light at all, the image being impressed in some way which is unknown to our present science, but possibly vaguely analogous to the present long distance wireless reproductions of faces. I have myself at Crewe received the impression upon a plate which I brought myself and handled myself, of the face of a sister who died 30 years ago, in a dark slide which was held between our hands and never put into the camera or opened. Such a psychograph – and I believe the normal psychic photograph is such – is independent of the laws of light, so that one can imagine how utterly at sea a photographic critic would be who judged its authenticity by shadows or any such tests. Mr. Traill Taylor made an exhaustive study of these psychic photos, using his own apparatus and chemicals. He was Editor of the *Journal of British Photography* and a non-Spiritualist. He received many extras under test conditions, but he observed that when he used a stereoscopic camera all else came out rounded, but the psychic face came out flat – showing that they were direct impressions upon the plate and not objective. I hope to show some of Traill Taylor's results in Leeds.

The photographic phenomena are only a small branch of a great subject, but they are important because they are the only proofs which can be shown to a large audience. It is difficult and unseemly to produce actual mediumistic results upon a public platform. In considering this particular pathway which leads to the central knowledge, I would implore your readers to put aside for ever those explanations of "fake" with which the public has so long been gulled. They are inexpressibly absurd to anyone who has actually worked upon the subject, and who is acquainted with those men of sanity and honour who testify to the facts. On the other hand there is a broad margin of thought form production which does afford reasonable ground for debate, especially when taken in conjunction with ectoplasmic moulds. Making every possible allowance for thought forms – as every cautious investigator has done – you come at last to the question whose thought, and the answer to that is the real crux of the question. Most of us, like Dr. Crawford, are forced to the absolute acceptance of the independent intelligent unseen co-operator, even when he produces, as he sometimes does, pictures which are reminiscent of, or facsimiles of, models which already exist. The problems are many, but mere stupid negation will not help us forward.

Yours, etc.,
ARTHUR CONAN DOYLE

Windlesham, Crowborough, Sussex, Sept. 30, 1921

Streatham Tragedy

SIR, – In your account of the youth who murdered two children you omitted to mention what religion he professed. That is reasonable enough, since no religion can always qualify an evil nature. But why, in the case of the Coates family do you mention in large headlines that they were Spiritualists?

As many hundreds of thousands in this country profess that belief there must be a weakling among them. This particular case showed no connection between their belief and the deed, which was pathetic rather than wicked.

ARTHUR CONAN DOYLE

Grosvenor Hotel, London, S.W.1

The Crushing of a British Industry

SIR, – I am a director of the Raphael Tuck Company, and as such have some inner knowledge of the picture post-card trade, which was originally developed in this country by their enterprise and energy. It employed a great number of people, both directly and indirectly. The ill-advised postal increases of Mr. Kellaway have reduced its volume to an extent which varies from 50 to 80 per cent. The result is that many a worker will have an unhappy Christmas who might have been comparatively well-to-do. The annoying part of it is that this sacrifice brings no possible good to the country, and that the postal receipts from this source are far lower than before. The thing is so indefensible that it must be altered, and no doubt the modified rates will be announced at the time of the Budget; but this delay will cause great unnecessary loss. If Mr. Kellaway is strong enough to admit that in this case he has made a miscalculation, and sets the matter right at once, he will benefit both individual interests and the national finance.

ARTHUR CONAN DOYLE

The Birthplace of Spiritualism

To the Editor of *The International Psychic Gazette*

MY DEAR LEWIS, – Our tour has been unprecedented in success, and all New York records were broken when for the seventh time I filled the Carnegie Hall, which is as big as the Queen's Hall. When we passed Rochester it occurred to me that it is no credit to us that we have no monument there to celebrate an event which has meant so much. My idea is an international subscription from all who have had benefit from it, so as to put up a fine inscribed obelisk. If we don't take ourselves seriously no one else will. I wonder if you would ventilate it in the *Gazette* and see how people take it. I would lead with fifty pounds. I thought of proposing it at Chicago where the Spiritualists have a big reception in our honour, but it will not be any use unless it is international. I know how badly we need money in every direction but really we should tap some of those wealthy people who have had good from this sacred knowledge.

ARTHUR CONAN DOYLE

Taking of Spirit Photographs

SIR, – Some little time ago you challenged me as to what I had to say upon this subject. I answered that I would write to you when fuller information was available. The case is not yet complete. When it is a pamphlet will appear covering all the facts. This should be ready in the course of the autumn.

In the meantime I take advantage of your having broached the subject in order to ask the public not to form premature conclusions about a man whom I believe to be grievously wronged, and who has no access to those legal means of redress which every Briton should command. These attacks would be much more circumspect if it was not understood that a medium in the present state of public knowledge enters a court with a crushing disadvantage.

While preparing a fuller statement, it is only fair to Mr. Hope to say at once that all the investigation which has been undertaken by his friends tends to show that the pamphlet issued with such indecent haste before he had any opportunity of furnishing a defence, is a document which will not for a moment stand impartial scrutiny.

The accusation, it will be remembered, was that the psychic photograph should have appeared upon a marked plate, since all the plates in the packet had been exposed to an X-ray process, without undoing the wrapper, which would leave certain marks upon them. The psychic photograph did finally appear upon an unmarked plate, and this was taken to be an absolute proof that the plates had been changed by Hope. There were several minor points, but this was predominant, and if this be eliminated the rest of the case becomes trivial.

We can claim now that this point has been eliminated. The investigators, Mr. Price and Mr. Seymour, acting as the agents of Mr. Dingwall of the Psychical Research Society, neglected to test the fact whether the X-ray markings were permanent or not.

One can excuse the others, but it really seems incredible that Mr. Dingwall, a so-called research officer, could have endorsed work which was done in so slovenly and unscientific a fashion.

Every effort was made to blast a man's good name and undo the effects of fifteen years of psychic demonstration upon the strength of an allegation which could easily have been tested, and which, when tested, has proved to be a complete fallacy.

Experiments made in several quarters by similar plates marked in the same fashion by the same firm, have shown that an exposure up to 15-seconds in a good photographic light leaves the marks intact. Beyond that point the marks fade and disappear, so that the plate becomes quite blank, though with a still longer exposure, say 25 seconds, the marks return in an inverted form.

Now, Mr. Price has left it on record that though the period of exposure was not taken (imagine this in a scientific experiment!) he counted slowly up to 19, so that by his own showing the exposure was just long enough to reach the point where the marks would disappear – and with them disappears all the main evidence, so far as at present revealed, upon which the case rests.

I will not encroach upon your space at present with the smaller points, as they are trivial in themselves, and will be fully dealt with in the pamphlet. It was felt, however, by Mr. Hope's friends that this interim statement should be issued, lest judgment should go by default. The matter will not be avoided, but will be thoroughly thrashed out in the most public way that can be found. Meanwhile, it is to be remembered that against the mere assertion of his enemies, Mr. Hope has sworn his affidavit as to his complete innocence of the alleged fraud.

ARTHUR CONAN DOYLE

The Green Ray

DEAR SIR, – I have twice seen the Green Ray, once in the Mediterranean and once in the Atlantic. One needs a perfectly clear sunset without a trace of haze. Then just as the upper rim vanishes – possibly a second later – there rises what is more like a puff of green smoke than anything else I can describe. I presume that it is an effect of refraction from the light shining through the curve of water, but I have never heard any scientific explanation.

As to the noise heard by the Irish ladies, I should guess that it was a meteorite flying low but slantwise to the earth's surface. That would, I think, produce the ever-increasing roar, and also enough atmospheric disturbance to bend the branches.

Yours faithfully,
ARTHUR CONAN DOYLE

LIGHT   18 November 1922

Spiritualism and the General Election

SIR, – Without presuming to interfere with the political convictions of my fellow Spiritualists, I would remind them that the present interpretation of the Witchcraft Act, as given by the Lord Chief Justice, is an intolerable one, since it makes the exercise of psychic gifts which are well attested as criminal as the fraudulent imitation of such gifts. Personally I will vote for no candidate who does not pledge himself to vote for the abolition of so reactionary a law. Those who are interested in psychic matters are now a very numerous body, and if they all take a determined line they may, even at this last hour, exert considerable influence.

Yours faithfully,
ARTHUR CONAN DOYLE

Windlesham, Crowborough, Sussex. November 13th, 1922

THE TIMES   9 December 1922

The Channel Tunnel

SIR, – Mr. Skeus discusses in your columns the question of what would have happened had we had the Channel Tunnel during the war, and raises the bogy that it would have been seized by the Germans.

Surely we have sufficient information at our disposal to show us that the German right wing was very nearly cut off by stretching itself as far as Amiens, and that, if it had extended to the coast, it could hardly have got away. The end of the tunnel would, of course, have been fortified, and a comparatively small garrison could have held it secure, for it would constitute a fortress unique in the history of war – a fortress into which reinforcements and supplies could always be introduced, and from which wounded could be evacuated. With the smooth fields of fire which lie everywhere in that chalk country, it should be impregnable. If the very worst had happened, the cost of a destroyed tunnel would be less than that of a week of war.

On the other hand, so long as the tunnel existed, we could pass over reinforcements to France in all weathers with no danger of submarine attack, we could pass stores and munitions without breaking bulk, we could save all the shipping and all the escorts which were used in the Channel, and we could bring back our wounded swiftly and without discomfort. In money alone it is impossible to compute how much was wasted by our insane policy of obstructing the boring of the tunnel in pre-war days. We came badly out of the Suez Canal business, but our mistakes there were venial compared with those which we have made over the Channel Tunnel.

Now the matter has, as it seems to me, ceased to press. The mischief is done. It was only in view of a great Continental war that it was of really vital importance.

Yours faithfully,
ARTHUR CONAN DOYLE

Windlesham, Crowborough

THE TWO
WORLDS   19 January 1923

The Hydesville Memorial.

SIR, – When I was in America it was suggested that a memorial should be raised by the subscriptions of Spiritualists all the world over to the great occurrence at Hydesville in 1848 which has modified and glorified the lives of so many. A subsequent resolution of the National Association of America decreed (wisely, I think) that a memorial in Washington would be of more service to the Cause than one in a place so difficult of access as Hydesville. I was asked to be Secretary and Treasurer for the movement in Great Britain, and it is my ambition when I return to America at the end of March to take with me a handsome sum as our contribution to the undertaking.

I have in hand at present £100 subscribed by my wife and myself. If any of your readers would send me sums, however small, they would be gratefully received. I will keep the addresses of the donors and retain the money in my own hands until I have absolute assurance that the scheme is going through. Our help would be particularly appreciated at present, as the Americans realise how great the pressure is upon us, and the self-sacrifice which is involved in a subscription towards a monument which so many of us will never see. It will, however, dignify the Cause, which means so much more than money. Private gifts or church collections are equally welcome.

Yours faithfully,
ARTHUR CONAN DOYLE

Windlesham, Crowborough, Sussex.

LIGHT   8 February 1923

The Washington Memorial

SIR, – When I returned from the United States in June I brought with me some £2,000 of American money, nearly all of which has now been expended upon the Spiritualist cause. I am asking those who believe in that cause, and who approve of my work, to show that approval in a practical way by sending me subscriptions which I can take with me, when I return to America in March, as a British donation towards the International Washington Memorial, which is to be erected in honour of the piercing of the barrier which occurred at Hydesville upon March 31st, 1848. Swedenborg and Davis had of course paved the way, but it is beyond question that the first of those direct communications, which have since then been of such priceless comfort to so many of us, was made upon that occasion, and that it is in truth the greatest date in human history since the great revelation of two thousand years ago. Let us show by our actions that we realise and appreciate it.

ARTHUR CONAN DOYLE

Windlesham, Crowborough, Sussex

LIGHT   10 March 1923

The Washington Memorial

SIR, – The response to my appeal for some central memorial of our

Cause has been so scanty that I cannot bring myself to present it. I am, therefore, returning the money to the various subscribers, whom I hereby thank.

Yours faithfully,
ARTHUR CONAN DOYLE

Windlesham, Crowborough, Sussex. March 6th, 1923

THE NEW YORK
TIMES   2 September 1923

---

*Oscar Wilde's Communication
Accepted as Genuine*

SIR, – You have occasionally allowed me to use your columns in order to keep the American public informed as to the progress which is being made in Europe upon the all-important subject of psychic evidence. Upon the last occasion I gave some description of Dr. Schrenck-Notzing's experiments with Willy at Munich, and I told how he had demonstrated that mysterious substance ectoplasm to 100 incredulous men of science, including twenty-six professors of universities, and that all without exception had been compelled to accept the evidence of their own senses.

A second similar mass demonstration has just been concluded at Paris and has received far less public attention than it deserves. Indeed, it is one of the curiosities of this controversy that when a negative result is obtained, which means, of course, nothing at all, it goes like wildfire through the press, while the positive results, which mean everything, are received with apathy. One is forced to the conclusion that the human instinct really shrinks from the idea that we do most certainly continue our existence, and do most certainly answer for our action, whether private or public.

The new demonstration has been carried out by Dr. Geley of the Metapsychique Institute of Paris. He assembled thirty-four men of distinction and in successive sittings demonstrated the usual physical phenomena of spiritualism, using as a medium one Jean Gusik, a Pole. The results were perfectly conclusive, and all the observers signed their acquiescence. The signatures include those of Dr. Rehm, scientific editor of the *Matin*; Cinisty, editor of the *Petit Parisien*: Huc, editor of the *Dépeche de Toulouse*: a dozen leading doctors from the Parisian hospitals; Marcel Prévost of the French Academy; Bayle of the Prefecture of Police; several men of letters, and finally, three great men of science – Richet, Flammarion and Sir Oliver Lodge.

The phenomena to which these gentlemen subscribe are

302

movements of objects without touch at a distance from the medium and taps received when out of reach of the medium. There were, however, many other phenomena. Their confession of faith ends with the words: "We simply affirm our conviction that the phenomena are not to be explained by illusions and that there was no possible cheating."

They certify to the fact that these various phenomena showed every sign of having an intelligence at the back of them. In fact, they answered requests and obeyed orders. Since these facts are surely indisputable, we are faced by the question, Whose intelligence is it? Is it that of the unconscious medium acting independently? Is it the collective consciousness of the company? Or is it an outside independent intelligence which is directing the experiment?

It is only fair to say that even among the most experienced psychic researchers the answer to their question is a varied one. We have to remember that many of the best Continental minds start from a position of extreme materialism. Sir David Brewster said: "Spirit is the last thing which I would give in to," and though he said it sixty years ago, it still represents a common phase of thought. Such men as Richet or Notzing have been converted from materialism to a sort of super-materialism, which needs one more step, but a very vital one, to elevate them into spiritualism. To get that step they would need, I think, to turn from those physical phases where they have done such splendid work and to examine more carefully the mental and religious sides of the question, without neglecting those methods of analysis and exact thought which they have applied to the lower phenomena. No faith is needed, but simply an extension of their present experimental methods to another class of evidence. As they are already prepared to admit that an ectoplasmic figure can move about a room, can talk and can claim an individuality, it would not seem a great gulf which they have to cross in admitting that claim to be true, and that the discarnate soul can indeed find means to manifest itself in this lower world of matter.

An interesting mental and literary problem has presented itself lately in England by the appearance of a script which claims to be from Oscar Wilde. Wilde was a man with a very peculiar quality of thought and of expression. The latter may be parodied, but the former can hardly be copied in its fullness, for to do so would imply that the copyist had as great a brain as the original. Yet both in thought and in expression this script rings true. There are passages in it which Wilde in his best movements has never bettered. He had in life a very fine cue for colours which often manifested itself in his writings gave them a peculiarly vivid touch. Thus in a private letter to me he spoke of the "honey coloured harvest moon." The script shows this rare quality to a remarkable degree. "In eternal twilight I move, but I know that in the world . . . red sunset must follow apple-green dawn." Then again, "The rose-flushed anemones that star the woodland ways," or again, "Already the May is creeping like a white mist over lane and hedge now, and year after year, the hawthorn bears blood-red fruit after the white death of its May."

The other characteristic of Wilde was his freakish, paradoxical humour. This also is much in evidence in the script. "Being dead is the most boring experience in life, that is if one excepts being married or dining with a school-master!" Those last four words are Wilde all over. "My life was like a candle that had guttered at the end."

I defy any man of real critical instinct to read that script and doubt that it emanates from Wilde. One may imitate a man's features, one may forge his name, but it is impossible to sustain a deception in a prolonged communication from a great writer. Verily, there is no sort of proof under Heaven which has not been accorded to us, and those beyond must despair sometimes of ever penetrating our obtuse intelligence.

ARTHUR CONAN DOYLE

London, England, Aug. 15, 1923

THE TIMES   25 October 1923

A Recompense for the Dardanelles

SIR, – There is one aspect of Mr. Churchill's wonderfully lucid and powerful statement about the Dardanelles expedition which should be noted. In case of success, we had pledged Constantinople to Russia, regardless of the just claims of Greece, who is obviously the rightful owner. If we had won, how terrible would our position now be! We should have seen a Bolshevist republic with its right flank at Archangel and its left at Constantinople – a fearsome portent! Failing this, we should have had a Russian military empire overhanging Europe from the same high points and ready at any moment to roll down upon it. Either alternative would confront us with a menace as dangerous to civilisation as the pre-war Germany.

Thus, as always, Providence has wrought more wisely than man, and it may well console us for our losses to reflect that victory would ultimately have meant defeat, while defeat has meant comparative victory. In all Mr. Churchill's closely-reasoned argument which led up to the expedition, the one flaw seems to me to have been that in grasping at an immediate advantage there was not sufficient appreciation of the dangers prepared for our posterity.

Yours faithfully,
ARTHUR CONAN DOYLE

Crowborough.

LIGHT   10 November 1923

"Outward Bound"

SIR, – It is so seldom that even an approximation to our psychic views is shown upon the stage that I think we should support it. Those who see "Outward Bound" at the Garrick Theatre will, I am sure, thank me for calling their attention to it, for it is the most daring, original and arresting play which has been seen in my time upon the London boards.

Yours, etc.,
ARTHUR CONAN DOYLE

Windlesham, Crowborough, Sussex. November 4th, 1923

THE ADVERTISER AND ECHO,
          THANET   16 February 1924

A Letter to "Psychono"

SIR, – Congratulations on the good work you are doing in Kent.

I was deeply interested in the "Second Coming" script, because I have had the same through the hand of my wife. The year 1925 is given, and even the day of the angelic demonstration – harvest festival of that year.

I must get the continuation.

Yours sincerely,
A. CONAN DOYLE

Windlesham, Crowborough, Sussex.

OCCULT REVIEW   April 1924

Oscar Wilde

SIR, – I should wish with all courtesy, but also with all decision, to express my dissent from Mr. C.W. Soal in what he says concerning the style of Oscar Wilde. He had, as has frequently been pointed out, two separate styles, each very marked and individual, and each quite different from the other. The one is poetic, ornamental and artificial, with lovely word effects and a profuse use of colour.

It is shown in the Script by such phrases as "from russet eve to apple-green dawn" or "the rose-flushed anemones that star the dark woodland ways" or "the May is creeping like a white mist over lane and hedgerow." The second style is epigrammatic, witty, cynical and full of paradox. Here we have it in "Death is the most boring experience in life – if one excepts being married or dining with a schoolmaster." "It is always bad advice that is given away." "Even God does not know what to do with the industrious." "The woman who was content merely to be was always charming." It is difficult to note these close analogies of style and to doubt that an Oscar Wilde brain is at the back of them.

The idea that a weekly prize competition could produce a flood of Barries and Stevensons, with all the marks of the original, is surely untenable and could hardly have been meant to be taken seriously. It is easy to produce a short comic parody, by exaggerating the features of a style, but to write or talk in exactly the same style and with equally good matter, argues an equal brain, which would certainly exhibit itself in something more ambitious than parody.

Mr. Soal claims that he has traced all the allusions to their "probable sources." In the case of a man whose life was so public and who has been the centre of a whole literature, it is difficult to imagine that there is anything of any importance in his life – anything which would now emerge from his own memory – which was not directly or indirectly alluded to in some quarter or another. But such an explanation would mean that the automatists had ransacked all the Wilde literature. We have their assurance that this is not so, and that their acquaintance with it was very limited. As to the suggestion, put into the mouth of a suppositious critic, that the writers memorise great sections of script, that would of course be a direct accusation of deliberate fraud which is not justified by the character and position of the writers. Such suggestions are made far too readily and should be banished from the controversy.

When I consider the various corroborations in this case of Oscar Wilde:

1. The reproduction of his heavy style.
2. The reproduction of his light style.
3. The reproduction of character.
4. The recollection of incidents, some of them quite obscure, in his own life.
5. The reproduction of his handwriting.
6. And (not least in my eyes) the similarity of the conditions which he describes upon the other side with those which our psychic knowledge would assign to such a man I consider that the

306

case is a very powerful one indeed. I quite agree that George Pelham and The Ear of Dionysius are very convincing, but to me the Wilde case is even more so.

Yours faithfully,
A. CONAN DOYLE

THE TIMES   23 May 1924

Wembley on Sundays

SIR, – It is to be hoped that a democratic Government will see to it that the poorer people have a fair chance of seeing the wonderful show at Wembley. For many, indeed most, of them Sunday is the only clear day available. If legislation is needed then a Bill would surely pass without serious opposition. Personally, I think that the Amusement Park is on quite a different footing from the Exhibition itself, and might well be closed on Sunday. Both adults and children should find enough to interest and amuse them without swings or roundabouts. But better throw it all open than have it wasted on the best day of the week.

Yours faithfully,
ARTHUR CONAN DOYLE

Athenæum Club, May 21

THE MORNING
POST   26 September 1924

Mr. Maskelyne and the Slade Case

SIR, – I observe in your columns the statement that Mr. Nevil Maskelyne's father, together with Professor Ray Lankester, exposed Mr. Slade in 1876. I will say nothing as to the alleged exposure save to remark that Mr. Slade went straight to Leipzig, where he gave before Professor Zollner and three colleagues one of the fullest demonstrations of psychic power ever recorded by a scientific observer. It seems improbable – though not impossible – that he was a counterfeit in London, but the real thing in Germany. His performance was checked by Bellachini, the Court Conjurer, who declared that it was far beyond the reach of art.

The point, however, on which I wished to comment was that the accusers were Dr. Bryan Donkin and Professor Lankester, and that Maskelyne's evidence was indirect. In the course of it he deposed that the table used by the medium was a "trick" table. This no doubt affected the verdict. As a matter of fact, this table is now to be inspected at No. 5, Queen's-square, the Headquarters of the London Spiritualist Alliance. It will be found to be quite an ordinary table with no trick whatever.

Those thousand pound challenges from conjurers to which your contributor alludes are mere advertisements, without any real meaning whatever. When I was in America last year the famous Houdini proclaimed in similar fashion that he could do anything which a medium had ever done. I at once accepted the challenge and stipulated that he should show me the presentment of a near relative who had passed out of life, and that it should be so clear that I and others who sat beside me could recognise it. I need not say that I heard no more of the challenge.

Yours, &c.,
ARTHUR CONAN DOYLE

15, Buckingham Palace-mansions, Sept. 25

THE TIMES   28 October 1924

Merits of Baseball

SIR, – As one who has sampled most British sports, may I say a word upon baseball? It seems to me that in those Press comments which I have been able to see too much stress is laid upon what may appear to us to be a weakness or a comic aspect in the game and not nearly enough upon its real claim on our attention. I fully agree that the continual ragging is from a British view-point a defect, but baseball is a game which is continually in process of development and improvement, as anyone who reads Arthur Mathewson's interesting book on the subject is aware.

The foul tricks which were once common are now hardly known, and what was once applauded, or at any rate tolerated, would now be execrated. Therefore, this rough *badinage* may pass away and it is not an essential of the game. What is essential is that here is a splendid game which calls for a fine eye, activity, bodily fitness, and judgment in the highest degree. This game needs no expensive levelling of a field, its outfit is within the reach of any village club, it takes only two or three hours in the playing, it is independent of wet wickets, and the player is on his toes all the time, and not sitting on a pavilion bench while another man makes his century. If it were taken up by our different Association teams as a summer pastime I believe it would sweep this country as it has done America. At the same time it would no more interfere with cricket than lawn tennis has done. It would find its own place. What we need now is a central association which would advise and help the little clubs in the first year of their existence.

Yours faithfully,
ARTHUR CONAN DOYLE

Windlesham, Crowborough, Oct. 25

THE TIMES   December 17, 1924

Thought Transference

SIR, – Dr. Haldane claims that telepathy is really the result of subtle sound waves. In very many cases which have been recorded the phenomenon consisted of the reproduction of drawn diagrams. Does Dr. Haldane really consider that the sound of the pencil can indicate the shape of the figure?

ARTHUR CONAN DOYLE

15, Buckingham Palace-mansions, S.W.1, Dec. 16

LIGHT   24 January 1925

The Psychic Bookshop and Library

SIR, – It has long seemed to me that one of the weak points in our psychic movement is the complete disconnection between our splendid literature and the man in the street. He is as a rule absolutely unaware of its existence. In an endeavour to get past this difficulty I am engaged in starting a psychic bookshop and library in one of the most central positions in London. It is in Abbey House in Victoria-street, opposite to Dean's Yard, and within a stone's throw of Westminster Abbey. I would ask the support of all psychic students for this venture, so far as it can be given without encroaching upon the trade in psychic books already done by the London Spiritualist Alliance, or by the office of the "Two Worlds." I wish to open up new fields, not to encroach upon the old ones. Nothing but psychic books will be sold, and a large stock kept in hand, while every effort will be made to meet the wants of customers. Should any reader have duplicates which he could spare for the library he would do me a service if, after the beginning of February, he would send them to the manager at the address given.

Yours, etc.,
ARTHUR CONAN DOYLE

January 16th

309

THE NORTHERN WHIG
AND BELFAST
POST   12 May 1925

Sir. A. Conan Doyle and the
"Fairy Photographs"

SIR, – In your issue of to-day I notice some allusion to the "Fairy Photographs" as if they had been in some way explained or discredited. This is not so. A number of inquiries both as to the girls and as to the negatives, the latter conducted by some of the best experts in Great Britain, have failed to shake the evidence in any particular, while fresh facts have appeared which strengthen the case. Prominent among these is a letter written by one of the children, aged 10, to a friend in South Africa, telling the story at the time – though it only leaked out to the public some years later. What these little figures are, and how far they may be thought forms is, as I state in my book, an open question, but the honesty of the girls is assured, and the evidence has never been in any way shaken. Of course the matter has nothing to do with spiritualism, which is concerned only with the destiny of the human soul.

Yours &c.,
A. CONAN DOYLE

Midland Station Hotel, May 10, 1925

LIGHT   4 July 1925

A Proposed Psychic Museum

SIR, – I am establishing a small museum of psychic objects under the Psychic Bookshop, Abbey House, Victoria Street. The situation is so central that such a collection cannot fail to attract attention and to form a powerful propaganda centre. I should be greatly obliged if any of your readers will either give, lend or sell suitable objects. I have at present the two wax gloves lent me by the Psychic College and I have the Garscadden collection of photographs with some other pictures. With such a nucleus I should have no difficulty in getting together a worthy collection. Perhaps those who wish to help me will send me a line first so that I may tell them how far, with our limited space, their kind offers can be taken advantage of.

ARTHUR CONAN DOYLE

"Psychic Photographs"

Sir, – I have noticed that my name is quoted in a contemporary psychic paper in connection with the photographs of the young mediums Falconer, of Edinburgh. May I say that I have no experience at all of the work of these mediums and cannot vouch for the bona fides in any way. There is a reproduction of one alleged spirit photograph in the same pages which is undoubtedly an out-of-focus picture of Albert Moore's well-known study called "Blossoms." Such cases of transference may be honest, but they are disconcerting and awaken not unnatural suspicions.

Yours, etc.,
ARTHUR CONAN DOYLE

Crowborough. September 4th

Soldiers Who Have Come Back
The Return of "Dead" Sons

Sir, – My Kingsley was not killed in the War. He was badly wounded at the Somme, but he died just before the Armistice in London from pneumonia.

It was about a year or more afterwards when I was sitting with Evan Powell that he came back. His voice sounded, very intense and earnest, before me. He said his own name, and my wife, his step-mother, heard it before I did. I listened very intently. Then I heard the word "Forgive!" in a loud whisper. I realised that he was alluding to the fact that he had opposed Spiritualism, for certainly there was nothing else in his manly and beautiful life which could possibly have hurt me. I, of course, assured him that I had nothing to forgive, and that he was right to form his own opinion. I then said, "Are you happy?" He answered, "I am happy *now*." I felt a heavy hand upon my head, which was bent forward, and I felt a kiss upon my brow. It would seem, therefore, that he was partly materialised. The medium who knew nothing of my relations with my son, was bound in his chair, and could not approach me. All the sitters heard the dialogue, so there was no hallucination. I have had several communications since, but none which moved me so much as this first one.

Yours sincerely,
ARTHUR CONAN DOYLE

The Psychic Museum

SIR, – The article by your representative upon this museum is so genial that I should be churlish indeed if I were to take serious exception to it.

In it he couples my name with Sherlock Holmes, and I presume that since I am the only begetter of that over-rated character I must have some strand of my nature which corresponds with him. Let me assume this. In that case I would say (and you may file the saying for reference) that of all the feats of clear thinking which Holmes ever performed by far the greatest was when he saw that a despised and ridiculed subject was in very truth a great new revelation and an epoch-making event in the world's history.

There are many more now who would subscribe to this opinion than a few years ago, and I am convinced that a very short time, at the rate of its present progress will bring about the considered comprehension of it on the part of the whole human race.

My great difficulty with inquirers who come to my museum is that often they know nothing of the subject – worse than nothing in many cases, for they may be filled with prejudices and misrepresentations. Then in a few minutes I have to try and convey to them the elements of a great science. Fancy a man coming to a geological museum who knew nothing of the science and imagined that he was competent to correct the curator upon the order of the fossils. That is a fair analogy to what is a constant experience.

To show the untenable nature of the views which they put forward I will take those of your correspondent concerning the experiment which produced the original Geley gloves. Let us take the facts as recorded in the Journal of the Institut Metapsychique, which is the organ of that body – a scientific and not a spiritualistic institution in Paris.

First of all we will take the fact that the report of what occurred was signed by Charles Richet, Professor of Physiology at the University of Paris, Gustav Geley, who was the head of the Institute, and of European reputation, finally by the Count de Grammont, an experienced investigator, none of the three a professed Spiritualist.

They observed what occurred under a fair red light, and all were agreed as to their observation. Their scientific reputation depended upon the truth of their statement. Now I ask your representative for a fair answer to this question. Were these three men deliberately and senselessly lying? I will assume, as he is a sane man, that his answer is no.

Then the only alternative is that they were deceived. Let us see if this is credible. They had locked the door, and as the room was their own (I know it well, and it is in a basement) there was no secret entrance.

When Kluski, who is a Polish banker, had sunk into a trance, and when the ectoplasmic figure was formed from him in a fashion already recorded and photographed on many occasions with other mediums, it was asked to dip its hand into a pail which contained warm paraffin. All the observers saw it do so, and controlled the medium at the same time.

When the wax had encrusted the hands of the phantom it was asked to disappear. It did so, leaving the wax gloves which had formed over its hands upon the table.

And now comes the point which your correspondent has overlooked, and which is fatal to his theory of impersonation. The wax gloves, as anyone can see for themselves, are in one solid piece, and are much narrower at the wrist than across the hand. How, then, could the hand have been withdrawn save by dematerialisation inside the glove. No one has ever yet suggested any feasible way in which this could have been done.

To show the care taken by the researchers, Geley had put cholesterine in the pail of wax. An independent chemist analysed a portion of the glove and reported cholesterine. This, of course, is proof positive that the glove was not brought ready-made into the room.

Impressions were taken of the spirit hand and of that of the medium, with the result that a certificate was obtained from M. Bayle, of the Paris police, that there was no resemblance.

The experiment was repeated with various sitters, Mr. and Mrs. Hewat McKenzie being among those who obtained the gloves at the Psychic Museum. Some 28 impressions were taken in all on different occasions. Is it to be supposed that in every case these observant circles were unable in a red light to see that a stranger had come through the locked door and was walking about the room?

It is a foolish thing to be too credulous, and it is an equally foolish thing to be too incredulous. The balanced judgment holds its poise between.

I can well understand that a reporter may find it impossible to attain in half an hour the experience and knowledge which 38 years of work have given to me. That is natural. But it is not natural or reasonable that a novice who was not present should ascribe to fraud or folly events which were observed and guaranteed by some of the first intellects of Europe.

ARTHUR CONAN DOYLE

THE INTERNATIONAL
PSYCHIC GAZETTE   April 1926

The Mediumship of Mr. F.T. Munnings

SIR, – The most puzzling and disconcerting cases which we ever encounter are those where a medium has intermittent psychic powers – sometimes of a high order – which are accompanied by a total want of moral perception, so that he is prepared to supplement such powers by cold-blooded and deliberate artifice when it suits his purpose. Mr. F.T. Munnings is an example of this type of medium, and it is our duty, after having some experience of his work, to warn the public that they sit with him at their own risk. We know of cases where the psychic result has been beyond suspicion and we know of others – notably one recently in a private family – where he has been exposed in obvious fraud with the tools of deception in his possession. We trust that this warning may prevent any such incident in the future.

Yours faithfully,
R.H. SAUNDERS
H. DENNIS BRADLEY
ARTHUR CONAN DOYLE
ABRAHAM WALLACE, M.D.

March 3, 1926

THE MORNING
POST   12 April 1926

The "Photograph" of Lord Combermere

SIR, – Mr. Campbell Swinton has criticised in your columns the psychic photograph which I showed at the Queen's Hall, and which exhibits a figure, supposed to be that of the late Lord Combermere, seated in a chair.

I received the photograph through the great courtesy of Lord Combermere himself, and he apparently accepted the facts as I

314

have stated them. I also hold a letter from a near relative giving further particulars and adding the name of the lady visitor who took it. He concludes with the words, "I am quite sure the negative was not faked. I got it direct from her."

The idea that this perfectly clear figure of a seated man is a defect in the plate is too absurd for argument, but it shows the extreme lengths to which our opponents will go in their frantic search for a materialist explanation. "Ex uno disce omnes."

Yours, &c.,
ARTHUR CONAN DOYLE

P.S. – I was careful to point out that this figure was not necessarily the spirit of the deceased, but might be one of those mind forms or memory forms which do appear to exist.

Athenæum Club, April 10

THE MORNING
POST
 19 April 1926

The Combermere Photo

SIR, – I should be happy to allow you to publish this photograph, but Lord Combermere has shown me great courtesy in allowing me to screen it, and I hesitate to go further until I have his express permission. For the moment it seems difficult to communicate with him, but I hope I may presently be able to respond to Mr. Campbell Swinton's challenge.

Meanwhile may I say once more that I received the photograph direct from Lord Combermere through the intermediary of a mutual friend. On the back is written:

"This photograph was taken of the library by Miss Corbet on December 5, 1891, on the afternoon of the funeral of Wellington Henry 2nd Viscount Combermere. The figure on the chair on the left of the photograph (legless) is supposed to be a likeness of him."

In view of this endorsement your readers are in a position to judge how far Mr. Campbell Swinton was justified in applying so insulting a term as "photographic fraud" to a picture which I had exhibited in public.

I would add that a comparison of features is impossible, since the face is shadowy. It is the time and the place which connect the photograph with the deceased.

The possible explanation that someone sat for a short period in

315

the chair while the exposure was being made has, I understand, been completely negatived.

Yours, &c.,

ARTHUR CONAN DOYLE

April 14

THE MORNING POST

23 April 1926

The Combermere Photograph

SIR, – I beg to enclose the Combermere photograph. I am advised that it will not reproduce, but you will be the best judge of that. Meanwhile you are at liberty to show it to any whom it may interest.

I notice with concern that one of your lady correspondents, with the spacious address of South-West London, complains that she was devil-ridden through a sentence in one of my works. As the same lady has appeared in one or more controversies, with the same story we may reasonably conclude that her case is an isolated one. Since, on the other hand, I have boxes and drawers filled with letters which tell me of hopes renewed and faith strengthened through these same works, I venture to hope that the balance is upon the right side.

It is strange to see some disputants urging the diabolical nature of spirit intercourse. Does it not strike them that if the Devil were to teach mankind he would infallibly urge that we should concentrate upon the affairs of life, and suck the last drop of pleasure from it, since there was nothing beyond and no retribution to be feared? Certainly the last thing he would preach would be that we continue our existence, and that the quality of that future existence is regulated by our conduct here. If instead of using the catchword "familiar spirit" they were to substitute "guardian angel," people would get a clearer view of what Spiritualism means. The Bible, too, would become more intelligible if they would realise that a "prophet" was an inspired medium and an "angel" a high spirit. Old records would then be brought into line with modern thought, and people would understand that God is not dead nor sleeping, but that He works for the education of His poor human children even as He did in the days of old.

There has never, in my opinion, been a time in the world's history when divine inspiration was more obvious than at present, but it is a common human error to magnify and idealise that which is distant and to fail to appreciate that which is near. In a century or two this Spiritualistic movement will be viewed with reverence as one of the great turning points of human thought.

Yours, &c.,
ARTHUR CONAN DOYLE

15, Buckingham Palace-mansions, S.W.1, April 21.

[The photograph could not be reproduced for technical reasons, but it was to be seen at the office of *Morning Post.*]

THE CHRISTIAN
SPIRITUALIST   2nd June 1926

The Bible

SIR, – Your correspondent who mentions my name in connection with the Bible must understand that a Moslem or a Hindoo can be a Spiritualist even as a Christian can. My view of the Bible, as of all other sacred books, is that they are gold in clay and that it is left to our intelligence to separate the one from the other. The Old Testament has more clay than gold. The New has very much more gold than clay.

Yours faithfully,
ARTHUR CONAN DOYLE

May 26th

THE MORNING
POST   14 June 1926

Conjurers and Spiritualism

SIR, – There is an abnormal frame of mind which may be called the Conjurer's Complex or Houdinitis. It is based upon several fallacies. The first is that Spiritualism depends upon physical phenomena for its proofs, whereas the more cogent are mental. The second is that manual dexterity bears some relation to brain capacity and enables its possessor to sit in judgment upon the Crookes, the Wallaces, and the Lombrosos. The third is that people who were not present are better judges of an episode than those who were present.

Now and again a conjurer is brought into contact with real psychic forces, and then realises his limitations. Kellar endorsed Eglinton, Bellachini endorsed Slade, and Howard Thurston endorsed Eusapia Palladino. But as a body the conjurors have not

317

a good record in this long-drawn battle between the new knowledge and the old.

Yours, &c.,
ARTHUR CONAN DOYLE

15, Buckingham Palace-mansions, S.W. June 10

"Alarmist Prophecies"

SIR, – You have published two letters, one from Mr. Howard and the other from Major Tudor Pole, both to the effect that prophecies of the future of the world which may alarm people should be suppressed. It is a subject to which I have given much anxious thought, as I have not only received such prophecies in a very consistent and detailed form, but also so large a number of independent corroborations that it is difficult for me to doubt that there lies some solid truth at the back of them.

One's own reason must always be the ultimate judge in such a case; but one cannot altogether disregard the views put forward by the unseen communicators, especially when their other communications indicate wisdom and knowledge. If one takes their information seriously one must also take seriously their advice as to how such information should be used.

Rightly or wrongly – only the future can prove that – they take the view that certain changes, spiritual and physical, are shortly coming upon the earth. Also that such changes might be modified by a lessened materialism and an increased spirituality – in a word, a more serious appreciation of the objects of human existence. If the messages are in any degree to effect this change of mind it is clear that they cannot be entirely suppressed.

Again, they declare that if such events should occur in a sudden and overwhelming manner, and be utterly unexpected and inexplicable, their result would be far more shattering to the human mind than if they had been foreseen, even in the vaguest fashion, and their ultimate purpose understood. This purpose, as explained in the messages, is remedial and altogether beneficial, however rough the treatment may seem, which is to rouse the world from the sleeping sickness which weighs it down.

Therefore I hold that we cannot lightly dismiss their considered conclusion, which is that the matter should not be discussed in a sensational manner, but that a quiet preparation should be made by the conveyance of information "where there is an ear to hear" and a general but gradual diffusion of the news and the evidence amongst those who might lead and steady the people in the event

318

of any cosmic crisis. I get occasionally more drastic counsel. "Make the people alive to these things. Never mind if it does frighten them. They are lethargic and sleeping." None the less I feel that the time has not yet come for such action, and that the advice of my own chief informant, as outlined above, is the course which I should pursue. I entirely understand the point of view of your two correspondents, but after reading this they will realise that the decision is not a simple one, and does not rest entirely with ourselves.

Yours, etc.,
ARTHUR CONAN DOYLE

Athenæum Club.

THE SUNDAY
TIMES   29 August 1926

The History of Spiritualism

SIR, – May I say a word upon the courteous review by my friend Sir Ray Lankester which appeared in your issue of the 15th inst.? He states there that I was converted to Spiritualism by the experiences of other men. This is very far from the fact. If he had said that my attention was drawn to Spiritualism and my interest first aroused by the testimony of Crookes, Wallace, and others, he would be within the truth. But my own actual convictions are based upon my own personal experiences in a research which extended over many years, but did not reach an absolute conclusion till the close of 1916. From that time onward I have *known* that communion and survival were true with an amount of definite objective proof which would have satisfied Professor Clifford or any other man who is capable of weighing evidence and is unclouded by invincible prejudice. I am sure that if Sir Ray Lankester, with his keen intellect, had devoted the same time to the research, and had enjoyed similar experiences, he could not have failed to come to the same conclusion.

In the chapter of my history which is headed "Some Modern Mediums," I give a short synopsis of personal experiences which cover, I think, as wide a range as those of any investigator with whom I am acquainted. I cannot understand how anyone could read that chapter and afterwards state that I was indebted to any other man for my knowledge of psychic truth.

I may add that there is no single fact in my book which I have derived from Mr. Podmore, as Sir Ray Lankester seems to think.

ARTHUR CONAN DOYLE

Lyndhurst.

319

Two Notable American Novels

SIR, – Americans give a generous welcome to good English novels. It is difficult for us sometimes to reciprocate, because their output is large and much of it passes us by. I happen to have read two of their books in succession, which seem to me to be on a very high level. The first is *A Stepchild of the Moon*, by Fulton Oursler (Harpers). The second has the uncouth name of *Teeftallow*, by T.S. Stribling, published by Nisbet. I have no axe to grind in the matter and no motive save to put two really good books under the notice of your readers.

I am, Sir, &c.,
ARTHUR CONAN DOYLE

15 Buckingham Palace Mansions, S.W.1

Houdini and the Spirits

SIR, – Mr. Clodd has given you a story of Houdini which I should wish to modify. It has always been the custom of Mr. Clodd to swallow without question anything which is against Spiritualism however absurd, and to refuse to give credence to anything, however well authenticated, which is in its favour. In this case he quotes from Houdini's book as though it were an authority, whereas it has been shown to be packed with inaccuracies from end to end.

What really occurred in the case to which Mr. Clodd refers was published by me on page 180 of my *American Adventure*. The account was written at the time, and was not disputed by Houdini when I met him in America next year. He tacitly accepted it then and never dreamed of disputing it until he began his campaign against Spiritualism.

We were together at Atlantic City and he was talking in moving terms of his mother. Knowing how strong an inspiration comes at times upon my wife, I asked Houdini if we should try and get him some comfort. He eagerly assented. It was a pure act of humanitarian pity which prompted my wife's acquiescence, and it is strange that he could ever have alluded to it in slighting terms.

My wife wrote rapidly some fifteen block sheets of paper, and Houdini, reading it page by page as I tossed it across, grew white to the lips. He was then told to ask a mental question. An answer was written and he said, "That is right." He was moved to the core at the time, and when we met him three days later in New York he said, alluding to the episode, "I have been walking on air ever since."

When he undertook his frenzied campaign against Spiritualism, which has had so deplorable an ending, Houdini had to deal with this episode. He could only find two points on which he might make this courtesy extended to him seem ridiculous. The one was that my wife had put a cross at the head of the paper whereas his mother was a Jewess. The other was that she spoke Yiddish whereas the message was in English. These seem plausible, but they really only serve to show the unfamiliarity with the methods of psychic communication which was characteristic of the man.

First as to the cross. We were aware, of course, that Houdini was a Jew. My wife *always* puts a cross on her paper when she writes under inspiration, as she believes it to be a protection against deceit.

Then as to the language. In the case of an inspirational writer it is the thought, the ideas, which are poured through her brain, and so to the paper. She does not give a verbatim message in a strange language. Such a feat might be possible to a trance medium, but not to a normal inspirational one.

Thus Houdini's objections fade into thin air. There is one other tragic point which I might add. On the same day as this seance we held a second one in the evening, as recorded on page 189 of the same book. On that occasion, through the lips of the wife of a well-known American lawyer who was present, there came a long message purporting also to come from the mother, mourning over the premature end which she saw approaching for her brilliant son. As we were all on friendly terms with Houdini at the time, we were shocked at the message. We did not pass it on to him, as we hoped it might prove mistaken, but that hope has now been dissipated.

Yours, etc.,
ARTHUR CONAN DOYLE

Bignell Wood, Minstead, Lyndhurst, 19 November

THE DAILY
EXPRESS   7 December 1926

Black-list the Tax Shirkers

SIR, – The hotels on the South Coast are at present half empty, while those of the Riviera are, I believe, filling fast. Is there not some sort of moral obligation in these days of economic pressure for those who make money in this country to spend it in this country?

I would go the length of stopping by law this dangerous leakage. Let there be a heavy poll tax upon those who go abroad, unless they can give good reasons of health or of business for their absence from this country.

As to the shirkers who live in the Channel Islands, or abroad, in order to escape taxation, and so put a heavier burden upon the shoulders of their more honest and patriotic fellow-countrymen, their names should be blacklisted in the *Gazette* and, if still recalcitrant, they should be deprived of all rights of citizenship.

The times are serious, and drastic methods are needed.

ARTHUR CONAN DOYLE

Crowborough, Sussex

THE MORNING
POST   20 December 1926

Sir A. Conan Doyle and Christie Case
Psychometry and Detective Work

SIR, – The Christie case has afforded an excellent example of the use of psychometry as an aid to the detective. It is, it must be admitted, a power which is elusive and uncertain, but occasionally it is remarkable in its efficiency. It is often used by the French and German police, but if it is ever employed by our own it must be *sub rosa*, for it is difficult for them to call upon the very powers which the law compels them to persecute.

In this case I obtained a glove of Mrs. Christie's, and asked Mr. Horace Leaf, an excellent psychometrist, for an opinion. I gave him no clue at all as to what I wanted or to whom the article belonged. He never saw it until I laid it on the table at the moment of consultation, and there was nothing to connect either it or me with the Christie case. The date was Sunday last. He at once got the name of Agatha. "There is trouble connected with this article. The person who owns it is half dazed and half purposeful. She is not dead as many think. She is alive. You will hear of her, I think, next Wednesday."

Mrs. Christie was found on Tuesday night but it was actually Wednesday when the news reached me, so that everything in the reading, so far as I could test it (there was a good deal about character and motives which was outside my knowledge) proved to be true. The only error was that he had an impression of water, though whether the idea of a Hydro was at the bottom of this

322

feeling is at least arguable. I sent the report on to Colonel Christie that evening.

Arthur Conan Doyle

The Psychic Bookshop, Library and Museum, 2, Victoria-street, Westminster, S.W. 1. December 16

THE TIMES   15 February 1927

Kitchener's Army

Sir, – One could not read the last paragraphs of Mr. Winston Churchill's accounts of the Somme Battles, as given in your issue of February 12, without rejoicing that Kitchener's Army has at last received a worthy panegyric. Personally, I have long recognised that Winston Churchill had the finest prose style of any contemporary, and it is indeed a splendid thing that he should use it to do that which seemed impossible – namely, to give an adequate appreciation of that glorious Army of patriotic volunteers who gave themselves so ungrudgingly to their country's service.

Yours faithfully,
Arthur Conan Doyle

Windlesham, Crowborough, Sussex, Feb. 14

G.K.'s WEEKLY   11 June 1927

"Pheneas Speaks"

Sir, – Your views are always of interest to me save when you touch upon religion, for there they may be predicted. Naturally you think of Spiritualism as your school of thought thinks of it. I only object to one sentence in your article upon *Pheneas Speaks*. It is that in which in some strange way you link up the Boer war and my views upon religion. The Boer war began in 1899. It was in 1879, or just twenty years earlier, that I came to the conclusion that the Almighty was not the Patron of any one sect, and that all were equally His children. What this has to do with the Boer war is beyond my comprehension.

Arthur Conan Doyle

THE TIMES   25 August, 1927

The Irish Oath

Sir, – It seems to me that the tension in Ireland on the subject of the Oath would be relieved if we could bring home the fact that this declaration of allegiance to the Crown does not concern England alone, but that it is an affirmation of comradeship with Australia, Canada, South Africa, and all those other scattered units of Empire where Irishmen have settled. Without the Oath Ireland would be quite isolated and an Irishman would find himself a foreigner in all the great Colonies. There is a sentimental argument there, but it may also be a very practical one when the question of Imperial preference comes more to the front.

Yours faithfully,
ARTHUR CONAN DOYLE

Bignell Wood, Minstead, Lyndhurst

LIGHT   1 October 1927

"The Mystery of Edwin Drood"

SIR, – The Edwin Drood case seems to me to be so important, both from a psychic and from a literary point of view, that I was about to interrupt my brief holiday in order to send you an account of it, but I find that it would be a superfluous act, since Mr. von Reuter has done it so clearly and accurately. I would only add that my hands were not on the instrument and that I had not discussed the question with the von Reuters.

Yours, etc.,
A. CONAN DOYLE

THE DAILY EXPRESS   6 October 1927

Police Evidence and Mediums

SIR, – Now that the Home Secretary is examining the value of uncorroborated police evidence, it is to be hoped that he will extend his inquiry into the cases where policemen, and police-women, appear against mediums.

There are no doubt some frauds among fortune-tellers and clairvoyants, but no one can have much wider experience of the matter than I, and I know that a good medium is the greatest source of consolation and the most cogent proof of immortality that can be found in the world today.

Yet these wonderful and sensitive instruments are worried by the unintelligent application of laws which were made before spiritualism was ever heard of, and were intended, as their name implies, to check vagrancy in the country.

ARTHUR CONAN DOYLE

Minstead, Lyndhurst

The Oscar Slater Case
Helen Lambie's Statement

Sir, – I have read the document, which, I understand, comes direct from Helen Lambie, and can be certified by an affidavit from the interviewer. The matter is of enormous importance. Indeed, it is not too much to say that it must mark the end of the Oscar Slater case.

In this document Helen Lambie admits that when she saw the murderer she recognised him as being one with whom she was familiar as a visitor to the house. She then confirms the statement of Lieut. Trench, that she mentioned the name of that visitor to other people that night.

She tells us that the police would not receive her plain statement as to who the murderer was, and that they called her "an auld gossip" when she tried to make the point clear. She shows that gradual pressure was brought to bear upon her until she was finally placed in the position of joining the cabal against the unfortunate and innocent Slater.

What recompense can now be given to the man for a life which has been wasted by the folly of his fellows? And what atonement for the honest Detective Trench who died, ruined and broken-hearted, when he was punished for trying to right the wrong?

ARTHUR CONAN DOYLE

Oscar Slater
The Farce of 1914

Sir, – I observe that in your Parliamentary column you give certain remarks about the Oscar Slater case as from an official source, which can, of course, only be Sir John Gilmour, since no one else is empowered to talk with authority from the Scots Office.

As the observations are made under quotation marks I may treat them, I suppose, as the actual words of that gentleman. If this be indeed so it fills me with amazed contempt that one who is in such high office should either be so negligent in learning the facts of the case, or else in seeing their bearing.

He says that no fresh evidence has been produced, and that the 1914 inquiry confirmed the original verdict. He should be aware that the 1914 farce was never an inquiry at all.

The terms of reference were such that the police conduct, the main point at issue, was excluded, the Press was not present, and witnesses were not sworn. To quote such a proceeding as a serious inquiry is a misuse of words.

Therefore all the original abuses of the trial, the serious mis-statements by the Lord Advocate which were uncorrected by the judge, and which brought about the verdict, the suppression of at least one important witness, and all the other irregularities still remain as before.

The one thing gained at the "inquiry" was that the best detective in Glasgow showed, to his own ruin, that he was convinced of the innocence of Slater, and stated that the chief witness, Lambie, had named another person as the murderer, a statement which has since been confirmed by Lambie herself.

But when we sum up the new evidence since that inquiry it is perfectly convincing, and one feels that the Scots Office must be deaf, dumb and blind if it does not respond to that which everyone else can sense so clearly.

In the whole Press I have hardly found one dissentient voice. How is it that everyone else can see so clearly what is invisible to the Scots Office? Is it not simply that bureaucratic protection of official by official, which would rather throw justice to the dogs than have it admitted that mistakes in high places had to be set right by outsiders?

I am sorry Sir John Gilmour has taken such an attitude. . . . He had the chance to play a noble part, and he has missed it. He has been the weak mouthpiece of the officials behind him.

Let us see what the new evidence is which Sir John Gilmour waves aside as if it was of no account.

1. There is an entirely new witness, a lady who is ready to depose on oath that she saw the murderer that night emerge from the entry, and that he in no way resembled Slater.

2. Helen Lambie has given a statement to the Press in which she corroborates the story told by Trench, the detective, that she did recognise the murderer, and that it was not Slater. An affidavit is being got from the responsible journalist who took the statement. The narrative bears truth in every line of it, for who but she could speak with such accuracy of Miss Gilchrist's household? As the story tells against herself it is vain to pretend that it is not the truth. If we have a difficulty in turning the statement into an affidavit it is due, I learn, to the alleged fact that the British Consul in Pittsburgh called upon Lambie and warned her to say no more.

3. Barrowman, the most positive witness to identity, has signed a statement before four witnesses to say that she was never sure that it was Slater, and that she was coached into saying so by fifteen interviews with the official in charge of the case.

4. An excellent witness has come forward to depose that Helen Lambie a week before the murder told her that Miss Gilchrist was expecting to be murdered, and was taking precautions against it. This cannot be fitted into the theory that Slater was the one whom she feared.

These are the chief of the new evidences. The signed statements of three out of four are in our hands, and can be shown to the Scots Office, who have already received copies.

How, then, can any sane and honest man say, as Sir John is reported as saying, that "nothing which could be regarded as evidence has been produced from any quarter"?

The original case depended upon two witnesses to identity. Both have recanted. And yet we are told that nothing is changed. I am sure that Sir John is riding for a fall. I do not believe that the deeply rooted love of justice and fair play which lies in the hearts of our people, and which is reflected in the conscience of Parliament, will allow this iniquitous business to continue any longer.

ARTHUR CONAN DOYLE

THE MORNING
POST   26 November 1927

Habitual Criminals

SIR, – I think that our admirable Home Secretary opened up a most important line of thought when he suggested that the habitual criminal should be treated as the abnormal man that he is, and *never* let loose upon the community.

If a man has been in prison, let us say, six times for violent assault, and then commits yet another one, on whom does the guilt lie – on the man or on the authority who set him free? I should say the latter, since the man may not be master of his own actions, but the release of so dangerous a person is deliberate.

Let us suppose that an annexe was built to the Dartmoor Prison, and that the really hopeless criminals were gradually segregated there after they had served their ordinary term. Their conditions might be those of comparative comfort, but there should be no question of release. By the time you had 1,000 in this cage imagine the relief it would be to the police force and the courts. There is also the question of eugenics, and that of the contamination of the young by the example of the hardened crook. It would take a rather ruthless man to carry the matter through, but there are times when ruthlessness to some means kindness to others.

ARTHUR CONAN DOYLE

Windlesham, Crowborough, Sussex

LIGHT   26 November 1927

The Hydesville Memorial

SIR, – I appealed to your readers to help me with subscriptions for the Memorial which is being erected at Rochester in memory of the birth of Spiritualism in the neighbouring hamlet of Hydesville. It is important that this Monument, a handsome obelisk, should be international in character. Up to date I have received 22s. 6d. from our British community. Will they leave me to send that in as our British contribution?

Yours, etc.,
ARTHUR CONAN DOYLE

Windlesham, Crowborough, Sussex

THE OCCULT
REVIEW   December 1927

Alleged Changes in Ocean Depths

SIR, – I agree with Mr. Hubert Stringer as to the necessity of verifying such reports. I did so in the case of the story of the deep-sea cable and was assured by the company concerned that there was no truth in it.

I should be glad, however, to have further assurance upon the Bay of Biscay soundings. They were originally taken, as stated, from the transport *Loiret*, Commander Cornet being responsible for the statement. He found thirty fathoms where he expected to find a mile. His results were pooh-poohed by Professor Lacroix, and were contradicted by soundings taken by Dr. Charcot. Some months later, however, another ship, *La Bourdonnais*, when about eighty miles from land, found forty-four fathoms where the chart gave eighty, and this over a wide area.

Personally, I cannot understand how there could ever be an

appreciable rise in the bed of the ocean without a corresponding change in high-water mark – unless, indeed, the rise was accompanied by sinkings elsewhere.

Yours faithfully,
ARTHUR CONAN DOYLE

THE TIMES   13 January 1928

The Death of Mr. Hardy
A Tribute

Thomas Hardy came nearer to nature in his writing than any other contemporary writer, in my opinion. He was a combination of Richard Jefferies and a great novelist. I remember years ago – about 25 I should say – producing a play while Thomas Hardy was staging his *Three Strangers* at the same theatre in London. They were both one-act plays. Sir James Barrie produced one of his short plays at the same time. The *Three Strangers* always stands out in my mind. It was a delightful piece. A hangman, as it happened, was the hero. Hardy was a lovable man then and he always remained so.

A. CONAN DOYLE

THE DAILY NEWS
AND WESTMINSTER
GAZETTE   21 July 1928

The Oscar Slater Case

SIR, – Of all the daily papers who have taken up the case from time to time, the *Daily News* has played the most honourable and effective part. By concentrating on it, getting detailed and accurate information, and declining to let the matter drop, it did more to strengthen my hands than any other paper. Much credit is due to it for the result.

ARTHUR CONAN DOYLE

THE TIMES   17 September 1928

The Oscar Slater Case

SIR, – At the conclusion of this case I applied to the Scottish Office to find out how far they would contribute to the costs of the appeal. As the appeal was successful and they were the defeated party, it seemed only just that they should do so. I have now received a somewhat curt intimation that they do not intend to make any additional payment. This seems a very unfair decision, and I hope that some lover of fair play will raise the question in the House. The Scottish Office itself is the cause of all the trouble and expense, since at any time during 18 years it could have found out what the five Judges have unanimously pronounced – namely, that the legal procedure was at fault and that the verdict could not stand. No trial was needed to show that, but merely an examination of the records by a competent lawyer. It seems to me that it is they individually who should be liable for the money, since it was their stupid obstinacy which created the situation. I am quite ready to meet my own promises and guarantees – and the lawyers engaged have been most generous in their treatment – but it seems a shocking travesty of justice that, having worked so long to set this wrong right, I should now be asked to pay a considerable sum in addition.

ARTHUR CONAN DOYLE

15, Buckingham Palace-mansions, S.W.1

THE MORNING
POST   17 September 1928

The Houdini Case

SIR, – With reference to Sir William Bull's question I do not know that there was any sequel to the Myers experiment. On the other hand there have been many cases of documents, wills, &c., being found by information given apparently by the deceased and coming through mediums. An outstanding case is that of the code word agreed upon between Houdini and his mother, which came through the agency of Arthur Ford, the well-known medium, and was admitted to be correct by the only person in the world who knew it – namely, Mrs. Houdini, the widow of the great magician.

A. CONAN DOYLE

15, Buckingham Palace-mansions, S.W.

THE CAPE TIMES   21 November 1928

A Happy Creed

SIR, – Your correspondent, "Confirmed Agnostic," need not be depressed. We are told that every man eventually gets his heart's desire in the other world, and if his ambition is really annihilation, as he states, then perhaps something of the sort, if only temporary, may be arranged.

But he should not continue to repeat the often-refuted statement that Spiritualism breeds insanity. It is absolutely untrue. Of course there is a certain type of mind which is put off its balance by any form of religion. But religious mania usually attacks those who have melancholy beliefs – such as predestination. Spiritualism is a very happy creed and in all my forty years of experience I have hardly ever known a person the worse for it.

The legend of insanity was started by Dr. Forbes Winslow, who said there were 10,000 people in asylums through Spiritualism. Winslow afterwards became an ardent Spiritualist, and admitted that his figures were imaginary, but the evil lived after him and the assertion is still made. Dr. Eugene Crowell made an analysis of the asylums of four States, including New York, and among many hundreds of cases of religious mania could only find four Spiritualists. Morselli, the famous Italian Alienist, made a similar inquiry with the same result. I hope, therefore, that your correspondent will either withdraw his statement, or give some definite figures to support it.

I am, etc.,
ARTHUR CONAN DOYLE

November 20

THE CAPE TIMES   5 December 1928

The National Women Monument in Bloemfontein
An Apology

SIR, – I hold myself responsible for anything which I may write, but I do not feel the same responsibility towards the words reported in an interview, for, however honest and correct it may be, much depends upon the circumstances, and the way in which it was said. No one has written more sympathetically of the Boers than I, and I paid my due respects, hat in hand, at the grave of General De Wet.

When, however, I examined the monument, my ignorance of Dutch led me astray, and deciphering the words, which seemed to be to attribute the death of those poor women and children to their treatment by the British, I used a rather warm expression with regard not to the monument but to the statement which would naturally pain any Briton.

It has been shown me that I misinterpreted the real meaning of the phrase, and, this being so, I cannot do less than express my regret and withdraw the remark. I would be sorry, indeed, to leave Bloemfontein after causing pain to any section of its inhabitants.

Yours faithfully,
ARTHUR CONAN DOYLE

THE EAST AFRICAN
STANDARD
2 March 1929

Success and Failure

SIR, – Mr. Sharpe Hillman's suggestion that Spiritualism should be judged by its failures and not by its successes is the exact opposite to all scientific methods – and I may add to common sense. It is as if I denied the Atlantic Cable because I have once or twice received misdirected or unintelligible cablegrams. In all science it is the positve result and not the negative which counts. The Chemist empties his failures down the sink but he builds upon his successes.

Yours, etc.,
ARTHUR CONAN DOYLE

Nairobi, Feb. 22, 1929

THE JEWISH
CHRONICLE
19 April 1929

Oscar Slater's Costs

SIR, – In your issue of February 22nd, I am asked about the Slater costs. There is little I can tell you about them since you have yourself handled all that the public subscribed. Everything which reached me I sent on to you, including a sum from the *Jewish Graphic*. If there was, as you say, any other collection, I am not aware of it. I, however, subscribed £100 from my own purse, half of which I sent to the law agents, and the other half to pay the out of pocket expenses of my friend the late Mr. William Park, who played such a noble part throughout. I may add that I have never allowed one shilling for my own expenses extending over seventeen years during which I worked for this man's pardon.

I am still liable for about £200, but have had no application from the law agents. Slater is, of course, ultimately responsible for all costs, and though I clearly pointed out to him what my own personal liability was, I have never received any offer from him to relieve me of it. The total quoted, £1,500, is extraordinarily low when one considers that there were really two trials, great researches to be made, and three Counsel employed, one of whom spoke for thirteen hours. Slater has owed his success to the wonderful work done by these men. The costs would have been four times as great had the trial been in England.

I am, &c.,
ARTHUR CONAN DOYLE

Aden, March 21st

THE EMPIRE NEWS   5 May, 1929

Bitter Dispute Over Appeal

SIR, – You have been so valuable a friend to Oscar Slater, and have seconded so admirably my attempt to get justice for this man, that I should wish you to know the result of these proceedings so far as I personally am concerned.

To start the wheels of the law I made myself responsible for costs up to £1,000. The Jewish community with the help of a few outsiders, subscribed £670 towards relieving me of this burden. The money was collected and forwarded to the law agents by the *Jewish Chronicle*. That left the sum of £330, which I have spent out of my own pocket.

Early in the proceedings I had a letter from Oscar Slater in which he declared that no one should be out of pocket over his defence. That was before he got his verdict. Since then I have written to him several times pointing out the facts, but have received either no reply or an evasive one. The lawyers have now, very properly, applied for the money, and of course I have honoured my personal guarantee and have paid in full.

Had Slater lost his case I would have cheerfully taken this heavy expense upon myself, but as he has received £6,000 compensation it seems a monstrous thing that these charges should be met by me.

Legally he is, of course, responsible for the money, but I am loth that so sordid an aftermath should follow a successful fight to vindicate British justice. I am not prepared, however, to submit to such treatment, and I shall be reluctantly driven to assert my rights in a court of law unless this man has the common decency to pay his own debts of his own free will and without compulsion.

Yours faithfully,
ARTHUR CONAN DOYLE

May 2, 1929

The Nairobi Ghost Photograph

Sir, – I notice that in your issue of April 18, you accuse me of making "another bloomer," in connexion with the Nairobi photographic incident. It is in truth yourself who make the bloomers, for I have never seen a statement about Spiritualism in your paper which was not either untrue, or else one of those half-truths, the nature of which is proverbial. For example, in this instance, you tell half a story, the whole of which is told in the enclosed extract. This tells how Mr. Palmer, after claiming to be the ghost, admitted to the audience (and to me in a subsequent letter) that the real ghost had afterwards appeared and terrified him. "When I had seen and felt its power," he writes, "I had no heart for further posing." If you believe him in one point, how can you discredit him on the other, and how can you sustain your contention that the incident disproves the existence of this particular ghost?

ARTHUR CONAN DOYLE

The Nairobi Photograph

Sir, – I am sorry to trouble you again upon this matter, but it was you yourself who brought it up, and Mr. Palmer now continues the attack. It may interest you both to learn that the photograph was originally obtained by me from Mr. Melton, of Nottingham. When Mr. Palmer claimed it at Nairobi, it was impossible for me to confute his claim. But now I have referred the matter to Mr. Melton, and he assures me that the photograph was indeed taken by him, that it is truly psychic, that he has the original negative, and that Mr. Palmer is quite mistaken. So it would appear that I have been right from the first.

ARTHUR CONAN DOYLE

The "Witch" of Endor

Sir, – It is curious that so exact a scholar as Bishop Barnes should speak of the "Witch" of Endor. No such person is mentioned in the Bible. She was always the "woman" of Endor. The opprobrious name is given to her in the chapter heading, which reflects the ignorance of psychic matters which prevailed among the high ecclesiastics who did the translation, and which has not entirely disappeared from among their successors.

Personally, I could never see anything of evil in the episode in which Saul consulted the seer. She was what we should call a clairvoyante, for she had to describe to the King what it was she saw. As a medium she had first to get a promise of immunity, for the laws of Israel were as barbarous as those of England are today in the matter of Spirit intercourse. She then was the means of conveying a direct message from the Lord, together with a prophecy which was duly fulfilled. What is there reprehensible in such a transaction?

Bishop Barnes talks of the strong current of materialistic thought which sets against miracles. But he says nothing of the very notable and increasing minority who understand that there are really psychic laws which produce results which might well appear to those who saw them to be miraculous, though they only meant that a lower law was temporarily in abeyance owing to a higher one, as when gravity seems to be contradicted when the steel bar springs up to the magnet. It is amazing that all the well-attested results of modern psychical research seem to be completely ignored by Dr. Barnes and the school which he represents. It is a school, I think, which has already passed its zenith and is on the downward grade.

ARTHUR CONAN DOYLE

Bignell Wood, Minstead, Lyndhurst

THE MORNING
POST   17 June 1929

"The 'Witch' of Endor"

SIR, – The letter of the Archdeacon of Chester seems not to refute but to confirm my assertion that the opprobrious word "witch" does not occur in the text of the Bible, but is inserted in the chapter heading to humour the well-known weakness of James the First. As the medium was made the direct messenger from God it is difficult to see why the incident is always quoted as if it were a scandalous one.

ARTHUR CONAN DOYLE

Windlesham, Crowborough, Sussex

Hardened Offenders

Sir, – A case tried recently at Quarter Sessions brings up in a very clear form the question as to what should be done with the irreclaimable criminal. The case was that of a burglar and a motor thief. He has again and again committed the same offences, for which he has spent eight years out of the last nine in gaol. He has now received a further sentence of three years, and in receiving it he passed a note up to the Judge to say that he had no intention to reform. This means that when he regains his freedom the community is warned that it will have to put up with this man's depredations. Being so warned is not the community very foolish to give the man the chance of putting his threat into execution?

Sir W. Joynson-Hicks, during his occupancy of the Home Office, mentioned in one of his speeches that the idea had been discussed of perpetual segregation for irreclaimable criminals. Personally, I have always been of opinion that this should be done. We segregate our lunatics and we segregate our infectious cases, and the hardened criminal is a mixture of both. He is a man with a dangerous *idée fixe*, and he is a man who is likely to infect others by exerting his influence upon those who are younger or weaker than himself. The world has no use for him. He is the enemy of society. It is folly, therefore, to give him successive sentences, which mean intervals when we have to pay the penalty for our own weak and illogical leniency. The true method of guarding ourselves is to eliminate him altogether. From the time that his true character is established the prison doors should never open again.

But this prison need not be a severe one. It should be rather on the lines of Broadmoor Criminal Lunatic Asylum. No great hardship need be involved. But since liberty has been abused, liberty should for ever be taken away. Suppose that such a law were at once enforced, and that two or three thousand hardened offenders were weeded up from the roots, what a relief it would be to the police, to the Courts, and, finally, to the public. Having got these obstacles out of the way for ever one could see one's way more clearly to social reform. It seems to me that if a man has been convicted three or four times of a penal offence he is a fit candidate for such a permanent asylum as I suggest.

Yours faithfully,
ARTHUR CONAN DOYLE

15, Buckingham Palace-mansions, S.W.1, June 18

Hardened Offenders

SIR, – Might I add one postscript to the discussion upon the subject of "hardened offenders"? I would have done so before but I wished to read all that others could say. The criticism, which has been widespread, divides itself into two contradictory assertions, the one that a measure of segregation would be too severe, the other (led by the honoured name of Sir Henry Dickens) that it would be too kind, and put a premium upon crime. This divergence of opinion seems in favour of the view which is attacked. Several papers have exclaimed that it is "un-Christian" but if we grant that any penal measures are justified, then it is hard to see why continuous segregation should be less Christian than a long succession of incarcerations with short intervals of crime against the community. As to moral reform, that is surely more likely to take place under the supervision which such a system would ensure than if the criminal returns to the society of other malefactors who are actively employed. I had a note of one case where a man had been condemned 30 times for physical assaults which involved severe injuries to the person assaulted. If this man had after the fifth offence been segregated, then it is clear that 25 people would have escaped broken heads. Why should we be so sensitive as to the fate of the criminal and pay no heed to his victims, whose persons or property are the forfeits paid for our own negligence?

Yours faithfully,
ARTHUR CONAN DOYLE

Windlesham, Crowborough, Sussex, July 13

Justice at Mark Cross

SIR, – My son was fined £5 for speeding by the Mark Cross magistrates at their last session. It was admitted by the police that the road was clear at the time, and that no danger was caused to anyone. This being so, one would have thought that a less excessive fine would have met the case. It was an offence which did not involve any moral guilt of any kind. On the same day a man was had up before the same Bench for gross cruelty to a horse. It was his 13th conviction, and it was asserted that he had flogged it for half-a-mile. For this horrible action he was fined £2. He paid no costs, while my son had to do so.

How can anyone excuse such judgments as these, and is it a wonder that many of the younger generation look upon the administration of the law with contempt? They do not blame the action of the police, but they can find neither justice nor sense in the rulings of the magistrates, who seem to consider a harmless burst of speed upon a motor as a more serious offence than the repeated torture of a helpless animal.

ARTHUR CONAN DOYLE

THE SOUTHERN DAILY ECHO, SOUTHAMPTON   19 August 1929

The Bignell Wood Fire

SIR, – Will you allow me to use your columns in order to express my gratitude to the strangers who helped to move the furniture from my house to the lawn on the occasion of the recent lamentable fire? One or two, I regret to say, showed a disposition to remove the goods even further, but the greater number gave me invaluable assistance. The Southampton fire brigade was hard working and efficient.

Yours faithfully,
A. CONAN DOYLE

Bignell Wood, Minstead, Lyndhurst, August 16

THE OCCULT REVIEW   December 1929

Convent Scandals

SIR, – I am glad to have the assurance of Mr. Thomas Foster that stories of escaped nuns and the occasional scandals in convents "have been long since exploded." One would certainly not wish to counter false accusations against spiritualism by advancing false ones against our critics. But if it is really as Mr. Foster says then why these sad tales from those who have got out, why these prison-like walls, and above all why this determined opposition to inspection? I am convinced that the Roman Church would be in a stronger position if these matters were open to public inquiry and that her true interests lie that way.

Yours faithfully,
ARTHUR CONAN DOYLE

Propaganda in India

Sir, – An eminent Frenchman remarked that no nation was so bad at defending itself as the British. We usually, out of a misplaced pride, put up no defence, and let our case go by default. Those whose memories go back to the Boer War may remember how there was actually at one time a danger of a Continental coalition against us, founded entirely upon false information, and how it was private rather than public propaganda which eased the situation, as many foreign newspapers admitted at the time.

It is a recollection of this which makes one apprehensive lest at this most critical time our case should not be fairly stated to the various very diverse elements of Indian life. We hear of the agitation for independence, but we hear nothing of that counter-agitation which could, one would think, be so easily evoked. For example, have the Mohamedans of India been asked whether they are prepared to obey laws which are passed by a permanent majority of Hindus? If not, why do they not say so? Will the great native Princes of India state definitely whether they wish their lands to be isolated islands in an independent country? Has it been explained to the Punjab that it will be left bare, without British help, to face any invasion from the north? Have the Parsees been asked to state publicly whether they prefer the security of British rule, or the century of chaos which would follow our departure? Have the 60,000,000 "untouchables" been asked whether they would wish to be left to the mercy of the Brahmins? Have the agitators themselves been reminded of the lesson of the Moplah rebellion, where the local Mohamedans, the moment they broke loose, massacred, not the white people, but the Hindus? All of these are cards in our hand, but they are no use unless we play them.

Yours faithfully,
Arthur Conan Doyle

Windlesham, Crowborough, Sussex, Jan. 10

THE JOURNAL OF
THE SOCIETY FOR
PSYCHICAL RESEARCH   March 1930

Resignation from the Society for Psychical Research

Dear Sir (or Madam), – I had occasion recently [on the 22nd of

January 1930.] to send the following letter to the Chairman of the Council of the S.P.R.:–

"Dear Sir,

"I have just read an article in the January number of the *Journal* by Mr Besterman upon the Millesimo sittings. It is, in my judgment, such a series of misrepresentations and insulting innuendoes that it tends to lower the good name of the Society. The insolence by which the considered opinion of a man like Professor Bozzano, who was present, is set aside and treated with contempt by one who was not present, and who has had very little experience of psychical research, makes one ashamed that such stuff should be issued by an official of a Society which has any scientific standing.

"To appreciate the full absurdity, as well as the gratuitous offensiveness of Mr Besterman's alternative theory of fraud, one has to visualise what it exactly implies. It means that an Italian nobleman of old family, a member of the legislative body, has invited a circle of friends to his home in order to practise a succession of complicated frauds upon them. That he is himself implicated is shown by the fact that levitation of his own body and other personal phenomena are among those most clearly recorded. Having assembled his guests he causes the voices of his own dead relatives and others to be sounded in the room. A lady confederate conceals under the short modern skirt a long medieval rapier, a matador's sword, a big doll and other objects quite unseen by a critical company. She or some other confederate produces a large balloon-like object which hovers above the company, and in some unspecified way produces blasts of ice-cold air. All these and many other wonders are brought off so successfully that in a succession of sittings the company, including Professor Bozzano, are completely deceived, and the latter stakes his scientific reputation upon the truth of the phenomena. This is the picture which Mr Besterman's theory of fraud would compel us to accept, the whole being done with no conceivable object. Can we dignify such nonsense as this by the name of Psychical Research, or is it not the limit of puerile perversity?

"A further example of prejudice is to be found in the allusions on page 15 of the same *Journal* to the real psychic researcher, Mr Dennis Bradley, and to George Valiantine in Berlin. The assertions of the opponents of Spiritualism are at once accepted on their face value without the slightest attempt at discriminate examination.

"I have long waited hoping that the Podmore, Dingwall, Besterman tradition of obtuse negation at any cost would die away. But as there is no sign of it, and the obsession seems rather to become more pronounced, my only resource is, after thirty-six

340

years of patience, to resign my own membership and to make some sort of public protest against the essentially unscientific and biased work of a Society which has for a whole generation produced no constructive work of any kind, but has confined its energies to the misrepresentation and hindrance of those who have really worked at the most important problem ever presented to mankind.

Yours faithfully,
ARTHUR CONAN DOYLE"

Those of us who are conscious of the extreme importance of the movement called "Spiritualism," or even those who are desirous to see fair play in the matter, must be aware of the way in which the Society, originally intended to be a sympathetic and fair centre for inquiry, seems to have become simply an anti-spiritualist organisation. Everything which tends to prove the truth of that cult, no matter how honourable or sane the source may be, is assailed by suppression, misrepresentation and every sort of unreasonable and vicious opposition.

For a generation, since the death of Myers and the end of the Piper sittings, the Society has done no constructive work of any importance, and has employed its energies in hindering and belittling those who are engaged in real active psychical research. This latest article of Mr Besterman may be insignificant in itself, but it is a link in that long chain of prejudice which comes down from Mr Podmore, Mrs Sedgwick [sic], and Mr Dingwall, to the present day. It is necessary, as it seems to me, to call a halt, and to make inquiry as to how far the Society is to be for ever in the hands of this small central body of reactionaries, or whether they really represent the opinion of the members. It is not desirable that the Society should lose its independence or become a Spiritualistic body, but it is most essential that it shall not treat what so many regard as a matter of supreme importance with the irresponsibility and levity which have been shown hitherto, where it has been the custom again and again for a commentator to jeer at phenomena which he has not witnessed, in the face of the most cogent evidence of their having actually occurred.

I would ask those who would wish to appreciate what I say to read Mr Besterman's article in the January *Journal*, and then Professor Bozzano's measured and dignified preface to Mrs Hack's *Modern Psychic Mysteries* (Rider), which treats of these sittings.

This matter is of more importance than would at first sight appear, for I say deliberately that these Millesimo sittings are on the very highest possible level of psychical research, both from the point of view of accurate reporting, variety of phenomena, and purity of mediumship. Therefore, if they can be laughed out of court anything we can produce will be treated with similar contempt. I can hardly believe, as I read Mr Besterman's criticism, that he has actually read the book. It bristles with errors of fact. He complains that we are not told where the sword was apported from. On page 93 may be read: "The weapon had been lying on a large table on the second floor of the palace. In a direct . . . thirty yards." He talks of the apports as if their extreme length was two feet (in order to insinuate that they could be concealed by the lady). On page 176 is a picture of a lance 6 feet long, and on page 208 of a plant 4½ feet high – both apports. He complains that he does not know what a flexatone is, and yet it is described on page 97. Yet this slovenly critic takes advantage of his official position in order to warn the reading public of the S.P.R. away from this most important book.

I have waited long in the hope of some reform but I have now concluded that it is not to be expected, and that the influence of the Society is entirely for evil. I have, therefore, resigned my membership, and the protest would be more effective if those who agree with me would see their way to follow my example. It need not hamper their psychic studies. In the British College of Psychic Science, 15 Queen's Gate, W., they will find an Institution where they can participate themselves in real positive psychical research, with mediums at hand to be tested, a good library, an excellent quarterly magazine, and an atmosphere which is progressive and not stagnant.

I write this under a strong sense of duty, for I am now one of the oldest members of the S.P.R. I am convinced, however, that they have long been not a help but a hindrance to the psychical knowledge of the world, and that a strong protest is called for.

I may add that, having uttered such a protest, I cannot undertake to enter upon prolonged argument or correspondence, nor can I attend meetings, as my health hardly permits me to leave the house.

Yours faithfully,
ARTHUR CONAN DOYLE
M.D. (Edin.), LL.D.

January 1930.

I would remind members of the words of that great pioneer, Sir William Barrett: "A scepticism which is too lofty to see the existence of a mass of evidence under its very eyes is anything but healthy. It calls for medical attention."

A Strange Experience

Sir, – In the early morning of February 3 I was lying awake when I became aware of heavy steps approaching along the passage which leads to my room. They were quite as well marked as those of the butler when he brings me my early morning cup of tea. They paused outside my door, and I then heard clearly a short cough as of someone clearing their throat.

I turned up the light and noticed that it was 3.30 a.m. I then rose and went to the door. I flung it open fully expecting to find some person on the other side. The light from my lamp shone down the passage and there was no one there. Having made sure that this was the case, I returned to bed in a somewhat shaken state, as I was a sick man and in no condition for such nocturnal adventures.

In a quarter of an hour or so my heart palpitation passed away and I fell into a deep sleep.

Two days later my wife received a letter from Mrs. Osborne Leonard, the well-known medium, saying that she had never dreamt of me before in her life, but that between 3.30 and four o'clock on Monday morning she had had an extraordinarily vivid impression of having visited me and actually seeing me and administering some healing treatment to me. "It was all so real," she said, "that it cannot be classed as a dream." In this letter Mrs. Leonard offered to come to Crowborough and to give me a special seance, which she did three days later nobly fulfilling her promise, which involved a drive of thirty miles partly through deep snow.

The seance was a very wonderful experience, but it makes a story by itself. When it was over I discussed with Mrs. Leonard the happenings of Monday morning, and I mentioned to her the short cough which I had heard outside my door. She said: "That is really final. I seldom have anything the matter with my throat, but that night every time I woke I found myself coughing in the very way you describe. It was so unusual that it impressed itself upon my memory."

These are the facts, and they seem to me beyond all range of coincidence, and to present a very clear case of bi-location. Mrs. Leonard was sleeping at Kenley, but undoubtedly her double or etheric body had visited me at Crowborough.

A. Conan Doyle

Lord Balfour

SIR, – In the various obituary notices of the late Lord Balfour I have not observed that any reference has been made to his keen interest in the things of the spirit.

As early as 1894 he was president of the Society of Psychical Research, and his presidential address of that year showed how keen was his understanding of the problems at issue. He had already amassed considerable practical experience of mediumship, for it is mentioned by Mr. Campbell Holmes in his "Facts of Psychic Science" (page 388) that as early as 1875 he had investigated materialisations in a series of seances with Miss Wood and Miss Fairlamb, some of which were held in his own house.

He was exceedingly cautious in expressing his convictions, and, though on one occasion I interchanged letters with him upon the subject, I am unable to say that he fully accepted the theory of communication, although I am quite certain that he did not absolutely reject it. As a proof of this I may mention that some years ago he was asked to address the annual conference of the Spiritualists' National Union, and he accepted the invitation. This, of course, would not imply full acceptance of the spiritualists' view, for spiritualists are always keen to get sane and intelligent outsiders' criticism. He was, however, prevented from carrying out his intention by an illness which entailed a visit to a Continental health resort.

I think that I am right in stating that he had even some undeveloped psychic gifts of his own and that he obtained some results in an experiment in crystal-gazing. Andrew Lang mentions the fact in one of his books.

Yours faithfully,
ARTHUR CONAN DOYLE

Windlesham, Crowborough, Sussex, March 27

The Use of Great Names

SIR, – It might interest your readers to know that some weeks ago I had a communication which professed to come from Thomas Hardy. It came through an amateur Medium from whom I had only once before had a message, which was most veridical. Therefore, I was inclined to take Hardy's message seriously, the more so as intrinsically it was worthy of him. I should place it on the same level of internal evidence as the Oscar Wilde and the Jack London scripts. Hardy gave a posthumous review of his own work, some aspects of which he now desired to revise and modify. The level of his criticism was a very high and just one. He then, as a sign of identity, sent a poem, which seems to me to be a remarkable one. It describes evening in a Dorsetshire village. Without quoting it all I will give here the second verse which runs thus:

> Full well we know the shadow o'er the green,
>   When Westering sun reclines behind the trees,
> The little hours of evening, when the scene
>   Is faintly fashioned, fading by degrees.

The third and fourth lines are in my opinion exquisite. I do not know if they were memories of something written in life. I should be glad to know if anyone recognises them.

ARTHUR CONAN DOYLE

THE DAILY
TELEGRAPH   7 July 1930

Constantinople

SIR, – It makes one's heart bleed to read Mr. Churchill's account of our unnecessary failure to force the Dardanelles.

Mr. Churchill writes with such power – he is, in my opinion, the greatest living master of English prose – that he may produce a greater effect than the facts warrant. For consider the situation if we had then taken Constantinople and driven Turkey out of the war.

The possession of Constantinople had been promised to Russia, and we should now have been faced with a mighty Power which faced Europe upon a front extending from Archangel to the Mediterranean. If this Power were Bolshevik the situation would be terrible.

But even if we assume that a victorious Russia would have remained Imperial, would not that also have been a mighty danger when the counterpoise of Germany had been removed?

It may be that our failure was really more beneficial in the end than success would have been, and that this is one more instance where the wisest plans of man have been set aside by that which is wiser still.

Yours, &c.,
ARTHUR CONAN DOYLE

Crowborough, July 4

345

NOTES

———◆———

Since, by definition, the letters collected in this volume deal with public affairs, and the context is generally self-explanatory, the following notes deal only with characters and episodes now largely forgotten.

LIST OF NOTES

'THE CONTAGIOUS DISEASES ACTS'
Medical Times and Gazette, 16 June 1883

The Two Acts of 1866 and 1869 had granted powers for the compulsory and periodic examination of women suspected of harbouring contagious diseases. Objections were first raised in 1870 and a Royal Commission had been appointed which suggested that alterations would be desirable. A Select Committee was therefore established and in 1883, after a three-year inquiry, produced two conflicting reports, one in favour of retaining the existing arrangements and the other seeking their abolition. The latter reflected the policy of many Liberals who had pledged to work to this end during the election of 1880 which had brought them to power.

The majority report in favour of the Acts had the backing of the medical profession and the Army Medical Corps, but it was rendered null and void when a resolution was passed in Parliament on 20 April 1883 by 182 to 110 votes which stated 'That this House disapproves of the compulsory examination of women under the Contagious Diseases Acts', and thereby effectively destroyed the Acts.

The districts or 'protected stations' where officers had been posted were the major Dockyards like Woolwich, Chatham, and Portsmouth. Various petitions in favour of the Acts were sent during the weeks which followed; these included a memorial from doctors in Portsmouth, of which Doyle would have been aware and very probably a signatory.

Although it was a distasteful subject, it was also a question of morality, whether the hygienic advantages could justify enforced examination and compulsory detention of suspects in locked wards.

Doyle returned to the subject in February 1916 when, in letters to *The Times*, he advocated the internment of prostitutes to prevent the spread of venereal disease among soldiers on leave.

'THE PORTSMOUTH YOUNG MEN'S CHRISTIAN ASSOCIATION AND THEIR REV. CRITIC'
Evening News, Portsmouth, 27 March 1884

On 7 March 1884, the actress Mrs. Adeline Billington appeared at the Circus in Bow Street, Landport, in 'An Evening of Grand Dramatic Recitals' under the auspices of the Portsmouth Young Men's Christian Association. It was the first of six entertainments designed to raise money to establish a Portsmouth scholarship in the Royal College of Music. The programme included such favourites as 'Billy's Rose' by G.R. Sims and 'The Charge of the Light Brigade'. The audience, among whom were the Prince and Princess of Saxe-Weimar and a party from Government House, judged the evening to be a complete success.

The controversy began on 19 March when a public meeting was called to discuss the establishment of a Y.M.C.A. in association with St. John's in Portsea. The vicar, the Rev. H. Lindsay Young, stated that he was totally opposed to the idea as the Association had so recently secured the services of Mrs. Billington who, he believed, was an actress. Indeed, it was his opinion that it was high time for the word 'Christian' to be expunged from the title of the Association.

W. Ridout was the first to criticise the vicar's intolerance and bigotry. Then, two days later, on 24 March, Alderman J.G. Whitcombe, who had helped to arrange the event, wrote to complain about the actress's 'traducer'. She was a lady of most estimable character and no one who had heard 'Billy's Rose', for example, would 'forget the lesson taught by the love of the sister and her fondness and devotion to her dying brother'. The leading article the same day was outspoken in its condemnation of the vicar's 'stupid blunder', calling him a 'veritable Ishmael' whose services would not be missed should he leave the area. That, in its turn, led three correspondents to write in the vicar's defence. Among them was 'Veritas' who recalled an old proverb, 'The truth may be blamed, but can't be shamed', and 'R.' who suggested that the Association might more appropriately be called 'The Borough of Portsmouth Young Men's Mutual Improvement Association'. It was at that point that Doyle entered the fray. Although in a light vein, recalling Sir Toby Belch's criticism of Malvolio, 'Dost thou think, because thou art virtuous, there shall be no more cakes and ale?' it made a serious point and reflected some of his own spiritual uncertainties.

AMERICAN MEDICAL DIPLOMAS

The diplomas offered by dubious institutions, for an average fee of $25, were first mentioned in the Portsmouth *Evening News* in a letter on 15 September 1884. Further letters were published the following day attacking them, and these led William Edwards Wymond 'M.D., Philadelphia, United States of America and Associate of the Arts of the University of Oxford' to write in their defence. The degrees given after his name thereupon became the subject of renewed controversy.

In his letter of 23 September 1884, Doyle refers to three leading medical men from the United States: Lewis Albert Sayre (1820–1900) who trained at the College of Physicians and Surgeons in New York and was the first American surgeon to operate successfully for hip-joint disease; Austin Flint (1812–86) who trained at Harvard and was President of the American Medical Association during 1883–4; and Gross, either Samuel David Gross (1805–84) who was the founder of the American Medical Association, or Samuel Weissell Gross (1837–89) who was one of the first to use antiseptic surgery in America.

'WORKING MEN'S LOYAL JUBILEE MEMORIAL'
Evening Mail, Portsmouth, 26 March 1887

A Jubilee Memorial meeting had been held at the Victoria Hall, Landport on 3 March 1887 when various possible schemes had been considered. These included a statue, a bust in the new Town Hall, or a portrait, also for money to be given to the Royal Portsmouth, Portsea and Gosport Hospital, to the Imperial Institute – as had been suggested by the Prince of Wales, and for a 'demonstration', decorations and arches at the time of the Golden Jubilee.

General T.N. Harward, in a letter on 25 March 1887, complained that the meeting had been held merely to endorse a prearranged plan. He expressed the belief that working men, who had been unable to attend as it was held during the afternoon, would desire a 'modest memorial bearing a suitable inscription, and ornamented or not, with a statue, bust, profile, or medallion of the Queen', which need cost no more than £200–300. Doyle, writing in support of General Harward, allowed his patriotism to extend beyond his professional interests which, as with his friend, R.W. Ford, who had seconded the resolution, might otherwise have favoured the hospital. If a little sentiment was excusable on this occasion, a great deal was called for at the time of the Queen's death. He was to give his patriotic fervour full scope in an obituary article for the New York *World*, and in 1910 did no less for her son, the late King Edward VII, in an article for the *Daily Mail*.

The loyalty of 'democratic Birmingham' refers to the vast display of affection shown towards the Queen during a visit on 23 March 1887 when she had laid the foundation stone of the Victoria Assize Courts.

' "ESTHER WATERS" AND THE LIBRARIES'
Daily Chronicle, 1 May 1894
'THE BOYCOTT OF "ESTHER WATERS" '
Daily Chronicle, 3 May 1894

On 27 April 1894 the 'Writers and Readers' column of the *Daily Chronicle* announced that the Society of Authors was contemplating action against W.H. Smith and Son's Circulating Library over the boycott imposed on George Moore's novel, *Esther Waters*. Although Walter Besant, the founder, admitted he had not read the book, another member, Doyle, had done so. It seems that the Society had discussed the subject and decided that the boycott was intolerable especially as a ban by the Library meant that the railway bookstalls would also refuse to take the book.

The ban was not the first which had been imposed on George Moore's novels. Mudie's had refused to take *A Modern Lover* and *A Mummer's Wife*, while Smith's had refused *A Drama in Muslin* and *Vain Fortune* (even though, as the author pointed out, they had taken the magazines in which the stories were serialized). The refusals had led Moore to fight a running battle against such 'censorship'. There was an article, 'A New Censorship in Literature' (*Pall Mall Gazette*, 10 December 1884), a pamphlet, 'Literature at Nurse, or Circulating Morals' (1885), and the introduction to Zola's *Piping Hot* (1886) where he accused Mudie and Smith of being 'the authors of our fiction' who were alone responsible for throwing it 'into the abyss of nonsense in which it lies'. It was, however, the boycotting of *Esther Waters* which, its author believed, led to the final destruction of the already moribund system.

Moore had tried to interest Henry James and Bernard Shaw in his cause, but it was Doyle who brought the matter to a head, and for this Moore was grateful. In a letter of 4 May he thanked his fellow author for his generous defence and for having thrown 'the weight and authority of his name on the side of justice.'

A day after Doyle's first letter, Frederick Pollock, the chairman of the committee, explained that the Society of Authors had been desired by Moore not to proceed with the matter, for which there was, in any case, no legal remedy. There was also an interview with William Faux, the head of Smith's library department. He had elsewhere explained that the book had been banned on account of about twenty lines of pre-Raphaelite hastiness. He now compared the book with Hardy's *Tess of the d'Urbevilles* (which had suffered problems at the time of its serialisation, though had been taken by Smith's after publication). Where one had been 'delicately inferential', the other was 'precisely positive'. Another explanation was given to Moore personally during a visit which he described in *A Communication to My Friends*. Faux told him that the readers were 'not used to detailed descriptions of a lying-in hospital'. Faux stressed in the *Daily Chronicle* interview that out of 15,000 subscribers only one had written to complain. At the end, he was asked if the intervention of Sherlock Holmes had made him quake, by which, the reporter explained, he meant Mr. Conan Doyle's letter to the *Daily Chronicle*. To this Faux replied: 'I read it, and I wondered that one who is so great an artist himself did not see the blemishes in "Esther Waters" which led to our rejection of it.'

The correspondence continued during the days which followed, especially as Hardy's novels had been introduced into the discussion. Among those who wrote were the novelist, Sarah Grand, the critic, William Archer, Edward Clodd (later a critic of Doyle's spiritualism) who suggested the wording for a formal letter of protest to Smith's, and L.F. Austin who, with his tongue in his cheek, suggested that Moore would have to prepare a special bowdlerised edition of his novel which might be called 'The Blemishes of Esther Waters: A Moral Tale of A Faux Pas'.

Moore, with the aid of an accountant, later estimated that Smith's had lost in the region of £15,000 on account of the boycott. He had obtained the best possible advertisement for his novel (which was into its eleventh thousand by 12 May), and was particularly gratified that, as a result of an announcement in the *Westminster Gazette* that Gladstone had read the book and expressed his approval of it, Faux was severely reprimanded for his decision by the partners of the firm.

'THE CASE OF MRS. CASTLE'
The Times, 10 November 1896

Walter Michael Castle, a respectable businessman from San Francisco, and his wife Ella were arrested on 5 October 1896 at the Hotel Cecil in London on a charge of shop-lifting. When the police entered the room Mrs Castle immediately locked a wardrobe in which, after a second key had been procured, were discovered furs, gold watches, fans, brooches, china, and other goods, many with their original sale tickets in place. The Castles had been intending to sail for America on 7 October and one of their trunks was found to contain two silver-plated toast racks, a cream jug, and a towel belonging to the hotel.

After being released on £40,000 bail, their case came up at Clerkenwell on 7 November. Mr. Castle, who pleaded 'Not guilty', was discharged, but Sir Edward Clarke, who appeared for his wife – by then hysterical and unable to speak – entered a plea of 'Guilty' to each of the seven indictments of having stolen furs from six shops and of having purloined property from the hotel. He also produced medical evidence to show that her physical condition was unlikely to withstand imprisonment, explaining that the week she had spent in Holloway gaol had seriously effected her. The judge, aware of the difficulty he faced and of the need for sympathy, sentenced her to three months imprisonment without hard labour, at which the defendent went out of control and was taken from the Court screaming and sobbing.

The medical evidence at the trial from Dr. Grigg, Senior Physician at Queen Charlotte's Lying-in Hospital, Dr. Savage, Senior Physician at the Bethlem Hospital, Dr. Scott, Medical Officer at Holloway Gaol, and Dr. Gabriel, who had examined Mrs Castle shortly after her arrival in England in May 1896, was soon afterwards supplemented by further evidence. The Home Secretary was advised by the Medical Officers from Holloway and Wormwood Scrubs, and by the former superintendent of the Broadmoor Lunatic Asylum of her adverse mental state, and on 10 November he ordered her immediate release into the care of her husband on the understanding that he would take her back to the United States without delay.

When Doyle returned from Egypt in May 1896 his new house at Hindhead was still unfinished, so he took the furnished house called Greyswood Beeches where he remained until early in the following year when he removed to Moorlands, a boarding house close to the site of his new dwelling.

352

As Doyle was staying at Morley's Hotel in Trafalgar Square, he was only too aware of the preparations being made to celebrate the 92nd anniversary of the Battle of Trafalgar on 21 October 1897. The Navy League, which had arranged similar festivities the previous year, was decorating the Nelson column with garlands and floral tributes. There was a naval crown half-way up and a number of shields carrying mottoes, the whole being illuminated at night by searchlights. The League hoped to make the anniversary an annual event similar to 4 July in the United States.

On the day itself, there were ceremonies throughout the Empire in places associated with Nelson or where the League had branches. It was recognized that such an occasion might arouse unpleasant memories in the minds of former opponents, but the intention was to honour those who had died for their country.

Arnold White, in response to Doyle's first letter, pointed out that Joan of Arc's memory was celebrated in a similar manner in France, and Admiral R.V. Hamilton, having expressed surprise that the author of *Rodney Stone*, 'a work that certainly induces the very act that he complains of – keeping green in the hearts of the nation the love for Nelson', should have written as he did, stated that Trafalgar had saved Europe from the tyranny of Napoleon and marked the triumph of right over might. He also believed that Englishmen would not take offence if the French were to celebrate their victory at Fontenoy or elsewhere.

After Doyle's second letter a number of people wrote on the subject. 'J.R.T.' considered that the recent celebrations had been tawdry, that 'silent meditation and solemn thankfulness' would have been more appropriate. But he judged Doyle's idea to be 'little short of grotesque', as it would be a form of hypocritical deference which would not conceal the true object of the celebration. One letter drew comparisons with the Diamond Jubilee, and another noted that working men had an insatiable appetite for knowledge which such occasions helped to gratify. Mrs. C.R. Whitte, a descendant of Nelson, complained that the 'milk-and-water policy' advocated by Doyle would logically require all the ships captured from the French to be renamed.

Doyle's reference to Lord Roseberry's words at Stirling were also the subject of a letter. The former Liberal Leader had been at Stirling on 9 October 1897 when he received the freedom of that ancient and Royal Burgh. R. J. Friewell, in his letter published on 25 October, pointed out that Doyle had completely changed the significance of Lord Roseberry's speech by substituting 'Britain' for England. What he had actually asked was, why did Scotland celebrate the victories of Wallace and Bruce, or Stirling and Bannockburn, when the English did not commemorate Flodden or Dunbar; and the answer was, he believed, that in the vast roll of her achievements, England could afford to pass over such victories as those.

A reply by Dr. William Robertson Nicoll was published on 16 May 1899 in answer to the attack on his ethics. He explained what had caused Doyle's letter: 'In two papers, under recognisable pseudonyms,

I have criticized his latest book as, in the first place, unworthy of his genius, and in the second place, fitted to mislead the public.' That as a result of one chapter 'to which serious moral exception might be taken'.

The reviews had appeared in the *British Weekly* on 6 April 1899, under the pseudonym of 'Paternoster Row', and in the 'Literary Lounger' column of the *Sketch* on 26 April 1899, under the pseudonym of 'O.O.' In the first, *A Duet* was judged to be only 'passable' and very 'stuffed out'. As a result of one episode, which taught 'the devil's own lie', the reviewer considered that Doyle would henceforth be a 'doubtful author' whose works would need to be scrutinised before being admitted freely into an ordinary English household. It would have been better had the book not been published. In the second review, the critic dismissed the two main characters as 'particularly uninteresting young people'; the book was full of inanities and crude jokes, and there was 'one chapter neither conceived nor written in good taste'. 'O.O.' felt that the author had no qualifications for entering into 'the complexities of humanity' and would be well advised to refrain from similar attempts in the future.

Doyle's criticism was answered in detail by Nicoll. He acknowledged that he was both 'Claudius Clear' and 'The Man of Kent' in the *British Weekly* (though he did not admit to being 'Paternoster Row' as well). 'The Correspondence of Claudius Clear' was, in most cases, a long review, while 'The Man of Kent' was responsible for a gossip column of 'Rambling Remarks'. He also confirmed that he had been the editor of the *Bookman* since its inception in 1891, but had never used it as a vehicle for his own opinions and had written no more than a dozen reviews, all of which had been signed. His letter to the New York *Bookman* appeared under his own signature and consisted of literary news. And finally it was the policy of the daily paper for which he occasionally worked to preserve the anonymity of reviewers (it appears to have been the *Daily Chronicle* itself, which had, for example, sent him G.A. Smith's *Life of Henry Drummond* for review the previous December).

As well as the letter from 'The Editor of "The Bookman" ', there was one from Shan F. Bullock defending Nicoll and suggesting that the real scandal was the existence of 'such mediocrity in the ranks of criticism' elsewhere.

Doyle's second letter restated what the editor had discreetly removed from the first, that Nicoll had for some time acted as an adviser to a publishing house (this being Hodder and Stoughton) and that he might therefore have an interest in securing the success of certain books. Nicoll's reply appeared the following day, and began: 'I have hesitated as to whether Dr. Doyle's supplementary letter would not be answered more properly in a court of law than in a newspaper.' But he had chosen the latter. He received no pecuniary advantages from the sale of books; he recalled that James Payn had been in a similar position; and he concluded by commending to Doyle 'the wise saying of Bentley, "No man was ever written down save by himself." '

Nicoll, as 'Claudius Clear', discussed 'The Pleasures of Reviewing' in the *British Weekly* on 18 May, and made references to Doyle's 'excited imagination'. Then in July he allowed the whole subject of 'Multiple Reviewing' to be aired in a symposium for the *Bookman* (see p. 54).

Doyle, for his part, was to describe the episode in his autobiography written nearly a quarter of a century later. His account has served as the basis for the many inaccurate versions given in subsequent biographies. *A Duet*, he recalled, led to 'a public bickering with a man who has done good work as a critic, Dr. Robertson Nicoll. He took exception to some passage in the book, which he had every right to do. But he wrote at that time for six or seven papers, under different names, so that it appeared as if a number of critics were all condemning me when it was really only one. I thought I had a grievance, and said so with such vehemence that he stated that he did not know whether to answer me in print or in the law courts. However, it all blew over and we became very good friends.' (*Memories and Adventures*, p. 145)

354

GEORGE EDALJI

George Edalji was born in 1876 and was the son of a Parsee who had joined the Church of England. A series of anonymous letters, the first of which had been sent nearly twenty years before, and a bout of cattle maiming culminated in his arrest on 18 August 1903. He was tried at the Stafford Assizes and sentenced to seven years in prison. His case was then taken up by R.D. Yelverton, a former Chief Justice of the Bahamas, and by other influential people including Sir George Lewis and the editor of the crusading magazine, *Truth*, and on 19 October 1906 Edalji was released on a four year ticket-of-leave. He immediately began 'protesting his innocence' in a series of articles in the Manchester *Umpire*, and it was these which brought the matter to Conan Doyle's attention. Doyle had been made a member of Arthur Lambton's Crimes Club, which included among its members George Sims, who in 1904 had defended Adolph Beck by publicising the case in the *Daily Mail*, and John Churton Collins, who was well versed in the Edalji case and other aspects of criminology. Sims provided Doyle with a model and Collins provided advice. Doyle considered that there had been a gross miscarriage of justice and, having met Edalji and paid a visit to the scene of the crime, Great Wyrley in Staffordshire, he became convinced that a man suffering from acute myopia could not have committed the crime. His articles in the *Daily Telegraph* and the other publicity helped to persuade the Home Office to re-examine the case. The charge of cattle maiming was dropped, but the other charges remained. Doyle therefore prepared a statement identifying the people whom he considered were the true culprits, but his evidence was deemed inadequate for a prosecution to be brought. Edalji's total innocence, though widely assumed, was never proved. He was reinstated on the roll of solicitors and died on 17 June 1953 after an otherwise uneventful life.

OSCAR SLATER

Oscar Slater was arrested in New York on 2 January 1909 and accused of having murdered Miss Marion Gilchrist in Glasgow on 21 December 1908. His trial was held at the beginning of May and he was sentenced to death by execution on 6 May. A Memorial on his behalf was presented shortly afterwards by Ewing Spiers and on 25 May the sentence was commuted to penal servitude for life. Conan Doyle was approached in the early summer of 1912 and his booklet, *The Case of Oscar Slater*, was published that August. In April 1914 an official inquiry was held in Glasgow but the Scottish Secretary delcared afterwards that no case had been made which would justify a new trial or any interference with the existing sentence. In October and November 1927 two of the key witnesses retracted their evidence and on 14 November 1927 Slater was released. An appeal was lodged in Edinburgh (being made possible by a special Act of Parliament) and on 4 August 1928 Slater was awarded an *ex gratia* payment of £6,000 which he accepted. He died on 3 February 1948 at the age of 75.

THE COTTINGLY FAIRY PHOTOGRAPHS

The first three fairy photographs were taken in Cottingley Glen in Yorkshire during July and September 1917 by two girls, Elsie Wright and her cousin,

Frances Griffiths. The fairies were copied from drawings by Claude A. Shepperson which had appeared in *Princess Mary's Gift Book* (and which incidentally bore a strong resemblance to those used to advertise Price's Night Lights. They were cut out and held up by hat-pins.

A fairy photograph made by the same method was published in the *Sphere* on 9 February 1918 without causing any comment, but when Elsie Wright's mother mentioned her daughter's photographs at a Theosophist meeting, they came to the attention of E.L. Gardner and he in turn brought them to the notice of Conan Doyle, who was looking for pictures to illustrate an article on fairy lore. Neither of the girls would admit that the photographs were fake, so Doyle and Gardner accepted them as genuine and together wrote an article on the subject which appeared in the *Strand Magazine* in December 1920. Further photographs were taken and these were reproduced in Doyle's original article which appeared

later, and the photographs and articles served as the basis for *The Coming of the Fairies* which was published under Doyle's name in September 1922.

Many critics recognised at once that the photographs were fake, but Doyle could not believe that the girls had lied to him and therefore wasted his energy checking the negatives – a waste of time, as the negatives had not been tampered with in any way. To the end of his life he remained convinced that they must be genuine, though he did say on at least one occasion that if the girls were not telling the truth, then the fairies could only have been cut-out figures. The girls, who had each accepted £20 in bonds from Doyle, remained silent until March 1983 when Mrs. Elsie Hill (as she then was) ended the absurd controversy by revealing the truth. What had started as a childish prank had grown into a serious matter from which the girls could think of no way of extricating themselves.

'OUTWARD BOUND'

The letter in *Light* on 10 November 1923 refers to the fantasy in three acts by Sutton Vane which was first performed at the Everyman Theatre, Hampstead, on 17 September 1923 and revived at the Gar-

rick Theatre on 15 October 1923. The play is set in the bar room of a ship where the characters gradually realise they are in limbo between life and death.

THE MYSTERY OF EDWIN DROOD

Conan Doyle's letter in *Light* in 1927 appears in the same issue as Florizel von Reuter's account of the seance at which 'contact' was made with Dickens. Doyle gave a further account in his 'Psychic Notes' in the *Sunday Express* on 6 May 1928 where he describes the two evenings which Florizel von Reuter and his mother spent at Bignell Wood, and refers to the various unseen presences which made themselves known. Of these, Dickens was the most notable and in the course of his conversation with Doyle said of Drood: 'I was sorry to go across before I got him out of his trouble. The poor chap has had a

hard time. I always hoped that you would put Sherlock on his track. I don't know which is better – to solve your mystery in your notebook or let it remain a mystery.'

In 1912, Doyle had a quite extensive correspondence with W. Robertson Nicoll, the two having by then become friends, after he had received a copy of Nicoll's *The Problem of Edwin Drood*. He then described the Drood case as 'one of the great problems and also one of the tragedies of literature, for what could be more dreadful than to be haunted at the moment of death by a task half-done which no other man can complete?' And he sent Nicoll his own views. These filled six pages of typescript and used the methods he was employing in the Slater case, but they came to no definite conclusion.

A full account of the 1927 seance, based on Doyle's original description which was given at a lecture at the Grotrian Hall on 4 September 1927, will be found in Florizel von Reuter's *Psychical Experiences of a Musician* (pp. 312–16).

CATEGORICAL INDEX

A. HOME AFFAIRS

1. MEDICAL
Gelseminum
  'Gelseminum as a Poison', *British Medical Journa*, 20 September 1879.
Leucocythaemia
  'Notes on a Case of Leucocythaemia', *Lancet*, 25 March 1882.
The Contagious Disease Acts
  'The Contagious Diseases Acts', *Medical Times*, 16 June 1883.
Sham American Degrees
  'American Medical Diplomas', *Evening News*, Portsmouth, 23 September 1884.
Gout
  'The Remote Effects of Gout', *Lancet*, 29 November 1884.
Compulsory Vaccination
  'Compulsory Vaccination', *Evening Mail*, Portsmouth, 15 July 1887.
  'Compulsory Vaccination', *Hampshire County Times*, Portsmouth, 27 July 1887.
Dr Koch's Consumption Cure
  'The Consumption Cure', *Daily Telegraph*, 20 November 1890.

2. POLITICS
Liberal Unionists in Portsmouth
  'The Unionist Platform', *Evening News*, Portsmouth, 6 July 1886.
  'The Liberal Unionists', *Hampshire Post*, Portsmouth, 27 April 1888.
Edinburgh Central Division
  'To the Electors Central Edinburgh', *Edinburgh Evening Dispatch*, 25 September 1900.
  'Dr Doyle and the Reform Club', *Daily Chronicle*, 28 September 1900.
  'Dr. Conan Doyle and the Catholic Church', *Scotsman*, 16 October 1900
The Border Burghs Election Campaign
  'The New Protection', *Spectator*, 4 July 1903.
  'The New Protection', *Spectator*, 18 July 1903.
  'Sir Arthur Conan Doyle on the Tweed Acts', *Hawick Express*, 18 December 1903.
  'Mr Balfour and the City of Bradford', *The Times*, 29 December 1903.
  'The Tweed Trade', *Southern Reporter*, Selkirk, 4 February 1904.
  'A Plea for Protection', *Daily Chronicle*, 4 Feburary 1904.
  'A Further Plea for Protection', *Daily Chronicle*, 6 February 1904.
  'Mr A.L. Brown and Sir Arthur Conan Doyle', *Border Advertiser*, Galashiels, 11 April 1905.

'Sir Arthur Conan Doyle's platform', *Border Advertiser*, Galashiels, 5 September 1905.
'Fiscal Policy', *The Times*, 31 October 1905.
'The Free Trade Debate', *Farnham, Haslemere, & Hindhead Herald*, 9 December 1905.
'The Fiscal Controversy', *Farnham, Haslemere, & Hindhead Herald*, 30 December 1905.
'To the Electors of the Borders Burghs', *Border Telegraph*, Galashiels, 9 January 1906.
'Sir Arthur Conan Doyle on Tariff Reform', *Hawick Express*, 9 March 1906.

3. SPORT
A new Portsmouth sports ground
    'The Proposed Recreation Ground at North End', *Evening News*, Portsmouth, 7 May
        1886.
Local rifle clubs
    'The Undershaw Rifle Club', *Farnham, Haslemere, & Hindhead Herald*, 5 January 1901.
    'Rifle Shooting as a National Pursuit', *The Times*, 14 June 1905.
The Olympic Games (London, 1908)
    'To Honour Dorando', *Daily Mail*, 25 July 1908.
Prince Henry Motor Race
    'The Prince Henry Tour', *The Times*, 11 July 1911.
The Olympic Games (planned for Berlin, 1916)
    'The Empire and the Games', *The Times*, 18 July 1912.
    'Our Olympic Failure', *Evening Standard & St. James's Gazette*, 22 July 1912.
    'The Olympic Games', *The Times*, 30 July 1912.
    'Britain and the Olympic Games', *The Times*, 8 August 1912.
    'Olympic Committee', *Sporting Life*, 25 March 1913.
    'Olympic Games Lethargy', *Daily Express*, 24 May 1913.
    'The British Olympic Council', *Daily Express*, 5 July 1913.
    'The Olympic Games', *The Times*, 27 August 1913.
    'The Olympic Games Fund', *The Times*, 13 September 1913.
    'The Olympic Games Fund', *The Times*, 11 October 1913.
    'Some Views on the Olympic Talent Fund', *Stock Exchange Christmas Annual*, 1913–
        1914.
Boxing
    'The Fighting Spirit – Letter to "Jimmy" Lowes', *Evening Chronicle*, Newcastle-upon-
        Tyne, 15 June 1920.
American baseball
    'Merits of Baseball', *The Times*, 28 October 1924.

4. THE LAW
The case of George Edalji
    'The Case of Mr George Edalji', *Daily Telegraph*, 9 January 1907.
    'The Question of Eyesight', *Daily Telegraph*, 15 January 1907.
    'The Edalji Case', *British Medical Journal*, 19 January 1907.
    'The Edalji Case', *Daily Telegraph*, 19 January 1907.
    'The Edalji Case – Summing Up', *Daily Telegraph*, 26 January 1907.
    'The Edalji Case', *Daily Telegraph*, 11 March 1907.
    'Edalji Case', *Daily Telegraph*, 20 May 1907.
    'Edalji Case – Statement in the House', *Daily Telegraph*, 29 May 1907.
    'The Edalji Case', *Daily Telegraph*, 1 June 1907.
    The Edalji Letters', *Daily Telegraph*, 20 June 1907.
    'The Edalji Debate', *Daily Telegraph*, 25 June 1907.
    'Case of George Edalji', *Daily Telegraph*, 20 July 1907.
Divorce Law Reform
    'Marriage Problems', *Daily Mail*, 16 January 1912.
    'Sir A. Conan Doyle on Divorce', *Daily Mail*, 23 January 1912.
        'On Divorce', *Daily Mail*, 25 January 1912.
    'Divorce Law Reform', *Morning Post*, 9 December 1913.

'Lord Hugh Cecil and Divorce Law Reform', *Morning Post*, 4 April 1914.
'Divorce and Separation', *The Times*, 8 September 1917.
'Marriage Cruelties', *Empire News*, Manchester, 16 September 1917.
'Divorce and Separation', *Spectator*, 20 October 1917.
'The Synod and Divorce', *Sussex Daily News*, Brighton, 9 February 1918.
'Divorce and the Bishops', *Daily Mail*, 15 November 1918.
'Divorce Law', *The Times*, 30 March 1920.

Oscar Slater Case
  ' "The Case of Oscar Slater" ', *Daily Mail*, 2 September 1912.
'The Slater Case', *Spectator*, 25 July 1912.
'The Slater Case', *Spectator*, 26 October 1912.
'The Oscar Slater Case', *Spectator*, 25 July 1914.
'The Oscar Slater Case – Helen Lambie's Statement', *Empire News*, Manchester, 23 October 1927.
'Oscar Slater – The Farce of 1914', *Daily News*, 14 November 1927.
'The Oscar Slater Case', *Daily News & Westminster Gazette*, 21 July 1928.
'The Oscar Slater Case', *The Times*, 17 September 1928.
'Oscar Slater's Costs', *Jewish Chronicle*, 19 April 1929.
'Bitter Dispute Over Appeal', *Empire News*, Manchester, 5 May 1929.

Habitual Criminals
'Habitual Criminals', *Morning Post*, 26 November 1927.
'Hardened Offenders', *The Times*, 20 June 1929.
'Hardened Offenders', *The Times*, 13 July 1929.
Local Magistrates
'Justice at Mark Cross', *Sussex County Herald*, Eastbourne, 20 July 1929.

5. OTHER ISSUES
Queen Victoria's Golden Jubilee
'Working Men's Loyal Jubilee Memorial', *Evening Mail*, Portsmouth, 26 March 1887.
Distribution of British Intellect
'Hampshire Worthies', *Evening News*, Portsmouth, 2 August 1888.
'Hampshire Celebrities', *Hampshire Post*, Portsmouth, 17 August 1888.
Income Tax
'Income Tax Assessment', *Evening News*, Portsmouth, 1 November 1890.
'Black-list the Tax Shirkers', *Daily Express*, 7 December 1926.
Preservation of Nelson's Flagship
'For Nelson's Sake', *Daily Chronicle*, 22 September 1892.
Shorter Hours for Shop Assistants
'Dr Conan Doyle on Early Closing', *Grocers' Assistant*, November 1900.
'Dr Conan Doyle Supports Our Cause', *Grocers' Assistant*, January 1901.
Motor Cars
'Sir Conan Doyle and the Motor Car', *Spectator*, 1 August 1903.
'More Motorphobia', *Daily Mail*, 21 September 1905.
Farms for Small Holders
'Yeomen Stock', *Daily Express*, 21 November 1908.
Bernard Shaw and the Sinking of the Titanic
Mr Shaw and the Titanic', *Daily News*, 20 May 1912.
'Mr Shaw and Sir A. Conan Doyle', *Daily News*, 25 May 1912.
Labour Unrest
'The Labour Unrest – A Rejoinder to Mr Wells', *Daily Mail*, 20 June 1912.
The Channel Tunnel
'A Channel Tunnel', *The Times*, 11 March 1913.
'The Channel Tunnel', *Daily Express*, 19 April 1913.

'The Channel Tunnel', *The Times*, 14 August 1913.
'The Channel Tunnel', *The Times*, 26 December 1913.
'The Channel Tunnel Scheme', *Glasgow Herald*, 26 June 1916.
'The Channel Tunnel', *The Times*, 9 December 1922.
Preservation of Endangered Birds
'The Importation of Plumage Prohibition Bill', *Spectator*, 28 February 1914.
Kent Coal
'Prophecy – and Finance', *Pall Mall Gazette*, 5 March 1914.
Kent Coal', *Pall Mall Gazette*, 7 March 1914.
Inflation and Profiteering
Profiteering', *The Times*, 9 July 1919.
'The Vegetable Market', *The Times*, 12 July 1919.
'Growers, Sellers, and the State', *The Times*, 17 July 1919.
Postal Increases and the Postcard Trade
'The Crushing of a British Industry', *The Times*, 9 December 1921.
The British Empire Exhibition
'Wembley on Sundays', *The Times*, 23 May 1924.
Conan Doyle's New Forest House
'The Bignell Wood Fire', *Southern Daily Echo*, Southampton, 19 August 1929.

B. FOREIGN AFFAIRS

1. AMERICA
'Britain and the Chicago Exhibition', *The Times*, 24 December 1892.
'Mr Conan Doyle and America', *Daily Chronicle*, 1 January 1895.
'Lecturing in America', *Author*, July 1895.
'A Letter from Dr Doyle', *Critic*, 21 September 1895.
'England and America', *The Times*, 7 January 1896.
'The Case of Mrs Castle', *The Times*, 10 November 1896.

2. THE BELGIAN CONGO
'England and the Congo', *The Times*, 18 August 1909.
'England and the Congo', *The Times*, 28 August 1909.
'The Congo Question', *The Times*, 4 October 1909.
"Belgian Denials", *Daily Express*, 8 October 1909.
'The Congo Question', *Pall Mall Gazette*, 15 November 1909.
'The Congo', *Tablet*, 20 November 1909.
'The Crime of the Congo', *Daily Graphic*, 23 November 1909.
'The Congo Loan', *The Economist*, 27 November 1909.
'The Congo Rforms', *The Times*, 3 December 1909.
'Germany and the Congo', *Daily Mail*, 8 December 1909.
'The Congo Reforms', *Daily Express*, 13 April 1910.
'Belgium and the Congo', *The Times*, 17 February 1911.
'Great Britain and Belgium', *Daily Express*, 9 March 1911.
'Rubber Atrocities', *Daily News*, 5 March 1912.

3. IRELAND
'South County Dublin', *Irish Times*, 3 October 1900.
'The South Dublin Election', *The Times*, 19 October 1900.
'Conan Doyle and Home Rule. "How I Stand in the Matter"', *Belfast Evening Telegraph*,
    22 September 1911.
'Sir A. Conan Doyle and Home Rule', Morning Post, 28 September 1911.
' "Peaceful Ireland" ', *Daily Express*, 26 March 1912.
' "Peaceful Ireland" ', *Daily Express*, 28 March 1912.

'Home Rule. Letter to R.J. Kelly of Dublin', *Irish Times*, 4 April 1912.
'Nationalists and Exclusion', *The Times*, 25 March 1914.
'Irish Compromise. Catholic Counties in Ulster', *The Times*, 16 July 1914.
'Irish Compromise. Concession as the Alternative to Force', *The Times*, 20 July 1914.
'On Ireland and the Empire', *Treeman's Journal*, 3 August 1914.
'Sir Roger Casement', *Daily Chronicle*, 30 November 1914.
'Justice in Ireland', *Daily Chronicle*, 9 May 1916.
'Ireland and the War', *Freeman's Journal*, 31 October 1916.
'Record of Sinn Feinism', *Belfast Evening Telegraph*, 17 July 1917.
'Ireland & Conscription', *Daily Chronicle*, 18 April 1918.
'A Voice from the Grave', *Freeman's Journal*, 27 June 1921.
'The King's Speech', *The Times*, 29 June 1921.
'Irish Separatism', *The Times*, 9 September 1921.
'The Irish Oath', *The Times*, 25 August 1927.

4. *OTHER COUNTRIES*
France
    'Nelson Day', *The Times*, 20 October 1897.
    'Nelson Day', *The Times*, 23 October 1897.
Japan
    'The Case of the Caroline', *The Times*, 28 November 1904.
Portugal
    'Political Prisoners in Portugal', *The Times*, 13 May 1913.
    'The Portuguese Prisoners', *Daily Chronicle*, 16 May 1913.
India
    'Guinea Pig or Man?', *Daily Express*, 1 November 1910.
    'Thyssen's Revelations', *Financial News*, 16 July 1918.
    'Propaganda in India.', *The Times*, 20 July 1920.
    'Propaganda in India. *The Times*, 14 January 1930.

C. LITERARY

---

1. *A. CONAN DOYLE*
My Friend the Murderer
    'A Protest from Dr Conan Doyle', *Critic*, New York, 2 December 1893.
    'Another Letter from Dr Doyle', *Critic*, New York, 27 January 1894.
Strange Secrets
    'Strange Secrets', *Critic*, New York, 26 October 1895
Rodney Stone
    'Dr Conan Doyle's Latest Case', *Saturday Review*, 2 January 1897.
    'Dr Conan Doyle's Latest Case', *Saturday Review*, 9 January 1897.
Sir Nigel
    'The Book War – Protest by Sir A. Conan Doyle', *Standard*, 20 November 1906.
    'Sir Arthur Conan Doyle and Mr Perris', *Daily News*, 24 November 1906.
The Poison Belt
    'La "Force Mysterieuse" ', *Le Temps*, 1 May 1914.
    ' "The Poison Belt" ', *The Times*, 2 May 1914.
'Danger!'
    ' "Danger!" ', *Daily Mail*, 29 October 1914.

2. *OTHER SUBJECTS*
Thomas Carlyle
    'Carlyle: His Character and Philosophy', *Hampshire Post*, Portsmouth, 29 January 1886.

George Moore
    ' "Esther Waters" and the Libraries', *Daily Chronicle*, 1 May 1894.
    'The Boycott of "Esther Waters" ', *Daily Chronicle*, 3 May 1894.
Hall Caine
    'Literary Etiquette', *Daily Chronicle*, 7 August 1897.
Multiple Reviewing
    'The Ethics of Criticism', *Daily Chronicle*, 15 May 1899.
    'The Ethics of Criticism', *Daily Chronicle*, 16 May 1899.
    'The Ethics of Criticism', *Daily Chronicle*, 18 May 1899.
The *Boy's Own Paper*
    'Completion of Twenty-Five Years of the "B.O.P." ', *Boy's Own Paper*, 31 October
        1903.
Laurence Housman and Stage Censorship
    'Mr Housman and the Censor', *Pall Mall Gazette*, 3 October 1910.
Bogus Literary Agents
    'A Warning', *Bookman*, March 1911.
Critical Commendations
    ' "Outward Bound" ', *Light*, 10 November 1923.
    'Two Notable American Novels', *Spectator*, 13 November 1926.
Thomas Hardy
    'The Death of Mr Hardy – A Tribute', *The Times*, 13 January 1928.

D. MILITARY

1. SALISBURY PLAIN MANOEUVRES (1898)
Recollections of Lord Wolseley
    'Lord Wolseley', *The Times*, 3 April 1913.

2. SOUTH AFRICAN WAR
Langman Field Hospital
    'The Epidemic of Enteric Fever at Bloemfontein', *British Medical Journal*, 7 July 1900.
    'Dr Conan Doyle and His South African Services', *Scotsman*, Edinburgh 3 October
        1900.
Civilian Riflemen and Other Lessons of the War
    'Volunteers and the War', *The Times*, 18 December 1899.
    'The Lessons of the South African War', *The Times*, 1 November 1900.
    'The Lessons of the South African War', *The Times*, 6 November 1900.
    'Mr Conan Doyle and Army Reform', *Westminster Gazette*, 12 November 1900.
    ' "Burghers of the Queen" ', *Glasgow Evening News*, 19 December 1900.
    'Civilian Riflemen', *Westminster Gazette*, 27 December 1900.
    'Civilian Riflemen', *Westminster Gazette*, 5 January 1901.
    'The Undershaw Rifle Club'. *Farnham, Haslemere and Hindhead Herald*, 5 January 1901.
    'Rifle Shooting as a National Pursuit', *The Times*, 14 June 1905.
    'Mr Chamberlain and Mr Burns', *The Times*, 26 January 1906.
High Angle Fire
    'The War Office and Inventors', *The Times*, 22 February 1900.
    'Mr Conan Doyle and High Angle Fire', Westminster Gazette, 26 February 1900.
Cricketers from South Africa
    'South African Cricketers', *Spectator*, 20 April 1901.
    'South African Cricketers', *Spectator*, 4 May 1901.
Deterrent to Boer Sabotage
    'The Derailing of Trains', *The Times*, 5 September 1901.
    'Train-Wrecking', *The Times*, 14 September 1901.

The War in South Africa: Its Cause and Conduct
  'Dr Conan Doyle on His Defence', *Daily News*, 31 January 1902.
  'The Lizzie Van Zyl Photograph', *Daily Chronicle*, 1 February 1902.
  ' "The Cause and Conduct of the War" ', *The Times*, 4 February 1902.
  'The War and Continental Opinion', *Daily Messenger*, Paris, 23 February 1902.
  'Dr Conan Doyle to our Readers', *German Times*, Berlin, 3 March 1902.
  ' "The Cause and Conduct of the War" ', *The Times*, 11 April 1902.
  ' "The Cause and Conduct of the War" ', *The Times*, 5 June 1902.
National Women Monument at Bloemfontein
  'The National Women Movement in Bloemfontein. An Apology, *Cape Times*, Johannesburg, 5 December 1928.

3. HOME DEFENCE
Motor-Cars
  'Motor-Cars and Home Defence', *The Times*, 12 April 1906
Cyclist Cavalry
  'Yeomanry of the Future', *Daily Express*, 8 February 1910.
Cavalry Training
  'Cavalry Training', *Pall Mall Gazette*, 6 April 1910.
  'Sir A. Conan Doyle and Cavalry Training', *Pall Mall Gazette*, 13 April 1910.
  'The Amateur Soldier Agin', *Saturday Review*, 4 November 1911.
  'The Amateur Soldier Again', *Saturday Review*, 2 December 1911.

4. THE GERMAN WAR (FIRST WORLD WAR)
Civilian Volunteers
  'Our Latent Forces', *The Times*, 8 August 1914.
  'Civilian National Reserve', *Daily Mail*, 13 August 1914.
  'Civilian Volunteer Reserves', *The Times*, 4 november 1914.
  'Volunteer Training Corps', *Crowborough Weekly*, 28 November 1914.
  'Volunteer Training Corps', *The Times*, 3 December 1914.
  'Volunteer Uniforms', *The Times*, 13 February 1915.
  'Home Guards', *Spectator*, 29 May 1915.
  'The Use of the Volunteers', *Spectator*, 13 November 1915.
  'An Opportunity Missed', *The Times*, 20 March 1916.
  'Volunteers and Their Uniform', *Volunteer Training Corps Gazette*, 29 July 1916.
Submarines
  'Sumarine Mines', *The Times*, 8 September 1914.
  'The Submarine Menace', *Daily Chronicle*, 2 May 1917.
Lifebelts and Lifeboats
  'Lifebelts in Men-of-War', *Daily Mail*, 29 September 1914.
  'Lifebelts for the Navy', *Evening Standard and St. James's Gazette*, 7 October 1914.
  'Saving Our Seamen', *Daily Chronicle*, 22 January 1915.
Armour for Trench War
  'The Use of Armour', *The Times*, 27 July 1915.
  'Modern Armour', *The Times*, 4 August 1915.
  'Mr Wells's Prophecy', *Daily Chronicle*, 21 January 1916.
  'Body Armour of Shields', *The Times*, 28 July 1916.
  'Body Shields again', *The Times*, 4 August 1916.
  'Body Shields', *Observer*, 20 August 1916.
Recruitment and National Service
  'Recruiting in Eastbourne', *Eastbourne Gazette*, 14 October 1914.
  'Recruiting and Publicity', *The Times*, 18 November 1914.
  'Compulsory National Service', *Daily Chronicle*, 23 August 1915.
  'Compulsory National Service', *Daily Chronicle*, 25 August 1915.
Campaign against Drink
  'Advertisements against Drink', *The Times*, 5 May 1915.

Soldiers and Venereal Disease
  'Soldiers in London', *The Times*, 6 February 1917.
  'Soldiers in London', *The Times*, 10 February 1917.
  'Soldiers in London', *The Times*, 17 February 1917.
Riot by Canadian Soldiers
  'The Epsom Incident', *The Times*, 23 June 1919.
The British Campaigns
  'The Surrender of Kut', *Daily Chronicle*, 2 May 1916.
The British Campaign in France and Flanders
  ' "The British Campaign in France", *New York Times*, 2 March 1917.
  'The British Campaign of 1915', *Times Literary Supplement*, 26 July 1917.
Films of the Front Line
  'The Somme Films', *The Times*, 4 September 1916.
Britain and Germany Compared
  'General Von Arnim's Report', *The Times*, 11 October 1916.
  'Supremacy of the British Soldier', *Daily Chronicle*, 19 April 1917.
German Policy
  'Germany's "Policy of Murder"', *New York Times*, 6 February 1915.
  'Murder Deliberate', *The Times*, 8 February 1916.
  'The German Criminals', *The Times*, 12 November 1918.
  'The German Criminals', *The Times*, 6 February 1920.
Prisoners of War
  'The Treatment of Prisoners', *The Times*, 13 April 1915.
  'The Case of Our Prisoners', *The Times*, 28 June 1918.
  'Our Prisoners', *The Times*, 8 October 1918.
Air Raid Reprisals
  'Reprisal', *The Times*, 15 October 1915.
  'The Policy of Air Raid Reprisals', *The Times*, 18 October 1915.
  'A Preventive of Air Raids', *The Times*, 18 January 1916.
  'Air Raid Reprisals', *The Times*, 22 January 1916.
  'Reprisals', *Saturday Review*, 26 February 1916.
  'Hospital Ships', *The Times*, 16 March 1918.
  'The Outrage on the Hospitals', *The Times*, 27 May 1918.
Divorce for British Wives of Germans
  'British Wives of Germans', *The Times*, 23 August 1917.
  'British Wives of Germans', *The Times*, 28 August 1917.
Anti-German Hatred
  'The Uses of Hatred', *The Times*, 26 December 1917.
  ' "The Uses of Hatred" ', *The Times*, 31 December 1917.
  'Records of German Crime', *The Times*, 16 January 1918.
Post-War Feelings towards Germany
  'British Attitudes towards Germany', *World of Trade*, Frankfurt, 15 January 1920.
The Dardanelles Expedition
  'A Recompense for the Dardanelles', *The Times*, 25 October 1923.
  'Constantinople', *Daily Telegraph*, 7 July 1930.
Winston Churchill's Panegyric
  'Kitchener's Army', *The Times*, 15 February 1927.

E. RELIGION AND SPIRITUALISM

---

1. RELIGION
Portsmouth Y.M.C.A.
  'The Portsmouth Young Men's Christian Association and their Rev. Critic', *Portsmouth Evening News*, 27 March 1884.

Modern Theism
  'Mr Shutte's Critic', *Portsmouth Evening News*, 20 November 1889.
Sport on Sunday
  'Sunday Rifle Shooting', *Farnham, Haslemere, and Hindhead Herald*, 28 April 1906.
Religious Faith
  'Are we becoming Less Religious?', *Daily Express*, 7 August 1906.
  'Are we becoming Less Religious?', *Daily Express*, 11 August 1906.
  'Are we becoming Less Religious?', *Daily Express*, 31 August 1906.
Roman Catholics and the Coronation Oath
  'The King's Declaration', *The Times*, 12 May 1910.

2. *CONAN DOYLE AND SPIRITUALISM*
Personal Experiences
  'A Test Message', *Light*, 2 July 1887.
  'Where is the Soul during Unconsciousness?', *Light*, 11 March 1916.
  'Where is the Soul during Unconsciousness?', *Light*, 13 May 1916.
  'A Prophecy', *Journal of the Society for Psychical Research*, January 1919.
  'Soldiers Who Have Come Back', *Christian Spiritualist*, 11 November 1925.
  'A Strange Experience', *Morning Post*, 6 March 1930.
Australian Lecture Tour
  'Sir Arthur Conan Doyle's Tour', *Two Worlds*, 1 October 1926.
  'Wake Up, Australia!' Sir Arthur Conan Doyle's on his Australian Tour', *International al Psychic Gazette*, January 1921.
  'Sir Conan Doyle's Book', *Evening Standard*, 14 September 1921.
  'Darkey of Christchurch', *Times Literary Supplement*, 29 September 1921.
Psychic Bookshop and Museum
  'The Psychic Bookshop and Library', *Light*, 24 January 1925.
  'A Proposed Psychic Museum', *Light*, 4 July 1925.
  'The Psychic "Gloves" ', *Daily News*, 9 December 1925.
The History of Spiritualism and *Pheneas Speaks* 7 June 1926.
'The History of Spiritualism', *Sunday Times*, 29 August 1926.
' "Pheneas Speaks" ', *G.K.'s Weekly*, 11 June 1927.
Resignation from the Society from the Society for Psychical Research
  'Resignation from the Society for Psychical Research', *Journal of the Society for Psychical Research*, March 1930.

3. *SUPERNORMAL PICTURES*
Spirit Photography
  ' "Psychic Photographs", *Light*, 12 September 1925.
The Cottingley Fairy Photographs
  'Fairy Photographs', *Light*, 18 June 1921.
  'Psychic Photographs', *Yorkshire Weekly Post*, 8 October 1921.
  'Sir A. Conan Doyle and the "Fairy Photographs" ', *Northern Whig and Belfast Post*, 12 May 1925.
The Crewe Circle (William Hope, Mrs Deane)
  'Taking of Spirit Photographs', *Evening Standard*, 9 August 1922.
The Combermere Photograph
  'The "Photograph" of Lord Combermere', *Morning Post*, 12 April 1926.
  'The Combermere Photo', *Morning Post*, 19 April 1926.
  'The Combermere Photograph, *Morning Post*, 23 April 1926.
The Nairobi Photograph
  'The Narobi Ghost Photograph', *Freethinker*, 5 May 1926.
  'The Nairobi Photograph', *Light*, 22 June 1929.
Inspirational Painting
  'Women "Spirit" Painter', *Daily Mail*, 16 December 1919.
  ' "A Disclaimer" ', *The Times*, 30 December 1919.

4. THE DEFENCE OF SPIRITUALISM

Proofs of Spiritualism
' "Spookery" ', *Daily Mail*, 7 February 1917.
'The New Spiritualism', *Nation*, 8 February 1919.
'Mrs Piper's Credibility', *John O' London's Weekly*, 27 March 1920.
'Success and Failure', *East African Standard*, 2 March 1929.

Spiritualism and the Church
'Father Vaughan and Spiritualism', *Pall Mall Gazette*, 11 June 1917.
The Bible', *Christian Spiritualist*, 2 June 1926.
'Convent Scandals', *Occult Review*, December 1929.

Spiritualism and Insanity
'Spiritualism's Peril', *Evening Standard*, 6 November 1919.
'Spiritualism and the Church', *Southport Visiter*, 22 January 1920.
'Spiritualism and Insanity', *Southport Visiter*, 12 February 1920.
'Spiritualism and Insanity', *Southport Visiter*, 2 March 1920.
'Streatham Tragedy', *Daily Express*, 4 November 1921.
'A Happy Creed', *Cape Times*, 21 November 1928.

Spiritualism and the Law
'Spiritualism and the General Election', *Light*, 18 November 1922.
'Police Evidence and Mediums', *Daily Express*, 6 October 1927.
'The "Witch" of Endor', *Morning Post*, 12 June 1929.
'The "Witch" of Endor', *Morning Post*, 17 June 1929.

5. MODERN SPIRITUALISM AND ITS CRITICS

Mediums
'The Naked Truth', *Daily Express*, 2 November 1917.
'The Character of D.D. Home', *Sydney Daily Telegraph*, 16 November 1920.
'Mr Maskelyne and the Slade Case', *Morning Post*, 26 September 1924.
'The Mediumship of F.T. Munnings', *International Psychic Gazette*, April 1926.

Messages from the Beyond
'Oscar Wilde's Communication Accepted as Genuine', *New York Times*, 2 September 1923
'A Letter to "Psychoro" ', *Thanet Advertiser and Echo*, 16 February 1924 ('Second Coming')
'Oscar Wilde', *occult Review*, April 1924.
' "The Mystery of Edwin Drood" ', *Light*, 1 October 1927.
'The Use of Great Names', *Light*, 5 April 193; (Thomas Hardy).

Psychic Phenomena
'The Cheriton Dug-Out', *Daily Chronicle*, 11 February 1918.
'The Green Ray', *Occult Review*, October 1922.
'Thought Transference', *The Times*, 17 December 1924.
'Alarmist Prophecies', *Light*, 26 August 1926.
'Sir A. Conan Doyle and Christie Case', *Morning Post*, 20 December 1926

Psychic Propaganda
'The Maintenance of "Light" ', *Light*, 26 January 1918.

Memorials
'The Birthplace of Spiritualism', *International Psychic Gazette*, July 1922.
The Hydesville Memorial', *Two Worlds*, 19 January 1923.
'The Washington Memorial', *Light*, 10 March 1923.
'The Hydesville Memorial', *Light*, 26 November 1927.

Critics of Spiritualism
'Modern Miracles – Reply to Jerome K. Jerome', *Common Sense*, 12 July 1919.
'Mr Jerome and Spirits', *Common Sense*, 16 August 1919.
'Houdini and the Spirits', *Westminster Gazette*, 22 November 1926.
'The Houndini Case', *Morning Post*, 17 September 1928.

'Lord Balfour', *The Times*, 29 March 1930.
'Conjurers and Spiritualism,' *Morning Post*, 14 June 1926.

INDEX

literary etiquette, 52–3
Liverpool, smallpox in, 30
Lodge, Sir Oliver, 251, 272, 286, 290, 302
Loiret (transport), 328
Lombroso, Cesare, 272, 278, 290
London, 266; air raids on, 227, 229; soldiers in, 245, 246–8
London Conference (1902), 113
London Spiritualist Alliance, 308, 309
London, Jack, 345
Lonsdale, Hugh Lowther, 5th Earl of, 178
Loos, battle of (1915), 249
Louvain, 217
Lovell & Co. (publishers), 42
Lowes, Jimmy, 286
Lowe (*Titanic* officer), 166
Lusitania, s.s., 205, 279
Lyon, Mrs., and D.D. Home, 288–9
Lyttelton, Edward, 197
Lytton, Bulwer, 289

Macaulay, Lord, 28
MacBrayne, Duncan, 206
McCabe, Joseph, 293
MacCammond, D., 162, 163
McIvor, Sir Lewis, 66
Mackarness, Mr., on train-wrecking, 83
Mackay, Edgar, 184
McKenzie, Mr. and Mrs. Hewat, 313
MacNeill, John Gordon Swift, 204
McNeill, Ronald, 185
Magee, Rev. A.V., 280
Margaret Ogilvie (Barrie), 52
Mark Cross (Sussex), 337
Marks, Mr., and Doyle's views on South African War, 83–4
Marmont, General, 232
Marne, battle of (1914), 249
marriage problems, 160–1, 254. *See also* divorce law reform
Martyrdom of Man, The (Reade), 33
Mary (queen of William III), 28
Maskelyne, John Nevil, 307
Mathewson, Arthur, 308
Maugham, W.S., 154
Maxwell, Sir Herbert, 197
Medical Defence Association, 17
medical diplomas, 17
Melton, Mr., and Nairobi photograph, 334
Methuen, Algernon (later Sir), and Free Trade, 111, 112
Micah Clarke (Doyle), 124
military inventions, 58–60
Militia, 72, 74, 78

Millesimo sittings, 340, 341–2
mine-laying, 216
Modern Psychic Mysteries (Hack), 341
Monaghan, County, 203, 204
Mons, retreat from (1914), 249
Moore, Albert, 311
Moore, George, 43
Moplah rebellion (1919), 339
Morel, E.D., 142, 155
Morrison, Mr (Congo missionary), 147
Moseley, Alfred, 110
motor boats, 215
motor-cars: manufacture of, 95, 96–8; and coast defence, 116–17; Prince Henry rally, 156–7
motorphobia, 108, 337–8
mounted riflemen, 150, 151, 152
Munnings, F.T., 314
Musgrave, Mr. (of *German Times*), 91
My Friend the Murderer (Doyle), 42
Mystery of Edwin Drood, The (Dickens), 272, 322

Nairobi, ghost photograph, 334
National Council for Combating Venereal Diseases, 248
National Health Society, 32
National Reserve, 208–9, 228
national service, compulsory, 223–6, 266–7
National Zeitung, 91, 93
Navy League, 53, 54
Nelson, Horatio, Lord, 41, 53–4
Nettleship, Edward, 129
New Revelation, The (Doyle), 270
New York, 297
Newell, Colonel, 242
Nicoll, Dr. (later Sir) William Robertson, 56–7
Northcliffe, Lord, 287; and Olympic Games, 183
Norway, 113; and *Cause and Conduct of the War*, 86, 89–90, 93

ocean depths, alleged changes in, 328
Ogilvie-Grant, W.R., 197
Olympic, S.S., 216
Olympic Association, 174
Olympic Committee, 178, 183–5, 189–91
Olympic Council, 182–5
Olympic Games, 171–5, 186–8; Stockholm (1912), 172, 174, 188, 190; Berlin (planned for 1916), 171–5, 178, 188, 189, 190, 191
Olympic Games Fund, 188–91
Omdurman, battle of (1898), 179
Our American Adventure (Doyle), 320

374

375